Decentralization

PUBLICATION OF THE SCIENCE CENTER BERLIN
Volume 21

Editorial Board

Prof. Dr. Karl W. Deutsch
Prof. Dr. Meinolf Dierkes
Priv. doz. Dr. Hans-Jürgen Ewers
Prof. Dr. Frieder Naschold
Prof. Dr. Fritz W. Scharpf

International Institute for Comparative Social Research

Decentralization

Sketches Toward a Rational Theory

Manfred Kochen
University of Michigan

Karl W. Deutsch
*Harvard University
and
Science Center Berlin*

HM
131
.K68
West

Oelgeschlager, Gunn & Hain, Publishers, Inc.
Cambridge, Massachusetts

Verlag Anton Hain
Königstein/Ts.

Copyright © 1980 by Oelgeschlager, Gunn & Hain, Publishers, Inc., and by Verlag Anton Hain Meisenheim GmbH., Königstein/Ts. All rights reserved. No part of this publication may be reproduced, stored in a retrieval system, or transmitted in any form or by any means, electronic mechanical photocopy, recording or otherwise, without the prior written consent of the publishers.

International Standard Book Number: 0-89946-022-4 (U.S.A.)
3-445-02068-x (Germany)

Library of Congress Catalog Card Number: 79-27059

Printed in the United States of America

Library of Congress Cataloging in Publication Data

Kochen, Manfred.
  Decentralization.

  Includes index.
  1. Organization. 2. Decentralization—Cost effectiveness—Mathematical models. 3. Decentralization in management. 4. Decentralization in government. I. Deutsch, Karl Wolfgang, 1912–   joint author. II. Title.
HM131.K68   302.3'5   79-27059
ISBN 0-89946-022-4

Contents

List of Figures	xi
List of Tables	xiii
Foreword	xv
Preface	xvii
Acknowledgment	xxi

Chapter 1 Decentralization: Approaches and Dimensions 1

- 1.0 Introduction   1
- 1.1 A Cost-Effectiveness Approach   2
- 1.2 Some Value Considerations   2
- 1.3 The Concept of Service: What It Is and for Whom   7
- 1.4 Direct Participants: Clients and Services   13
- 1.5 Indirect Participants: Beneficiaries, Sufferers, and Supporters   14
- 1.6 The Concept of Decentralization   16
- 1.7 Uses of Decentralization   18
- 1.8 The Dimensions of Decentralization   21
- 1.9 Relation to Decentralization Indexes and Hypotheses   27
- 1.10 Formulation of Central Problems   29

Chapter 2 Pluralization and Dispersion — 35

- 2.0 Introduction — 35
- 2.1 The Simplest Case: No Fluctuation in Demand and No Dispersion of Facilities — 36
- 2.2 Economies of Scale — 39
- 2.3 Simple Case with Uniform Spatial Dispersion and No Fluctuations — 41
- 2.4 Pluralization to Cope with Congestion — 50
- 2.5 Dispersion with Spatial Unevenness: Can It Favor Pluralization? — 59
- 2.6 The Effects of Fluctuations in Time and Space — 64
- 2.7 Pluralization, Redundancy, and Error Control — 66
- 2.8 Using Pluralization to Manage Fluctuations in Request Load — 67

Chapter 3 Functional Specialization — 69

- 3.0 Introduction — 69
- 3.1 Optimal Number of Functionally Specialized Agents — 72
- 3.2 "Fine Tuning": Dynamic Adjustment Through Feedback Cycles — 73
- 3.3 Adjustment Space and Geographic Space Combined — 75
- 3.4 Some Technological and Social Trends — 78
- 3.5 Functional Specialization Combined with Dispersion: Uneven Service Loads over Space and Time — 80
- 3.6 Summary — 82

Chapter 4 Responsiveness and Higher Service Quality — 85

- 4.1 Conversational Interaction — 85
- 4.2 Genuine Dialog — 88
- 4.3 Convergence and Divergence — 90
- 4.4 Effect of Decentralization on Feedback and Vice Versa — 92
- 4.5 Technology and Remoteness — 94
- 4.6 Some General Implications — 96
- 4.7 Informational Distance — 98
- 4.8 Transportation vs. Transmission: The Bulk of Objects and the Length of Messages — 99
- 4.9 Informational Distance in Service Systems — 103

Contents / vii

4.10	Quality of Service and Value of Time	106
4.11	Some Implications for Organization Theory and Politics: Some Secular Changes in Key Variables	114

Chapter 5 Hierarchical and Network Structures: Clustering and Hierarchies from Interaction 119

5.0	Introduction	119
5.1	Hierarchies in General: From First-order to Higher-order Clustering	120
5.2	Hierarchies in Service Organizations	122
5.3	Hierarchies from Coordination and Communication	125
5.4	Should Hierarchical Organizations Grow Taller?	127
5.5	A Basis for Calculating the Optimal Number of Hierarchical Levels: An Illustration	129
5.6	Organizational Design	133
5.7	The Optimum Number of Hierarchical Levels Determined by Computer Simulation	138
5.8	Dependency on Nature of the Input Load: Span of Control	162
5.9	Decentralization and Innovation	163
5.10	Concluding Remarks on Flatness as an Aspect of Decentralization	165

Chapter 6 Delegation and Control 167

6.0	Introduction	167
6.1	Control, Delegation, and Participation: The Notion of a Response Machine	170
6.2	Organizational Pattern Maintenance: Natural Control Mechanisms Shape Structure	174
6.3	Organization Design: How Should Decision Making and Memories Be Distributed Over Levels?	178
6.4	Organizational Change: When Does It Pay to Shift Memory Downward?	181
6.5	When Does It Pay to Refer Requests Downward?	182
6.6	Overall Considerations	183

viii / Contents

Chapte 7	Decentralization and Political Power	185
	7.0 Introduction	185
	7.1 Power: Clarification of the Concept	186
	7.2 Aspects of Power	195
	7.3 The Distribution of Power and Decentralization	198
	7.4 The Conservation of Power	200
	7.5 Effects of Decentralization on Power and Vice Versa	201
	7.6 Conclusions	204

Chapter 8	Political Values: Participation and Equality	207
	8.0 Introduction	207
	8.1 Political Background	207
	8.2 The Concept of Decisional Participation	208
	8.3 Participation in Organizational Redesign	210
	8.4 Value Aspects	211
	8.5 The Probable Consequences of Participation	214
	8.6 Impacts of Trends in Technology, Society, Culture, Economics, and Politics	218

Chapter 9	Conclusions and Perspectives	223
	9.0 Introduction	223
	9.1 The Concept of Decentralization Reconsidered	224
	9.2 Summary of Conditions Favoring Decentralization	238
	9.3 Overall View	241
	9.4 Recommendations	246

Appendixes

2.1	Derivation of the Optimum Degree of Pluralization	249
2.2	Location of Service Facilities in the Plane	252
3.1	Derivation of Optimal Number of Functionally Specialized Facilities	253
3.2	Joint Minimization of Cost with Respect to n_d and n_f	255
3.3	Effect of More Dimensions and Economies of Scale	256
5.1	Effect of Load on Optimum Flatness	259

5.2	Effect of Number of Sorters and Diagnosticians	265
5.3	A Model for Calculating Optimum Flatness Analytically	267
5.4	The Optimum Number of Hierarchical Levels Determined by Computer Simulation	275
6.1	Delegation and Suboptimization	283
6.2	Derivation and Analysis of Expression for Net Utility of a Service Organization with Distributed Memories	284
6.3	Model for Determining Shifts of Memory to Minimize Cost	292
6.4	Derivation of the Amount of Memory to Be Transferred	294
6.5	Does It Pay to Delegate More Than One Level Down?	297
9.1	Suggestions for Future Research: A Proposed Analytic System	299

Notes   307

Bibliography   317

Index   337

About the Authors   357

About the Science Center Berlin   359

List of Figures

1.1	Enlarging the Circle of Direct Participants in Agency Decisions: A Schematic Presentation of Marginal Value Gains and Costs	15
2.1	Total Cost vs. Number of Servers	39
2.2	Discount Fraction vs. n	40
2.3	A Centralized Organization	43
2.4	A Two-Facility Organization	44
2.5	Cost of n Facilities	46
2.6	Simplified Plot of Optimal Number n of Facilities for the Load L at Variable Operating Cost k	48
2.7	Distribution of Service Centers in a Plane	49
2.8	Average Waiting Time with n Facilities ($a = 600$ Requests per Month)	52
2.9	Average Waiting Time with n Facilities ($a = 2000$ Requests per Month)	53
2.10	Total Cost vs. Number of Facilities	54
2.11	Components of Response Time	55
2.12	Illustration of "Multiuniform" Service Request Distribution	60
2.13	Deviation of "Multiuniform" from Uniform Distribution	61

xi

3.1	Distribution of Demand over Geographic and Functional Space	76
3.2	Distribution of Service Stations over Geographic and Functional Space	77
3.3	Distribution of Requests over Nonuniform Distribution	81
4.1	Quality of Service vs. Cost	108
4.2	Utility vs. Number of Facilities	110
4.3	Utility vs. Number of Facilities for Various Request Loads	111
4.4	Utility vs. Number of Facilities for Various Values of a Client's Time	112
4.5	Utility vs. Number of Facilities for Various Values of Parameter A	113
5.1	Functional Sketch of a 5-Stage, 7-Level Service Organization	137
5.2	Total Cost vs. Error Rate for a Variable Number of Hierarchical Levels	157
5.3	Optimum Total Cost vs. Error Rate for Variable Probabilities of Client Appeal	158
5.4	Optimum Number of Hierarchical Levels vs. Client Load	159
5.5	Optimal Unit Cost vs. Client Load	160
5.6	Total Cost vs. Effectiveness of Vertical Communication for Variable Flatness	161
8.1	A Prisoner's Dilemma	210
9.1	Out Concepts of Decentralization and Organizational Structure	225
9.2	An Ordering of Structures on the Eight Dimensions of Decentralization	227
9.3	Display and Ordering Structures by Degree of Decentralization	233
A2.1.1	Illustrating a Skew (Pareto) Income Distribution	250
A5.1.1		263
A5.4.1		280
A5.4.2		281
A6.4.1		295

List of Tables

1.1	How Decentralists and Service Society Advocates and Members See Themselves and One Another	6
1.2	Key Parameters for Clients	30
2.1	Demonstrating the Importance of Variance in Number of Waiting Customers	57
5.1	Parameters Used in Computer Simulations to Compute Costs in Varying Conditions	141
5.2	Effect of Error Rates at Level 1, on Total Cost	142
5.3	Effect of Error Rates on Cost	144
5.4	Effect of Error Rates on Cost	146
5.5	Effect of Error Rates on Total Cost	148
5.6	Varied Opportunity Cost to Client	150
5.7	Varied Opportunity Cost to Client	151
5.8	The Effect of Client Load on λ^*, the Optimal Number of Hierarchical Levels	152
5.9	Variation of p_v (Horizontal Communication)	153
5.10	Variation of A, B, C (Coefficients for Relating Communication)	154
5.11	Variation of Amount of Time Needed in Vertical Communication	156

List of Tables

7.1	Consequences of Various Combinations of Power, Authority, and Responsibility	194
9.1	Eight Aspects of Decentralization	228
9.2	Examples of Feasible Structures with Varying Degree of Decentralization	230
A5.3.1	Relations among Communication and Work Times	270
A5.4.1	List of Variables	278
A5.4.2	Model Based on These Assumptions	279
A6.1.1	Key Variables and Implications	288

Foreword

Decentralization: Sketches Toward a Rational Theory has been written by a director and a collaborator of the International Institute for Comparative Social Research of the Science Center Berlin. It is included in the Science Center's series of publications as a contribution to the continuing search for, and debate about, a rational degree of decentralization of organizations performing any kind of service. It attempts to offer ways to identify its dimensions, its optimal extent, its limits, and some key conditions influencing all of these.

If this book serves to move the discussion of these matters somewhat further, it will have served its purpose.

For the Board of Editors
Karl W. Deutsch, Director
International Institute
for Comparative Social Research
Science Center Berlin

PREFACE

The purpose of this work is to explore the common structure of many problems of decentralization in large service organizations in government, business, and administration. In addition to helping persons responsible for decisions about organizational matters, it may help to raise the level of public debate. We are also trying to open, for further exploration, a line of research that can help shape policies of decentralization in various institutions and organizations, primarily in the public sector, but also with potential application in the private sector.

We approach this study from the viewpoint of the general theory of systems. We look upon any large service organization as an interdependent *service system*. Its participants include its personnel, clients, sponsors, and supporters. They are interconnected by a configuration of channels that distribute flows of communication and control. Insofar as this is relevant to the organization's existence and functioning, these participants and components must be understood in relation to their larger environment. By *service* we mean any operation performed regularly by the personnel or equipment of the organization, or both, for, or done to, its clients. Library users, telephone subscribers, hospital patients, traffic participants, university students, users of information and computer services, and government subjects in this sense are all "clients" of their respective organizations.

How much to decentralize has become a major issue in many discussions about the future of such services. In many countries, service sectors have increased their share of manpower and resources so that some writers have spoken of a coming, information-rich, "service-oriented," or "postindustrial" society (Machlup, 1962; Bell, 1973; Oettinger et al., 1977; Porat, 1976; Zeleny, 1978) in which the structures and problems of service organizations are often becoming more important.

The systems approach also has implications for the *values* that motivate our work. We start with the assumption that institutions that will survive during the next quarter- or half-century must be designed to serve people, rather than merely expecting people to serve them.

The main thrust of decentralization theory is to develop, organize, and analyze basic concepts and mathematical models in order to gain deeper insights into some of the social and organizational effects of current trends toward more powerful technologies and mounting demands for services. Another aim is to infer the likely consequences of various decentralization policies. These policies could then be compared with either "optimizing" or "satisficing"[1] policies. The derivation of such policies is a major, long-range aim of the theory we are developing in this book. Above all, we are concerned with developing a consistent theory that can help elucidate value positions for decentralization.

More specifically, we are concerned with three basic questions:

1. Given certain conditions, what degree of centralization or decentralization is desirable in a service system, if one considers generalized costs and benefits to the clients as well as to the service agency and the community that pay for it?
2. What necessary choices and terms of tradeoff among different dimensions of performance and values may be expected? In other words, to what extent will service agencies respond adequately or acceptably to the needs and wishes of their clients and to what extent will clients themselves be required to make compromises in dealing with agencies? How do agencies shape the needs of clients?
3. Which of these conditions is changing or is likely to change, and in what direction, under the impact of current or expected trends in technology, politics, and prevailing cultural values?

Our method is relatively abstract; we have tried to construct a systematic theory, aimed at general ideas about decentralization. We stress the identifiably *common* aspects of different service networks, such as government authorities, law courts, fire, police and ambulance systems, hospitals, mail order houses, libraries, and computer networks. Within the set of their common aspects, however, we attempt to identify the most crucial distinguishing features of each system, such as the need for a low rate of error in law courts, speedy response from fire stations, or quick and correct first aid from ambulances and their personnel.

Though many of our arguments have been aided by mathematical reasoning, they are presented here so that a general reader can follow them. More specific mathematical arguments are presented in the appendixes. Though we appreciate the complexity of most decentralization issues, we have come to recognize that the core of decentralization in a service system is its responsiveness, the shortness of its communication time, and the directness of its channels between servers and clients.

Even so, this is a book about timber lines rather than about trees. The details covered are few, and our mathematics are approximate. We know that any specific policy or case will have to be studied more thoroughly in particular detail. But anybody undertaking such a study would do so with general ideas or images in mind as to what decentralization means, why it matters, and which of its aspects are likely to prove important. We hope to present our view of these ideas or images, illuminating some aspects of decentralization too often relegated to the realm of bitter experience.

It seems to us, until now, that such general ideas have been insufficiently developed. Yet they are indispensable for policymakers, executives, citizens, or clients who have an interest in the shape of the organizations with which they must deal. We hope to help our readers clarify their general ideas about the concentration or dispersion of services, resources, and power, and to indicate the considerations involved in the redesign and reordering of many of the organizational patterns by which much of our lives are ruled, and which often could be modified for the better.[2]

M.K.
K.W.D.

Acknowledgment

We are grateful to many colleagues who helped us in the various stages of the work reported here during the past five years. Howard Fredrick wrote all the computer programs and provided us with the results of simulations and computations; he also checked the analytical work and contributed a number of valuable passages. Paul Eitner helped with some of the analytical work. Pietro Nivola prepared a glossary of mathematical variables. Barbara Perkel and Flora Wallace coordinated the work in compiling this manuscript, and we are particularly indebted to Mrs. Perkel for her expert and dedicated help. Robin Crickman, Clare Raizman, Amy Spitzer, and Brian Kuttner all helped in compiling references to the literature. Brian Kuttner also provided stimulating discussions, though our views did not coincide with his. Barbara Perkel's and Evelyn Neumark's editorial assistance and advice helped us improve the style. The expert, dedicated typing of several drafts of the entire manuscript by Barbara Perkel and Esther Washington made it possible to produce this manuscript. A special acknowledgment is due to Murray Aborn of the Special Projects Division at the National Science Foundation. NSF support, under grant number GS-43385, helped us to complete this work. We are especially grateful to the Mental Health Research Institute of The University of Michigan for its generous support for the time of both authors and the use of its facilities, as well as to the International Institute for Comparative Social Research of the Science Center Berlin.

We also wish to thank the *American Political Science Review*, the *Journal of Regional Science*, *Operations Research*, *Management Science*, *Behavioral Science*, and the *American Association for the Advancement of Science* for the use of excerpts from prior publications by the authors.

Chapter 1

Decentralization: Approaches and Dimensions

1.0 INTRODUCTION

The study of decentralization has reached a stage characterized both by challenge and opportunity. The opportunity derives from the considerable lore of conventional wisdom, insight, and experience from managers in business and government. At the same time, an impressive array of mathematical techniques and results have accumulated in such areas as economics, operations research, location theory, queueing theory, and organization theory. These developments suggest that a synthesis, focused on a cost-benefit analysis of client-centered service organizations, now may become an attainable goal.

The challenge stems from the growing disparity between (a) the complexity and multitude of problems that our institutions face and (b) the simplistic attitudes and glacierlike slowness of many of their leaders, sponsors, personnel, and clients in adopting new structures to cope more effectively with their growing tasks and burdens. Many observers of school, health, and other service systems have urged revising the organization of these institutions to improve their abilities to cope with the increased loads of more complex problems. Impressed by the increased capacities of modern transport and communication, some observers have concluded that the thrust of technological development by itself will promote ever more centralized patterns of organization in many fields, from local government and private business enterprise to international politics and global military strategy.[1] Some have advocated greater centralization as a value, hoping for gains in power, professionalism, and efficiency. With equal passion, others have advocated decentralization to bring about greater responsiveness to individual and community needs.[2]

This difference in viewpoint is dealt with by confrontation, letting the side with the greatest power or the strongest advocates prevail—sometimes only until the results of this kind of decision making are overridden by the impact of subsequent experience. Is there a less costly way to make such decisions?

1.1 A COST-EFFECTIVENESS APPROACH

We propose to examine the conditions under which decentralization is more cost-effective than centralization. What are the costs involved and what are the benefits? Can each of these be measured and on whom do they fall? Where is the point at which no substitute exists for ethical and political values?

To proceed with this approach, we need to specify a general class of client-centered service institutions with sufficient precision to characterize the degree of decentralization associated with its organizational structure.

In our attempt to obtain insights into the effect of decentralization on costs and benefits of services, we are frequently guided by analogies between man-made and natural structures. (The human nervous system, for example, shows a relatively high degree of decentralization and redundancy together with considerable coherence and coordination.) We occasionally find it useful to consider special kinds of service organizations, such as library, computer, and communication networks, as vehicles for analysis, illustrating and testing their realism.

1.2 SOME VALUE CONSIDERATIONS

To be of use to planners, what considerations should be included in a cost-benefit analysis beyond purely economic concerns? How can planners take account of human values?

As an example of how values and cost-benefit considerations interact, consider a health service. In a centralized system, where the

1.2 Some Value Considerations / 3

number of cases requiring heart-lung machines, for instance, is sufficiently large, expensive equipment is justifiable and there is also a sufficient concentration of resources (e.g., capital) to afford it. If the total of all resources available for all health services, centralized or decentralized, were fixed, resources allocated to centralized facilities are then resources not allocated to decentralized facilities. Decentralized facilities are exemplified by numerous first aid stations, roving ambulances, or helicopters to provide emergency aid to, say, highway accident victims. Shifting the balance of resources allocated to centralized facilities thus may cause premature deaths or disablements of certain client classes (e.g., highway users) while avoiding premature deaths or disablements in another client class (e.g., those requiring heart-lung machines). This requires trading lives. While an economic value could be assigned to a life, as might be done by an insurance company, profound moral and ethical problems need to be considered. These considerations also arise in deciding between policies that cost more but avoid extra deaths or disabilities and less costly, life-wasting policies.[3]

One possible solution would be to estimate the instrumental value of money in saving human lives and to compare the life-preserving potential of an identical sum of money allocated to different types of activities in public health or safety. We could compare the "purchasing power" of a sum of money spent in several alternative ways in pursuit of the same value for the same group of people. But such comparisons are harder when resources are to be spent in pursuit of different values or even of the same value but for different groups of people.

We could deal with the second problem by deciding arbitrarily to value equally all human lives and all human recipients of values. But we would need additional information before we could decide how much of a change in the probability of the delivery of a specified value would be accepted as equivalent to the delivery of another value to the same actor or acting group.

A familiar view of decentralization is to see it as a matter of power. According to this view, the strong tend to centralize in their own hands as much power as they can; they then delegate to the weak only as much power as they must. In this perspective, centralization and power of the key agent are assumed to coincide, and concentration of information flow and decision-making responsibilities means both power and centralization. In our view, though power can affect centralization, the reverse holds to a much lesser extent. Thus, centralization does not necessarily enhance or even maintain the key agents in power. The same holds for other values. Increased centralization will not necessarily help the decision maker to get more.

4 / Decentralization: Approaches and Dimensions

The purpose of our analysis is to help planners and decision makers become more aware of possible inconsistencies in their behavior. The content of political decision making is critically dependent on what the decision maker values. The results of analysis are if-then statements. They are the logical consequences of the decision makers' value orientations. They assert that *if* they seek benefits of a certain kind and in a certain amount more highly than they value saving costs of a certain quality and quantity, *then* they would probably choose a course of action that promised to maximize—or at least increase—what is of greatest net value to them.

The following values are implicit in our analytic approach. Logical consistency is preferred to inconsistency. Statements with empirical content that can be independently and replicably verified are preferred to statements that cannot be verified. Means and ends that are valued by each member of a larger community are rated more highly than would be true for a smaller community, *if no other considerations apply*. Actions that are valued and that affect a longer time horizon are valued more highly than actions with a shorter time horizon, again with other considerations assumed as fixed.

The difficulties arise when other considerations intervene simultaneously. The most important considerations omitted so far are "absolute" ethical principles, such as those embodied in the Ten Commandments. Then tradeoffs should be made (or are supposed to be made) without violating basic ethical constraints. There are trades between what a small group values highly, but which is less valued by a larger community. There are trades between what is highly valued if attainable immediately, but much less valued if attained later. But we must not compromise fundamental ethical principles that may be partly or largely invariant under changes of time or culture.[4]

Insofar as decentralization has been widely used as a slogan, instead of a property of organizational structure to be investigated scientifically, it is a near-synonym of terms like "democratization" and "self-determination." It then denotes an ideology: a system of beliefs and values. Followers of the decentralist "secular religion," as Daniel Bell calls it, are faithful to its dogma and do not need the arguments presented here to persuade them about the most likely and most desirable direction for the evolution of society. Decentralization, as a near-synonym of "postindustrialism," is such a direction.

As characterized by Marien (1977), postindustrialism has two opposite meanings. The first is that of a technological, affluent, service society, a vision widely associated with Bell. The second is that of a decentralized agrarian economy, a vision that Marien has traced to Belloc (1913), Penty (1917), and the Jefferson-Hamilton debates. As

1.2 Some Value Considerations / 5

Schumacher (1973, p. 229) puts it, "Centralization is mainly an idea of order; decentralization one of freedom. The man of order is typically the accountant and, generally, the administrator; while the man of creative freedom is the entrepreneur. Order requires intelligence and is conducive to efficiency; freedom calls for and opens the door to intuition and leads to innovation. Actually, however, the entrepreneur, like the artist, wants freedom for himself but central and controlling power over his team or organization, in order to preserve the integrity of his vision."

The world has had a long and bizarre history with decentralization, usually after one-man empires like that of Alexander, Ghengis Khan, Charlemagne, and Hitler. The urgency of today's issue is due to the rapid technological changes we have witnessed since 1945. Factories and skyscrapers may be destined to disappear as the U.S. labor force shifts to 15 percent manufacturing and 65 percent services by the year 2000 (Wheeler, 1974). With computerization of manufacturing and of many bureaucratic functions, the present maze of suburbs strung together by freeways are no longer needed; smaller autonomous communities organized on the basis of cultural amenities rather than commercial values can take their place.

If the decentralists are a "secular religion" or ideologues, then so are the adherents of the view that postindustrial society (the next stage in social evolution) is a service society, according to decentralists.[5] The ideological bias attributed to Bell, for example, is his reliance on science, technology, and professionalism in their present forms. We find it difficult to compare science, which would be a necessary basis of Bell's service society and the method of inquiry by those who hold that view, with "self-sufficiency," "values," and "alternative futures," which presumably are the counterparts of science. In our view, science is a uniquely successful human enterprise, an unsurpassed method of inquiry and of attaining valid knowledge and communicable understanding, at least of nature. Whether it can create an equally satisfying understanding of society is not as certain. But after all societies are part of nature too, and there is little reason to believe that such alternatives to science as proposed and practiced by some extreme decentralists can do any better.

Table 1.1, which is based on Marien (1977), shows the contrast between service society advocates and members (SSAMs) and decentralists. This table resembles that of Meehl for how clinical and experimental psychologists see themselves and one another. Marien suggests the possibility and desirability of a next stage of social evolution that is both a service and agrarian society, with 10 to 20 percent of the labor force in agriculture. Our conclusions are remotely analogous if

6 / Decentralization: Approaches and Dimensions

Table 1.1. How Decentralists and Service Society Advocates and Members See Themselves and One Another

	SSAMs as:	Decentralists as:
SSAMs See:	Scientific	Nihilistic, apocalyptic
	Objective	Romantic
	Quantitative	Antiscience
	Professional	Antiprogress
	Harnessing technology	Ineffective
	Bureaucrats	Moralistic
	Interdependent in the global community	Hedonistic
Decentralists See:	Amoral technocrats	Striving for self-sufficiency as the good life
	Elitist experts	Independent in small communities
	Reductionists	Yearning for return to agrarian life
	Middle-class welfare careerists	Acting on their values, freely expressed
	Tools of big government	Ecologically minded
	Tools of big business	Appreciating that small is beautiful
	Ignorant of the real world	Future-oriented

we substitute for agrarianism a lifestyle characterized by intimate and highly responsive social bonds among people in need of one another's services. Returning to an agricultural life is neither the most likely nor the best way to achieve this.

Skinner (1971) has argued that freedom and dignity are meaningless and antiquated notions to which modern organizations should pay little heed. Indeed, one of the arguments for centralizing control within an organization at the top is that this is the most efficient way for the organization to attain its behaviorally specified objectives. Presumably service providers who choose to remain affiliated with the organization and clients who continue to come back for service have behaviorally specified objectives that are met when those of the organization are met. This might lead one to think that what is good for GM or IBM is good for its employees and its customers. Their freedom and dignity are not behaviorally specifiable and play no role.

Yet, advocates for decentralization in municipal services, such as schools, seem to value not only the autonomy for local decision making in its own right, but also the freedom and dignity they feel to be part of that autonomy. Thus, local decision makers prefer the freedom and the right to make mistakes, that is, to criticize *themselves*. They often value this more highly than the presumably more error-free services they could receive from a central agency. An important aspect of "bringing government closer to the people" characterizes the ideals of federalism.

An interesting parallel to the relation between the values of science and the values of an ideology is the relation between the value of autonomy and the value of an ethic, such as affirmative action to attain racial equality. Many people, particularly decentralists, value their autonomy, freedom, and independence very highly. Deans or department heads in certain universities jealously guard their rights, as well as the rights of their colleagues, to decide whom to hire and what to investigate and teach. While they might also highly value a universitywide affirmative action program, the two values could conflict if some departments chose not to implement the program as fervently as others. Would they be willing to limit the autonomy of departments in order to permit enforcement of the more highly valued affirmative action program uniformly across all departments? Or would they value the autonomy of each department more highly than the affirmative action program? The preference between these two valued policies is a third value that transcends the other two.[6]

This suggests a hierarchy of values or value scales, with any individual employing as many levels as needed to behave and believe consistently. In as much as science has thus far shown itself capable of resolving what were paradoxes, contradictions, and anomalies at lower levels of explanation, science as a value may have a similar power in relation to ideologies. Individuals may "resolve" value conflicts and resulting consistencies without resorting to higher level values by deliberate or inadvertent lack of logical precision, that is, by confusion. Alternatively, they may live with inconsistent beliefs, which is a very prevalent but not natural condition. So far as organizations are concerned, evolutionary trends may favor the maintenance of consistency in the most precise, conscious, and economical manner possible.

1.3 THE CONCEPT OF SERVICE: WHAT IT IS AND FOR WHOM

The central object of our book is a service organization, or *agency,* for short. From one point of view, this is an "if-then" machine that receives inputs from its environment and produces an output of decisions or services. From another point of view, it is more than a passive respondent; it can initiate actions as well, causing its environment to "respond." Indeed, it often contributes vitally to the climate of that environment. Both the active and passive modes can be types of service. Strange as it may sound, from this point of view policymaking is service in the active mode, whereas firefighting is service in the passive mode.

Passive services, those services regarded as input-output devices, can be further classified according to the fraction of inputs they receive from the external environment as distinct from inputs generated within the agencies. Northcote Parkinson's image of a large bureaucratic office in which the clerks are too busy communicating with one another to tend to the long waiting line of clients is an all too familiar example of an agency that manages to generate most of its input through internal processes (Parkinson, 1957).

1.3.1. Single vs. Plural Services. Some agencies, such as gas filling stations, perform only a single service (or very few), whereas others, such as clinics, perform multiple services. What, however, is a single service? Filling a car's gas tank? Checking the oil? Administering vaccines? From an economic point of view, a service is labor that benefits someone but does not produce a tangible commodity. It involves the creation of capital or of a relatively durable consumer good—for example, the barbered head for barbershop services—that can depreciate or decline (Boulding, 1955). From a sociopolitical viewpoint, a service is an operation performed by one agent or agency at the command of another. A single service is a class of operations defined by the client's dependence (possibly temporary) on the agency to satisfy some expressed need.

Occasionally, the agency may exercise, for the duration of the service, some authority and responsibility over the clients or some of their belongings or resources. Thus a doctor is responsible for a client's health and has authority about decisions affecting it while the doctor ministers to the client. On the other hand, the collectivity of clients, or a pressure group within it, often is capable of exerting strong pressure on the agency.

1.3.2. Consonant vs. Dissonant Services. Suppose two or more services are performed for the same client at more or less the same time and place. Administration of anesthesia and surgery are compatible and not only can but also ordinarily must be performed together. Serving a restaurant customer wine or coffee at the same time that the meal is served illustrates two consonant services. Providing one consonant service makes performance of the other service easier or more probable. Two services are dissonant if providing one reduces the probability of successfully delivering the other service, or makes it more difficult.

1.3.3. Self-Service. Advanced societies are believed to be in a transition from service to self-service (Skolka, 1974; Zeleny, 1978). Services, such as those provided by barbershops, are not likely to increase in productivity because of advances in technology even though an increased need for these services will be met, in part, by the clients themselves. This is due to new products from highly productive industries, such as those making kits for shaving and haircutting. In part, it may be met by clients providing mutual help. Even science-based professional services, such as health maintenance, are likely to involve novel linkages of services provided at all levels between the client and a highly specialized expert. Partial self-service results in a greater distribution of control and accountability among all the service providers and clients, including those servicing the equipment used in self-servicing.

1.3.4. Bundles of Services. It is not unusual for a firm to decentralize its marketing and centralize some of its accounting functions. If a firm has branches, each branch may have its own accounting system, with separate journals and ledgers. The way accounts are classified may, however, be specified by the home office, which also keeps a general ledger and enforces conformity with the classification. It is a widespread problem, especially in developed countries (Fesler, 1965, p. 557) that functions fail to be treated as entire bundles of services.

1.3.5. Units of Measurement. For the most part, our analysis deals with passive services that respond to requests from outside the agency, that is, the *request* or presenting case. The basic variable characterizing the agency's environment is the request *load* or number of requests per unit time, such as a month. Requests may originate in simple *desires,* such as a customer's asking for a mystery story in a lending library. Or it may stem from a real *need.* That is, the service may be indispensable to the client in order to save the client from probable observable damage, such as medical attention in severe illness or supply of foods containing nutrients such as calcium, protein, and vitamins, all of which are among the nutritional needs of children.

The unit for measuring the gross *work load* put upon a service agency is the *request* for service. When a significant number of requests are rejected from the outset by the agency, the unit for measuring the net load is the *case.* This is defined as any request that leads to relevant activity by the agency beyond some minimum threshold. Thus, requests made erroneously by someone to the wrong agency—for example, a fire reported to a hospital—will ordinarily not produce a case but only a formal or informal referral of the client to the appropriate agency (such as the fire department).

For analytic purposes, we work with *average* numbers of requests and cases in terms of the time and resources they engage. The number of cases, multiplied by their average time or cost, corresponds to the agency's total load or cost.

Most services show a skewed distribution of service time and costs—similar to the well-known Yule, negative binomial, or lognormal, distribution—in which the median case takes less time and money than the mean. Correspondingly, of course, a smaller portion of cases engages a relatively large part of the time and resources of the service agency. Reporting the median, or even the modal, case of service will give a more favorable image of the performance of the agency than would the mean; and the most lengthy and costly, or perhaps the poorest cases of service, such as the extreme 5, 10, or 20 percent, may remain unrepresented. On the other hand, performance in remote areas, or in the great majority of cases, may have a greater effect on the likelihood that the agency will continue to be supported by its sponsors and the community at large.

1.3.6. Responses and Responsiveness. Another basic notion is that of a *response* of acceptable quality within an acceptable time of delay. The response to an explicit request is usually well defined and clearly recognizable by the client as meeting or not meeting the client's need. The *form* in which the service is delivered is often beyond the client's power to control. He or she cannot always recognize good or poor service, as in the case of professional service. Responses to implicit requests are usually arrived at in a sequence of successive feedbacks or negotiating cycles that terminate when the last version of the request is satisfied.

Response Deviation. In measuring the responsiveness, we may be concerned with the degree to which the *original* desire or need of the client is satisfied. We may also take into account the redefinition or adjustment that the client has made in his or her request in the course of repeated negotiation or queries and the client's growing knowledge of what may be reasonably expected from this agency. One cannot get apples by shaking a plum tree but one might be quite willing to settle for plums. To what extent are the actual needs of clients met and are these needs adjusted to reality or distorted into a standard formula?

Ideally, we should endeavor to ascertain the extent to which the client finds satisfaction with the service provided by the agency. This means that very subjective considerations are involved. A regular user of the agency may adjust to the procedures and forms required. He or she may have established contact and made friends with the agents. This user may even have delivered "a letter of introduction from the secretary of the treasury"—in Gogol's words. Such a user may find the agency perfectly responsive simply because the agency has succeeded in shaping his or her needs to fit its capacity to respond. Another, more naive user may experience a high degree of frustration with the impersonal, mechanical procedures of the same agency, repeatedly being sent to the back of queues for failing to have the appropriate forms filled out correctly and finally being fobbed off with a formula. We need to gauge the relation between the final service and the original need of the client. Was this need suppressed completely in the face of the grim "reality"? For instance, a black woman suffering from discrimination may eventually make do with food stamps if she is unable to find suitable employment through institutional aid. To what extent is this responsiveness? This possible *deviation* of the agency's final response from the client's original request or need can be measured by the time and cost of the adjustment required from the client.

Response Time. In simplest terms, *responsiveness* is measured by the time needed to deliver an acceptable response. Since that time is generally a random variable, a more sophisticated characterization of responsiveness is the probability distribution of such response time, that is, the likelihood with which various delays occur.

Several factors contribute to response time. To clarify the notion, consider the client's turnaround or total elapsed time, T, measured from the moment the client recognizes a need for the service to the moment the client is satisfied that it has been met by the service. For example, T for the client of a clinic may be the several weeks between the moment when he or she first notices a pain that motivates this client to seek the clinic's services, through a possible hospital stay, to the time when the case is considered closed by everyone concerned.

Alternatively, we could measure the agency's T from the moment the client presents him- or herself at the clinic and the record is opened to when the record is closed (for further clarification, see Figure 2.11). The agency devotes a total service rate S to servicing the request for which the client is charged. This may be spread intermittently throughout the total turnaround time. This service time is generally less than T. The period of convalescence or waiting for laboratory tests is not part of the direct service time by the clinic. Most service agencies sell their time. The cost per unit time depends in part on the investment necessary to prepare and maintain the agency's ability to render the service. The price per unit time, like any wage, depends not only on this fixed cost but also on the supply of labor and the demand for the service and the agency's capacity to regulate the market. Presumably, the higher the quality of the service the greater the costs, for the required abilities are more rare.[7]

1.3.7. The Service System. A service agency, viewed as an "if-then" machine responding to requests from clients, is a network of components that themselves are smaller if-then machines. For example, in a clinic we may view these components as belonging to the following classes of agents: (1) Sorters, who are the first to receive requests, recognize them as belonging to certain classes in which other agents are experts and refer the request, or the client, to those experts; (2) Diagnosticians, who are the first experts to receive requests from the sorters or the clients (who must repeat their requests in more detail), must specify correspondences between various operations that have to be done simultaneously in a coordinated way and also correspondences between operations that must be done in a time sequence; (3) Load schedulers, who receive, for each request, the orders from a diagnostician specifying what operations need to be done, when, how, and with what priority; they must know the status of the various resources (e.g., machine or human operatives) needed to perform these operations and then they must specify which operatives are to perform the operations and when. In this scheduling task they are expected to minimize idleness and congestion without violating constraints on maximum turnaround time and numerous other variables; (4) Operatives, who perform the various operations specified by diagnosticians and are signaled by load schedulers; (5) Inspectors, who check the output of operatives to ascertain that they conform to the specifications set by the diagnosticians and give final approval to a response before it is sent to the client. They enforce quality control standards. Some of them may check and reverse the output of sorters, diagnosticians-designers, and schedulers as well; (6) Tactical supervisors, who coordinate, by communication with superiors, lateral colleagues, and subordinates (by controlling the latter) in order to implement plans requiring complex correspondences of operations; (7) Strategists, who plan longer range policies; formulate standards, regulations, budgets, guidelines; execute strategic plans and judge performance with a view toward continued viability of the organization in providing services responsive to the needs.

These seven classes should be regarded as categories of functions rather than of agents. The same agent may perform several of these functions. Conversely, some functions may be performed by several types of agents. Thus the tasks of control may be divided among groups 5, 6, and 7, which we called inspectors, supervisors, and strategists, respectively.

1.4. DIRECT PARTICIPANTS: CLIENTS AND SERVERS

There are pressures, both private and public sectors, by the clients and their servers at the lower levels of the service organization for greater participation in both reallocation of organizational resources and in redesign of performance and structure. Both social workers and their "cases" or interns and their "patients" want to have more to say about possible decentralization or centralization of their agency. Public school boards must cope with the pressure from parents, students, teachers, and maintenance personnel. This is true for many enterprises in the private sector as well. Textbook publishers, owners of theaters, and newspaper editors all face pressure from a variety of direct participants. The direct participants in the automobile industry are the car buyers and owners who need repairs and maintenance, as well as engineers, salesmen, service station managers, and many others. In the latter case, potential car buyers may opt for another make of car or for another type of transportation. The more difficult or costly it is to find such an "exit" from the limited field of choices offered by a service agency, the stronger the possible interest of the client to obtain a "voice" in the agency's decisions (Hirschman, 1970).

Some participants suffer from the deficiencies of agencies but are powerless to apply pressure to the authorities. These include applicants for assistance of various kinds who cannot afford to offend the agents for fear of prejudicing their requests. These people are a latent source of pressure. Given sufficient organization, they may become capable of bringing about large changes in the institutions.

One-sided advocacy is unlikely to solve problems. Wider participation improves responsiveness to those to whom it is extended; it may strengthen the values of autonomy and self-respect among them, and it may provide additional inputs of useful information to the agency. But it is also likely to increase the risks of congestion and overload in the agency's channels of communication, thus increasing its rates of error and delay as well as the cost of its services.

Often the assumption may be justified that those to whom participation is most valuable are also those to whom it is extended first. If so, the marginal value of adding further participants will tend to decline while the marginal cost of adding more participants will tend to rise, as shown in Figure 1.1, Case A. The intersection between these two curves will then indicate the best solution, if all other conditions remain equal; the larger region enclosed by the two curves above it indicates the region of relatively small gains or losses, where acceptable compromises between costs and participation may be found. In Case B of Figure 1.1, however, no such overlap and room for compromise exists: the marginal value of participation here is still very high—perhaps for some particular group—while marginal costs are already prohibitive.

1.5. INDIRECT PARTICIPANTS: BENEFICIARIES, SUFFERERS, AND SUPPORTERS

Some people are indirectly affected by the external economies or diseconomies, benefits, or deprivations brought about by an agency. Again, pressures from such indirect groups arise both in the private and public sectors. Real estate agencies may change the character, as well as the real estate prices, of a neighborhood.

Until recently, it was sufficient to heed only the first-order effects in evaluating how an agency was performing its service. More often, however, with the increasing scale and power of its operations, its second-order effects are becoming too large to ignore. The first-order effect of the car industry is to provide owners with convenient, rapid, cheap transportation. Road congestion and air pollution were second-order effects. They were relatively insignificant until a few years ago when the number and concentration of cars made the quality of air in many urban areas unacceptable. Persons affected by the secondary effects are the indirect participants.

Distinguishing between the direct and indirect participants is increasingly important for decentralization policies because response priorities of various parties may differ as well as their need to be articulated. Whose benefits should be maximized, with what emphasis, and how should any conflicts be handled? The "beneficiaries" of a genetic counseling service include the unborn; the clients are a couple who may want to decide between nurturing offspring with a chance of congenital disease (that they, in turn, could pass on to their offspring),

1.5 Indirect Participants / 15

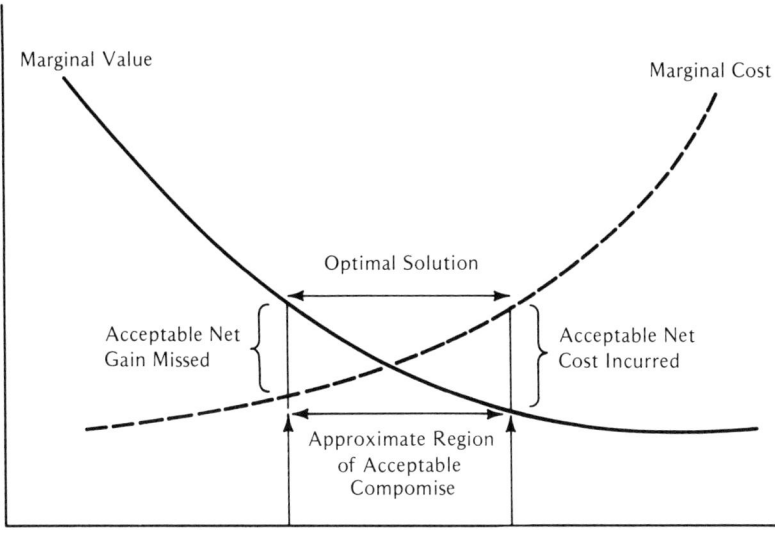

Case A. Wide Overlap of Acceptable Costs and Value Gains

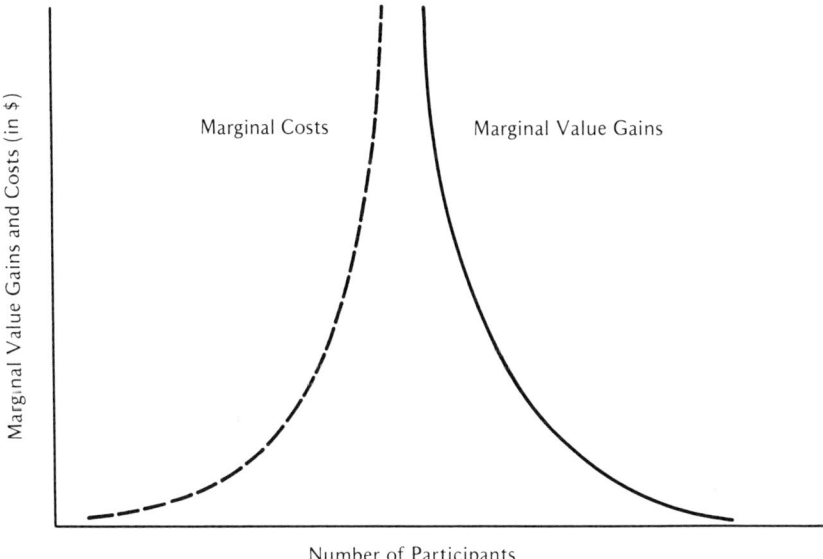

Case B. No Overlap

Figure 1.1 Enlarging the circle of direct participants in agency decisions: a schematic presentation of marginal value gains and costs.

adoption, or other acceptable options. Should all the weight be given to the interests of the direct clients, on the assumption that this benefits the future "beneficiaries" as well? This is in part an empirical question of the values that various individuals and groups of people hold, and which predominate in a given time and community. It is also in part a question of who is able to forecast the interests of the unborn, and of the probable degree of uncertainty and error of any such forecasts, whoever may make them.

1.6. THE CONCEPT OF DECENTRALIZATION

The most highly centralized system we can imagine would be one in which, given a domain of space or clients and a scope of functions, all decisions and services were made and performed by a single compact actor-as-an-individual located at one point. He or she completes each operation as a single act without any sequence of negotiations or other feedback interactions with the client. For perfect service, maximum centralization thus would require an actor who ideally, within his or her domain and scope of service, would have to be omnipresent, omnicompetent, inexhaustible, and infallible.

Few, if any, organizations or agencies exist in this extreme form. The single location, identity, and functional omnicompetence of an individual has been approximated more or less imperfectly by the emperors of ancient Rome or medieval Byzantium, some Muslim khalifs, Western medieval popes, and in later ages by absolute monarchs or modern dictators. Each individual, however, had subordinates in a hierarchy of power and authority and had to concern him- or herself with problems of the delegation of decision-making powers and the day-to-day control of limited amounts of resources. None of these relatively extreme forms of centralized decision making has endured.

Extremely centralized organizations have some points of strength. Their assets include a good chance of achieving and maintaining concentration of resources, speed and consistency of decision-making, high visibility, and easy orientation for their clients looking for service.

The weaknesses of such extremely centralized organizations, however, most often are larger and more serious. Their liabilities include overload and congestion of their communication channels and facilities, with resulting long delays or partial or general breakdowns of the system. Some frequently used methods of coping with overload are themselves sources of further liabilities, such as the growth of long waiting lines, frequent errors, and the chunking or stereotyping of

1.6 The Concept of Decentralization / 17

more or less diverse cases into a few categories that are often likely to prove inappropriate.

On the average, a *service system* catering to a varied set of clients with diverse needs is more decentralized, with less communicative distance between its clients and the relevant portions of the system serving them. Hence a network of agents is decentralized if they are distributed and strategically deployed, thus shortening lines of communication and control between the system and its clients. Considered in greater detail, as we shall do later in this chapter, decentralization will turn out to be a structural concept with several distinct dimensions. But the notion of short, fast, cheap, and capacious communication channels between a service system and its clients remains at the core of our approach.

For us, decentralization is not a value in itself. Our key values are quick responsiveness, reliability, adequacy, and quality of the needed or requested service. In this view, a service system will be more efficient with more of these values delivered at a lower cost. In relation to these goal values, the various structural patterns of centralization and decentralization are mere instruments, to be judged by the benefits they are apt to bring under each set of particular conditions.[8]

Decentralization of service facilities may be viewed in two broad ways. The first includes *pluralization* and *dispersion,* where the central issue is to find the optimum number and location of identical service facilities in order to meet a certain demand throughout the system. Problems in this category include determining the number of service stations that should be available along a highway. The second category involves not only the duplication of facilities but also the design of *hierarchies* of communication and control within the service system, and the differential *allocation of tasks, decision making, and resources* to the agencies at the various hierarchic levels, so as to determine their efficiency in providing service. These preliminary considerations suggest a set of eight distinct dimensions of decentralization, discussed in 1.8, below.

Decentralization is not fragmentation. Fragmentation no longer forms a system. Once disassembled or disjointed, its parts may remain scattered without mutual interactions, common tasks, and common sources of support. In the late 1960s and early 1970s, some young people seemed to believe, to a greater extent than did their counterparts in previous generations, that events in their lifetimes were unprecedented, that they had to come up with novel responses of their own to their unique challenges, that they had little to learn from the "outdated, irrelevant" experiences of their elders. They also felt powerless and alienated, holding their elders to be responsible for their problems and believing that the elders were in control but should not be. Thus, they formed mutual support groups, same-age peer groups, and other fragments of society, at the loss of historical continuity. Many of the dissident groups struggling for lifestyles of their own arose in affluent society and while they are the most vocal in their rejection of, say, Pareto optimality, they insisted on getting what *they* want (Samuelson, 1970). But links among them remained fragmentary.

By contrast, a decentralized system still remains a system, with its parts linked by bonds of mutual transactions and interdependence, common tasks of service, and common sources and bases of support. If decentralization leads to a less unequal distribution between clients, say, in central and peripheral locations in regard to time, attention, resources, and kinds and quality of services, it still remains committed to the rendering of a specific class of services, and not merely to some general redistribution of power, wealth, or other values, regardless of how and to what ends these may be used by the recipients.

The guiding principle of decentralization thus remains the performance of a service, not the scattering of handouts. Adherents of general equalitarian leveling may favor decentralization, but decentralization has rational limits and does not necessarily favor general leveling. Rather, it will continue to be achieved as cost-effective performance, of which the breadth of the delivery of service is but one important dimension.

1.7. USES OF DECENTRALIZATION

If we analyze the verb "decentralize" logically and completely, we should try to insert appropriate terms into the blanks of the following sentence: " __(A)__ decentralizes operation or function __(B)__ in service organization __(C)__ at level __(D)__ to extent __(E)__ at time __(F)__ by means of __(G)__ and in order to __(H)__ ."

1.7.1. Who Decentralizes. It is primarily managers who make decentralization decisions. In a highly centralized organization, the chief executive alone may be faced with such a decision, possibly because of antitrust decrees by the government (e.g., IBM in the 1950s) or for other reasons. In a less centralized organization, several managers may participate in the decision. If it is a large organization, it is unlikely to be a viable decision unless there is consensus about it among the key people who must carry it out. Sharing in decision making, as in a council of executives, results in identification, which improves the quality and quantity of the participants' contributions

(Suojanen, 1956). Groups with "employee-oriented" general supervisors have the highest outputs, even down from the policy level. Organizations with a given degree of decentralization may decide in favor of greater or less decentralization or they may decide to remain at the existing level. It would be interesting to determine empirically the correlation between the degree of decentralization that prevails and the degree that is opted for. *Who* decentralizes is a very critical question that cannot be easily separated from the question of who controls.

1.7.2. What Is Decentralized. In large complex organizations some functions or operations (B) may be decentralized while others are not. When in 1969 it was decided to decentralize federal assistance programs in the United States so that decisions could be made as closely as possible to where services are delivered, agencies were also warned to avoid "overfragmentation" of service-type functions (Ink and Dean, 1970). Legal, procurement, data processing, and engineering appraisal functions exemplified what was not to be decentralized. Research and development tend to be centralized in firms whose corporate structure is centralized, and decentralized or a combination of centralized and decentralized functions are found in firms with a like organization structure (Rubenstein, 1964). Programs administered by the U.S. government have been decentralized for some time. The field-initiated research proposal, judged by peer review, is a major factor in the success of U.S. science. In 1970, staffing of community mental health centers was decentralized. This meant a real break between policy formulation and operational activities in the review/approval process. It also fed fears that the delegation of operational authority to the regional offices would lead to "political control."

1.7.3. Where Centralization Occurs. The question of what is decentralized, of the unit (C) to which decentralization applies, is quite complex. Service organizations include business and industrial organizations, educational institutions, and governments, to mention but a few. Not all business firms are service organizations; most are still primarily manufacturing goods. Most of the literature on decentralization deals with manufacturing organizations. Insofar as some of the functions performed in a manufacturing organization—selling (order procuring and fulfillment), managing inventories, financing, packaging, producing, delivery, installing, maintaining, billing, accounting, managing, and planning—have analogs in service organizations, this literature sheds light on our problem. In particular, selling may correspond to identification of clients' needs, inventory management to the maintenance of clinics, fire, police stations, parks. Both are sensitive to distance between clients and servers. Production is analogous to therapy, diagnosis, and teaching; these are sensitive to capital and functional specialization. Health maintenance and research organizations perform services, but in the case of an institute engaged in long-range basic research, stress on service in its usual connotation is not evident; indeed, many scientists engaged in basic biomedical research make a sharp distinction between research and service. Government, including its regulatory functions, is a service to the community at large, or to some section of it, even though many people find it difficult to view it as such.

There is clearly an interaction between the mixes of functions (B) and the administrative organizational units (C) to which decentralization applies. Thus, the U.S. national and state governments perform many common functions except for defense, diplomacy, and postal service (Fesler, 1965, p. 557).

There are many types of decentralization. Within the gross category of governmental decentralization, we (Furniss, 1974) can identify: *economic* decentralization (to best utilize the country's resources for maximum, low inflationary output of the host of industrial enterprises controlled or regulated by government, funded by 35 to 50 percent of the total national income); *industrial* decentralization (transfer of authority control, initiatives and incentives regarding public enterprises from political ministries to more autonomous managerial boards of directors); *regional economic planning* decentralization (delegating responsibility for optimal utilization of regional resources as well as allocating the needed authority/power (including money) to regional projects, providing for more inputs to national planners); *administrative/internal* decentralization (vertical delegation); *administrative/spatial* decentralization (dispersion); *administrative/functional* decentralization ("autonomous" boards, councils by problems); *political* decentralization (participation, smaller units); *legislative* decentralization (creation of new, more proximate elected bodies or transfer of power from the center); *corporate* decentralization ("worker control"); *millenial* decentralization (decentralism as a creed, see 1.2).

Furniss concluded from his analysis of these eight different ways of decentralizing that they often impede and obstruct one another, and many of the decentralization efforts are unrewarding. When they raise unproductive conflicts between control and efficiency, decentralization does not appear as a superior strategy. "There appears to be no alternative but to face the problems of the modern state in terms of substance, not process" (Furniss, 1974, p. 982). This conclusion is less than persuasive because it is based on the very imprecise and confused categorization of the types of decentralization, but it does reflect some of the prevalent thinking about what is to be decentralized.

1.7.4. On What Level We Decentralize. We can have different degrees of decentralization at different hierarchical levels (D) of the same organization. Voters now vote by districts, and the votes are bundled by major parties. There may be centralization at a high level of aggregation, with more decentralization at the level of government and even greater decentralization among voters and interest groups.

The extent of decentralization, (E), is described in terms of the eight aspects we have analyzed and the scale implicit in Figure 9.1. Whenever we describe a move to decentralize or centralize we should, of course, specify when (F) that was done. The means (G) for bringing about decentralization can be analyzed according to: (1) technological/ economic feasibility; (2) political feasibility; and (3) psychosocial feasibility. Decentralization is not likely to happen unless key political leaders and elites agree that it should and will occur. Nor can it happen unless it is acceptable, at least not objectionable, in a major way to the rank and file of those affected and to their most concerned opinion leaders. It must also be logically, technically, and economically feasible.

Finally, the purposes (H) of decentralizing should be explicit. We have discussed decentralization as a desideratum, value, or end in its own right. It is more fruitful, however, to specify both the practical immediate-survival related purposes as well as the longer-range humanistic ideals, and view decentralization as a means to those ends.

1.8. THE DIMENSIONS OF DECENTRALIZATION

In our attempt to characterize the degree of decentralization by a number or a set of numbers, we try to specify the main groups of variables that are related to decentralization. We could approach this task as an exercise in geometry, as did Bavelas (1951), when he studied communication nets in small groups and viewed a star net ✶ to be more centralized than a wheel net ◌. Decentralization refers to the functional and structural properties of a network. The primary function of the network is to identify requests or needs of clients, and to provide services in response to them. Our main concern is with the shortness and *directness* of lines of communication and control. In addition to geographic distance, we are interested in all sources of costs and delays, and hence in the paucity of points of relay, switching, or recoding.

We propose to analyze the concept of decentralization in terms of eight dimensions: (1) pluralization of agents; (2) dispersion; (3) functional specialization; (4) feedback fitting; (5) hierarchization; (6) delegation; (7) participation in decision making; and (8) participation in redesign.

1.8.1. Pluralization of Agents. This can be measured by the number of agents of the same type in the organization. A bank with ten tellers and teller windows has 10 as its degree of pluralization. The number of telephone terminals or ticket counter positions in a large airport are two more examples of this simple type of variable. The crucial point is that these facilities are provided in parallel (and not in "sequence" or "cascade"), and thus delays in any one facility do not slow up service at any other.[9]

This point becomes important when the case load is such that a larger number of persons is required to perform the services requested. This number of servers could be arranged in sequence to form a single—and hence centralized—service or production line, with each request moving down the entire line, and each agent performing some part of the overall service on each case. Here the agents are arranged in sequence or cascade.

This may be efficient in terms of economizing in the frills and equipment of each server, but the effect of congestion and delay will accumulate along the line. Alternatively, the same number of servers may be arranged in parallel, with each of them constituting a separate service line, fully equipped to perform the entire service. In this case—which we call pluralization—delays or errors in any one line will not interfere with service in the other line; on the average, some time of the clients may be saved, but the time of the servers may be utilized somewhat less efficiently. In one sense, the problem of optimal pluralization of service facilities resembles the problem of optimal redundancy.

1.8.2. Dispersion in Space. The degree of dispersion is, in its simplest version, the number of *different* geographical locations over which a plurality of agents of the same type are distributed. This cannot, of course, exceed the degree of pluralization.[10] Beyond this simple count of the number of distinct sites is the geographic spread, measured by the mean, median, and modal distance between them. If two receptionists are 10 feet apart, the degree of dispersion may be less than it would be if they were 3000 miles apart. If, through a tie line they could communicate with one another to achieve all the *essential purposes* as efficiently and as effectively as when they were 10 feet apart, their degree of dispersion would still be different in the two cases as long as their accessibility to clients would be different.

The next six dimensions will be referred to briefly here:

1.8.3. Functional Specialization. This can be characterized by the number of specialized functions performed by specialized agents. The distance from one such function to another is measured by the cost of retraining and/or reequipping a server, already competent for the first, to perform also the second. Another measure is the time and cost for a server of shifting from performing one function to performing the other. These matters are particularly relevant where performance of different specialties demands the deployment of costly equipment or personnel.

1.8.4. Feedback Fitting and Responsiveness. The lapse in time between a client's presentation of a request and a satisfactory response is a measure of responsiveness. This is the average, median, and modal number of negotiating passes and the average rate of improvement; still other measures will be introduced later.

1.8.5. Flatness of Hierarchization. That is, most simply, the inverse of the number of levels of supervision, where agents at different levels coordinate actions of agents at other levels. A flat rather than steep pyramid is a correlative of decentralization.

1.8.6. Coordination and Delegation. The number and nature of decisions that may be taken on lower levels of the hierarchy are considered in this dimension. This implies a decentralization of (1) memory, that is, information storage and recall; (2) decision points that utilize this memory; and (3) access to or by the clients; as well as (4) time and resources devoted to lateral communication of acceptable effectiveness.

1.8.7. Participation in Decision Making, Performance, and Reallocation of Services. This refers to the probability of access to the agency by clients in determining the "intake channels" or avenues of approach, the making of particular decisions, and the time and resources provided for such access, with the resulting shift in the probability distribution of outcomes.

1.8.8. Participation in Structural Redesign. This can be defined as the extent to which possibilities for broader review exist, facilitating input to changing the general staffing and structure of the organization, together with the resulting shift in the probability of such outcomes.

A summary index combining the first four dimensions might be most relevant for the accessibility and quality of service to clients; a second index, combining dimensions 5 to 8, might tell us primarily about the distribution of power within the organization and some of the conditions of people working in it.

Developing and testing any particular disaggregated or partly aggregated indices, however, clearly would go beyond the limits of this book.

These last two dimensions have been stressed, but not consistently separated, by Levy and Truman (1971). They refer to them as supposedly characteristic of governmental organizations in contrast to private organizations. In our view, this public-private distinction is overstated. Many services are occasionally performed in the public sector, and others occasionally in the private sector. Customers of private monopolies, such as airlines or telephone companies in the United States, may have to raise their voices in complaint rather than "exit" from the clientele of a private firm by taking their business elsewhere. The relative costs and benefits of "exit" and "voice" strategies in each such situation are more important in determining the outcome than are the governmental or business character of the service organizations concerned.[11] Similarly, the concepts of work load, systems capacity, service costs, response time, delay and error rates, queueing and congestion problems all cut across the public-private distinction. What major differences, if any, should still be ascribed to these two categories—such as public versus private systems or agencies of transport, education, broadcasting, and the like—empirical studies should reveal.

Something similar applies, in our view, to statistics and other measures of organizational performance. Some services, public or private, are performed in discrete and readily identifiable acts or units, such as ambulance services or vaccinations against certain diseases. Other services, public or private, come in poorly delimited and highly interactive combinations, such as the cumulative cultural content of radio and television programs by private networks in the United States or by the public British Broadcasting Corporation, or the educational impact of private or public schools and universities.

While Levy's and Truman's stress on the supposedly fundamental

1.8 The Dimensions of Decentralization / 25

difference between private and governmental service systems seems to us not particularly helpful for the understanding of decentralization, their stress on *participation* does not promise to be fruitful. For that concept, we should like to suggest some possible further operational distinctions:

Participation by whom refers to the possible participation by members of the service organization, its direct clients, and by those indirectly affected by its external economies and diseconomies, benefits, or deprivations. Which of these possibilities materialize is a question of empirical fact in each particular case. Such pressure for participation by indirectly but substantially affected parties may occur in the world of private business decisions no less than in the public sector. In this respect, not so much the differences but the commonalities of many problems in the private and the public sectors seem to us characteristic of many highly developed industrial countries.

Participation in what refers to the scope or the category of decisions, such as those distinguished in points 7 and 8 above.

Participation with what weight refers to the difference that participation by some particular person or group will make in the probability of some particular outcome.[12]

Some Recent Literature. Blau and Schoenherr (1971) were among the first modern social scientists to study the problems with this cost-effectiveness approach. The voluminous earlier literature still discoursed on the subject as "the zoning of power" (Merriam, 1934; Hariou, 1892; Harris, 1925; Lowrie, 1922). Truman (1940), for example, analyzed the problem as "so arranging the constituent elements of the body of politics that its human resources may be employed to the full, that no single group shall be so poorly articulated with the whole as to desire the destruction of the established equilibrium, and that the entire organism may adjust to change without violent rupture or dissolution." Blau and Schoenherr, however, began to ask how size and automation of an organization affect the number of authority levels and the degree to which authority is centralized. They measured this by who makes decisions about personnel and budget, delegation to local managers, and spread of influence. They regarded performance on the lower levels as predictable and reliable.

Nordlinger (1972) articulated three goals for decentralization: increased governmental responsiveness; amelioration of political alienation in citizens; and improved municipal services. He summarized four "models" or types of neighborhood decentralization: bureaucratic (delegation to neighborhood civil servants); representational (political participation, direct or indirect, by residents-clients); governmental (combination of the above two); and Little City Halls, the permanent location of municipal facilities in a city's neighborhood.

Yates (1972) has examined block associations, community task forces, neighborhood corporations, and community school boards for their initiatives. He found that decentralization produces a greater awareness of community needs; that all these experiments in decentralization except community boards have introduced some innovations, but that no experiment has produced quick or dramatic solutions to major neighborhood problems. By and large, the experiments did not impose great cost burdens on the taxpayers, and they did not bring out the worst fears of decentralization critics: corruption, patronage, and abuse of power. Corruption may be viewed as behavior in response to a probabilistic reinforcement schedule that deviates from the goals of the organization as a whole, such as the greatest good for the largest number. The more the goals of an organization are socially unjustified, however, the more socially beneficial is its corruption or inefficiency, or both (cf. B. Brecht, 1967, vol. 5, pp. 2081–2086). Overall, the community boards, which are advisory bodies in New York City concerned with physical planning and capital budgeting and provide a forum for articulation of grievances and sporadic protest, showed the greatest power and impact.

Child (1973) examined relations between centralization and conforming behavior versus conflict behavior in 78 British business organizations through interviews with 787 senior managers. He found that centralization tends to encourage conformity and low levels of conflict through the prescribing of roles.

An important exception was the development of a methodological approach for comparing the formal structure of bureaucracies, but not specifically with regard to decentralization (Samuel and Mannheim, 1970). They used four dimensions to characterize and classify bureaucracies: (1) Structural control, reflected by the hierarchy of authority. This is similar to the measures we use in Chapter 5, in that status, measured by the number of immediate subordinates, may vary from level to level. (2) Functionalization measured by (a) the number of distinct jobs; (b) the extent to which positions are dispersed among the jobs; (c) functional specialization, by which they meant the proportion of specialized jobs relative to simplified ones. A specialized job was defined as requiring at least four years of formal, professional, or technical training. (3) Interlevel impersonality, measured by the extent of universalistic, specific, affectively neutral relations among superiors and subordinates. (4) Normativity, measured by the weighted number of rules, regulations, and procedures in a formal or compulsory form that existed. Profiles of 30 Israeli production plants that included, in addition to these four dimensions, age, size of parent enterprise, size of plant, kind of ownership (mass, process, unit), were analyzed by a multidimensional scalogram procedure. The 30 profiles could be mapped into a two-dimensional plane and grouped into three meaningful clusters, indicating six types of bureaucracies: (1) rudimentary (low normativity, little functionalization); (2) emergent (high control); (3) interpersonal; (4) balanced; (5) managerial; (6) technical. These findings are not yet definitive, but the methodology is promising. It may prove fruitful to combine this with some of the techniques we develop in this book and adapt it to the analysis of decentralization. It seems to us that both rudimentary and technical bureaucracies could be centralized or decentralized. It would be necessary to adapt this typology to service organizations and to stress responsiveness to clients' needs, as we have done.

On the more theoretical level, outstanding analyses of decentralization issues have been contributed by Arrow and Hurwicz (1960) and Marschak and Radner (1972). Arrow and Hurwicz pointed out, for example, that a completely centralized organization would need enormous information processing and storage capacities, whereas decentralization is the result of a competitive process. Marschak and Radner show that centralization cannot hurt and may help if all decision functions are feasible and of equal cost, a condition that is rarely met. Morris (1968) presented a series of models and a valuable summary of the literature (pp. 18-22) in terms of 43 hypotheses, such as "the tendency to decentralize is related to the size of the organization," "the greater the urgency of a decision and the shorter the time in which to make it, the greater the tendency to centralize," and "the greater the potential consequences of a decision, the more likely it is to be centralized."

1.9. RELATION TO DECENTRALIZATION INDEXES AND HYPOTHESES

The relation between decentralization and measures of the extent to which the aims of decentralization were attained have been investigated empirically. One such measure (Neghandhi and Reimann, 1973) is organizational effectiveness in terms of: (1) ability to hire and retain high-level manpower; (2) employee morale and job satisfaction; (3) turnover and absenteeism; (4) interpersonal relations; (5) interdepartmental relations; and (6) utilization of high-level manpower.

To examine this relation, a composite index of decentralization was proposed. It employed nine factors:

1. Hierarchical layers, from top executive to blue-collar worker; this corresponds to our "flatness of hierarchy" aspect or dimension.
2. Locus of decision making with respect to major policies (e.g., mergers, diversification decisions), from chief executive/owner to broad representation of stockholders; this corresponds to a part of what we called participation in organizational redesign.
3. Locus of decision making with respect to sales policies.
4. Locus of decision making with respect to product mix.
5. Locus of decision making with respect to standard setting in production.
6. Locus of decision making with respect to manpower policies; together, items 3 through 6 correspond to much of what we called participation in current decisions.
7. Locus of decision making with respect to selection of executives.
8. The degree of participation in long-range planning; items 7 to 9 again correspond, like item 2, to parts of participation in organizational redesign.
9. The degree of information sharing, from little, where all information is kept secret from everyone except a few top executives, to considerable, where there are general memos on all major aspects; this is an aspect of what we called "delegation," here applied to the task of receiving information.

By locus is meant the level in a vertical hierarchy (our flatness dimension) with some delegational and specialization aspects implicit. Information-sharing also is remotely related to our feedback dimension. Our aspects of pluralization and dispersion do not seem to play a role in the composite index used by Neghandi and Reimann. Their findings suggest that decentralized firms may stay more effective: firms with longer-term perspectives prefer flatter hierarchies with more consultation. As mentioned earlier in this book, these findings have not been confirmed by subsequent studies. The discrepancies are due partly to different interpretations.

Another index that has been proposed (Kaufman, 1963) is the degree to which subordinates in an organization are subjected to central directives that spell out the work to be done, the way it is to be done, and the standards of quality, speed, and cost the final services must meet. If top management spells out such instructions in detail, the organization is called centralized; if only a few guidelines are given, leaving interpretation and provision of details to the field units, it is called decentralized. The organization is called centralized if top management controls completely the selection, advancement, and discipline of other servers, with the appearance of appeals channels and immunity to leadership sanctions being signs of decentralization. A third aspect of centralization is the existence of a central treasury in which all revenues are deposited, with disbursements authorized only by top management, whereas units in a decentralized structure have their own sources of income and credit, spending part or all of their resources as they see fit. Fourth, in centralized organizations there is a great deal of reporting, inspection, and central record keeping, while top management of decentralized organizations does not necessarily know, in detail, what their subordinates are doing. Fifth, servers in centralized structures refer major decisions upward for review and prior clearance by superiors. Sixth, centralized organizations develop loyalty to top management by such devices as rotation of personnel from unit to unit and special training and indoctrination programs.

As we point out in Chapter 9, rotating potential executives from unit to unit is favored by a decentralized structure, and vice versa as well. The inculcation of loyalty to top management is a separate aspect. The other five of Kaufman's attributes of centralization correspond to our flatness, delegation, and, to some extent, feedback dimensions. The notions of participation and specializations appear only marginally, with pluralization and dispersion seemingly absent altogether. Here, too, there is a conspicuous absence of any mention of the client, and that is one of the main differences between most other indexes and our approach.

1.10. FORMULATION OF CENTRAL PROBLEMS

To state the key problems to be analyzed we need to formulate the general model that represents our point of view. First, we list the variables that seem to us most essential for a structural and functional description of a service organization. For each variable we indicate the approximate range of values each is now likely to take, and the plausible trend its present value is likely to take if all the other variables stay fixed. Second, we make explicit our assumptions about relations among these variables and general optimization criteria. Finally, we formulate the problem to be solved; this involves primarily the derivation of formulas expressing various measures of the optimal degree of decentralization in terms of other variables, like the request load, so that we can estimate likely trends.

According to Cairncross (1971), no one can lay down from first

30 / Decentralization: Approaches and Dimensions

Table 1.2. Key Parameters for Clients

		Range	Trend
N_o	Number of clients in a region	10^3–10^{10}	Increasing to a limit
L_o	Number of requests per client per month	1–10	Increasing to a limit
D	Distance or average diameter of a region where clients are located (miles)	1–10^5	Constant
c'_{wa}	Average cost of a client's time, in dollars per hour	1–50	Increasing
u	Average utility to a client of an adequate response to his or her request, in dollars per request	1–10^3	Constant
R	Value of the client's time, in dollars per hour he or she is willing to pay for a service with 1-hour turn-around time	1–100	
Parameters for Service Agents			
c'_{op}	Average cost of an agent of a certain kind, in dollars per hour	10–100	Increasing
w	Average time an operative agent, working alone, has to spend to produce his or her share of a satisfactory response to a request, in hours per request	.1–10	Decreasing
l	Level of command at which the agent works	1–10	Increasing with age
T^u	Time, in hours per request, that agent spends in upward communication		
T^d	Time the agent spends in downward communication, hours per request		
T^l	Time spent on lateral communication		
T^s	Time spent in thinking, hours per request		
b	Amount of memory, in chunks of information		
a	Probability that a random request is met by one chunk of memory		
S	Service rate of an agent, request per month		Increasing

Table 1.2. (Continued)

	Key System Variables	Range	Trend
v	Average speed it takes to forward a request, client, or server over a physical transport channel, miles per hour	3–1000	Constant
λ	Number of levels in a hierarchical organization	1–10	
C	Cost of fixed capital investment in system (amortization plus interest) dollars per agent per month	1–1000	Increasing

principles the exact point beyond which further centralization of control in a large firm is counterproductive, even though it is everyday experience that there is such a point. He states that "the great secret of efficient management of a national economy as of an industrial concern is to recognize that fact." Cairncross's claim that no one *can* determine the optimal degree of decentralization is a challenge. In a modest way, that is the central problem we try to solve.

First, we shall consider a set of variables describing the clients to be served; second, variables describing the functional characteristics of serving agents; third, variables describing the structural characteristics of the service agency. These variables are listed in Table 1.2.

These are only the most important of the variables to consider. The choice and selection of variables already make many fundamental assumptions and represent our point of view. We now make explicit some of our most important additional assumptions that are necessary to derive an expression for the total net utility of an organization. These are used to calculate values of the variables characterizing decentralization that optimize that net utility. The utility of a satisfactory response to a client's request is commensurate with: (a) that of all other clients (and an average is a meaningful measure); (b) disutility of receiving unsatisfactory service; and (c) costs and prices of providing the response. We know very little about how much clients value services. Willingness to pay is a crude measure. It can be improved if it is weighted by the inverse of the client's ability to pay and by the client's propensity to spend rather than to save.

Even less is known about how to combine the utilities of two or more clients into a measure for the group according to a social welfare function. The average is a plausible function. Maximizing the average, however, may not help. It may even hurt some clients whose utilities are already below acceptable limits.

Disutility of failure to get an adequate response could be simply the negative of utility of getting an adequate response. But this does not take into account the opportunity that the client may have lost—and certainly the time that was lost—of getting more satisfactory service from another source. Moreover, the disutility of a harmful response, such as the new disease caused by side effects of improper medical treatment, may add a considerable amount. Like utility, this disutility could be measured by a client's willingness to avoid the undesired consequences. These are not always known to the client, and the client may not have the wisdom to make an accurate judgment.

The distinction between disutility, cost, and price is well known. For each quantity, however, we need to append "to whom and judged by whom." They may be judged subjectively by the client, or by someone dependent on the client. Or else it is tempting to estimate a social or economic disutility by the cost of replacing the victim in roles he or she can no longer fill.

A utility approach to our central problem could be to calculate those values of decentralization variables that, within given limits of cost, would maximize or at least increase some social welfare function, such as the average net utility of service. A cost approach toward the same result seems preferable. For a given volume and level of service performance, it is to find those values for the relevant variables that will minimize costs. This assumes that communities want the levels of services and benefits that they are actually getting, and to ask how they could get these at less cost. This bypasses the need to take up here the more complex question of what level of services they ought to get, or might like or learn to like.

How do the optimal degrees of decentralization change as certain key parameters, such as the request load, vary according to known secular trends? The general conclusions will also be discussed for their ethical and policy implications. If there is a natural trend toward decentralization under specific conditions, which seems ethically sound as well, one should make policies to conform with and abet the trend. If there is a major trend of the times that does not seem ethically sound, we should seek to develop policies to reverse it.

Here, one should try to distinguish between short-run and long-run trends. A policy that conforms to long-run trends may be considered preferable to one that conforms to short-run trends; temporary sacrifices are often made in the hope of a better life for future generations or even for a greater chance of national survival or because of

1.10 Formulation of Central Problems / 33

belief in an afterlife. Actions that bring immediate pleasures but suffering in the long run have been called social traps (Platt, 1973). Our own point of view leads us to distinguish from the outset between what we want and what we think is likely to happen. Our values are humanistic and concerned with truth as well as with ethics. Our cognitive effort is concentrated on those effects of technological and social development that by the evidence are revealed to be the dominant short-term trend today and for the next two or three decades.

Chapter 2

Pluralization and Dispersion

2.0 INTRODUCTION

To say that a service is delivered in a decentralized manner is to evoke in the minds of many people an image in which those who perform the service are close[1] to the clients. This image involves numerous servers dispersed among the clients. It is natural, therefore, to begin to think of decentralization in terms of the number of service providers.

We will henceforth refer to servers as agents or facilities, with the understanding that an agent is the smallest stand-alone unit in a service organization. This does not mean that an agent can meet every request for service without other agents. Nor does it mean that agents are always human servers; they could be small, stand-alone computers, intelligent terminals, or man-machine systems. A machine that changes coins or bills is an example; a possible check-cashing machine is a future possibility; automatic tollbooths on the highway and telephone booths at an airport are other examples.

If we replace a single agent—for example, a bank teller, telephone booth, or information desk agent—by several essentially identical agents in order to prevent congestion, we shall call that *pluralization*. Insofar as the availability of more agents should appear to waiting clients as a service that is more responsive to their individual needs, whereas a single agent would be viewed as a central point for service delivery, it is reasonable to identify pluralization as *one* aspect of decentralization. The greater the degree of pluralization, the more decentralized the service organization, *if other factors stayed unchanged*. One of these other factors, for example, is *dispersion*. If several bank tellers or telephone booths are distributed over a large area rather than concentrated in one location, we have an even greater degree of decentralization than if that same number of agents are all in one place. The organization is also decentralized if the number of agents is increased, even without changing their placement.

The simplest concrete instance of a pure pluralization *problem* is determining how many telephone booths to place at the same location, such as in a large airport. Formally identical problems are obtained when the telephone terminals are replaced by teller windows in a bank, toll booths on a highway, or ticket booths at a theater. For purposes of analysis, we will assume that there are n agents (i.e., facilities or servers) located at the same point, with n to be determined. A newly arrived client is served by any free agent. While initially we neglect the effect of dispersion, we introduce it later in the chapter.

2.1 THE SIMPLEST CASE: NO FLUCTUATION IN DEMAND AND NO DISPERSION OF FACILITIES

Clearly, the cost of maintaining agents increases with pluralization. But there are many components to the *total* cost. It is characteristic of our approach that we attempt to include in our total cost all the factors that determine what is reasonable for the *community as a whole* and in the *long run*. Thus, we include such factors as disutility to clients of not having enough agents. Clients, requesting service from an organization that engages fewer agents than necessary to cope with the load, must wait. Unless they have a way of occupying themselves in ways they consider a valuable use of their time, they incur a cost proportional to the value of their lost time.[2] If a society chooses to consider only the costs to a service system and to the taxpayers or other sponsors who pay for it, and to disregard or discount the costs to the clients, the calculations of what it will consider cost-effective behavior can be made by correspondingly modifying our formulas. The power aspects of this problem will be treated in Chapter 8. In some cases, such as waiting for medical attention in an emergency, delay may harm the

2.1 The Simplest Case / 37

client far more than in proportion to the time, whereas in other cases, such as settlement of a court case, delay may work in the client's favor.

In Chapter 1 we introduced the *load* as our main dependent variable. We denoted it by L, the number of requests for service that clients generate in one month. In terms of the variables introduced in Section 1.10.1, $L = N_o L_o$. We now start our analysis with the assumption that L is the same for each month, that $L/30$ is the same number of requests that must be serviced each day and $12L$ the number each year. The conclusion derived from this simplifying assumption—that increased loads favor pluralization—holds only in situations where the effect of fluctuations in load or availability of agents, and the effects of dispersion or other variables that are now ignored, do not lead to a reversal or contradiction of this conclusion.

Our central dependent variable is n, the *plurality* or number of *service-providing agents*. It is to be determined in its dependence on L, so that total costs are least and net benefits are greatest. We must keep in mind what the total costs include and how important the benefits may be. Two kinds of situations in which the relation of n to L does not depend on the other variables that characterize an organization are (1) the controlled experiment, where all variables other than L and n are kept fixed, and (2) the survey based on a statistical design, where the sample of organizations studied is such that all values of important variables other than L and n are equally represented so that their effects cancel one another without affecting the n-L relation.

Both the controlled experiment and the scientific survey are not only very costly, but are also limited by the assumption that L and the variables that are kept fixed should be statistically independent.

The simplest relation between n and L is based on selecting enough agents to cope with the load but no more than necessary. Let S be the rate in requests per month at which an agent can service a request. As in the case of L, let us assume that S does not vary with time or the request and that it is the same for each agent. If one agent can service S requests per month, and the agents operate independently, the n agents can service nS requests per month. If each agent is to be fully occupied and never overloaded, then nS should be made equal to L. Hence

$$n = L/S$$

Frequently, the capacity of an agent is measured by the time it takes to service one request rather than the requests per month the agent can service. This is simply $1/S$ months per request, and if we assume a

38 / Pluralization and Dispersion

time-scale factor, such as τ hours per month, then the *service time* is τ/S hours per request. Similarly, the demand or required time per request would be τ/L hours per request. Let us abbreviate τ/S by T, the service time.

If $n > L/S$, there will be unused or reserve capacity. If $n < L/S$, there will be demand that is not met. Suppose it costs C dollars per month to maintain each agent, regardless of whether used or unused. This is a *fixed cost* and if it is paid when the agent or facility is first acquired, it is amortized over its useful life with straight-line depreciation, at the rate of \$$C$ per month. The total fixed cost is then nC dollars per month, assuming no economies of scale.

Added to that may be an *operating cost* that varies with the number of requests serviced. For example, maintaining a car repair station may cost C dollars per month, but each car serviced may incur an additional cost in parts and labor. Suppose that it costs c_{op} dollars per request to service it on top of the fixed cost. Then the total operating cost is Lc_{op} dollars per month if there is a simple linear increase with L. This cost component does not depend on the number of agents n, provided that each of the n agents processes $1/n^{th}$ of the load.

Demand not met generates a third cost component. Let c_{sf} be the *cost of suffering* endured by the client and those attending the client due to a request for service that is not met. If $n < L/S$, then $L - Sn$ requests per month will be unmet, resulting in cost of $(L - Sn)c_{sf}$ dollars per month. Hence, the total cost is:

$$Cn + Lc_{op} \quad \text{if } n > L/S$$

and (2.1)

$$Cn + Snc_{op} + (L - Sn)c_{sf} \quad \text{if } n \leq L/S$$

In Figure 2.1, we plot this total cost versus n. As long as $c_{sf} > C/S - c_{op}$ it pays to increase n up to L/S.

Now let us consider the cost reduction achieved by adding one more agent to a system in which there still is demand not met. Such an additional agent will serve S cases and reduce the unmet demand accordingly. It will be economically rational to add this agent if this will reduce the costs of unmet demand, Sc_{sf}, by more than the concomitant sum of the increase in fixed costs, C, and in operating costs, Sc_{op}. It will then pay to add further agents, as long as this condition holds, up to $n = L/S$. In this sense, increased loads will make it rational to increase the pluralization of agents. Increased loads on service facilities result from growing populations, especially populations

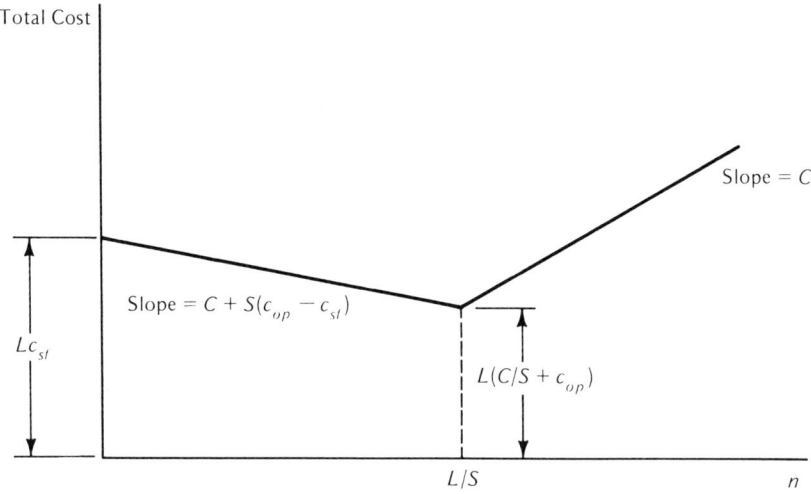

Figure 2.1. Total cost vs. number of servers.

whose levels of education and aspiration are increasing and whose demands must be given weight.[3] Thus, rising L may be the trend. Insofar as plurality is an aspect of decentralization, the prevailing trend would thus favor decentralization in that respect.

2.2 ECONOMIES OF SCALE

Placing an order for several facilities, rather than one, often reduces the unit fixed cost of a facility. Thus, the purchase of 100 telephone handsets, computer terminals, first-aid kits, school texts, and so on, may cost less than 100 times the cost of one. Similarly, the operating cost per request, c_{op}, or per hour in servicing requests, c'_{op}, may decrease if there are more facilities or agents using expandable resources than just one. Thus, the unit cost of electricity may decrease if larger quantities are consumed.

If C is the fixed cost in dollars per month of one facility, then the corresponding unit cost (C_n), when a batch order of n is placed, will be less than C by amount depending on n. The discount fraction is $(C -$

40 / *Pluralization and Dispersion*

C_n/C, and it would vary with n according to a curve with a shape like that shown in Figure 2.2.

Suppose now that there are economies of scale in operating costs. These may result from an increase in the number of cases processed by one agent due to increases in productivity via technological aids, for example. The economies of scale may also result from an increase in load that calls for more agents and resources to be utilized, with discounts for the use of larger resource levels, despite added distribution costs.

Both centralization and decentralization result in economies of scale (Hannan and Fried, 1977). The most frequent argument given in favor of centralization is that it results in economies of scale. Whether that reason is used to justify the desire to centralize for other purposes or whether it is valid can be ascertained by examining comparative data on cost reductions.

A third scale effect might be a nonlinear increase in the costs of demands not met with an increase in their number $(L - Sn)$ as $(L - Sn)c_{sf}$ in place of c_{sf}. If this cost is significant, it would tend to favor pluralization. Thus, an unchanged percentage of neglected and alienated adolescents in a small town may not suffice to sustain gangs and

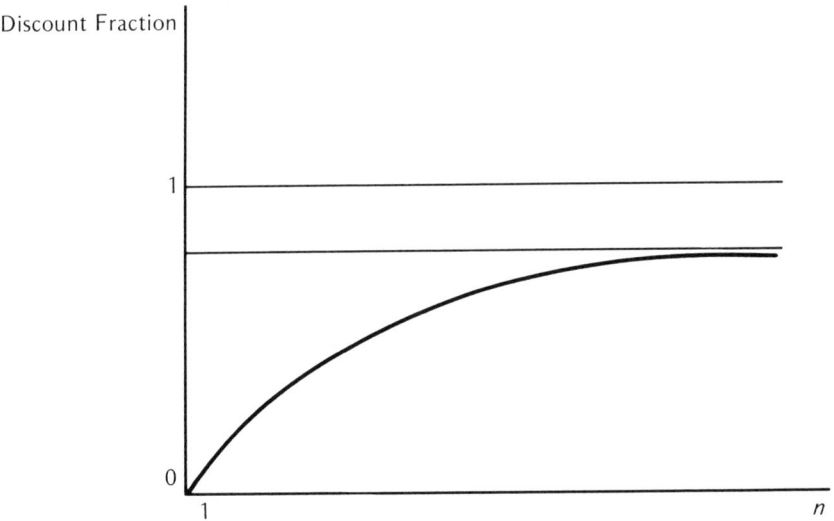

Figure 2.2. Discount fraction vs. *n*.

drug traffic, but it may suffice to produce these effects among the larger population of a big city. This may justify the provision of preventive social services in the latter case.

We argue later that economies of scale result from both centralization and decentralization. We also point out that spokesmen for centralization, observed in some trends toward greater chief executive authority and greater sharing of high-level financing (Haider, 1971, p. 113), tend to underestimate the attraction of "intimacy of scale" as opposed to economies of scale (Schumacher, 1973) to decentralizers.

2.3 SIMPLE CASE WITH UNIFORM SPATIAL DISPERSION AND NO FLUCTUATIONS

Pluralization was the first aspect of decentralization we considered because it best illustrated our approach. The concepts of centralization or decentralization are based on the idea of a center, and it has a geometric origin. Before advancing to notions of more general spaces, it is helpful to examine other simple cases of Euclidean geometry[4] as they would apply to the geography of a plane or line. For this reason, spatial dispersion of agents is the second aspect of decentralization that we consider. If the number of agents to be dispersed is fixed, and the distribution of demand over a region is given, deciding where to locate the agents is known as the *location problem*. The simplest example is that of a region consisting of a straight-line segment, with requests for service as likely to originate from any point along the segment as from any other. If there is only one agent, it should obviously be located at the center.

On the more general problem of where to locate a fixed number of facilities, there is a large literature and an active research community. Fermat and Steiner were two eminent mathematicians who studied optimal facility location problems many decades ago. Many problems have yielded to mathematically elegant solutions and have led to new challenges for mathematicians. Some of these challenges originate from such problems as the optimal location of noxious facilities, distinguishing between emergency and routine service facilities, round trip problems, and so on (see bibliography by Hsu, 1976). In the 1960s, such problems as finding the coordinates to locate activities so as to minimize $\Sigma_{i,j} w_i d_{ij} \lambda_{ij}$, where w_i = service demanded at location i, with λ_{ij} = 0 or 1 representing a spatial assignment, and d_{ij} = distance from i^{th} to j^{th} service site, led to problems of great computational complexity. An important early study of the "best" national pattern for locating all industries suggested that where there is more than one effective input restriction, the decision that is typically made is to split available capacity between two or more of the possible sites (Marschak, 1951).

The problem of primary concern to us, however, is not so much the optimal location of a given number of facilities but the optimal number of facilities, assuming that number to be optimally located. More generally, we ask for both an optimal number of facilities and their optimal location. The development of a computer program to study the deployment of services in a region, such as a state with a given demand distribution over the region, is relatively simple. The first and hardest step is to partition the region or to specify a set of service subregions that covers the regions (possibly with overlap, possibly with unsharp boundaries). The difficulty stems from specifying criteria for such a partition or covering. Should each service subregion have the same load? There may be infinitely many such partitions. Should the facility be located at the "center of gravity" of each subregion, that is, at the point where the average distance to any other point in the region is minimum? Why consider only averages? A finite number of points could be very far from the center while most are close by. Even if averages are used, should each subregion have the same average distance to its center? The problem of simultaneously specifying the number of subregions, their boundaries, and their centers seems impossible in its full generality. Appendix 2.2 suggests an approach to this general problem that uses computer simulation.

In practice, we are more often faced with the relocation of existing facilities. The items marked LC (location change) in the bibliography by Corey and Stafford (1969) illustrate the kind of work done along these lines.

To gain insight into our problem in a way that the literature does not provide, consider an extremely simplified situation in which the location problem has an easy solution but leads to a revealing formula for the optimum number of facilities, an optimal degree of pluralization.

A Case in One Dimension. Consider the following illustrative vehicle: to service motorists along a stretch of highway that is D miles long and of small constant width with first aid, gasoline, repairs, and so forth, through a single all-purpose service station, we would place that facility at the midpoint of the stretch (see Figure 2.3). Let us assume that at any time the sites at which requests originate are uniformly distributed over the D-mile stretch and that they arise at a rate of L requests per month. We can now ask whether there is an optimal number (n) of general purpose, identical service stations that would be rewarding to distribute uniformly along the D-mile strip.[5]

To answer that (Kochen and Deutsch, 1972) we need to know, in addition, the fixed cost, C, in dollars per month of maintaining each of

2.3 Simple Case with Uniform Spatial Dispersion / 43

the n stations; the variable cost, k, in dollars per hour; and the speed, v, in miles per hour, of delivering the service. The variable cost is $k = c'_{op} + c'_{wa}$ where c'_{op} is the operating cost as in the previous section, except that it is measured in dollars per hour rather than dollars per request; c'_{wa} is the cost of the client's time, in dollars per hour, that the client regards to be lost while waiting for the request to be forwarded and serviced. (The time of a patient waiting in a dentist's office may not be totally lost if this patient acquires information there from magazines he or she would otherwise not have seen. But the patient may regard it as a less valuable expenditure of time than had it been spent on the job.) The difference in the value of the time thus spent is c'_{wa}.

We assume a transportation medium that transports at a uniform speed of v miles per hour. This should be interpreted as an average speed, for the speed varies depending on whether there are or are not obstructions along the strip. Then the delivery time to a point at a distance of x from the station is x/v. Because the sites of requests are assumed to be uniformly distributed over the length D, and the station is in the middle, the maximum distance to the station is $D/2$ and the average distance between the site of a randomly selected request and the station at midpoint is $D/4$. Hence the average delivery time for a request is $D/4v$.

If we take account of both the time it takes to forward the request and the time it takes to deliver the response, and if we assume both to be equal, the average transit time is then $D/2v$ instead of $D/4v$, as above.

By a slightly less centralized organization we mean two stations with identical inventories (each containing a copy of each valuable

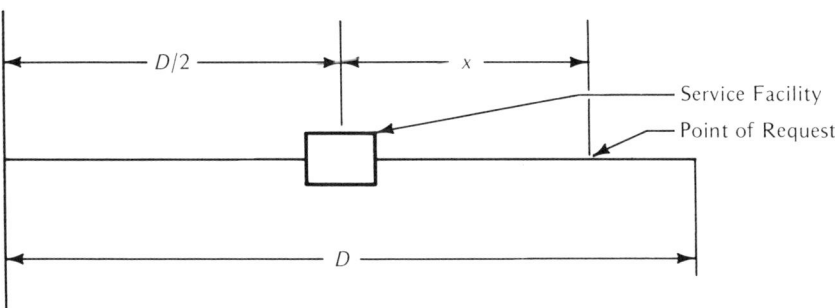

Figure 2.3. A centralized organization.

44 / Pluralization and Dispersion

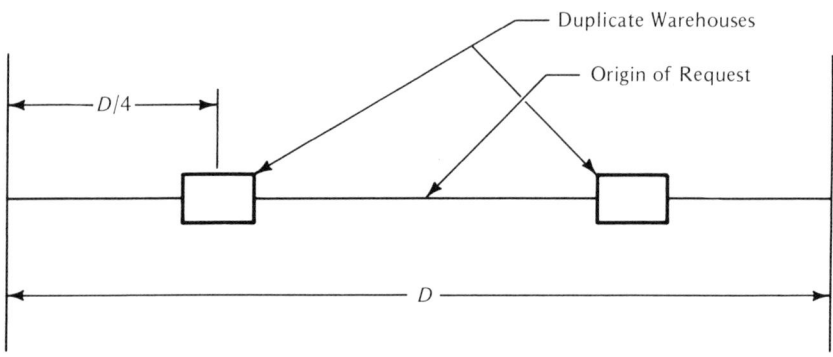

Figure 2.4. A two-facility organization.

object), located at the quarter points of our elongated region (see Figure 2.4).

The D-mile strip is then divided into n service regions, each D/n miles long. A service station is placed in the center of each, and it services any request in its service region. The maximum distance that any such request must be forwarded and the service delivered is $1/2$ D/n miles each way. On the average, it is half of that, or $D/4n$ miles. That will take $D/4vn$ hours. If we neglect the time to perform the service at the site where the request originated and the time to forward the request, but count only the time to deliver a response from the center to the site, the operating cost is then $Dk/4vn$ dollars per request or $DkL/4vn$ dollars per month. To this we must add the cost of maintaining the n stations, which is nC dollars per month. This fixed cost increases with n, while the operating cost decreases. Hence, there is an optimal n for which the total cost is least. We assume that the operating cost and maintenance costs are comparable in magnitude. The total cost is:

$$\text{Cost} = \frac{kDL}{4vn} + nC \qquad (2.2)$$

We seek that value of n for which the cost of increasing it by 1 (adding one more service station) is just offset by the marginal decrease in operating cost. This is equivalent to minimizing cost with respect to n, shown in Appendix 2.1. The optimal value of n is:

$$n = \frac{1}{2}\left(\sqrt{1 + \frac{kDL}{Cv}} - 1\right) \doteq \frac{1}{2}\sqrt{\frac{kDL}{Cv}} \qquad (2.3)$$

2.3 Simple Case with Uniform Spatial Dispersion / 45

The approximation holds if $kDL \gg Cv$. Thus $n \doteq 2$, if $kDL \doteq 16Cv$, an error of 3 percent.
Let us suppose the following possible values:

C = 10,000 dollars per month to maintain a facility
k = 10 dollars per hour to service requests
D = 1000 miles
v = 100 miles per hour to forward requests
L = 100,000 requests per month

Note how the middle curve, in Figures 2.5A and 2.5B corresponding to $C = 1000$ and 10,000 respectively, shows a decrease in the total cost (Equation 2.2) as n increases to a number near 2 and increases thereafter. The bottom curve corresponds to the total cost for $k = 0$ (fixed cost only) and the top curve for $k = 100$, for which the minimum n is about 6. In Figure 2.6, we see how the optimal number of pluralized facilities, computed according to Equation (2.3), increases with the request load.

These graphs demonstrate—as does, of course, the formula given earlier (Equation 2.3 above)—that this simple model is equally sensitive over a wide range to proportionate changes in k, D, L, C, and v, but is more sensitive to changes in C and v where these values are very small. The graphs also show that pluralization declines as capital costs and/or delivery speeds increase, but that it increases even at rising levels of capital cost and delivery speeds if the load of service requests and the costs of delivery have risen faster.

Secular trends favor an increase in L, while D stays constant, v increases only slowly, and k/C, the ratio of operating to fixed cost, may not increase as fast as L. Thus, on balance, secular trends tend to favor an increasing value of n, or pluralization.

This result tends to modify the suggestion of Herbert Simon and his associates that "improved methods of communication have made a much greater degree of centralization possible" (Simon, Smithburg, and Thompson 1956).[6] If we are to judge what is probable or rational, in addition to what is merely possible we now may consider that a society that produces telephones also produces higher request rates, service demands, and decision loads for public and private agencies. Such a society may become more affluent in regard to capital costs, and thus the optimum number of decentralized facilities actually may increase.

The optimum level of decentralization emerges as a system property in response to changes, not in one parameter, but in the *configuration* of several critical parameters. Such a configuration may favor the excellent telephone service and considerable political decentralization of present-day Switzerland rather than the slow messenger service and the much greater political centralization of ancient Egypt or of Tokugawa, Japan.[7] Even under the simplified assumptions of our

46 / Pluralization and Dispersion

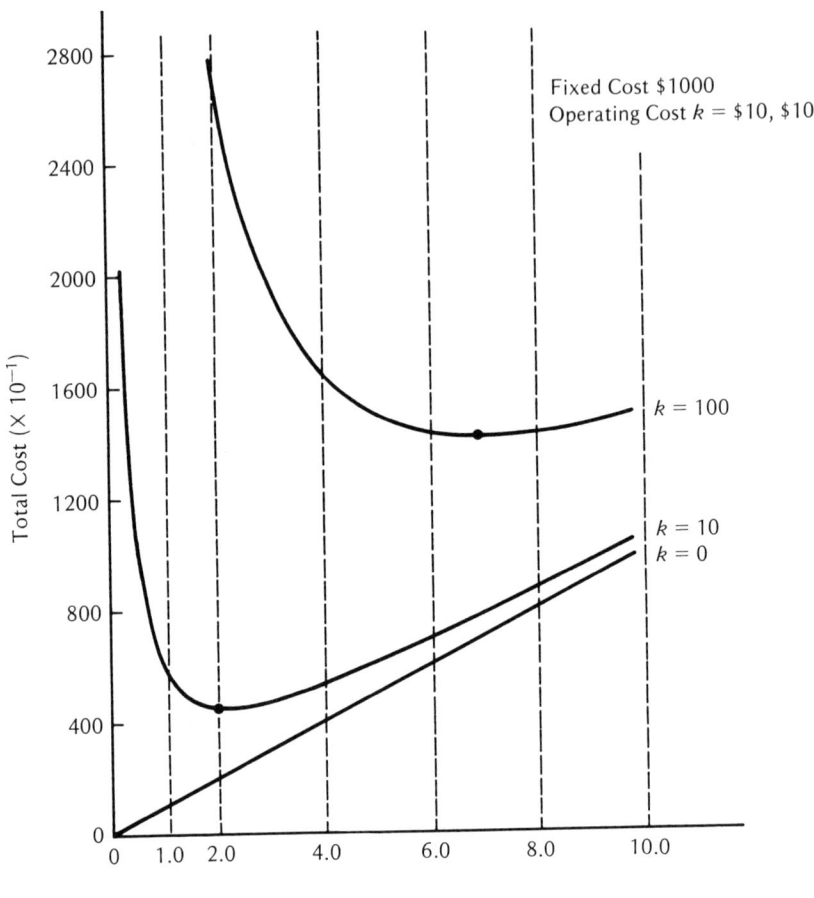

• *Optimum number of facilities.

Figure 2.5a. Cost of *n* facilities.

2.3 Simple Case with Uniform Spatial Dispersion / 47

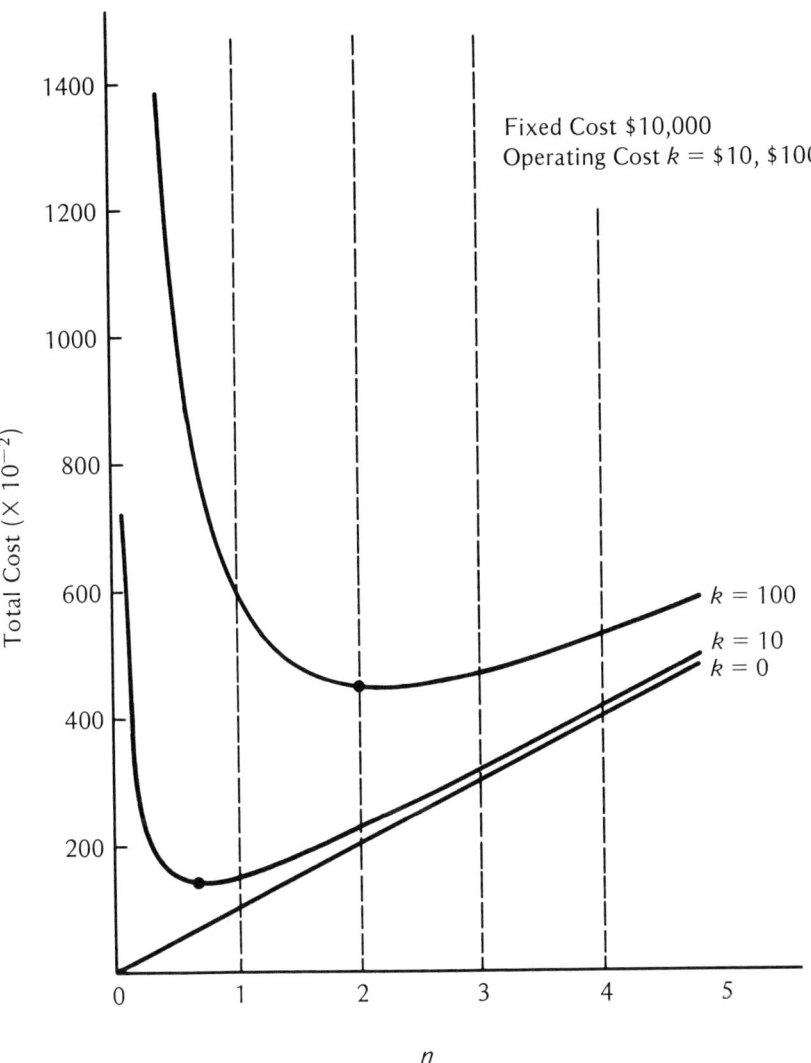

• *Optimum number of facilities.

Figure 2.5b. Cost of *n* facilities.

48 / Pluralization and Dispersion

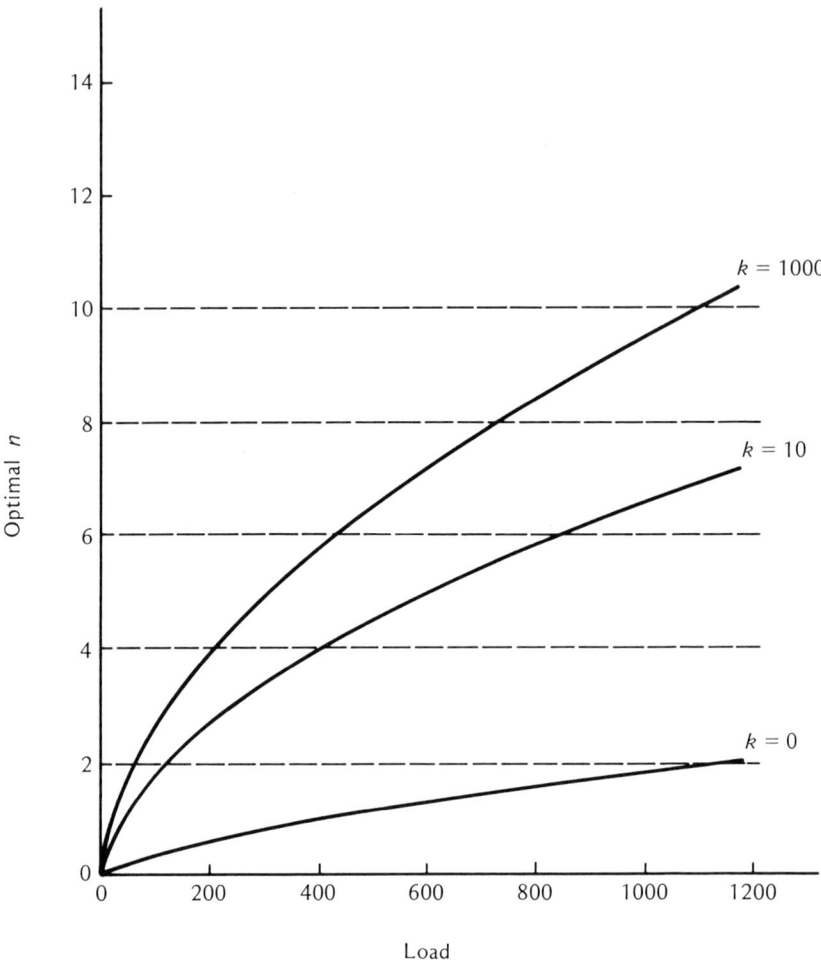

Figure 2.6. Simplified plot of optimal number *n* of facilities for the load *L* at variable operating cost *k* (in requests per month).

prototype model, we can see that service organizations of all kinds, including governments, could rationally decentralize or centralize depending on which of the relevant parameters grow at a greater rate.

A Case in Two Dimensions. We can now extend this analysis to two dimensions by considering the rectangular region shown in Figure 2.7. The ratio from its shorter to its longer side is ψ. As in the case of one dimension, we assume that demand is uniformly distributed over this rectangular region. If we were to deploy n facilities we would partition this region into n smaller rectangles (as close to squares as possible) and place a facility at the center of each. Let us assume that n can be written as a product of two numbers, n_1 and n_2 such that n_1 is proportional to D and n_2 is proportional to ψD. In general, since n, n_1, and n_2 must be integers, these conditions cannot all be met, but let us, as before, regard n as a continuously varying quantity. This will give us an approximate solution for n. If, for example, ψ were 2/3 and n turned out to be 6, we could take $n_1 = 3$, $n_2 = 2$, and divide the rectangle into six squares as shown in Figure 2.7.

In general, $n_2/n_1 = \psi D/D = \psi$ or $n_2 = \psi n_1$. Since $n = n_1 n_2$, $n = \psi n_1^2$ and $n_1 = \sqrt{n/\psi}$, $n_2 = \sqrt{n\psi}$.

Were we to take the Euclidean distance between two points, the problem of computing the average distance from the service center to points in the service region becomes mathematically unwieldy. We therefore use the "Manhattan" distance, or the shortest zigzag path using only vertical and horizontal segments from the center to any other point. The dimensions of each service region are D/n_1 and $\psi D/n_2$, or a square with side $D\sqrt{\psi/n}$. The maximum distance to forward any

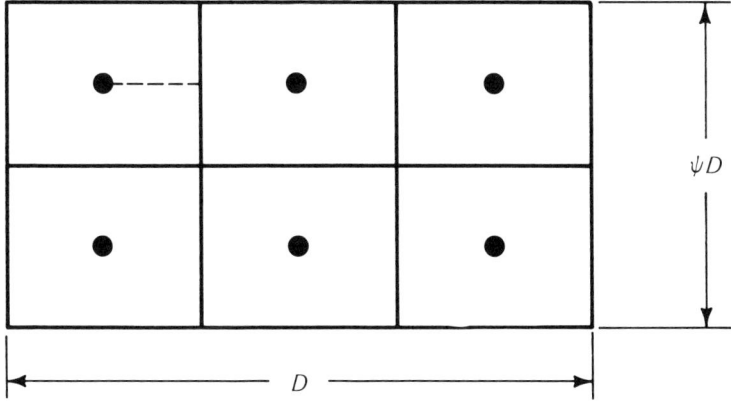

Figure 2.7. Distribution of service centers in a plane.

request within that service region to the center is $2 \times 1/2\, D\sqrt{\psi/n}$, shown by the dashed path in the figure. The average is half that, or $1/2\, D\sqrt{\psi/n}$. The average time to forward a request, at speed v, is then $(D/2v)\sqrt{\psi/n}$; at an operating cost (rate per unit time) of k, the cost per request is $(kD/2v)\sqrt{\psi/n}$. To get the monthly operating cost multiply by the load L (requests per month) and add to the fixed cost for n facilities, nC, to get a total cost of

$$\text{Cost} = nC + (kDL/2v)\sqrt{\psi}\, n^{-1/2}$$

Differentiate with respect to n and set to 0 to obtain:

$$n \doteq (kDL\sqrt{\psi}/4Cv)^{2/3} \qquad (2.4)$$

Three Dimensions. For a cubical region D miles on a side, the corresponding formula for n is

$$n \doteq \left(\frac{DkL}{4Cv}\right)^{3/4} \qquad (2.5)$$

The general conclusions that applied to a one-dimensional region apply also to two- and three-dimensional spaces.

2.4 PLURALIZATION TO COPE WITH CONGESTION

Thus far we have ignored the problem of congestion. Now, however, we present as much of it as necessary to show its use for computing n, the optimal number of pluralized service facilities, under conditions of congestion. We then draw some conclusions about decentralization under these conditions.

We begin our analysis of *waiting lines* by assuming that two numbers are known.

a = the *average* rate of requests for service, in requests per month. (We now regard L as a random variable, with a its mean or its expected value, EL.)

s = the *average* service rate (i.e., the number of requests one server can service in one month. Now S, too, is a random variable, and $s = ES$, its mean).

It is assumed that L and S are statistically independent and that

2.4 Pluralization to Cope with Congestion / 51

their means exist. They must be determined empirically from known data; a may be determined by sampling L (the load) or the expected demand for the service, and s may be determined from the nature of the service to be performed.

The first restriction on n is that $n > a/s$ must hold. This guarantees that there will be enough facilities to cope with the load. In certain cases this restriction is sufficient to determine the optimal number of facilities. But what happens if we take into consideration the cost of the clients' waiting time? Since a and s are only average rates, the situation may arise that sometimes requests for service are more frequent than usual, while service is taking longer than usual, so that some requests will not be met immediately. Then, either a line forms or clients must "try again later." Thus the cost of a client's waiting time becomes a factor. This cost may vary from negligible to practically infinite: to a seriously injured person awaiting medical care the cost of waiting may be infinite, while if a client's name only and not his or her physical person is placed in a queue for some trivial service the cost of waiting time may be minimal. In many cases, however, the cost of waiting time can be measured exactly in dollars. Consider a company that has contracted to perform a service whose completion is contingent upon performance of a service by a subcontractor. To quote the contractor, "Time is money!"

The analysis of waiting lines is well developed (Panico, 1969). It is applied to derive a formula for the average waiting time (in months) with n facilities.[8] The average waiting time $w(n)$ is a decreasing function of n for $n > a/s$ (concave upward) and approaches 0 as $n \to \infty$. Thus it has the following appearance (see Figures 2.8 and 2.9). So the total cost $K(n)$ has exactly one minimum if $C > 0$ (with no deceptive local minima) and looks like (see Figure 2.10).

These results hold under the following assumptions and definitions. Clients are assumed to arrive and take their place at the end of a queue, if there is one, at any of the n agents. By "arrival," we mean acknowledgment by the agent that a request for service has been initiated.

The response time, from the client's point of view, is a random variable T corresponding to the total elapsed time from the moment the client recognizes a need to the moment the client recognizes that it has been met; and t is the average of such response times. That includes the time to forward the request into the "arrival" state as well as forwarding the response back from the service to the client, with the number of possible feedback cycles taken into account (see Figure 2.11).

52 / *Pluralization and Dispersion*

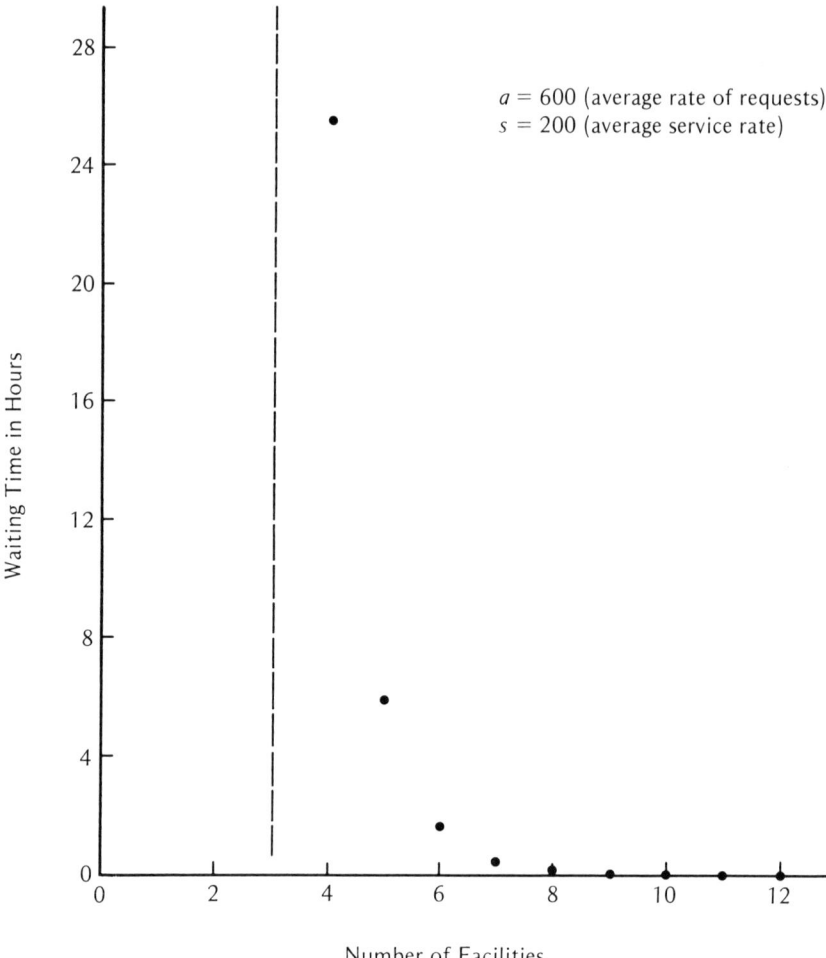

Figure 2.8. Average waiting time with *n* facilities.

2.4 Pluralization to Cope with Congestion / 53

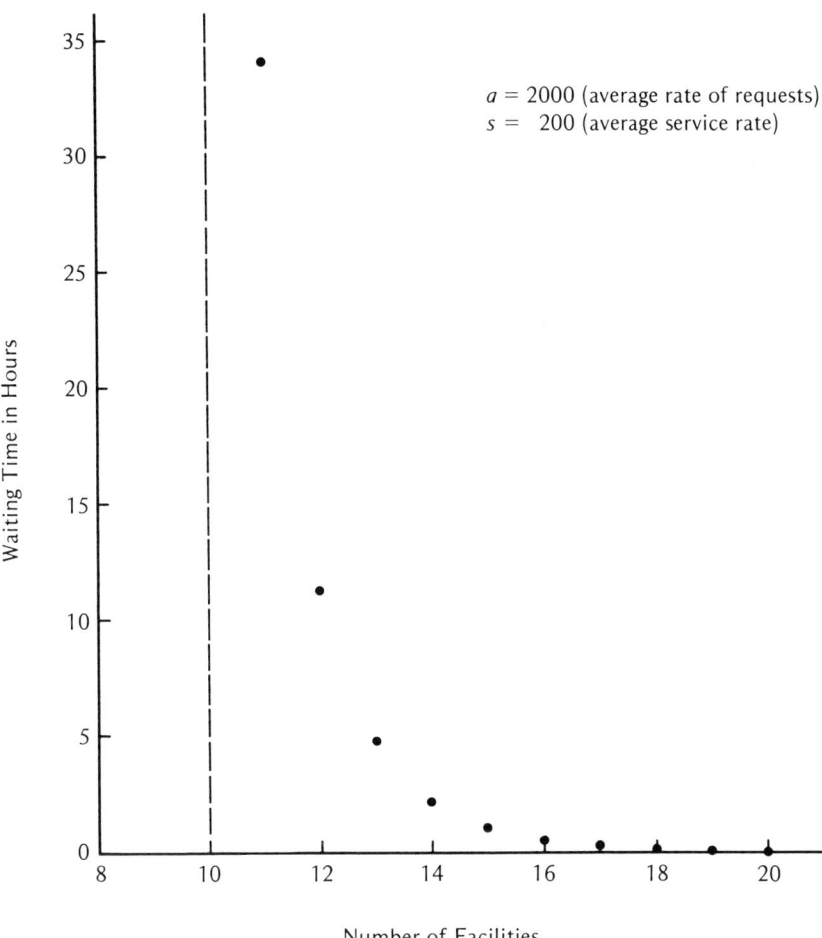

$a = 2000$ (average rate of requests)
$s = 200$ (average service rate)

Figure 2.9. Average waiting time with n facilities.

54 / Pluralization and Dispersion

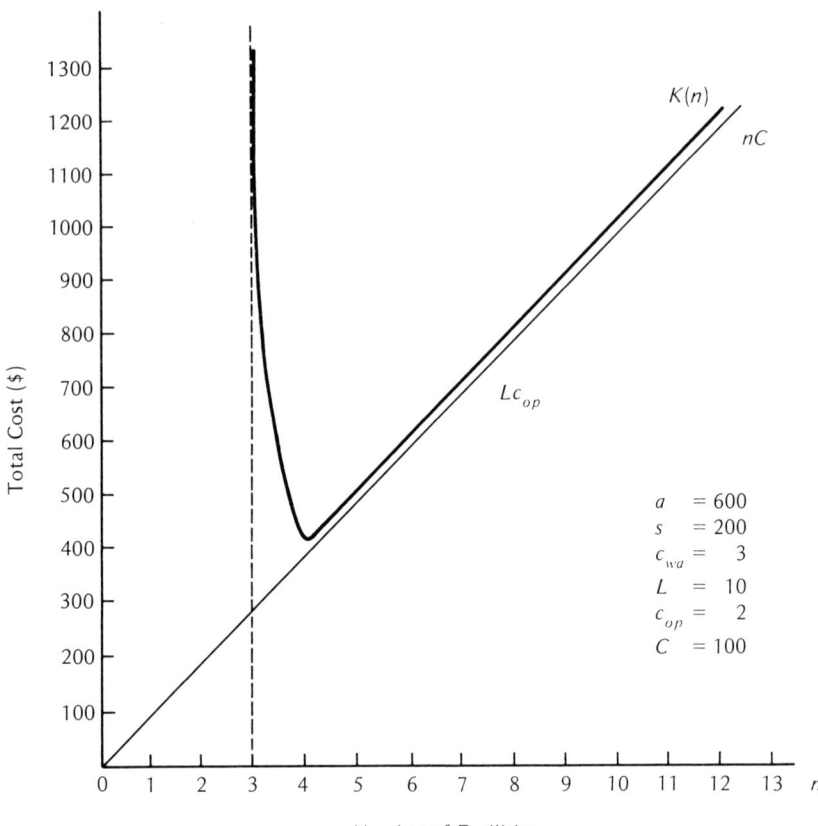

Figure 2.10. Total cost vs. number of facilities.

2.4 Pluralization to Cope with Congestion / 55

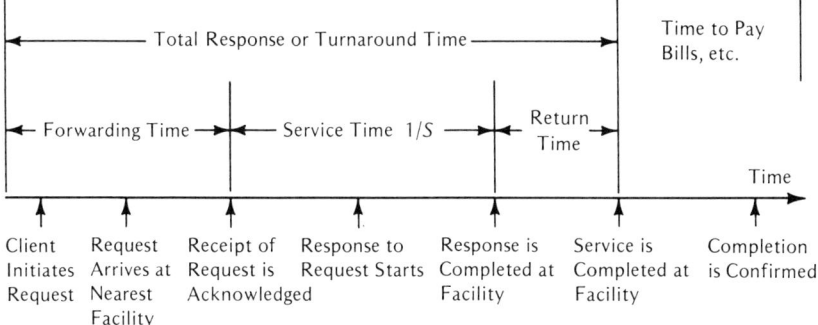

Figure 2.11. Components of response time.

We assume:

1. The probability laws or statistical characteristics of the stream of arrivals do not change with time.
2. The probability of an arrival in any time interval does not depend on the history of arrivals prior to the time interval.
3. Two or more events, such as two arrivals or an arrival and completion of service, and so on, can never occur simultaneously.
4. The same assumptions hold for service completion events, and the probability law governing the stream of these events does not depend on that of the arrival stream.

Mathematically, we assume that the probabilities characterizing the request rates providable by the server and demanded by the clients are statistically independent. Further, we assume that they are both Poisson processes, and have the form $S(t) = 1 - e^{-st}$, and $A(t) = 1 - e^{-at}$, respectively, where a is the rate at which clients arrive on average, and s is the average rate at which they are served. We also assume that events of arrival or service completion in nonoverlapping time intervals are statistically independent.

A new arrival, such as a customer in a shop or a patient at a clinic, engages the single server, if the server is free, and waits in a queue or waiting room, if the server is not. In the case where the client need not physically present him or herself but instead sends the request for service via a transport or communication channel, a "stack" of backlog requests or a computer-stored file takes the place of a waiting line or waiting room. Both require space and attention.

Analysis of 12 months of log data in an arthritis clinic (Hull, Saarinen, and Mason, 1975) showed that there is little variation in the patient load over the year. The average total patient time in the clinic was 128 minutes for all patients, with significant variation in time among the treating staff. Adding more examination rooms is not likely to affect total patient time in the clinic.

The simplest rule for the order in which clients are to be served, known in the literature as *queue discipline,* is that of "first come, first served." This implies the formation of a waiting line in which the first member is the next to be served and the latest arrival goes to the end of the line. This corresponds to a "queue" in computer terminology, as distinct from a stack, where the first client to be served is the latest arrival (Knuth, 1968). This question of priorities is, of course, important. If clients with top priority are allowed to delay or interrupt the service of others, there are likely to be political consequences.

If there are n servers, let us also imagine them to form a queue as in the case of telephone trunk lines or a group of waiting barbers. The first client on the waiting line is assigned to the first available server. Clients wait only if all n servers are busy. Servers wait only if there are no clients. Some clients may not wait and do without the service, incurring the cost c_{sf} introduced earlier in this chapter; there is a corresponding loss to the service organization, sometimes described by the Erlang loss formula used in telephone congestion theory (Syski, 1960).

The use of queueing theory can be incorporated into the search for an optimal n by starting with an estimate for the value of n exceeding L/s and searching, by computer, for that value of n that minimizes total cost. On the whole, the introduction of probabilistic analysis does not change the general conclusion that secular trends toward increases in the dominant variable, L, favor increased n or higher pluralization.

An important conclusion from the study of fluctuations that we will use later is the significance of variance in the waiting time. It is customary to plot the expected waiting time versus the load factor, which is defined as a/s. The idle fraction of service capacity, $1 - a/s$, is the redundancy or excess capacity of the system. As the ratio of arrival rate to service rate increases from 0 to 1, the expected waiting time rises slowly until it is near about .9, when it begins to rise toward infinity very steeply. Lest it be thought that a load factor of about .8 might be safe—with the server idle 20 percent of the time—it is instructive to inspect how not only the mean but also the variance of the waiting time increases with a/s. Consider the following table (from Feller, 1966, p. 199) for a single server for $s = 1$ (Table 2.1).

The average waiting time is given by $a/s(s - a)$. If $a = 1$ and $s = 3, 4,$

2.4 Pluralization to Cope with Congestion / 57

Table 2.1. Demonstrating the Importance of Variance in Number of Waiting Customers

Load Factor	0.5	0.6	0.7	0.8	0.9	0.95
Average waiting time (e.g., hours)	1.0	1.5	2.3	4.0	9.0	19.0
Variance of waiting time	3.0	5.3	10.0	24.0	99.0	399.0
Average length of busy period	2.0	2.5	3.3	5.0	10.0	399.0
Variance of busy period	12.0	25.0	63.0	225.0	1900.0	16000.0
Average number of customers in the system per busy period (queue length)	2.0	2.5	3.3	5.0	10.0	399.0
Variance in customers	6.0	15.0	44.0	200.0	1700.0	15200.0

Source: From W. Feller, *Probability Theory and Its Applications*, vol. 2 (New York: Wiley, 1966), p. 199.

5, 10, the waiting time is then 1/6, 1/12, 1/20, and 1/90, respectively. The mean duration of the busy period is $1/(5 - a)$ and its variance is $(a + s)/(s - a)$.[3] Enormous fluctuations in the busy period are likely, and sole reliance on averages is most dangerous.

If the average waiting time at a .5 load factor (twice as many servers as would be needed if each were occupied 100% of the time) in a mental health clinic were 1 month, however, it might rise to 19 months, if the clinic were busy to 95 percent of its capacity. With 20% redundancy, it would rise to 4 months and with only 10% redundancy to 9 months. These calculations suggest that a substantial degree of redundancy or excess capacity in service facilities may still have positive value within the context of other cost considerations.

A cost-benefit formula for *optimal redundancy* would then be sensitive to cost c'_{wa} to the client of waiting or delay in treatment. With L requests per hour and each service provider handling about s requests per hour but working only a fraction f of the time, it would take L/sf providers, or $(L/s)[1 - (1/f)]$ more workers than it would take if each were 100% busy. If each worker costs C dollars per hour, then it costs CL/sf \$/hr to provide this service. This clearly increases as f, the load factor, decreases. The delay costs the clients at least

$$c'_{wa} L \frac{f}{s(1 - f)} \text{ dollars per hour}$$

where

58 / *Pluralization and Dispersion*

$$\frac{f}{s(1-f)} = \frac{a/s}{s(1-a/s)} = \frac{a}{s-a}$$

is the average waiting time. The total cost to the providers *and* the clients is thus $CL/sf + c'_{wa} Lf/s(1-f)$. Differentiating with respect to f in order to find the value of f that minimizes this total cost, and solving for f that makes the derivative zero gives

$$f = \frac{\sqrt{C/c'_{wa}}}{1 + \sqrt{C/c'_{wa}}}$$

If the ratio of the service provider's cost to that of keeping the client waiting is 1, 4, 9, 16, 25, then the optimal value of f is $\frac{1}{2}$, $\frac{2}{3}$, $\frac{3}{4}$, $\frac{4}{5}$, $\frac{5}{6}$, respectively, with 50, 30, 25, 20, 16 percent of the providers to be redundant. As pointed out, using *average* waiting times is very dangerous.

These formulas apply if all clients can and do wait until served, and thus no costs of nonservice or nontreatment, c_{sf}, are incurred. If some clients give up, however, and if some of the costs of their fruitless waiting, c'_{wa}, and the costs of their nontreatment are higher, then the level of optimum redundancy will tend to be higher. For telephone systems, the proportion and cost of "lost calls" has been calculated (Syski, 1960). For fire departments or accident clinics, where long delays may be fatal, very high redundancy rates may still be optimal or acceptable.

If the agency is to accommodate clients who are waiting, it must supply a waiting room, a parking lot, and so forth. This is an additional cost that should be added to the equation for total cost. If the agency determines the size of the waiting room according to the *average* number of clients who are waiting at one time, there is a risk that, quite often, clients for whom there is no room will have to be turned away. This is shown by Table 2.1, which indicates the importance of the variance. The waiting facilities should therefore be sufficiently large to allow for fluctuations because there are additional costs to be added from clients being turned away. (As the number of patients waiting in a doctor's office increases, the probability increases that a communicable disease will spread, which favors small queues.)

The effect of increasing n is to decrease both the expected waiting time and its variance. Therefore, if the costs of a waiting room (dollars per square foot per month) and clients turned away are high compared with C, the cost of each server, then n should be increased. The costs of waiting space and clients turned away increase with L. Hence, taking these extra costs into account will accentuate the trend toward increasing pluralization even further.

2.5 DISPERSION WITH SPATIAL UNEVENNESS: CAN IT FAVOR PLURALIZATION?

It is noteworthy that the mayor of the city of New York called for decentralizing the delivery of most municipal services, including police and sanitation, but not fire protection, into 52 districts (*New York Times,* September 16, 1976, p. 52). Each was to be governed by a newly reconstituted community board. These boards replaced 62 boards that functioned for the past eight years but lacked real power over local service delivery. Each of the new boards was to hire a service manager to monitor services. Fire protection was excluded because the present organization was felt to provide the fastest response.

The 52 districts are a partition, cannot be gerrymandered, and vary in population from 100,000 to 250,000. They correspond to identifiable neighborhoods, but they follow population indexes that reflect the nonuniform population density of the city.

The general problem of determining both the number of agents and their location throughout a plane region with an arbitrary demand distribution is mathematically untractable. Even in the one-dimensional case, it is not a trivial problem.

In the case of a one-dimensional problem, the distribution of demand is at the opposite extreme from perfect uniformity. Case 1, as analyzed in Section 2.2, is also of special interest to us here. For if such an extreme departure from uniformity does not strongly favor centralization, it is likely that less extreme departures from uniformity would favor centralization even less strongly, if at all.

To start with an intermediate case, we consider once again a segment of length D, as in Figure 2.4, and we let $f(x)$ denote this frequency distribution, where x is a position on the D-mile stretch considered. In Figure 2.12, let the shaded area, $f(x)dx$, represent the probability that a request originate at a site located within $(x, x + dx)$. Of course, $f(x)$ is a density, and $\int_0^D f(x)dx = 1$. That is to say, the aggregate area under all the bars will be set equal to 1, so as to present this calculation of density as a probability. The basic idea is to divide a nonuniform distribution into subregions, where the distributions are uniform, and to treat each subregion by the previously developed method for finding the optimum degree of pluralization. We wish to characterize such a

60 / Pluralization and Dispersion

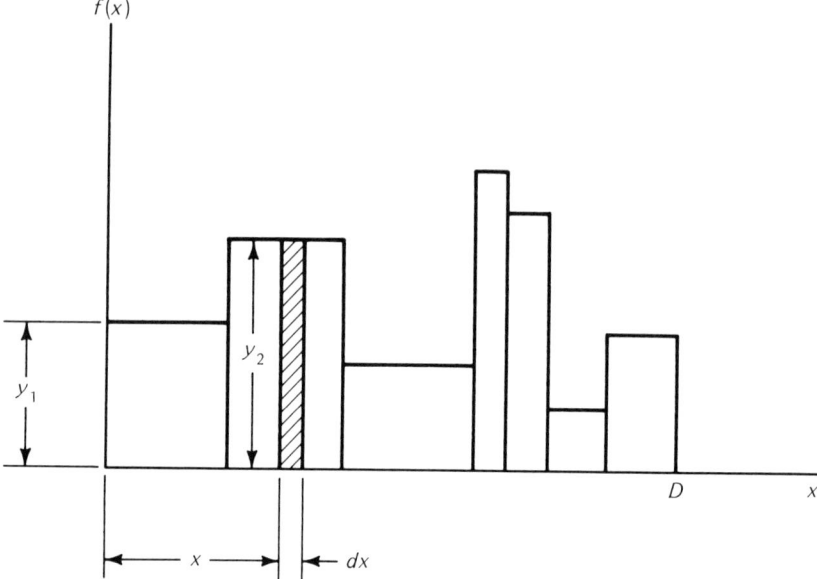

Figure 2.12. Illustration of "multiuniform" service request distribution.

multiuniform distribution in terms of its departure from a uniform distribution: that is, in terms of the departure from a completely homogeneous distribution of requests over space.

A uniform distribution would be characterized by the dotted line as in Figure 2.13. Let h_i be the departure of the height of the ith bar from $1/D$. For example, the bars might be interpreted as the population of apartment houses in a city, with a constant rate of requests being generated by each apartment dweller. Thus the first block or house has a larger population and contributes a greater fraction of requests than the last one. The area under the bar graph is the same as the area under the single dotted line bar, namely, 1 to indicate that 100 percent of the requests come from the D-mile strip.

We can imagine a bar graph in which there are no bars at all over certain intervals, corresponding to empty lots or stretches of desert. Let u denote that fraction of the D-mile stretch that is populated. Suppose that requests for service come from $100u\%$ of the D-mile stretch. For example, if only half the D-mile stretch were populated, then $u = .5$. The uD miles from which they come need not be contigu-

2.5 Dispersion with Spatial Unevenness / 61

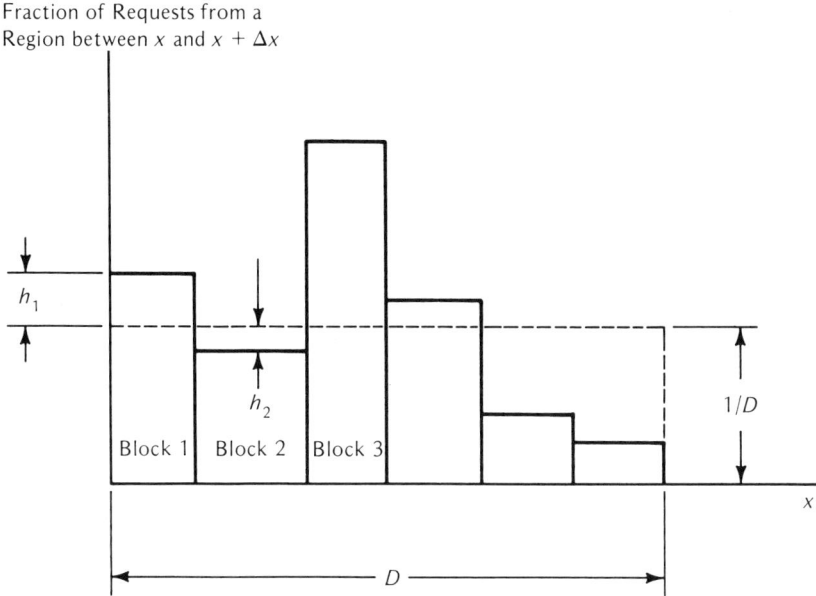

Figure 2.13. Deviation of "multiuniform" from uniform distribution.

ous, but we assume for this example that a request is as likely to come from any one point along these uD miles as from any other. Thus, if $u = .5$ they could come from any point in $[0, D/2]$, $[a, a + D/2]$ for any a, or from any point in $D/2d$ d-mile strips, to take but three examples. In each case if we were to compute the number of agents needed for the smallest connected region from which requests originate and add up these numbers, we would get fewer agents than if the demand came from the entire D-mile strip.

Thus, one of the d-mile subregions in the third example mentioned above contributes d/uD of the total load generated. We would therefore replace L by $(d/uD)L'$ and D by d in Equation (2.2), to obtain $d/2$ (cL/Cv) $(1/uD)$ for the approximate number of agents in that substrip. There are uD/d such strips. The total number of agents needed is approximately uD/d times the number in each strip. It is $1/2$ (cL/Cv) $\sqrt{uD}$.

Note that we would have obtained that number if we had viewed it as a single contiguous strip of length uD, as in example 1 or 2 above; here, all the load comes from that strip, and D is merely replaced by

uD. In the case where the demand density has the same height, suboptimization over subregions gives the same result as optimization over the entire region.

Compare this "optimal" number for the case in which demand for service arises uniformly from $100u\%$ of the region with the case in which it arises from the entire region, for $u = 1$. There, the optimum number was approximately $1/2 \, (cL/Cv) \sqrt{D}$. The ratio is $\sqrt{uD}/\sqrt{D}$ or $\sqrt{u}$.

This means that if requests originate from anywhere in only 25 percent of the region, then we should use only half as many facilities as if they came from anywhere in the region, regardless of the volume of requests. If the fraction of the region from which requests originate is, respectively, 81, 64, 49, and 36 percent, then the number of facilities needed is, respectively, 90, 80, 70, and 60 percent of the number that would be needed if requests could have come from anywhere in the entire region. If $D = 3000$ miles, $L = 30{,}000$ requests per month, $v = 10$ miles per hour, $k = 10$ cents per hour for operating or forwarding cost, and $C = 100$ dollars per month for fixed cost, then about 47 agents would have to be spread uniformly over the 3000-mile stretch when requests can originate anywhere along that route. If requests originated from just 4 percent of that stretch, we would need $\sqrt{.04} \times 47$ or $.2 \times 47$ or approximately nine agents spread uniformly over that 4 percent of the stretch. We would need just one center if the demand for service were concentrated in $1/(47)^2$ or within 1.3 miles of the entire stretch.

The difference between suboptimization[9] and optimization in a special case was analyzed by Kochen and Deutsch (1970). It shows that the number of agents that minimize cost where the demand distribution is multiuniform is less with the suboptimization approach than it would be for optimization. Thus, the error introduced by suboptimization rather than optimization tends to exaggerate the extent to which spatial unevenness favors centralization.

We now present an expression for this ratio as a function of a measure of nonhomogeneity that we call V. In the above-mentioned paper we show it to be approximately $1 - 1/8V$ where $V = D \sum_{i=1}^{s} d_i h_i^2$, where s, d_i, h_i are shown in Figure 2.12, for $s = 6$ spikes, of widths $d_1 \ldots d_6$ and deviating from $1/D$ by $h_1, \ldots, h_6$. $V = 0$ if and only if we have a uniform distribution. V can increase beyond any bound in several ways, though within the limits of our approximation, it can increase only up to 8, which represents the most centralized situation.

To see what kind of distribution is characterized by large V, consider a class of distribution of $s/2$ spikes of equal height and width so that with $y = 1/D + h$, $s = 2, 4, 6, \ldots$. Plotting V versus x indicates that the smaller x, the larger V. In words, a distribution with tall, thin spikes

2.5 Dispersion with Spatial Unevenness / 63

calls for greater centralization than one with shorter, wider spikes, regardless of the number of spikes. Suppose that we now keep $u = (s/2)(d/D)$ or $s/2$ constant. Then $V = 1/u(1 - x)^2 + 2u/x$, which also increases as x decreases from 1 toward 0. Thus, if the requests come from 50 percent of the strip ($u = .5$), as the spikes become thinner and longer there must also be more of them, and that favors centralization in inverse proportion to how thin the spikes are.

In general, highly predictable unevenness of the demand distribution tends to favor centralization at peak locations and periods, but not very strongly. In special cases irregular and unpredictable unevenness may favor decentralization. For example, we have calculated the cost of maintaining n agents uniformly distributed over a D-mile region with $s/2$ spikes of width d separated by gaps of width g. If $g > d$, then the cost for the spiked distribution is less than that for the comparable uniform distribution, with the same number of agents. Thus the spiked case can afford more centers (larger n) for the same cost than the uniform case. In this case, the number of spikes was taken to exceed the number of agents, in contrast with the preceding suboptimization analysis where we assumed several agents in the stretch under each spike.

In general, uneven spatial distribution of demand favors centralization, inversely as the square root of that fraction of the service area that is populated more densely than the average, and perhaps in some proportion to the difference in densities; or it leaves n, the optimum number of facilities, unchanged.

The same holds for the dispersion of facilities in space.[10] Uneven distribution of demand in space usually will reduce the optimal amount of dispersion, or leave it unchanged except where n is small and most of the demand is concentrated in a few widely separated settlement clusters scattered around the periphery of the area, as perhaps in the case of Australia and part of the Amazon basin.

An analysis of historical trends in the distribution of loads may reveal two reversals of direction. In very early stages of settlement, large territories may remain empty. Population is concentrated in a few regions; that favors centralization. Later, if the population increases and if predominant economic activities continue to be agricultural, there may be a trend for the people to distribute themselves more evenly; that favors decentralization. In a third stage, industrialization and urbanization may once again produce local concentrations of people and of demands for service. Finally, in a fourth stage, the countryside may again fill up with suburbanites and all kinds of dispersed settlements. Once again, people distribute themselves more uniformly and this promotes pluralization.

2.6 THE EFFECTS OF FLUCTUATIONS IN TIME AND SPACE

The use of plurality of service providing agents to cope with spatial fluctuations in demand is analogous to a similar use of pluralization to cope with fluctuations in demand over time. Indeed, our simplest result for the optimal number of agents when demand is evenly distributed over space has its counterpart in the simplest theory of inventories (Whitin, 1957, p. 32). An inventory is a plurality of goods that is kept so that a good will be available when a customer requests it, with the smallest possible response time.

Let Y be the number of items per year that are expected to be sold. Let Q be the number of items bought in one batch, or the maximum inventory size. Let C' be the cost per unit and E the cost of placing an order for Q items. Interest, risk, depreciation, and so on, are represented by a fraction I that is the fraction of each dollar's worth of goods in inventory that is contributed to the annual variable cost. If we assume that inventory decreases steadily from Q to 0, at which time a new batch of size Q arrives, then the average value of the inventory at any time is $QC'/2$ dollars, and this contributes $QC'I/2$ dollars per year to the cost. But a new inventory batch must be reordered Y/Q times per year, adding another YE/Q dollars per year to the cost. The value of Q that minimized $QC'I/2 + YE/Q$ is approximately $Q \doteq \sqrt{2YE/IC'}$. Here Q is analogous to our n.

Fluctuations of the load over time give rise to peaks at which there may be congestion at a fixed number of facilities, with idleness during the calm periods. To avoid congestion during *peak periods*, we must either pay the cost of having a fixed number of facilities idle much of the time or the cost of a variable number of facilities that can rapidly be pressed into service when a peak period is about to start. Large cities do this with the number of buses or subway trains during rush hours. If that reserve capacity had to sit idly until pressed into service, it would hardly differ from the case of fixed facilities. The variable-facility case is advantageous when the spare agents can be productively occupied in servicing requests of lower priority, or if there are several streams of incoming requests, the fluctuations of which combine to smooth the confluent stream.

If the distribution over space is uniform and the *peak load* is four times the average load, then at most we double the number of facilities. They then would still be spread uniformly over space but wholly or in part at different locations. If, at the other extreme, the distribution over space is concentrated at a single spike, a similar increase in the number of facilities may be required but with no need for dispersing

2.6 The Effects of Fluctuations in Time and Space / 65

them. Whether the dispersion also increases, therefore, has to be calculated separately.

The situation changes if peak loads occur at different times or different spatial regions. In the extreme case, peak loads for regions $a, \ldots, i$ might coincide with minimal loads for regions $j, \ldots, z$. If we retain our assumptions of very high redundancy so that each service facility still has the capacity to cope with the whole service load L for the entire space D, then such peak loads will reduce the underutilization of the rest. This will increase the proportion of requests serviced by the busiest centers, reduce the share of the rest, and shorten the length of the average round trip.

In general, if L_p is the peak load of $L(t)$ compared with the average load L (in the same units), then we can write $n_p/n = \sqrt{L_p/L}$. Here n is the optimal number of decentralized facilities for a distribution that is constant in time and space, while n_p is the optimal number of such facilities if peak load conditions are to be accommodated within the same average service time. Thus, if peak loads are nine times as high as average loads, three times as many facilities will be needed, and if L = 30,000 requests per month, and L_p = 72,000 requests per month (1000 per hour), $L_p/L = 72/3 = 24$. If the optimum number of facilities in the absence of fluctuations had been, say, 48, then n_p now would be $n\sqrt{L_p/L} = 48\sqrt{24} = 235$ facilities. Indeed, the experience of telephone companies suggests that a ratio of 5:1 for peak loads over average loads may be realistic (see Kochen, 1965, p. 50; and Syski, 1960).

There will be no change in n, however, if $n \leq L_p/L$, because up to that point peak loads would be absorbed by the unused capacity of the n facilities in the system. We shall call peak loads larger than nL *relevant* and peak loads less than or equal to nL negligible. Fluctuations of service loads in time thus always will either increase n or leave it unchanged. Since by definition $L_p > L$, peak load phenomena, so long as they are uniformly distributed over the entire space, cannot reduce the desirable number of facilities.

If we take into account the average *internal service time i* for servicing a request at a facility—as distinct from the time of forwarding a request from a client to the nearest facility and returning a response to the client —and if each facility is capable of serving the entire load L, but not more than that, then in the absence of fluctuations, $i = 1/L$. In the case of relevant fluctuations, congestion effects will enter and will promote a further increase in n_p and thus in the pluralization of facilities. If *waiting line effects* are taken into account, it will become desirable to keep service capacities about 20 to 25 percent larger than request loads, so as to prevent the development of long queues, particularly their variance.

66 / Pluralization and Dispersion

Suppose that $f(x, t)$ is not uniform in x. To take an example, suppose

$$f(x, t) = \begin{cases} h & \text{if } x_1 - \frac{d}{2} \leq x \leq x_1 + \frac{d}{2}, \text{ all } t \\ 0 & \text{otherwise} \end{cases}$$

This is a simple spike of height h centered at distance x_1. We must have $hd = 1$, but $h, d,$ and x_1 can all vary with t. Let $h_{\min}$ be $\text{Min}_t h(t)$; that is, the peak load. From the arguments of the previous section, the optimal number of service stations to be spread uniformly under the spike is given by

$$n = \frac{1}{2}\sqrt{\frac{c(dhL)d}{Cv}} = \frac{1}{2}\sqrt{\frac{cL}{Cv}} \, d\sqrt{h}$$

$$= \frac{1}{2}\sqrt{\frac{cL}{Cv}} \frac{\sqrt{h}}{h} = \frac{1}{2}\sqrt{\frac{cL}{Cv}} \frac{1}{\sqrt{h}} \quad (2.6)$$

If n_p is the number under the worst conditions—that is, the largest number of requests per unit time and least concentrated per unit area—then $n_p/n = \sqrt{(h/h_{\min})(L_p/L)}$. Here n is the optimal number of facilities under that spike if h were constant in time.

If x_1 varies with t, what is the optimal number and dispersion of facilities? It would, of course, be ideal if we could move the n facilities so as to always keep them under the spike as it moves, as in the case of roving police cars, ambulances, or bookmobiles. Our work, however, has been confined to a static deployment of decentralized facilities. We might, then, consider stationing facilities over a region of extent greater than d so as to maximize the time spanned by the spike over one of the centers.

2.7 PLURALIZATION, REDUNDANCY, AND ERROR CONTROL

If n identical agents serve the clients at one site, several opportunities for improved service are opened up if n is large. For one thing, if one agent does not function, this will not seriously impair the service. The other servers either speed up by $s/(n - 1)$ requests per month or the waiting time or cost of clients turned down increases somewhat. If the agents are unrealiable in the sense that probability of breakdown is high and the downtime long, then n should be larger to maintain a given level of service. The improvement and introduction of technology makes the agents more reliable and hence favors smaller n, a slight countertrend to the other trends already noted.

Downtime (delays caused by breakdowns) can be decreased, however, if some of the agents at the site are competent repairmen. This deviates somewhat from our assumption in this chapter that all the n agents are identical, and it will be discussed further in our later chapters on functional specialization and coordination. If we count such repairmen among the n agents, we may get a smaller n by utilizing such specialists instead of simply increasing the number of direct servers. This, too, is a countertrend to pluralization.

Two considerations, however, lead us to believe that the forces favoring pluralization outweigh those favoring the countertrend. The first is that reliability increases very slowly after a certain risk level has been reached, while request load continues to rise even with zero population growth. Many technologies already have very high reliability. In current communications, computers, aircraft, and so forth, the mean times between failures are of the order of decades. Human agents interacting with technological aids learn rapidly to decrease the error rate of the man-machine stations. In two or three decades even technologically unsophisticated societies seem able to work with advanced technologies at high levels of reliability. Increasing them further takes considerably more time and effort, which is not always warranted. Request loads continue to rise dramatically.

Second, as the request load increases and more clients acquire experience and intimacy with the service, they demand more reliable, better service. They refuse to settle for less than what they learn to be possible. Failure to provide service of the quality demanded incurs additional costs. This favors an increase in n.

2.8 USING PLURALIZATION TO MANAGE FLUCTUATIONS IN REQUEST LOAD

Another opportunity afforded by an organization with many agents is to balance idleness and congestion among the various agents and respond to special requirements for servicing the input stream of arriving requests. As long as n is sufficient to cope with the total load L, it does not affect the total cost if some agents are occasionally (or chronically) overloaded while others are idle. Without provision for smoothing loads, the costs of inferior service incurred by overloading some agents should be added to the equation for total cost. But there is also a cost incurred by keeping some agents idle; their skills may deteriorate from lack of practice; if they are machines, they may rust. It is therefore cost-effective to balance idleness and congestion within the organization.

This requires special agents who watch the loads on each agent and coordinate the assignment of newly arriving requests to agents.

68 / Pluralization and Dispersion

These coordinators must receive very up-to-date information about the likely duration of busy times from the agents to which they assign requests, and they must be able to respond rapidly by directing new requests appropriately. Whether each agent acts as his or her own part-time coordinator or whether there are specialized full-time load schedulers among the n agents, the effect is to increase the number of agents. Moreover, increasing n decreases the variance of the waiting time and of fluctuations in general, reducing the severity of the task of balancing idleness and congestion. These considerations will be taken up in further detail in Chapters 5 and 6 in dealing with hierarchy and coordination.

The powerful and elegant results of queueing theory apply mainly to simple queue disciplines, such as first-come-first-served. Queues with priority levels have been investigated and are of some relevance to our subject. Clearly, a request for emergency first aid has higher priority than a request for aspirin to alleviate a headache. The assignment of priorities helps manage fluctuations and control the flow. As mentioned earlier, it also has political consequences. The need to gain priority may motivate some clients to bribe agents, to engage in conflict with one another, and to harbor jealousy and resentment. The result of such tension is an added cost.

Scheduling the loads on agents in the organization to minimize idleness and congestion too rigidly can also be costly. We have already seen how making the load factor close to 1, which minimizes idleness, inordinately increases the mean waiting time and its variance, forcing the effects of congestion upon the clients. The attempt to utilize the total capacity of an agent can have other detrimental effects. In submarines, for example, where the crew sleeps in shifts, it might be thought that bunks could be shared, so as to keep them fully used, and thus lower the number of required bunks. Experiences with "hot bunks," however, have shown that this contributes greatly to lower morale. There is a great psychic cost to crewmen who live in tight quarters under water for long periods and who do not have a spot they can call their own. Similarly, many researchers dislike having to share microscopes, or even small computers, requiring delicate settings with which others might tamper.

If we examine all the factors considered so far, we find an overall trend toward pluralization in service organizations, providing service at one site. This often is a justifiable trend from a rational, normative point of view. That is, if the organization's director wishes to provide a service at the least possible cost to the organization and its clients, the director *ought* to use an increasing number of agents, stations, or servers. This conclusion holds only for the aspects we have considered so far. It does not appear to us to contradict any ethical considerations.

Chapter 3

Functional Specialization

3.0 INTRODUCTION

So far we have examined the degree of pluralization and dispersion of service-providing agents that make the service organization most responsive to its clients' needs at the lowest cost to society. We now take another step toward a more complete characterization of the decentralization concept. This is an analysis of the number of specialities a service organization should have and beyond which it becomes counterproductive to add more.

We consider all possible requests for service to be classified according to the specialized *kind* of service requested. An adjustable, general purpose facility would then have to undertake some steps of search or adjustment in shifting from performing one kind of service to another. We thus assume not only a geographic space, but also a second *adjustment space*, or *scope*, constituted by the different kinds of services demanded. Effective distances in geographic space are determined by existing transportation facilities between any two points; effective distances in adjustment space are set by the *number of steps* that either the service facility or the customer must take until the adjusted capability of the facility or the adjusted request match. By *step* we mean the equipment, personnel, or individual adjustment that must be introduced to cope with requests of different natures. Geographic distance and adjustment steps both translate into *cost of time and effort*; in this sense, they are commensurable.

This leads to the possibility of a plurality of separate, specialized facilities dispersed across any geographic region, as against one general purpose facility that can adjust to meet requests in several different categories of service. This generates four possible types of organizations: (1) centralized by service area and scope; (2) centralized by area but decentralized by scope; (3) decentralized by area but centralized by scope for each area; and (4) decentralized by both area and scope. We then search for logical conditions relating properties of a mathematical model under which it is preferable to organize a division of labor of type 2, 3, and 4 with separate specialized scope or service type centers rather than a centralized, general purpose facility of type 1.

We are leading up to a notion of decentralization in which decision making is dispersed in various ways while maintaining a necessary level of interaction. In this chapter we analyze but one other kind of dispersal. The main virtue of functional centralization is the increased efficiency, speed, and superior capacity made possible by the concentration of resources. The main virtue of functional decentralization, as of pluralization and dispersion, is responsiveness to local demand and sensitivity to environmental change.

Functional decentralization means the separation of the experts, files, and facilities over the various functions in specialized suborganizations that they serve. The suborganizations may also serve a more or less extensive service area, depending on the degree of geographic decentralization. Functional centralization is favored by two conditions: the different functions are not very disparate, and thus a shift from one to the other is effected by a few adjustment steps by the server and the high capacity of the server to shift from one functionally specialized service to another. This high adjustment capacity can be attained by a service center, either by high capacity for rearranging its limited resources—similar to the jack-of-all-trades pattern—or by a very rich repertory of specialized service facilities and capacities at the disposal of the server.

We start our analysis with a primitive mechanical model. We shall treat the requests as analogous to an assortment of bolts of varying sizes, with each bolt requiring tightening at some random time. A facility is analogous to a wrench used to tighten a bolt. A very specialized facility corresponds to a fixed size wrench fitting only bolts of one size. We assume its capacity to be such that it can handle all the bolts of that size in the time required. A multipurpose, less specialized facility in this example corresponds to an adjustable wrench. It can be used for bolts of sizes varying over a range.

3.0 Introduction / 71

Two bolts of nearly the same size are thus "separated" by a few adjustment steps of this adjustable wrench while bolts of very different sizes are separated by a larger number of such adjustment steps. (The same would apply to differences in the shape of the bolts, though we know of no wrenches that can adjust to radically different shapes.) We thus can map the differences in the size of the bolts (analogous to *kinds* of service requested) into a space consisting of adjustment steps or efforts that the server must make in order to cope with size (and shape).

For a slightly less primitive example, let us take the "little red schoolhouse" (or modern open classroom school) in a small settlement. Here children of 7, 8, 9, and 10 years may be taught in a single classroom to read third- fourth- and fifth-grade texts, respectively, by a teacher experienced in third-grade teaching. As the teacher shifts from working with third-graders to fourth-graders, he or she must make some mental adjustment, look for some different books, teaching materials, and some background information about how to teach children of this age group. If the teacher has to switch from a third-grader to a fifth-grader, we assume that all these adjustment efforts would have to be larger.

As a third example, consider a clinic. Some of its patients need orthopedic surgery. Others have problems in neurology or need psychiatric treatment. If there was only a surgeon in attendance, who nevertheless tried to do his or her best for every patient, then he or she might have to do some medical research or telephone a specialist for certain advice. This surgeon might have to take still more steps of this kind to cope with the psychiatric patients. In adjustment space, neurology would then seem to lie somewhere between surgery at the one extreme and psychiatry at the other. The precise nature of primitive steps that could serve as units for measuring distances among such diverse services has yet to be discovered.

Some of the literature (e.g., Morrill and Earickson, 1969, p. 131) states that "there is obviously little or no substitution possible among obstetric, pediatric and medical-surgical units of hospitals." Nonetheless, patients and physicians have been classified according to types and levels of demand, and this has been used for simulating allocations between clients and servers. In such a simulation, patients are initially allocated to physicians according to where patients would like to go, given the uneven distribution of physicians that exists. Then physician capacity is shifted, followed by a shift of patients from physicians who are too much in demand to those who are in less demand. Patients react to geographic distance by indifference up to about two miles, after which attractiveness decreases so that a physician twice as far away is viewed as much less than half as attractive. White patients,

72 / Functional Specialization

however, evaluate distance not only geographically but also "religiously." On the average, Jewish clients evaluate the distance to a non-Jewish hospital as about three times as far; Catholics evaluate the distance to non-Catholic hospitals as about twice as far; Protestants evaluate Catholic and Jewish hospitals as about twice as far, but they evaluate nonreligiously named hospitals about as far as Protestant hospitals (Morrill and Rees, 1968). A generalized concept of relative distance can be derived from frequency of transactions between any two points, groups, or countries and type of transaction (Deutsch and Isard, 1961).

Our preliminary analysis of function space cannot be applied directly to the latter two examples, but only to several subsets of cases resembling the first. It is most easily applicable to cases where there is only one relevant dimension of adjustment, and where this behaves like an interval scale (Stevens, 1951), regardless of whether the adjustment steps are discrete or continuous. It can also be applied to cases of two, three, or more dimensions, as long as these have adjustment properties corresponding to Euclidean[1] or near-Euclidean space. It is not directly applicable to adjustment problems corresponding to partially ordered or still less highly ordered types of space.

In such cases, our approach could be used at best as a kind of baseline or null model. This can reveal some possible limiting case, against which the deviations of the actual case could be appraised. It is possible, however, that even in such cases one adjustment dimension has near-Euclidean properties. This may be so highly salient that it can be used as a meaningful base for approximate calculation. Thus, a wider range of adjustments might require more extended facilities, staff additions, staff training requirements, and client referrals within the facility. There would be corresponding changes in the fixed costs per installation as well as in the time and money costs of individual services. These cases could then be treated as a near-Euclidean space. More complex spaces, such as nonlinear spaces, could be approximated by linear scales for part of the adjustment range.

If each specialty slot were filled by a specialized facility and if geographic distance among such facilities were negligible, requests for that service would be allocated to it and no adjustment is necessary.

3.1 OPTIMAL NUMBER OF FUNCTIONALLY SPECIALIZED AGENTS

We define the *scope* of a facility as the ordered ensemble of specialities—the spectrum of bandwidth—over which it can adjust. Denote the number of these specialties by ρ. The greater the number of specialties separating any two sequential requests, the greater will be the adjustment cost.

Let b denote the maximum adjustment range of a service facility. In the wrench analogy, this would mean that if f is the smallest size bolt that the wrench can fit, then $f + b$ is the largest bolt size it can also fit. In what follows, we shall maintain the assumption that there is a one-to-one correspondence relating the functional request space and the functional service space b, and that there are ρ specialty slots on which a metric is defined.[2] The distance between specialty slot f and specialty slot f' is simply $|f - f'|$.

The new variable, ρ, which we call scope can be interpreted as the specialty bandwidth. It is analogous to D, the total distance over which demand is spread, except that it is an integer. It can be viewed as the total number of rungs on the specialty ladder. Implicit in our model is the strong assumption that all the functional specialties comprise a totally ordered set and can be spread out with equal spacings, just as the rungs of a ladder are. We have not yet investigated how substituting the more realistic assumptions of unequal spacing or of a partial ordering would affect our conclusions.

The maintenance cost increases in direct proportion to the number of facilities. This cost increases by C, the fixed capital cost for investment, amortization, and maintenance, if the number of facilities is increased by 1. This marginal increase in maintenance cost is just offset by the marginal decrease in the adjustment cost if the number of facilities is increased by 1. The number of facilities at which these two marginal costs offset each other—at which the total cost is least—is approximately $1/2\sqrt{c_f \rho L/C u_f}$. This is derived in Appendix 3.1.

The optimal number of specialized agents increases as the square root of the request load, the total number of specialities, and the unit adjustment costs increase, all of which tend to increase in the course of social and economic development. It decreases with the cost of maintaining an agent and with adjustment speed. For example, if $c_f = 8$, $\rho = 16$, $L = 10,000$, $C = 1000$ and $v_f = 10$, then $n = 3$ facilities, each covering two specialty slots, should be spread over the 16 specialties. If $c_f = 80$ instead of 8, then n should be 5.

3.2 "FINE TUNING": DYNAMIC ADJUSTMENT THROUGH FEEDBACK CYCLES

A most critical determinant of responsiveness is the opportunity given users to interact with facilities: to converse, adjust, and reformulate their requests that may at first have been only vaguely

74 / Functional Specialization

stated. This opportunity is afforded by two-way channels allowing several passes to and from the nearest facility before the final response to a request is accepted.

If F is the number of times a request-bearing message is repeatedly forwarded, the effective interaction time is proportional to F. In the preceding analysis, the average time it takes a specialized agent to adjust to a request in its service region as it is received in one pass, disregarding geographic distance, was taken to be $\rho/4v_f n$ hours. If we assume that the agent is adjusted back to its midrange position when it has serviced that first pass, the total roundtrip time is $\rho/2v_f n$ hours; if the client requires F such roundtrips or passes before the request is considered to have been adequately dealt with, then the mean time is $F\rho/2v_f n$ hours per request. The resulting number of specialized agents that minimizes total cost is now:

$$n \doteq \frac{1}{2}(2c_f F \rho L/C v_f)^{1/2} \tag{3.1}$$

The number of passes per request would be greater if the specialized agent's interpretation of the request, as it is first posed, poorly matches the problem representation that finally leads to satisfactory service. The number of passes is thus inverse to the practicable economy of coding. It is small if the specialist is so specialized that he or she can spot instantly what needs to be done or if the client has such a clear-cut request that any agent could see immediately what to do. In the case of a highly specialized agent, for F to be small the client must also know just where to turn, and right away. Otherwise additional time and cost has to be expended in referral and runaround.

Suppose that each request goes first to a generalist who cannot render the service but refers the request to the appropriate specialist. The greater the number of specialties represented, the more specialized the agent and the closer to 1 is the mean number of passes per request: that is, the more immediate is the specialist's identification of what needs to be done. If the referring generalist makes an acceptable referral in one pass, the specialist to whom the request is referred renders the service in one pass, and F is 2 under these conditions. Then

$$n > \frac{1}{2}(2Lc_f \rho/Cv_f)^{1/2}$$

If ρ is small, F tends to increase. Thus the product, $F\rho$, may decrease on balance because of an upper limit to F. If a certain service cannot be performed by any of the n nonspecialists, that upper limit will not change no matter how large F is. The service will generally end, albeit unsatisfactorily, after a certain number of passes. An increase in either the request load or in the number of specialties tends to increase the optimal number of facilities, n, and those two trends seem to outweigh any likely decrease in C/c_f or v_f, so that the importance of being able to identify what needs to be done right away, in the first pass, appears to be diminishing except in cases where speed of an appropriate response is itself crucial.

Suppose that the agents are not completely time-shared. An agent, once seized by a client, may not have to readjust to the midrange of its service region in readiness for *any* request, but it may remain at the point of adjustment it had just reached. If the next request is a second pass of the request just serviced, it may not require so many adjustment steps.

These considerations hold both for messages communicated over transport or communication channels or messages representing control signals that cause a facility to adjust. In the latter case, the distance in adjustment space would be less for each successive adjustment cycle. In addition, F may be proportional to how poorly the nearest specialized facility matches the request when it is first posed.

3.3 ADJUSTMENT SPACE AND GEOGRAPHIC SPACE COMBINED

We now want to examine whether there might be trades between the number of functionally and the number of geographically dispersed facilities. We can picture the total volume of requests distributed over both the D miles of geographic space *and* the ρ request categories of functional space. It may then be shown as a slab with rectangular base of dimensions $D \times \rho$ and height $L/D\rho$. Its volume is L requests/month (Figure 3.1). The base of this slab is a space that we view partitioned into geographic-functional service regions. There is a service facility centered in each region (see Figure 3.2).

The total cost K of providing service is the sum of three terms.[3] The first is the *fixed cost*, nC_n dollars/month, where C_n is the cost of one of the n facilities. Hence C_1 is the fixed unit cost in a one-facility system, C_2 is the unit cost of a two-unit system, and so forth. The second term is the forwarding cost due to transport over geographic space. The third is the adjustment cost component. We ask how to make K smallest. If there is an unsaturated infrastructure that we can utilize, the cost of adding another specialized facility is less than the cost of building a new one.

Consider first the simple case where there are no economies of scale, and $C_n = C_1 = C$. We summarize our variables:

L is the total demand, in requests per month, for example, 30,000
D is the total distance, in miles, for example 3000
c_d is the cost of time spent in transporting a request, in dollars per hour, for example, 10
v_d is the speed of transporting a request, in miles per hour, for example, 10
C is the total fixed cost, in dollars per month, of maintaining one simple, general purpose facility, for example, 10,000
b is the number of specialized functions over which one facility ranges, for example, 2 to 10
ρ is the total number of specialized functions, for example, 10
c_f is the cost of adjusting a facility by one step to respond to a request, in dollars per hour, for example, 10
v_f is the speed of adjusting a facility, in steps per hour, for example, 10

Note: c_d and c_f correspond to what we have denoted by c'_{op} in Chapters 1 and 2. We omit clients' waiting costs for simplicity here.

To get from a randomly chosen point in the $D \times \rho$ rectangle to its nearest service facility, a request must move first a distance x and then

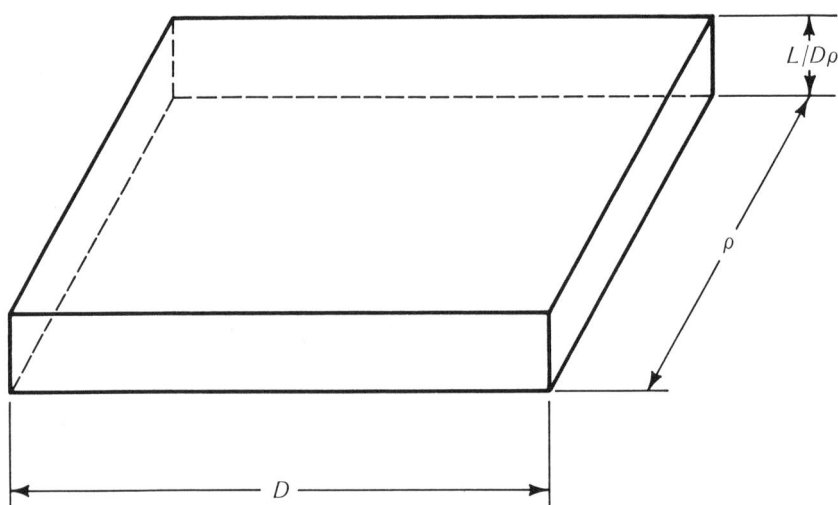

Figure 3.1. Distribution of demand over geographic and functional space.

3.3 Adjustment Space and Geographic Space / 77

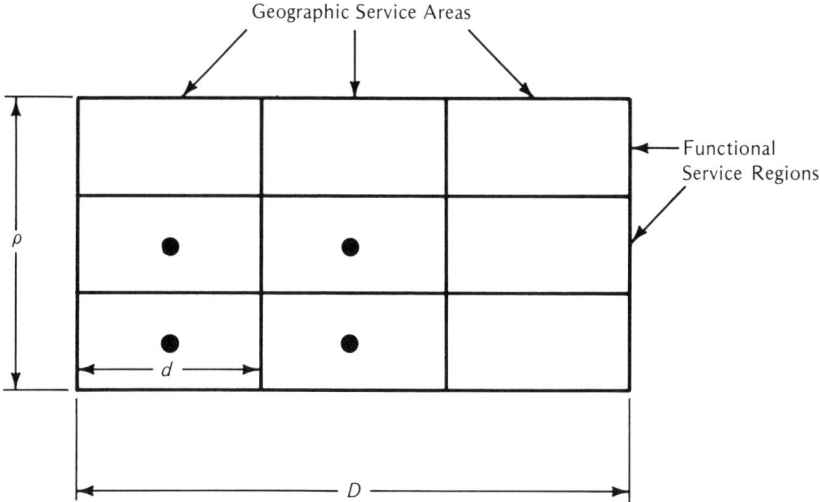

Figure 3.2. Distribution of service stations over geographic and functional space.

a number of steps Y. If the facility assigned to each center is in the middle of both ρ and D and the request distribution over the rectangle is uniform, the average forwarding distance is $D/4n_d$ and the average number of adjustment steps is $\rho/4n_f$. The corresponding average times are $D/4n_d v_d$ and $\rho/4n_f v_f$, and they must be added. The mean operating cost is then $Dc_d/4n_d v_d + \rho c_f/4n_f v_f$ dollars per request and the fixed cost is nC_n dollars per month. We seek n_d and n_f such that they jointly minimize the total cost, where n_d is the number of facilities dispersed in space and n_f is the number dispersed by function. Thus, the total cost is:

$$K = nC_n + \frac{L}{4}(c_d D/v_d n_d + c_f \rho/v_f n_f) \tag{3.2}$$

and $n = n_d n_f$, where n_d and n_f are determined implicitly in Appendix 3.2.

The result of this calculation, shown in Appendix 3.2, is:

$$n = (L^2 c_f c_d D \rho / 16 v_f v_d C^2)^{1/3} \tag{3.3}$$

and it holds when $(c_d/v_d)D$ and $(c_f/v_f)\rho$ are both large so that the error

78 / Functional Specialization

committed by using partial derivatives of cost with respect to n_f and n_d can be neglected.

Under the above assumptions and with illustrative values for L, D, c_d, v_d, c_f, v_f, C, and ρ taken to be 30,000, 375, 10.10, 10, 10, 10,000, and 128, respectively, the value for n according to Equation 3.3 is 30; this corresponds to $n_f = 3.2$ and $n_d = 9.375$ according to $n_f = 4v_d n^2 C/Lc_d D$ and a similar formula for n_d that follows easily from Appendix 3.2. Since n_f and n_d must be integers, we may interpret this result as 3 specialized clinics at each of 9 geographic sites, with 27 (rather than 30) 3-clinic hospitals covering the 375 miles and the 128 specialties to be a least-cost number of facilities. This compares with about 16 facilities that would result from the use of Equation 2.3, which holds if there were no functional specialties.

In Appendix 3.3, we derive and present the results of expanding the above analysis to situations characterized by more than one spatial dimension and more than one functional dimension. We also introduce the effect of economies of scale.

3.4 SOME TECHNOLOGICAL AND SOCIAL TRENDS

What long-term trends could be expected in regard to this value n? Population increase would tend to increase the service load, L, over time and thus support a trend toward increasing n, toward decentralization. Both D and ρ may stay constant in time, though ρ, the range of specialized functions, could be on the increase. The geographic cost-speed ratio, c_d/v_d, is very likely decreasing unless congestion effects should reverse it. (The time and cost of crossing midtown Manhattan on a weekday at noon have increased during the last half-century.) The cost-speed ratio of functional adjustments, c_f/v_f, related to the average learning capacity of individual servers or service facilities within the system, is also related to what is called *bureaucracy* and *rigidity* in human organizations; indeed, it could be used as a quantitative indicator.

Theories about the growing bureaucratization and rigidity of modern industrial societies would assert, therefore, a secular trend toward an increase in this ratio. Whether this is true or false is a matter for empirical research to decide. If bureaucracy and rigidity should increase the cost of adjustments, this would reward decentralization.

On this count, bureaucratic rigidity and centralization may direct funds toward greater functional decentralization, which may further reduce the resources available for greater geographic dispersal. If the

3.4 Some Technological and Social Trends / 79

adjustment cost-speed ratio, c_f/v_f, is high, a feedback process of this kind may lead to a highly specialized sedentary society or functionally decentralized stagnation. If it is low, functional decentralization may be compatible with experimentation and innovation.

It is interesting to consider how c_d/v_d, the cost-speed ratio of geographic dispersion, varies with the range of geographic distance that various technologies have permitted people to attain. Reaching out with one's hands enables humankind to traverse at high speed (large v_d) a very limited range at low cost (small c_d). Hence, c_d/v_d is small up to a few feet. To transcend this range, we resort to walking. This requires a greater expenditure of energy (larger c_d) relative to the possible speed, for we have to move more mass. Hence, c_d/v_d is slightly larger in the range from a few feet to a few miles. We then resort to wheeled vehicles—bicycles, cars, trains—which extend the range to hundreds of miles—and increase c_d/v_d even further. The bicycle is an exception in that it requires less energy expenditure (lower c_d) than walking while providing for greater speed. In terms of costs for shoe repairs, and so on, the actual dollar cost of walking has been found to exceed that of bicycling as well. Increasing the range beyond that of cars through the use of large jets appears to drive c_d/v_d down again because v_d grows to be very large and c_d does not grow as large any more. Thus there is a trend for c_d/v_d to increase.

Similarly, c_f/v_f may be small if the total range of adjustment steps is very small or if training and technology make it possible for a large number of functions to be served with little adjustment between them. However, as mentioned above, bureaucratization can have the opposite effect. It is interesting to note that Charles Perrow develops the idea of "unobtrusive controls" as a way to clarify the notion of decentralization (1972) to resolve the paradox that the more bureaucratized an organization, the more decentralized it is.

In systems where such conditions apply, we should find during an early period of development a trend toward centralization, followed by a reversal when decentralizing trends prevail, and a second reversal during a later period when movements toward unification and centralization once more would predominate. Further oscillations of long-term trends may well continue and deserve empirical investigation.

However, changes in either the geographic cost-speed ratio, c_d/v_d, or the functional adjustment-speed ratio, c_f/v_f, may be small in comparison to the secular increase in the *variety* of different functions and kinds of service that may be required. This range could roughly be estimated as proportional to the per capita gross national product (GNPC). Since GNPC has been growing in many countries at about 3 percent per annum, it has been doubling every 23 years; and a similar increase in the range of different responses and services demanded might provide a powerful impetus toward continuing functional specialization. However, if we consider the long-term effects of pollution and dwindling fossil fuel resources, it may be found that GNPC growth rates of 2 percent, with doubling times of 35 years or still lower rates of growth, could become realistic (Heierli, 1974/1976).

It is interesting to compare the formula for n without economies of scale but with one geographic and functional dimension, with a corresponding formula for n in which functional specialization was ignored. In the latter case n varies as the square root of the ratio of service load to capital cost, L/C. Here it varies as the two-thirds power of L/C. If historical trends favor an increase of L/C, $(L/C)^{2/3}$ increases more than $(L/C)^{1/2}$, and the introduction of functional specialization beyond geographic dispersion favors decentralization, if other factors remain the same.

Arguments for centralization (Davis, 1969) do not even make mention of such factors as L/C but list the key advantages of centralization factors like better reliability, better servicing, and more storage capacities. We have shown the first two to also be by-products of decentralization, and it is questionable whether the improved storage capacities derivable from centralization can compare with the results of secular increases in the load-to-cost ratio, L/C.

3.5 FUNCTIONAL SPECIALIZATION COMBINED WITH DISPERSION: UNEVEN SERVICE LOADS OVER SPACE AND TIME

Generally, the load of demand for service is distributed unevenly over both geographic sites and specialized functions. If all requests for one special function originate from the vicinity of one site, a facility capable of that special function should be located at only that site. More generally, if the distribution of requests over functions were concentrated at one point (just one spike) but the marginal distribution over geographic space had n spikes, we could disperse n identical facilities, each under one of these spikes. If the demand for a specialized service is strongly correlated with a particular location, it may pay to put a service facility at that location.

Suppose that requests were distributed according to the particular nonuniform distribution shown in Figure 3.3.

There are s spikes of dimensions a by b by y. Each spike has a volume of aby that denotes the probability of a request originating within the a

3.5 Specialization Combined with Dispersion / 81

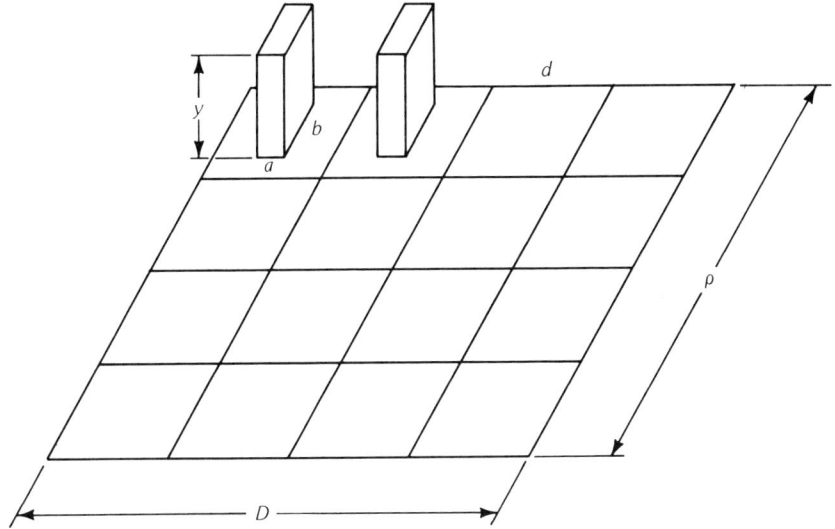

Figure 3.3. Distribution of requests over nonuniform distribution.

$\times$ b area. Consequently, $aby = 1$, since a request is sure to originate in one of the s areas of dimensions $a \times b$. If we were to suboptimize, the number of facilities that would go under each spike would be given by Equation 3.4 with D replaced by b, ρ and a and L replaced by $Lyab$. If we denote the resulting total number of facilities by n', then:

$$n' = \frac{s}{2} \left(\frac{(Lyab)^2 ab}{2C^2} \frac{c_d}{v_d} \frac{c_f}{v_f} \right)^{1/3} \qquad (3.4)$$

Now let u denote the fraction of the area from which requests originate. Then $u = (sab/D\rho)$ or $ab = (uD\rho/s)$. It can easily be shown that $n'/n = u^{1/3}$. Compare this result with the case without functional specialization, which was $n'/n = u^{1/2}$.

Thus, if there are four spikes, with $a/D = 1/4$ and $b/\rho = 1/8$, $u = 1/8$ and half as many facilities would be needed as in the case where the requests are uniformly distributed over $\rho \times D$.

Nonuniformity of the request distribution over both space and functions favors centralization, but not as much as would the same nonuniformity over space alone. Introducing functional specialization

82 / Functional Specialization

tends to reduce or undo the centralizing effect of nonuniformity, and thus it favors decentralization.

3.6 SUMMARY

In general, we find that the introduction of functional specialization in service systems, in addition to considerations of geographic dispersions, makes their optimum design more stable against—that is, less sensitive to—changes in any parameter. The general formula, in the absence of significant net economies of scale, shows that the optimum number of facilities, n, changes in response only to the cube root of the change in the request load, or of any other relevant parameter.

Large capital economies of scale indicated by the term, α, in the production and/or installation of service facilities, such as the case of automobiles or telephones, promote decentralization and make the optimal number, n, of facilities *more* sensitive to changes in the request load or other parameters. Large *service* economies of scale, indicated by β, will have the opposite effect, promoting centralization and making the optimum number of facilities less sensitive to parameter changes. Since the two types of economies of scale, α and β, have opposite effects, they are likely to cancel each other out, at least in part, and only their joint *net* effect needs to be considered. The assumption that this net effect, $\alpha - \beta$, or α/β, can be neglected may fit a wider range of actual cases, and the cube root formula may serve more often as an acceptable first approximation for $m = 2$. As m, the number of dimensions in functional adjustment space, increases in the absence of economies of scale, the most cost-effective number of facilities varies approximately as $L\rho c_f/4C$. Increasing loads and unit adjustment cost as well as greater spread of functional specialty slots favor decentralization, while increasing capital costs favor centralization.

The effects of uneven distribution of requests in two-dimensional space with one dimension of adjustment space also favor centralization; they decrease the number of needed facilities from what is most cost-effective in the case of an even load distribution. This decrease varies as the cube root of the fraction of the area from which requests originate. Nonuniformity over both space and function favors centralization but not as much as nonuniformity over space alone.

The questions we have asked arise in the design of computational facilities (Davis, 1969), library branches (Tauber, 1961), municipal services (Savas, 1969), and many other areas. In the organizational design of academic science libraries, for example (Cooper, 1968), decentralized subject departmental organization is held to be feasible only for large institutions, since they can afford to have library units serving one or two specialized departments. At Harvard, for example, decentralization is so complete that in 1955 there were at least 40 different cataloging centers with widely different rules. Information services are used by corporations in highly specialized and decentralized ways. In education, the question of providing minimal cultural uniformity through school integration and preserving cultural diversity through local matching can be seen as one of functional specialization. On balance, the trend toward greater functional diversity should thus reinforce trends toward decentralization.

Chapter 4

Responsiveness and Higher Service Quality

4.1. CONVERSATIONAL INTERACTION

An important reason for decentralizing a service organization is to make it more responsive to its clients in the sense in which the concept has been defined in Chapter 1. One way to do this is to shorten the lines of communication between servers and clients. Another way is to provide for a larger number of two-way conversational interactions with many cycles. A client may present a well-defined request for service, and he or she may also have a clear-cut criterion for recognizing when a response is satisfactory; this is communicated to the service system. The client may still receive an unsatisfactory response, or none at all, for any of the following reasons: (1) the service system does not have the capability; (2) it does not want to provide the response; or (3) it misunderstood the client's instructions.

The system's response should never consist of just one reaction to the client's initiative. Even if the client specifies all details about the nature of the response he or she wants, when he or she wants it, in what form, how much he or she is willing to pay, when, and so on, the system should first react by acknowledging the request, restating it according to how it was understood and agreed to by the system. Such acknowledgments can take the form of a contract or agreement. It is an early feedback to the client.

It is essential for responsiveness that the client feels that someone is listening and empathizes. This should be mandatory except in emergencies. Immediacy of the first reaction is usually of great importance though there are special situations where excessive rashness can be harmful.

Generally, at least two transactions with at least one feedback—the implicit contract—are required. The client, by informing the system whether the response was or was not satisfactory, should have the last word. The service organization should solicit this feedback from the client in discrete ways other than inferring it from the client's payment or repeated use of the system. While repeated use may be a good behavioral indicator of satisfaction, if the client is indeed satisfied, he or she may use it repeatedly even if the client is dissatisfied when there is no better choice. Recommendations to others and switching from a competitive service are even better indicators (Hirschman, 1970).

Conversational interaction is important not only between server and client but also among servers in order to coordinate their task roles to attain their organization's objectives: for example, render good, responsive service. Coordination can be achieved in two ways. The first is by programming, planning, and using preestablished rules, schedules, and standards, with reliance on sanctions. The second is through the continual flow of new information that is fed back to detect errors and aid in mutual adjustment, with reliance on socialization and peer pressure, and self-control rather than external control (Hage, Aiken, Marrett, 1971). The second method of coordination is favored by diversity in organizational structure, for example, by personal specialization and differentiation of roles. It is manifested primarily by increased horizontal communication (see Chapter 5).

An important aspect is the quality of the socioemotional bond between server and client, and between people in general. It involves such interpersonal relations as the need to include or be included, the need to dominate or be dominated, and the need to love or be loved (Schutz, 1967).

The socioemotional, as well as the professional, relation between client and service provider has always been delicate. There are important trends that are likely to affect it. Some insight into the nature of this relation can be acquired from an analysis of the simpler relation between the consumer and provider of a product rather than a service.

A man needing an item of apparel can go to a clothing store, state that he needs a dress suit, prefers a dark color, but does not know the exact size and knows little about various fabrics or styles. The salesman has more specialized expertise than the client, and the client relies to some extent on that. The client may not trust the salesman completely. He may assume that if there is a conflict between the interest of the salesman and his interest, the salesman will favor his own interest. Such a conflict might arise if the client aims to spend no more than a certain amount, yet wants to get the best possible value for his expenditure, while the salesman is aware of certain items that yield the highest return or that are overstocked and which he would prefer to sell.

A man who knows more about clothes may go to a custom tailor. He then specifies exactly what he would like. The tailor prepares the goods to order. In this case, the client is in a more authoritative position. The tailor still has expertise, know-how in the actual manufacture of the product, but is not likely to tolerate instructions by the client in how to tailor the suit.

Clients can acquire expertise about the properties of simple products that they consider important. Acquisition of such expertise is more difficult for complex products, such as computers, and an obstacle to the maintenance of clients' expertise is the great and increasing variety of products. These considerations apply to an even greater extent for services. Services tend to be more custom designed and individualized than products. If clients could specify with some precision and detail the service they wanted, they could often render it by and for themselves.

In the doctor-patient relation, the client trusts the doctor to not only perform but also to specify needed services. Most patients come to doctors with only a very general implicit request or need: to maintain or improve health or to alleviate a specific complaint. As patients learn more about medicine and health care, they can become sufficiently sophisticated to tell the doctor what services to perform. The ultimate responsibility for what services are to be performed, and by whom, rests with the client. The servers, doctors and other professionals included, report to the client. It is the client who sees the doctor, whom the client authorizes and pays to do certain work, not the doctor who sees the patient. The physician is increasingly concerned about helping his clients learn, guiding them in modifying their lifestyles so as to reduce the risk of major illnesses and acquire enough knowledge about their own bodies to initiate early detection of incipient illness and manage themselves wisely. Thus the clients increase their participation in the service. The relation becomes less authoritarian and possibly even more responsive in its socioemotional and human aspects.

That this is beginning to happen is evidenced in the creation of health maintenance organizations, the upgrading of nurse-practitioners, and other major changes in health care aimed at increased responsiveness at lower cost. Yet some older physicians, trained in authoritarian attitudes and beliefs, still cling defensively to dogmatic statements such as: "Thus, if a patient wishes to see me, and he truly is sick, he will have to come at my convenience" or "But I refuse to back down one inch to those patients who question the value of my services" (Kaplan, 1915).

4.2. GENUINE DIALOG

The services of a family physician who made house calls were appreciated primarily because of the responsive interactions, with many opportunities for dialog, in a half-hour visit. The modern medical specialist with an automated laboratory and large, specialized supporting staff can render instrumental services of higher technical quality, but spends less time in I-Thou dialog (Buber, 1958) at the patient's bedside. Automated procedures for taking medical histories, computer-aided diagnosis, and medical management could undoubtedly be made so that, as patients converse with the system through a console or terminal, they are provided with valuable feedback every few seconds in immediate response to their imputs. It is not obvious, however, that clients would pay as much attention to, or money for, this man-machine dialog as they would for human contact, provided that the latter were genuinely human. It is perhaps this human element, the I-Thou dialog, that is the major part of the essence of responsiveness in a human service organization.

Many dialogs of this kind are predominantly instrumental in character. The goals of the user, as well as those of the service system, remain fixed. The communication between them deals only with ways and means for each to realize the largest possible gains at the lowest possible cost. In the terms proposed by Anatol Rapoport, such dialogs resemble *games* in which the goals of both parties stay unchanged and only their strategies are flexible and subject to their choice. More rarely, such dialogs may turn into genuine *debates* in Rapoport's sense, in which not only the strategies but also the goals and values of the parties are subject to possible change in the course of their communication (Rapoport, 1960).

The problems or issues faced by a decision-making group may be simple or complex. Experiments with small groups (Harshbarger, 1971; see also Bavelas, 1951) suggest that groups with a decentralized decision structure are more accurate, if not faster, in solving complex problems than groups with centralized structures. Moreover, participants will like their task better because the decentralized structure is reportedly more satisfying. Left to themselves with free choices, however, members of a group will probably organize themselves into a centralized decision structure.

Most of these findings cannot safely be extended to large service organizations. It is known, for example, that large coalitions are very rare. The role of communication and information and its effects on the difficulty of forming and maintaining coalitions of varying size appears to be one of the key factors in explaining the rarity of large coalitions (Komorita, 1974). Another factor in the rarity of large coalitions, however, may be a "size principal," according to which it is rational to limit a coalition to the smallest size that still assures winning (Riker, 1962).

Communication may well become the primary instrument in the delivery of future services. This is illustrated by the health care service sector. It continues to grow in cost, but there is no correspondingly dramatic reduction in morbidity and mortality. Clients will soon realize that the benefits of advances in medical science, such as vaccines and antibiotics, cause major reductions in morbidity and mortality through public health measures rather than through medical practice. Such social programs aim at prevention of illness. Further preventive measures involve lifestyle changes such as improved nutrition, exercise, avoidance of noxious substances, avoidance of stress, and so on. Some modern physicians, whose professional behavior increasingly resembles that of businessmen, do not find it in their interest to engage in the educational services necessary to effect major changes in their clients' lifestyles. The future of the health care industry may lie in the employment of many health information professionals with responsibility for helping clients to utilize what is known in order to maintain health, after properly screening and synthesizing such knowledge. It is quite possible that we are moving toward a self-service society, in which control and accountability shifts from extreme concentration in the hands of individual service providers to a more even distribution among various types and levels of service providers and clients as well.

Other factors being the same, a service organization that provides more opportunities for education, communication, and especially I-Thou dialogs is preferred. Suppose now that there are a few servers with a rare gift for such I-Thou dialogs—or for giving such an I-Thou feeling to their clients—because of their warm, positive personalities, their integrity, moral strength, faith, and otherwise outstanding human qualities. Suppose they are in great demand and that their services could somehow be amplified by a centralized organization in which one such server interacts with numerous clients in a group. Examples in education are large lecture courses and videotapes.

As a very different alternative, consider clients meeting on a one-to-one basis with more abundant servers whose qualifications are lower from this humanistic point of view. The opportunity for more frequent, and perhaps more intense and rapid, client-server interaction may have to be traded against the intangible human quality of the interaction. This problem is similar to the quality due to concentration and dispersal trade studies elsewhere in this book in which the question provides clients with a specific arrangement and the best options. It must also provide them with wisdom to choose among options. The organization should contain enough I-Thou interactors to meet the demand for both large audiences and for private sessions with clients whose needs appear sufficiently urgent or are willing and able to pay enough, or both. It should also provide more moderately priced highly responsive "terminals" that offer less opportunity for I-Thou dialog.

4.3. CONVERGENCE AND DIVERGENCE

If a client does not present a well-defined request with a clear-cut criterion for recognizing a satisfactory response, considerably more dialog is required. Dialog, or conversational interaction with responsive feedback by both client and server, may be convergent or divergent. If it is convergent, it helps both the client and server arrive jointly at a statement of the client's need that represents the need with increasing accuracy and precision. This makes possible a more significant, relevant, valid, and useful response.

If it is divergent, the articulation of the need becomes increasingly confused as client-server interaction proceeds. The server's responses become increasingly irrelevant and useless in meeting the need. This may be due to a communication barrier, which could be worsened by affective or sociological factors such as the client's need to be shown affection and the server's inability to do so. When either the client or the server begins to sense the futility of further interaction or find that the emotional or other costs have become intolerable, the interaction is terminated, sometimes with a tragic outcome (Hollingshead and Redzich, 1958). In less serious cases, it is simply considered unsatisfactory. If feedback in either direction *worsens* an already existing obstacle, impeding progress toward a satisfactory response, it is called positive feedback. If it *lessens* such an obstacle it is called negative feedback, and in time the obstacle may disappear. If it is not sufficiently negative, oscillations between the same low and high levels of the obstacle may result, which is tantamount to divergence.

On the other hand, some phenomenon may help or catalyze progress toward a satisfactory response. Then positive feedback from server to client or from client to server can amplify the effect of this phenomenon and speed convergence. Here negative feedback can delay convergence or cause divergence. It is therefore extremely important for clients or servers to recognize whether a phenomenon is likely to help or to hinder progress toward meeting a need and whether the feedback is in the right or wrong direction.

Convergent sequences of such feedback cycles also tend to contribute to the adaptiveness or flexibility of a service system. Such adaptiveness or flexibility has been proposed as one of eight key variables that describe the formal structure of any organization (Hage, 1965). To measure it, Hage proposed indicators such as the number of new programs and techniques adopted by the organization in a year. Another of his eight variables was "centralization," which he operationalized as the inverse of the proportion of jobs that participate in decision making and by the number of areas in which decisions are made by decision makers. "Complexity" is another of his variables, which he defines as the number of occupational specialities at the level of training required, a mix of our functional specialization and delegation dimensions. He assumes that the higher the complexity, the lower the centralization; also, the higher the stratification (differences in income and prestige among jobs), the lower the adaptiveness. From six such assumptions he believes that certain "corollaries" follow. One is that the higher the centralization, the lower the adaptiveness. Another is the lower the adaptiveness, the lower the job satisfaction; and the lower the complexity, the lower the adaptiveness.

Hage then used evidence from published studies to test these propositions. He found that most of them were supported. For example, he cited a study by Cillié (1940) that used a scale of innovations in school techniques and programs as a measure of adaptiveness, comparing the degree of adaptiveness in 16 schools that were centralized and 16 that were decentralized but which were matched in socioeconomic characteristics. The decentralized schools had adopted more of the techniques and programs, particularly those that increased their capacity for change to allow greater individual attention to students, which included more varied teaching and greater teacher participation in decision making. The centralized schools adopted fewer programs and techniques, preferring those that increased efficiency.

4.4. EFFECT OF DECENTRALIZATION ON FEEDBACK AND VICE VERSA

Decentralization would increase the number and variety of servers available for matching with clients. It would also increase opportunities for heightened sensitivity in the client-server interaction. Of course, decentralization also increases opportunities for error, by sending insufficiently sensitive, competent, or appropriate servers to interact with clients. These servers could do more harm than good. But if enough servers, sufficiently well-qualified to prevent, check for, and correct such errors, are spread at strategic points in the service organization, such risks can be kept under control. The cost of doing this will go up as the organization is decentralized and would seem to limit how far it pays to decentralize.

A simple model to capture an aspect of these considerations is to regard the load of requests to be classified into m different types and the servers to be graded into ν classes. These classes resemble the functional specialties studied in Chapter 3, except that we are now measuring decentralization by ν. We ask how far it pays to increase ν. Ideally, $\nu = m$, with a server tailored for each type of request. Generally, $\nu < m$.

Assume that ν divides m, that all request types are equally likely, and that there is just one server in each of the ν classes. Then each server must deal with m/ν types of requests. To sort the type it is, the sorter-server must ask at least $\log_2 m/\nu$ yes-no questions or make that many conversational passes. Let k be the operating cost, as before, in dollars per hour, to engage in such sorting activity, and let T be the turnaround time per pass. Then $LTk \log_2 m/\nu$ is the average operating cost per month. Adding the fixed cost of maintaining servers at C dollars per month, the total cost is:

$$\nu C + LTk \log_2 m/\nu \text{ dollars per month}$$

Differentiating this with respect to ν, setting to 0, and solving for ν, we obtain as an approximation,

$$\nu \doteq \frac{LTk \log_2 e}{C} \qquad (4.1)$$

The optimal variety of servers increases with load, turnaround time per pass, and ratio of operating to fixed cost. The increase with load is plausible. Insofar as increased turnaround time may increase the

4.4 Effect of Decentralization on Feedback

chance of a more sensitive server-client interaction—a key attribute of responsiveness—there should be a positive correlation between ν and T. There may be a slight tendency for T to increase and for k/C to stay constant; L is likely to increase, favoring an increase of ν. Since ν is an aspect of decentralization, the secular trends appear to favor a shift toward decentralization from this point of view.

Clients' needs for service become more complex as technology advances. The car, for example, has led to a car-servicing industry, insurance services, and numerous new laws and their enforcement This increases the load L on the service system. It also requires greater sensitivity and special competencies on the part of servers if they are to meet these needs. There is demand, for example, for mechanics experienced with particular types of cars. This tends to increase, in effect, the fixed capital cost C that has to be invested in training each additional server. The trend toward an increasing load then favors decentralization up to the point where the counter trend toward a higher fixed cost per server, as well as the cost due to error control, will balance the benefits of increased sensitivity in client-server interactions. This point of marginal cost-benefit balance then determines the optimum degree of decentralization from this point of view.

Experiments (Harshbarger, 1971) with small groups have suggested that a decentralized interaction structure (the possible number of participating dyads in the group) is more satisfying to the members than a more centralized structure; also a decentralized decision structure (number of participating decision makers) leads to greater accuracy in solving complex problems. Coping with complex problems might sometimes require complex service organizations. An organization has been called complex (Hage, 1965) according to the number of occupational specialties and the length of training required by each. Such increased specialization is often accompanied by an increased use of technology, which in turn increases the complexity of the problems faced by both clients and servers.

The same balance also determines the expected number of feedback cycles and the duration of each. Let F denote the expected number of query negotiation passes or feedback cycles of conversational interaction until a satisfactory response is obtained or the request is abandoned. The effect of F is to multiply the effective distance over which requests and responses must be sent (or over which the clients must travel). It affects the optimal number of pluralized and dispersed agents, as derived in the previous chapters, as $\sqrt{F}$. The tendency to demand more cycles of conversational interaction thus favors decentralization.

4.5 TECHNOLOGY AND REMOTENESS

For clients who buy custom-tailored suits, F is the number of fittings required; for the clients of a portrait painter, F is the number of sittings; and for the clients of a psychotherapist, F is the number of sessions. Which services of this kind could be rendered equally well from a remote location?

We could imagine a psychiatric session governed by a computer program that the client may find indistinguishable from the behavior of some psychiatrists (Colby et al., 1966). The computer and tapes may be located remotely, as might a psychiatrist interacting with the client by telephone. We could even imagine a portrait of a New York woman painted by a painter in Boston as she poses over a picture phone. We might go even further and imagine a tailor in Hong Kong using a dummy, or in some future day, activating a robot on which a garment fits that is the exact size of the client.

Technologically, these feats are possible but it is unlikely that anyone would pay the price to obtain service this way. Even the great convenience of the telephone has not lessened people's need for face-to-face contacts. On the contrary it appears that cheaper, faster, more ubiquitous telecommunication devices are increasing the need for face-to-face contact. This may be due to the increased consciousness by clients that the serving agent is responding as a whole human being. Clients cannot express their possible anger at the agent by punching their robot surrogate, for they are aware that it is only a terminal and not the actual agent. And Joseph Weizenbaum asserts that a computer could never converse meaningfully about its own death or physical love because it lacks a body resembling that of a person (Weizenbaum, 1976).

This raises the question of what is to be called an agent or, for that matter, a client. The same programmed computer can interact with several clients simultaneously, serving them with responses to requests for computation, information, and so on. Is each terminal a serving agent or service station, as we called it? Or, if a surgeon operates on a patient's heart, he or she tends to focus on the damaged heart as the part to be serviced. The surgeon deals with only a fragment of the client as if that were the client. This would be less trivial as an example if the client were a man-machine system or a machine, with a machine part in the role of the heart. But can the notion of "client" and "server" apply to entities that are only part human or entirely nonhuman? One answer may be that, so long as the part treated or serviced remains in close and multiple connection with the rest of the client's body and personality, the client as a whole will have to be taken into account. Only those of the client's subsystems for which partial decomposability is high are more likely to permit more nearly separate treatment without severely damaging results (Simon, 1969). This degree of temporary decomposability, however, has been increased by recent medical advances (DeBakey, 1977).

The key point of this chapter is to express our predominantly humanistic orientation to the problems of decentralization. We are concerned primarily with human clients, and for us, their human concerns come first. Man-made artifacts or natural objects ordinarily are to be provided service only insofar as this is an indirect service to a human client or a human client has identified with them. This does not imply, therefore, that the clients of a veterinarian are only the human owners of livestock or pets and not the animals being treated. Once these animals have come to matter to people, their well-being may matter for their own sake to some human service organization. Most often, however, a *client* is anyone who is capable of posing a request that reflects a need, recognizing a satisfactory response, and aware of his or her own intentions. The client is also aware that the server who is responding is a free agent with intentions of rendering good service, and where appropriate, of entering into an I-Thou dialog with the client.

Similarly, a *server* is anyone capable of recognizing a request as an expression of need, or providing a satisfactory response, and aware of his or her own intentions. A server must also recognize that the client is a free agent with the intention of paying for the service or of being entitled to it on the community's or some other sponsor's behalf. Both server and client realize that each is capable of entering into an I-Thou relation with the other. (For further discussion of "intention," see Section 4.6 and Chapter 1.)

In the face of technological growth, people are becoming more aware of their distinctly human properties and needs. This tends to increase the need for more human feedback and interaction. Hence, from this point of view the trend is toward larger values of F, the average number of interaction feedback cycles, and toward more decentralization.

There is, however, at least one countervailing tendency implicit in this process. "I-Thou" dialogs take time, even among persons of highly similar language, memories, and cultural background who can use highly economical methods of coding for their mutual communication. If every request for a laundry ticket, a postage stamp, a quick restaurant lunch, or a seat in a theatre were to require an "I-Thou" dialog of even a few minutes, many social and economic transactions would slow to a degree where their opportunity cost in terms of the value of time to the client might become higher than the expected value gained from the transaction. More complex cases of the division of labor often require uniquely long sequences of transactions among sequences of actors. How many "I-Thou" dialogs might then be required in the process of assembling an automobile, which at present can be assembled quickly and cheaply by impersonal mass production methods?

The more redundantly time and resources are available, the more "I-Thou" dialogs can be afforded. For each client's needs there may be a best combination of materially productive but dialog-poor methods of interaction and other dialog-rich methods that are less productive in specific goods and services. The optimal mix may also depend on the service organization and general culture at each particular time and place.

Many complex sequences of economic, technical, or military cooperation require quick, impersonal, and dependable responses to commands or other messages. An example from the Ice Age is the teamwork of primitive hunters. A modern example is the quick cooperation of a modern surgical team. Some or all members of such teams must function, at least part of the time, not in "I-Thou" terms but with quasimechanical precision. To the extent that this is true, human beings always have had to accept some partial and temporary "dehumanization," as required by the speed, precision, and complexity necessary for their own operations. It is then a task for the design of their technical and social organizations to reduce this residual sphere of inescapable dehumanization as far as possible, particularly in regard to the work process as well as for many service organizations, and to provide for its further reduction in the future.

4.6. SOME GENERAL IMPLICATIONS

So far we have dealt primarily with physical distance as the barrier to greater responsiveness between server and client. We have also discussed the length of messages as a cause of delay in communication and with the bandwidth of communication channels as limiting the speed of information flow. In all cases we measured responsiveness in terms of time.

There are, however, important psychological and social obstacles that impede the responsive client-server communication and impose costs or delays. There is considerable literature on communication roles in small groups, such as information or opinion seeking and giving (e.g., Bales et al., 1951; Etzioni, 1961; Katz and Kahn, 1966; Likert, 1967; Wager, 1972).

One source of such impediments is *informational distance* between two communicators in terms of rates of transmission errors and requisite redundancy. This factor will be discussed later in this chapter.

A related type of distance may refer to the mismatch of the intentions of the parties (see also Chapter 7). An *intention*, according to the viewpoint of mathematical psychology (Miller, Galanter, and Pribram, 1960), is that part of the plan or program of an actor that has been postponed in regard to its execution. In this view, the depth of plans would seem to be a function of the number and complexity of postponed steps together with the length of postponement. This view implies, of course, that the acting person, organization, or system has already become committed to that plan or program, ordinarily by carrying out some part of it.

From the viewpoint of civil and criminal law, as well as from that of moral philsophy, the concept of intention is defined more narrowly as *conscious intention*. It then refers to the subset of deferred plans or programs that have been internally monitored and thus made conscious through the attachment of secondary symbols.[1] This implies that some human actor had an abbreviated image of part or all of the postponed program, its expected consequences, and its compatibility with the legal and moral standards of the society. In contrast, mathematical psychologists like Noam Chomsky and George A. Miller, as well as Freudian psychiatrists, seem to admit the possibility of nonconscious intention, consisting of postponed but not fully monitored parts of plans (see also Chapter 7).

The conscious as well as the nonconscious intentions of two human actors, such as a server and a client, may be either compatible or incompatible. Moreover, larger service organizations, as well as nonhuman serving machines, may include postponed programs in their structure, which may function as a quasi-intention, partly or wholly incompatible with the intentions of some of their clients. In such cases, therefore, the concept of *intentional distance* will be meaningful. Certain pairs of people may talk "past one another," in part because they cannot or do not want to recognize the intent in their partner's message.

Compatibility of values and viewpoints, if not intentions, favors the maintenance of consensus about standards and indirectly formalization, routinization, and uniformity. Delegation of authority to managers with diverse viewpoints, on the other hand, favors decentralization and innovation (Downs, 1967, p. 203). It increases the variety of responses for each server (Ashby, 1960).

If servicing the requests requires little information and the servers have very modest information processing capabilities, it is best to decentralize the way they are organized. If their tasks require more information, it pays to centralize to a limited extent because of the advantages inherent in sharing or pooling information while still maintaining a diversity of sources. Thus, major advances in the social sciences often have been achieved by small teams at large centers, including several universities and research institutions (Deutsch, Platt, and Senghaas, 1971). To improve the quality of rural education in isolated places, for another example, it has been proposed to centralize services that are less frequent and more costly by sharing certain educational services (Hessacker, 1970).

If servicing requests requires little information but the servers have very high information-processing capabilities and thus can handle many challenges, a decentralized structure will do well where servicing local variety at a fast rate counts a great deal; a more centralized structure may be needed to cope with tasks of exceptional difficulty and scope, requiring that only a few things at a time be attended to.

As in daily life, there is probably an optimal point between excessive heterogeneity in the services to be rendered and too much monotonous uniformity. An essential unity in diversity must exist in viable service organizations as in other natural systems. A minimal sprinkling of incompatibility and nonconformity must exist in every system to give it a chance for continual, self-testing, self-correcting maintenance of natural error-avoidance procedures. This manifests itself as unavoidable play or wobble in the best managed organizations.

But is not modern technology, as some writers assert, taking us in the opposite direction, toward an increasingly centralized, depersonalized, and alienated future?

4.7 INFORMATIONAL DISTANCE

A popular conception of technological development maintains that advances in technology lead inevitably to similar increases in the effectiveness and power of social control and hence to a suffocating tightening of social bonds. Orwell's *1984* is a well-known literary presentation of this image. In this view, centralization of state and commercial administration is supposed to be an unavoidable concommitant to advances in technology, particularly communications technology. Hence, increasing concentration of power is seen as inevitable as technological development continues, and human affairs are seen as subject to technological determinism.

Throughout this book we are stressing an alternative perspective on these matters. Control and informational proximity—the ease or difficulty of mutual communication—must be distinguished. They are correlated but not identical. Continuing control demands that the controllers be capable of communicating with the controlled and receive some information about the results of their orders. Such feedback information, however, can treat persons as if they were things. It need not include any initiatives from them. Thus physicians have some control over the treatment, but their patients can talk back to them. Veterinarians try to control and treat animal patients who cannot talk back—and some people favor a veterinarian's approach to politics. By contrast, lovers may engage in much mutual communication with only little mutual control.

The viewpoint of communication also involves the questions of tradeoffs between transportation and communication, which will become increasingly important. Recent experiences with computer conferencing, which is a means of nonsimultaneous communication among scattered people who share a common file, suggest that: (1) certain items of knowledge are exchanged and accessed more easily and flexibly; (2) the size of the common information base can be increased; and (3) the probability of discovering and developing latent consensus is increased.

Nonetheless, telecommunications have few dimensions, whereas face-to-face contacts have many more. The Bell Telephone Company of Canada has studied the extent to which potential travelers over their main travel corridors would forego being physically present, if they could transact their business over communication channels. They found that relatively few businessmen would give up traveling. Nonetheless, a suitable communication system could facilitate some exercise of power without direct face-to-face intervention.

4.8 TRANSPORTATION VS. TRANSMISSION: THE BULK OF OBJECTS AND THE LENGTH OF MESSAGES

Consider the following example of the relation between transportation and transmission channels. If a motorist's vehicle breaks down and requires repair service, the motorist must first forward the request for service from the site of the mishap to a site from which a mechanic can be dispatched; then he or she must wait for the mechanic to arrive. If the request is forwarded by telephone, this is an instance of combining a communication and a transport channel. If the mechanic who receives the call could furnish the client with enough information to help the client repair the car, thus perhaps eliminating the need for the mechanical breakdown service, only communication channels will be used.

Whether or not to service requests with a centralized or decentralized deployment of facilities depends to some extent on what is being requested: materials or information. These are transmitted through channels that vary primarily in the speed of transmission over unobstructed portions of the channel. In each case, however, these channels have limited capacities. They can, and usually do, become overloaded and obstructed with a resulting decline in the effective rate of flow.

Thus, congested roads may cut the effective speed of traffic flow from 60 to 15 miles per hour; congested airports may cut the effective speed of downtown-to-downtown jet air travel from 600 miles per hour to 300 miles per hour for airport-to-airport speed and 100 miles per hour for downtown-to-downtown speeds. Similarly, overloaded switchboards and relays reduce the effective speed of electronic transmission from the theoretical limit of 186,000 miles per second to an average effective speed varying from 1000 to 10,000 miles per hour. Even when delayed in this manner, however, electronically and optically transmitted information will tend to move on the average about 100 times as fast as would bulky material objects. Communication thus would differ from transport by several orders of magnitude in regard to its effect on the degree of centralization, or decentralization. But this would be the case only if the problems of channel distance and information distance did not exist.

The notions of "center" and "distance" do not have the same meaning for communication channels as they do for transport channels.[2] Regardless of the distance in miles between them, two points in space may be close in *channel distance* if they are separated by few channel nodes or switching points, and hence few opportunities for error and delay. But they may also be close to each other if their memories and communication codes are highly complementary and thus require few decoding steps and small decoding costs.

4.8.1 Informational Distance as a Problem of Codes and Memories.
It is this latter type of *informational distance* and closeness that will interest us here. We might call a source or service station *informationally close* to a client if (a) that client does not have to compose long, elaborate messages to communicate his or her request and (b) if the source can meet the client's need with a brief message. This notion is similar to that of a *complementarity of communication habits* that may be viewed as the essential element of membership in a people that enables the members to communicate rapidly, accurately, and eco-

nomically with each other and facilitates mutual trust and cooperation. Such complementarity, however, must meet the additional test of scope, or a range of specialized functions, as discussed in Chapter 3, for it must be applicable to a wide variety of topics (Deutsch, 1966, 1969).

If the client has to compose a sequence of lengthy messages over many feedback passes to specify his or her need, and if the responses are equally arduous, we call such a source informationally distant from the client. (For examples from the delivery of mental health care, see Hollingshead and Redlich, 1958.) The site of the request may be a few feet from the source and yet be informationally distant. That is, informational proximity is, in principle, independent of proximity via transport channels. Nearly every telephone in the world is equally close to every other telephone, but getting to some places or shipping goods to them is very much harder for some places than for others. In many social and geographic situations, however, protracted learning processes may produce some degree of positive correlation between the two (Deutsch, 1969).

The concept of *informational distance* may be operationalized by: (1) transmission rates, in bits per second; (2) error rates in transmission; (3) the amount of redundancy required to keep the error rate below a specified requirement; and (4) total costs of effective transmission, in dollars per 1000 bits understood by the receiver. The last three factors covary, but they are not the same in the direction from sender to receiver as from receiver to sender, for an expert may understand short messages from a layman but not vice versa.

4.8.2 Shipment of Goods and Transmission of Messages.

The delivery of services requires both the transmission of information and the shipment of objects. Even the transmission of information is often accomplished by shipping message-bearing objects, such as books, letters, and journals. As it costs more to ship a heavy and bulky object, thus does it cost more to transmit a voluminous message that requires communication channels of wider bandwidth. As we measure bulk in units of weight, such as kilograms, we measure the volume of a message in bits. As we measure the capacity of a transportation channel by the maximum amount M of mass it can move times the speed V that can move it under the best traffic conditions, we measure the capacity of the communication channel in bits per second that can be transmitted as a least upper bound to all possible transmission rates.

Telephone, telegraph, radio, television, and other communication channels differ mainly in their capacities. The capacities and costs do not vary greatly with geographic distance, and with automatic switching, neither does speed. Capacities vary from a low of 2000 bits per second for voice-grade telephone lines to several million bits per second for television channels.

While certain services are completed by the delivery of noninformational objects that could not be transmitted electronically as an alternative, information-bearing objects can be shipped or transmitted. A 300-page book is the equivalent of about 3 million bits, and a one-second picture on a normal television screen requires about 20 million bits.

The formula for the overall capacity of a transportation channel is MV and mv for its effective capacity in regard to the mass or size and actual speed of transmitting and/or servicing the average request. Both MV and mv are formally analogous to the concept of momentum in mechanics. As it takes an impulse to change momentum in mechanics, so it takes innovation—in the form of visible investment in capital equipment and/or invisible investment in new technology—to change capacity in a transport channel (e.g., to a supersonic transport aircraft). The change in capacity MV is then a possible measure of the effect (or "force") of innovation in respect to the overall capacity of a channel, and the change in mv similarly would measure its effect in regard to the servicing of average sized requests. The greater mv, the greater the amount of physical energy, hence cost, required for starting, stopping, and resisting obstructing forces by the vehicles moving in a transport channel.

Decentralization often depends critically on the effective service capacities of the available transport and communication channels. Technological changes in these channels effect changes in the optimum level of decentralization for a given organization, government, or service.

A typical administrative agency consults a file on each case for which it has to make a decision. Servicing a case may typically require either transporting, on the average, one pound of documents from the repository to the site of the request, or transmitting the information in those documents over a long-distance channel. The file to be transmitted is assumed to contain the equivalent of a 200-page book, about 4 million bits, or 4 megabits.[3] If standards of legal evidence improve, more statements by witnesses may have to be stored and forwarded or the trial may have to be moved or the witnesses transported to it. As medical standards improve, more elaborate medical records will have to be kept. The requirements of environmental impact statements cannot but increase the bulk of information needed for many decisions. All these long-term trends, therefore, may favor decentralization.

Using a formula for the optimal number of facilities for electronic transmission that minimizes total cost, resembling the previously used square root formulas and derived in the same way, we find this optimal number to be 16. This is more than three times as many as in the case where the transmission costs depended only on speeds and not on the amount of information being transmitted to service the average request.

Had we sent the four megabits by express messenger service at the rate of $.04 per pound-hour, the optimal number of facilities would be three. In other words, *under the assumptions of our example, a slower service based on messengers or mail delivery could be much more highly centralized than a fast service based on a computer-based or satellite-based communication net.*

It might be interesting to compare the total costs for these two kinds of service. We assume that each of them would have to cope with 3 million requests per month, each request requiring transmission of four megabits. The cost of servicing requests via "dataphone" transmission would be $1.05 per request, compared with $.20 per request for service by mail or express messenger. *The fivefold increase in cost, however, here would buy a sixtyfold increase in speed.* The dataphone replies would be available within little more than half an hour, in contrast to the response time of 30 hours required for the more highly centralized services based on messengers or mail.

If the faster transmission of bulkier memories facilitates centralization, it produces at the same time rising *costs of interpretation*—that is, decoding—and of storage, which have the opposite effect. In the case of transmission across boundaries of language or culture, or even across different scientific specialties, these latter cost effects may prevail and promote further decentralization. Thus, the development of ultrashort radio broadcasting enables Switzerland to develop special transmitters and programs for the 40,000 speakers of the Romansh language, in addition to existing transmitters and programs in German, French, and Italian.

4.9 INFORMATIONAL DISTANCE IN SERVICE SYSTEMS

Consider a community of potential clients for services such as health care. To communicate their needs is to transmit information. It takes an aggregate "memory" of information to deliver all of the needed services. We inquire into the number of decentralized service agencies, each having a fraction of the total required memory, that minimizes total cost.

Let N be the number of individuals or clients of a service organization. Assume that they rely on a common data base for their information needs. Since human needs are, by and large, socially determined, they also rely on each other. We can distinguish groupings among the individuals. Each subgroup requires *extra* facilities for storing and retrieving information that is necessary for its survival *as a group*. One nation sets itself off from another by its culture. Institutions develop traditions and "reputations" that they internalize. Families remain distinct entities to the extent that they maintain their identity—a shared, remembered history and sense of belonging. How is information shared within and between groups?

Clearly informational distance can account for part of the group identity—or vice versa, the one varying inversely with the other. A shared world view, a common mythology, and a like use of terminology all contribute to the group nexus. The nature of this sharing is of crucial importance if a coherent picture of informational distance is to emerge.

Many transactions that are conducted over transport channels could be conducted, to advantage, over communication channels. This might even apply to the movement of people to attend face-to-face meetings. For certain kinds of interactions, teleconferencing may prove to be more cost-effective. It should not be overlooked, however, that face-to-face meetings are wideband channels for communication, which also transmit among the participants gestures, postures, indications of mood and character, information interactions such as those occurring at mealtimes, and the like. Negotiating a contract, making new friends, or courting a woman are all different operations on closed-circuit television than they are in face-to-face situations.[4]

We would not like to present some insight into the number of *data bases* that minimize the cost to a community of data base users. To do this, we consider a community of N users of a service, such as the telephone network. A directory with N entries will include many more names than any user is likely ever to contact. If each user were to have his or her own directory—or the equivalent personal data base—a total of $320N^2$ bits will have to be stored if we assume 320 bits or about 40 bytes per entry (name, address, telephone number). If everyone accessed a central data base on line, only $320N$ bits of central storage would be needed. If each user's personal data base had only K entries, a total of $320KN$ bits would be required in the distributed system. That is less than $320N^2$ and greater than $320N$ if $1 < K < N$.

If we revised the above illustration to apply to a classified directory for access to goods and services, there may be much more commonality among the N callers, especially if their interests do not greatly diverge. To take an extreme example, suppose that a caller needs the service

4.9 Informational Distance in Service Systems / 105

that tells him or her what doubling time corresponds to various percentages of a geometric growth rate; the caller does not just want a telephone number but an answer. Thus, instead of 40 characters for name, address, telephone number, the caller wants "subject heading," such as "doubling time of various growth rates," followed by a more specific entry, such as "$r\%$," followed by an answer, such as "T years." Under the same subject heading may now be the equivalent of a table with as many lines as there are anticipated entries for r (or for T if the table is also to be used in reverse). Since requests for most values of r will be rare and there may be requests for values for r that are not anticipated, it may be best to store, instead of an $r-T$ table, a formula for computing T given r (and r given T), whichever has lower expected cost.

Let B be the memory requirement, in bits, of the least costly on-line storage to meet the information requirements of a group of N people. That is, they have sufficiently similar "memories" that a single source informationally close to each of these can serve *to some extent*. Presumably, the smaller N is, the more similar the members could be, and the less the informational distance between them and the source. If there are n subgroups and N is divisible by n, each subgroup on the average has N/n members. Each subgroup requires a common data base of B' bits. The n data bases will overlap to some extent because certain core reference data (e.g., basic legal information, elementary medical facts) must be present, redundantly, in each data base. Hence, B' will not be less than B/n.

We can now derive a simplified expression for n, the number of pluralized data bases that minimize total cost. This simple expression for the total cost now is the cost of maintaining the communication (or transport) channel plus the cost of using it. The first cost component is the number of servers times the monthly cost of maintaining the common data base per group using it, plus a fixed overhead rate. The second cost component is the average time it takes to service a request times the monthly request load and the average operating cost of using the channel. Under some plausible assumptions, we find that the optimal number of data bases increases, as the square root of: (1) the request load L; (2) the ratio of operating to fixed costs; (3) the storage requirement of a subgroup, B'; (4) the increased complexity of the data bases as reflected by the ratio of the subgroup's storage requirement B' to average message length. It decreases with communication capacity, as the inverse square root.

Actual trends in the specific variables used in this model are likely to favor further informational pluralization. These conclusions were derived for a particular set of assumptions. We tested the sensitivity of the conclusions to these assumptions and found them to hold quite generally.

There are several ways in which information can be shared. They include: (1) multiple use of available information channels as well as (2) circulation and (3) exchange. The use of available channels is obviously limited by the capacity of the channels. We would expect this first form of sharing to depend inversely on informational distance within the group. Circulation and exchange also depend on some common understanding as well as on the size of the group involved. A small group could be expected to circulate information more efficiently within the group than a large one, unless fixed costs are greatly increased to favor the large group. Altogether, limiting the size of the group appears to favor intra- (and possibly inter-) group sharing. Computer runs based on this more sophisticated model confirmed our previous conclusions. They helped us to see the importance of informational proximity and sharing of information, two factors that a planner ought to take specifically into account, even though in the short run the planner may have little power to influence them. It follows that differences of language and culture are not a matter of mere prejudice, but they may have direct influence upon the costs and capacities of service organizations.

4.10 QUALITY OF SERVICE AND VALUE OF TIME

Several attributes characterize quality in the provision of a service. First and foremost is rapport, that is, the extent to which the service rendered fits the client. This means: (a) how well it corresponds to the client's messages, how accurately his or her expressed request is interpreted; (b) how well and appropriately it meets his or her need; (c) how well it suits his or her desires, and the amount of spontaneity accepted and accommodated. All these imply short communicative distances.

The next most important attribute of service quality is *responsiveness*, as discussed before. Third, we proposed the richness or *multidimensionality* of the service, exemplified by color televisions versus black and white stills. Fourth is *breadth of variance* within the same dimension. This corresponds to Ashby's "requisite variety."

A fifth attribute of service quality is the inverse of error and risk margin, hence *precision* and *reliability*. Sixth is the extent of *desirable side effects* or phase changes in some dimension with gradual change at threshold in other dimensions. This may be how increases in quantity become improvements in quality, generating originality and creativity.

Finally, there are intangible aspects or *psychological effects,* such as the quality of music, art, architecture, or education. These seven dimensions enter, at least implicitly, with varying weights into what is called the "quality of life."

Certain services cannot be performed at all if a sufficient concentration of resources—human, capital, informational—cannot be mobilized. Alternatively, if there is a choice of distributing a fixed set of resources in various mixes, a trade must often be made between spreading them thinly to provide highly responsive but routine services to many and concentrating them to provide less responsive but very exceptional services to a few. The best computing centers used to cater to a few expert users who had the know-how for making excellent use of very high-quality facilities; the numerous less expert users could not expect to receive a great deal of highly responsive aids to meet their needs. Modern programmable pocket calculators, on the other hand, may be just what they need even though there are certain tasks they cannot do because of their limitations of memory and other functions.

It has been pointed out that the pace of technological advance necessitates large concentrations of financial and scientific manpower (Furniss, 1974, p. 963). Economic enterprises based on high technology are also capital-intensive. It takes a "critical mass," a certain minimum number of dollars and experts to successfully develop a new communications enterprise such as COMSAT, a new direct solar power space station, or fusion reactors. Generally, only governments can take such risks, and they attempt to minimize them by purposeful planning that may be a step in the direction of centralization.

How could such considerations be applied to a specific case? Consider a facility such as a hospital. A fixed cost of C dollars per month (amortized over its expected life) has been allocated to its construction and maintenance. Suppose now that a larger amount, C', becomes available, say $C' = 2C$. When would it pay to invest all of C' into making the originally planned hospital better and bigger as against building two hospitals of the kind originally planned? To analyze this problem, let $\phi(C)$ denote some measure of the quality q or "goodness" of the services rendered by a facility costing C. Assume that the relation between quality and cost is S-shaped, rising concave up as C increases from 0 to a transition point C_0 and then rising, but concave down, with diminishing returns as C increases, without bound beyond C_0, with quality leveling off at a quality index q_{max} (see Figure 4.1). The

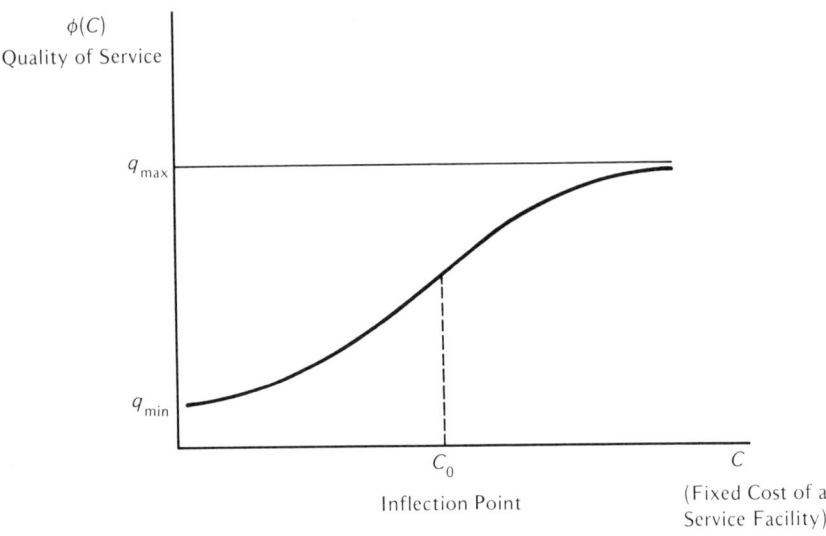

Figure 4.1. Quality of service vs. cost.

simplest mathematical characterization of such a relation is the symmetric logistic curve shown in Figure 4.1.

Since service quality increases monotonically with cost C, it is clearly preferable to concentrate resources into a single more expensive facility than to distribute them among several lower-quality facilities unless there were compensating gains in responsiveness. It is to those gains that we turn next.

Suppose that if several facilities were built they would be dispersed to be closer to the clients. Let us measure the closeness by the turnaround or total response time, T, of an adequately rendered service, averaged over all clients and their requests. Let $u(T, q)$ denote the utility to a client of a service characterized by turnaround time T and quality q, measured in dollars per request.

Assume now that utility of the service varies inversely with total response time but directly with quality,

$$u(T, q) = \frac{qR}{T} \qquad (4.2)$$

We take $q_{\max}$ to be 1. We substitute for q the formula of the logistic curve, shown graphically in Figure 4.1. We can then interpret R as the utility of top-quality service ($q = 1$) rendered with 1-hour turnaround time ($T = 1$). In a sense, R measures the *value of a client's time*. The higher is R, the more the client would be willing to pay for rapid responses, and the lower is R, the longer this client is willing to wait. The expression for the net utility is $uL - TkL - C$, shown in Equation 4.1, and the formula for the logistic curve substituted for u, and with $T = D/2vn$, as in Chapter 2. It was analyzed with the help of a computer. Figures 4.2 through 4.4 give the computed values of U for various values of n and for different values of the other parameters.

None of these figures shows a value of n for which U is maximum, and all three indicate that the larger n is, the better. Figures 4.2, 4.3 and 4.4 indicate that a value of n such as 30 is a point of diminishing returns: increasing n beyond that does not add much to the utility, especially for lower costs and lower loads. Increasing L favors making n larger.

Figure 4.5 shows U as a function of n according to a negative exponential rather than merely an inverse relation with total response time.

We can get some insight into the implications of the assumption $u(T, q) = qR/T$ if we take q to be 1 independently of n, assuming the rendition of the best service possible, with utility improving only as a result of decreased response time. The net utility is now:

$$U = 4RLvn/D - nC - kLD/4vn \qquad (4.3)$$

The value of n that maximizes that is easily shown to be, approximately,

$$n \doteq \frac{D}{2}\sqrt{kL/v(CD - 4RLv)} \qquad (4.4)$$

This is valid as long as $CD > 4RLv$ or $R < CD/4Lv$. If a client values his or her time in excess of $CD/4Lv$, no value of n can possibly maximize U. Clearly, n increases with the operating cost k and distance D (as a square root). If $R = 0$, the formula for n is just that of Equation 2.2, $1/2\sqrt{kDL/Cv}$. Increasing R increases n even further, favoring pluralization.

We can acquire additional insight by reanalyzing the simplest problem: to find the number of pluralized facilities n when the total cost is $K(L, n) = nC + DkL/4vn$, corresponding to the D-mile strip with uniform demand. We now treat L as a randomly fluctuating variable, with Avg L as its mean and Dev L as the square root of L's variance.

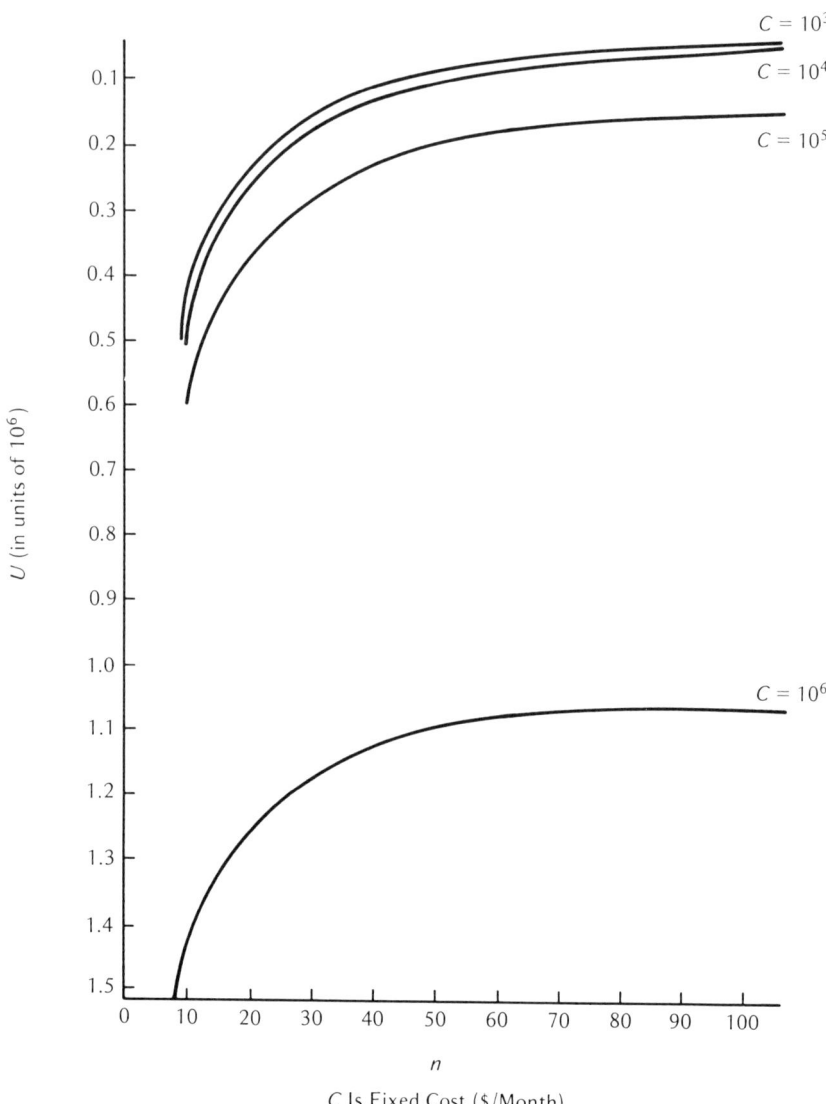

Figure 4.2. Utility vs. number of facilities.

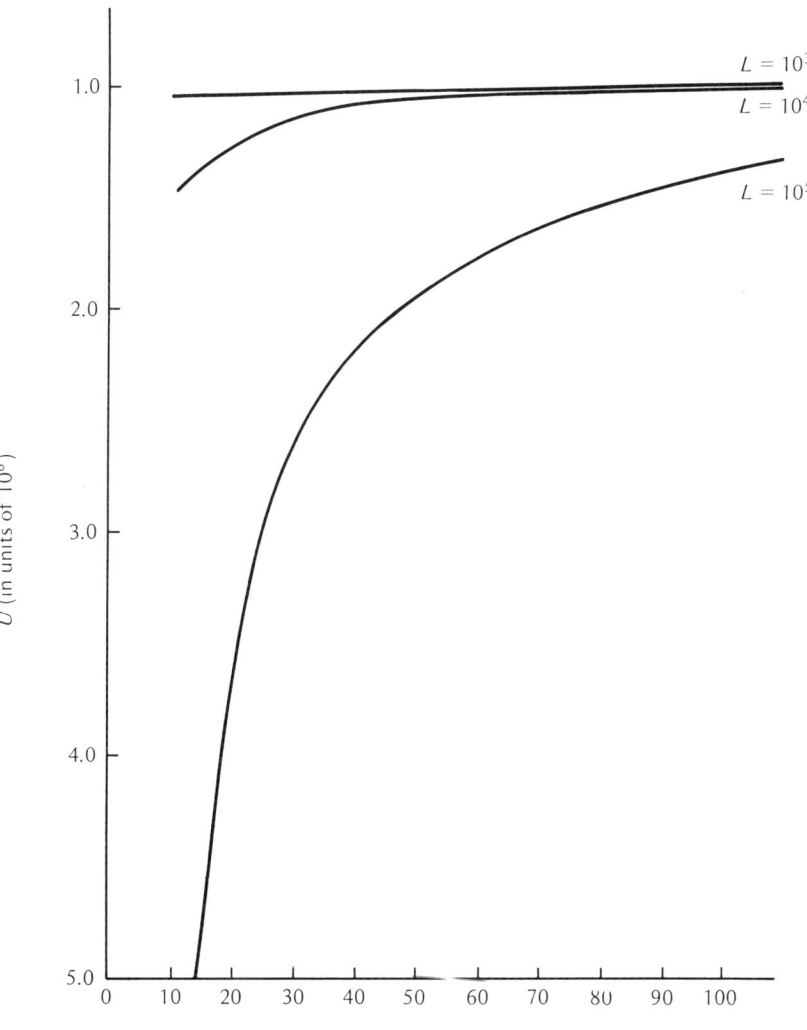

Figure 4.3. Utility vs. number of facilities for various request loads.

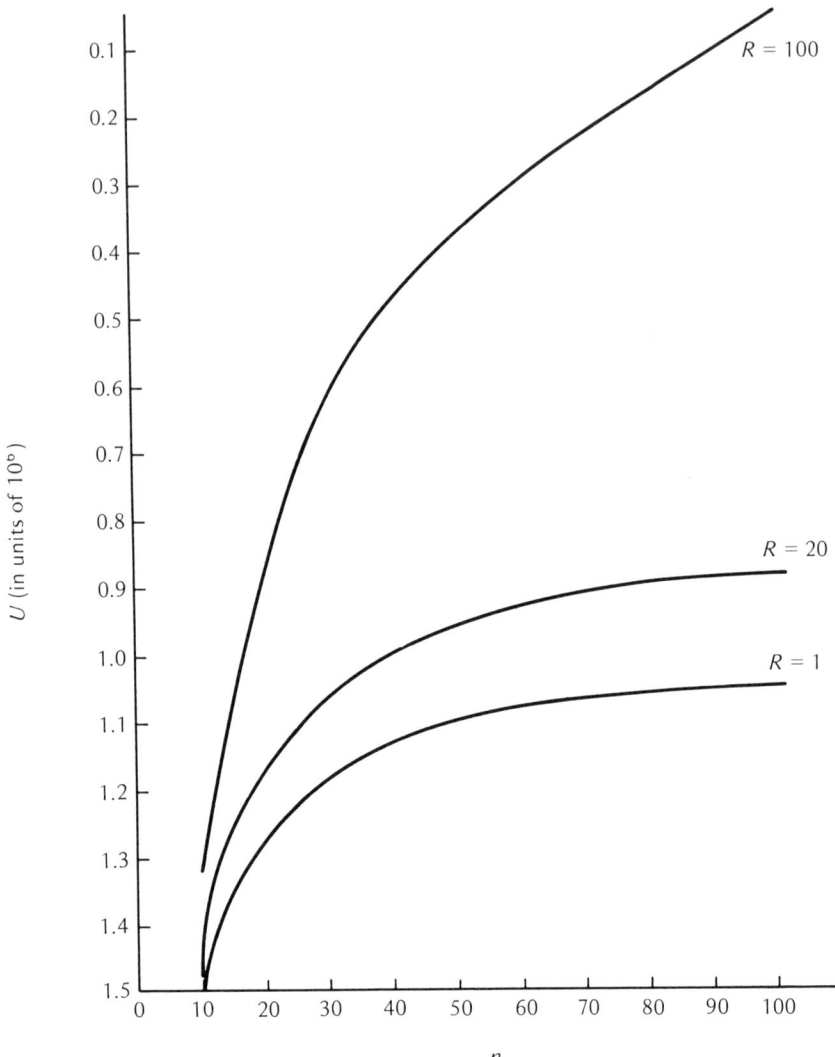

Figure 4.4. Utility vs. number of facilities for various values of a client's time.

4.10 Quality of Service and Value of Time / 113

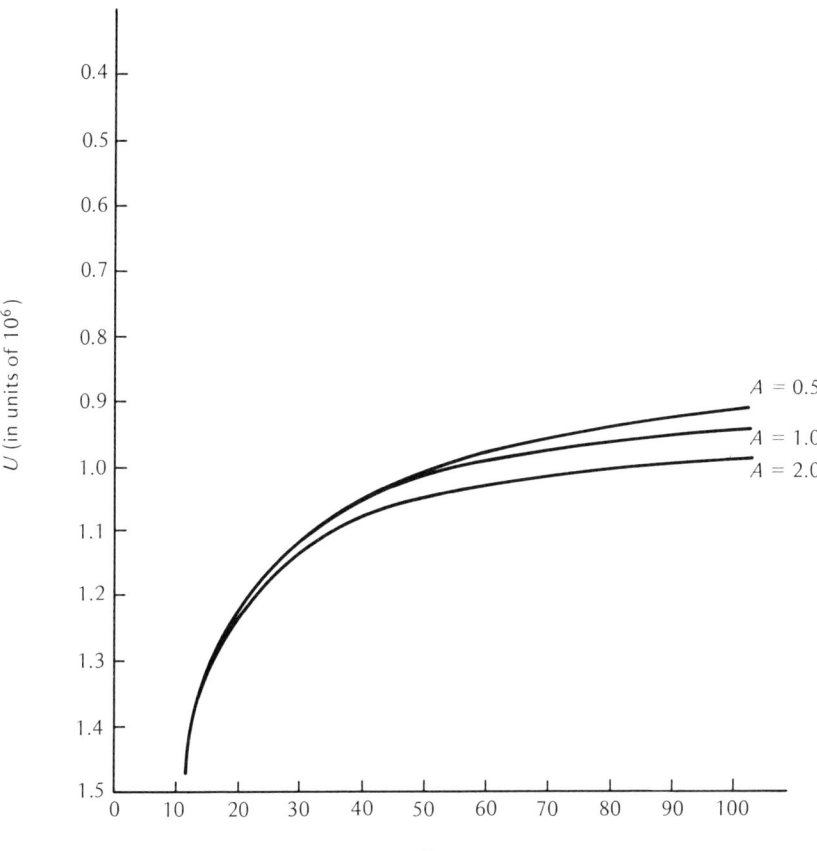

Figure 4.5. Utility vs. number of facilities for various values of parameter A.

The average total cost is $nC + (Dk/4vn) \operatorname{Avg} L = \bar{K}(n)$. The variance of the total cost is:

$$\int (K(L, n) - \bar{K}(n))^2 f(L) dL$$

where f is the probability density of L. This is:

$$(Dk/4vn)^2 \int (L - \operatorname{Avg} L)^2 f(L) dL = (Dk/4vn)^2 \operatorname{Var} L$$

The average deviation of the cost around the mean is $Dk/4vn \operatorname{Dev} L$. Suppose now that we seek n that minimizes both the average cost *and* the average deviation of the cost, but with weights w_a and w_d. We then need to minimize:

$$w_a(nC + (Dk/4vn) \operatorname{Avg} L) + w_d (Dk/4vn) \operatorname{Dev} L$$

The value of n that minimizes this is approximately:

$$n \doteq \frac{1}{2} \sqrt{Dk (\operatorname{Avg} L + (w_d/w_a) \operatorname{Dev} L)/Cv} \quad (4.5)$$

This is clearly what we had previously if no weight is given to the deviance of the cost, $w_d = 0$. The ratio w_d/w_a may be interpreted as the value assigned to insurance against risk of unpredictable fluctuations in load.

4.11 SOME IMPLICATIONS FOR ORGANIZATION THEORY AND POLITICS: SOME SECULAR CHANGES IN KEY VARIABLES

Our crude models suggest that a greater number of multiple service facilities, n, and hence a higher degree of decentralization, becomes rational with an increase in the load or volume of services demanded. In addition, a higher degree of decentralization becomes desirable with an increase in the value of time and in those portions of service costs that are related to time and/or distance.

Our models further suggest that this optimal degree of decentralization increases with a decrease in the proportion of the fixed capital costs of the service among its total costs. They also suggest that the optimum degree of decentralization increases with any decrease in the

4.11 Implications for Organization Theory and Politics / 115

margins of error and of breakdown that are considered acceptable in the performance of the service.

All these decentralization-promoting conditions will tend to increase with economic growth and technological development. Let us first consider changes in direct costs. If other things remain equal, the optimal number of decentralized facilities for a service increases in proportion to the square root of the ratio of its time-distance costs, k and to its capital costs C. Secular trends toward highly advanced levels of economic and technological development make human labor more expensive and capital goods relatively cheaper. Thus they may tend to increase this ratio, and hence the desirable degree of decentralization.

Some economic data suggest that this may have happened, both in socialist and nonsocialist countries. An increase in real wages normally represents an increase in the price of labor relative to the price of goods, including capital goods, and hence an increase in the k/C ratio. In many advanced countries of the world during recent decades, real wages have tended to grow on the average at about 3 percent per year, thus doubling every 23 years. If real wages were to grow fourfold in the course of a half-century, while capital costs would not, at the end of such a period the optimal number of decentralized facilities for a wide variety of services may well have as much as doubled during the same time. If capital costs were to grow somewhat, but less than real wages, there would still be a net tendency toward some decentralization, albeit to a lesser extent.

Similarly, if the service load, L, were to increase faster than the service speed, ν, there should be a trend toward somewhat greater decentralization. Is such a shift in the L/ν ratio in fact occurring?

There is some evidence that this may be the case. Demographic, economic, and technological growth in many countries in recent decades, very roughly speaking, has proceeded at annual rates of about 2 percent and 3 percent, respectively. This adds up to an approximate annual increase of 5 percent in the demands for many services. It doubles the load upon many of the public or private centers that have to supply them every 14 years. Such increases in loads include the volume of demands for many political, administrative, judicial, and quasijudicial decisions and responses, as well as for many services and for the communication and transportation they require.

In the 1950s, the average rate of per capita income growth in 68 countries, comprising 86 percent of the world's population, was about 3 percent, while the average rate of population growth in 111 countries, with 97 percent of her mankind, was 2.3 percent.[5] More recently, during 1960–1966, the world population increased at an annual rate of

116 / *Responsiveness and Higher Service Quality*

1.9 percent. During the last two decades, total GNP in many countries may have been rising, therefore, at about 5 percent per year, and thus doubling every 14 years. Request loads and service loads in many fields, including governments, may have grown at about the same rate as GNP.[6] During the same years, 1960-1966, the population of the United States increased at the rate of 1.4 percent, while its gross national product in constant 1958 prices grew at 4.8 percent. Murders and nonnegligent homicides grew at 2.3 percent, all accidents at 2.8 percent, domestic mail at 3.5 percent, daily telephone conversations at 5.0 percent, and automobile thefts at about 7 percent. In contrast to this, the average speed of motor vehicles increased only at 1.4 percent a year, and about the same low rate held for the 1945-1966 period. The average speed of aircraft on scheduled domestic air carrier routes increased at about 3.5 percent for 1950-1967 period, but rose more quickly, at 5.0 percent, during the years 1960-1967; the speed of aircraft on international flights in 1960-1967 increased at about 7 percent per year.[7]

These figures exclude the delays caused by getting to and from the airports as well as the delays caused by traffic congestion on the ground and in the air above many airports. If these delays are taken into account, it seems plausible that many activities, calling for public service, may be growing faster than our effective speed in moving persons and goods in daily practice. Something similar may apply to telephone communications; a telephone call from Washington to San Francisco during business hours does not get through much more quickly to the individual we want to reach in a busy office than it did in 1945.

Moreover, as technological progress speeds up transport and communication, it increases the *opportunity cost of time,* because more things now could be experienced in each unit of time than had been the case earlier.

In addition, highly modernized and automated technologies may require higher levels of accuracy and reliability of service. Thus they may need more redundancy of facilities as insurance against error and breakdown.

Perhaps most importantly, the growing need for greater precision and adaptability of responses to the increasingly complex, diverse, and changing needs of people will require, in many cases, more frequent dialogs and *feedback cycles of communication* between service centers and customers, agencies and clients, administrators and constituents, and the rulers and the ruled. This will multiply the effective distance D (regardless of whether it is measured in rules, switching points, or intervening obstacles or opportunities) by F, the average number of

4.11 Implications for Organization Theory and Politics / 117

feedback cycles of communication, travel, or transport required to ensure an acceptable fit between each specific demand and the particular response to it. The current demands for more popular participation, initiative, and communication "from below," if heeded, would have similar effects; it would increase the average number of feedback cycles needed, and hence often the importance of distance and proximity. Each of these changes makes for an increase in the degree of desirable decentralization.

Under the assumptions of our models[8] it seems quite possible that many of the highly modernized and automated societies and nations that we may find by the end of this century will by then require a much greater degree of decentralization in public and private services than the one to which we are accustomed now. Doubtless some of these assumptions will have to be replaced by more realistic ones. In particular, refining our simple concept of decentralization and introducing the notion of hierarchies of facilities may well modify some of our findings. This chapter already may suggest, however, that the naive images of a future of ever-increasing centralization in business organizations, public services, national governments, and the international political systems may have to be revised.

Chapter 5

Hierarchical and Network Structures: Clustering and Hierarchies from Interaction

5.0 INTRODUCTION

The notion of structure is widespread across many fields of inquiry (e.g., Deutsch, 1974; Mesarovic and Macko, 1969; Miller, 1971). There is hardly an aspect of nature in which definite forms and structures cannot be observed. "Structuralism" has recently become an increasingly prominent concept in literature, art, music, linguistics, psychology, anthropology, and many other humanities and sciences (Piaget, 1970). It is no surprise that "structure" is also central in the study of human service organizations and the theory of decentralization.

For our purposes, "structure" and "organization" are nearly synonymous. Structure has been defined as the design of organization through which enterprise is administered (Chandler, 1962). More generally, *structure* presupposes a set of elements and relations among them that changes so slowly that it can be identified and treated as relatively persistent for the time scale of the operations of interest (Fiske and Root, 1976). The organizational structure of a city's police department, for example, does not change often. Formally, structure among a set of elements is specified by relations and operations on that set. Thus, the set of natural numbers, 0, 1, 2, 3, . . . , is structured by the adding operation, +, which assigns to any two natural numbers a third number. A set of points in a plane can be structured by directed lines joining certain pairs, forming a network. Important relations that are found in most human service organizations include those denoted by phrases such as, "in communication with," "coordinated with," and "subordinate to." These may or may not hold among certain pairs of service providers.

There is little merit to a plurality of facilities if *each* has enough capacity to process the entire request load unless the facilities are dispersed (see Chapter 2), specialized (see Chapter 3), or otherwise related. In this chapter we consider facilities that comprise managerial organizational structures. These are hierarchical in various degrees and we ask what is the proper number of hierarchical levels for various purposes. We do not propose from a limited number of case studies, as does Gerlach (1970), that hierarchical structures are no longer adequate for coping with contemporary or future problems and that they are being replaced by structures that are segmented (i.e., pluralized), polycephalous (many control centers, leaders), and reticulated (connected into a network). We find that this is likely to be so, but we derive our results as an implication of plausible general assumptions.

5.1. HIERARCHIES IN GENERAL: FROM FIRST-ORDER TO HIGHER-ORDER CLUSTERING

A very common process by which structures emerge is that of aggregation and clustering. The result of that process is a local concentration of other primitive units or clusters. If the mutual attraction that brings units into clusters declines with distance and if there is also a decline in the capacity of clusters beyond some threshold size to interact with additional units, the size of clusters will remain limited. Possibly there may be forces that unite clusters into weaker but higher-order clusters; this regress will continue to higher system levels so long as additional types of interactions are available. Clustering can occur recursively. There can result clusters of clusters, perhaps in an indefinitely extended hierarchy.

In the work of scientists in many diverse fields, concepts of hierarchy are used (e.g., Whyte et al., 1969; Miller, 1971). Some philosophers have attempted to deny that hierarchies exist or that this concept can be adequately specified (Berlinski, 1976, p. 89; for an opposite view, see Deutsch and Kochen, 1977), while others (Gerlach, 1970) argue that the secret of survival of modern "liberation movements" (e.g., Women's, Gay, Palestine, Black Power, etc.) lies in the nonhierarchical, polymorphic structure of these organizations. Michael Polanyi (1968) has argued that the principles governing both living and machine systems may be represented as a hierarchy of boundary conditions. The pattern of organic bases in DNA, for example, is a boundary condition that cannot be reduced to physics and chemistry, according to Polanyi.

Social aggregations, too, may be treated as clusters, clusters of clusters, and so on, in a scale of higher orders, often linked by bonds of decreasing strength. The few members of nuclear families may be held together by strong but short-range transactions and psychosocial *bonds*. A larger number of families may be held together by weaker but further-range social bonds into a clan or kin group. Clans themselves were coupled to many other clans in the medieval kingdom of Scotland by even weaker bonds of longer range, and after 1603 and 1707, additional political bonds developed by linking Scotland and England in the United Kingdom of Great Britain (Deutsch, Burrell et al., 1957). In rarer cases, however, the bonds to larger systems and the attendant claims of nationalism, religion, or political ideology may override the bonds of family or friendship. To make the bonds to various hierarchical levels consonant, rather than dissonant, is part of the art of management and politics. Where this pattern of a declining strength of bonds to higher hierarchical levels exists, prudence will derive the *"subsidiary principle,"* in which each task should be delegated to the lowest hierarchical level at which it still can be effectively performed.

Self-preserving configurations are not limited to mechanics. They may also occur in human learning processes and organizational behavior. Thus, increases in interactions, communication, and amalgamated control devices among several relatively small human groups all may have rewarding side effects. These tend to reinforce further movement toward increased amalgamation and integration. If, however, the negative rewards or costs of interactions grow faster than the positive rewards or gains—perhaps through effects of increased congestion or more frequent failures of coordination and control—the movement toward integration will be stopped or reversed beyond a certain threshold. This reverse movement again may be stopped and reversed when transactions have declined below another threshold.

The result will then be a larger system of separate and partly autonomous—but interacting and thus partly interdependent—subsystems. This is similar to that of several nation-states in a region, all states in the political system of the world, or several subunits or departments within a larger private corporation or public agency.

There are revealing cases of persistent interdependence but resistance to amalgamation at the level of international politics (Katzenstein, 1976, Russett, 1969). In business organizations, structure has been said (Chandler, 1962) to emerge from several strategies. These include creation of an administrative office for one function in one local area, geographical dispersion that leads to a departmental structure of local field units administered by headquarters, vertical integration to perform new functions, and diversification to help new products.

There are three bases for specifying an ordering among servers in an organizational hierarchy. According to the first, agent A stands above agent B in the hierarchy if the jurisdiction of A includes and exceeds that of B. Secondly, if agent A prevails in case of a conflict between A and B, with a high probability, so that in effect A's program or decision is very likely to override that of B, A is also higher than B in the hierarchy. The third criterion for hierarchical ranking is the size of the resources that an agent can mobilize; if agent A's resources are at least one order of magnitude larger than agent B's, A is likely to be at a higher hierarchical level than B. These three criteria should coincide in normal cases but may differ in marginal ones (Deutsch, 1974). All three criteria imply a transitive relation on the agents and enable us to view hierarchies as partial orderings.

5.2 HIERARCHIES IN SERVICE ORGANIZATIONS

Service organizations are particular kinds of social aggregations that may have to develop more structure as the size and complexity of their request load increases. Each agent has a fixed radius in geographic and functional space beyond which he or she cannot readily interact with other agents in the performance of required services. As loads increase, an organization of partially decomposable subsystems (Simon, 1975) may begin to emerge. These subsystems may need to interact to some extent. This need, together with the number of subsystems, may increase the number of hierarchical levels. The maximum number of levels is determined when the interactions at higher levels are not needed for rendering adequate service. An organization providing decision-making services can be decentralized when it is partially decomposable into subsystems that themselves have some structure, yet without complete fragmentation.

In the formation of urban communities, a certain minimal set of vital services must be provided. If these are supplied from within the community, the clients of one service organization are likely to become the service providers for some other clients. In an autonomous urban community, everyone is the client of some service organization within the community and usually a service provider for others within the community, forming a network structure with interlocking closed loops.

Export-import bonds tie communities together into a larger network. Such a network may give rise to several central place hierarchies where numerous small communities provide the most primitive services and a few large communities provide highly complex and sophisticated services. Urban centers are organized functionally into a hierarchy for the purpose of spatially integrating the society, polity, and economy. In a developing region in the late twentieth century, there is usually one large city that has primacy; it provides the sophisticated services, whereas the bulk of the population is spread throughout the rural countryside with no services. Connections to the city are long and unresponsive, and there are few or no resources. We interpret this state of extreme single city primacy as one of centralization. As the region develops, the spectrum of hamlets, villages, small cities, and so on, should be filled and a central place hierarchy should emerge: the distribution of cities by size is roughly log normal or negative binomial like Pareto's law, which asserts that there is a long tail, with numerous towns of small size.[1]

We interpret this as more decentralized. Some scholars believe that this decentralization happens without deliberate interventions, through a process by which knowledge in and about backward areas filters down when transportation routes connect these areas and make them potential markets and production centers. Other scholars believe that present economic systems inhibit such filtering mechanisms. They believe that radical changes in the nature of urban systems must be introduced to overcome constraints of size, low growth rates, and colonial inheritance that account for the condition of primacy, viewed as a malaise.

According to Berry (1971), more urban and regional planners are arguing for programs of decentralization into new growth centers in less developed countries as the preferred policy to combat primacy. It is seen as a major cause of the social inadequacies in less developed countries because it maintains inequities that favor the advantage of the developed, large urban centers for concentrating funds and power. The most educated citizens and immigrants, overhead facilities and external economies are all concentrated in the single urban centers. To reduce the condition of primacy, it has been proposed to emphasize the growth of medium-sized cities and the allocation of public investments to create magnets for migrants.

As the members of a growing community with increasingly diverse interests (revealed preferences) become more involved in governing themselves, they tend to generate controversies about how to structure their service organizations, such as schools and health facilities.

Markets may also promote hierarchies. If capital and managerial talent in a country are scarce but highly mobile, automatic market processes will tend to drain them out of the hinterland into the primary city or cities where the effective demand for them is higher and primacy and centralization will tend to grow. If mobile capital and talent are abundant, however, and exceed the demand in the primary city or region, market processes will tend to spread them more broadly to secondary centers or across the country, and thus primacy will be reduced and decentralization will increase (Myrdal, 1957).

The tendency of market competition to promote at least some degree of primacy of large firms, as against smaller ones, is well known (Simon, 1957). Similarly well known is the tendency of human groups to segregate themselves more or less automatically into neighborhoods according to income and culture with a resulting relative primacy and concentration of resources in economically and socially favored areas (Schelling, 1978). Some reformers and disfavored groups wish to reverse these trends.

In establishing school subdistricts, for example, it has been proposed (Brownell, 1971) to include in each local unit a population that is racially, socioeconomically, religiously, and politically diverse, where the citizens of the district should have genuine responsibility and authority, with policy formation reserved for a central citywide board. This leads to a hierarchy in which the basic unit is the pupil-teacher group. Several of these groups are aggregated into a school, and a constellation of schools becomes an administrative subdistrict in a decentralized city school system. The latter, in turn, constitutes the citywide school district.

In general, the eventual appearance of internal conflicts, due to increased loads, gives rise to hierarchies. Conflict resolution is often performed by certain people in the organization who specialize in this function (Chapter 3) and who are so authorized. This requires at least two levels, that of disputants and dispute settlers. This leads to the "law of hierarchy"; "Coordination of large scale activities without markets requires a hierarchical authority structure" (Downs, 1967, p. 52), even though, as we just have seen, market processes also often produce hierarchies.

5.3 HIERARCHIES FROM COORDINATION AND COMMUNICATION

In the previous two sections, we discussed service organizations in which hierarchies arose because service-providing members of the organizations interact because of psychosocial or economic bonds among them with different strength and scope. Even if an organization had no services to perform, it could continue to exist as a social group, and its structure would reflect the extent to which it functions to meet the social and emotional needs of its members. For a service organization to continue to exist with some stability it must meet those needs, but to render useful services, it must also be task oriented.

Many service tasks require the activities of more than one individual service-provider in some definite spatial or temporal correspondence. Such correspondences are maintained through the operation of coordination or linkages among parts of the organization necessary to attain objectives. These linkages often take the form of communications in staff meetings, interlevel conferences, or their equivalent, where participants seek as well as give information and opinions. When such communication occurs among servers at the same level, we call it *lateral*; otherwise we call it *vertical*. Empirical findings (Wager, 1972) suggest that information and opinion *seeking* is more strongly correlated with hierarchic states than is information and opinion *giving*, with subordinates engaging to a much greater extent in seeking than superordinates.

Tasks performed by service organizations can have external or internal origins. Pure research organizations often formulate and choose the tasks they work on with minimal external input, even when their work is sponsored by an industrial client or a sponsor. Manufacturing organizations engage in production tasks. A consultant firm, on the other hand, relies heavily on its external channels to the client in selecting its tasks; it operates in a problem-solving mode based on knowledge. According to a report by Zand (1974), an organization that operates in the "authority/production mode" is much more hierarchical and centralized than an organization that functions in the "knowledge/problem mode." Moreover, when groups that operate in the knowledge/problem mode are given a series of well-structured problems and allowed to reorganize, they become more hierarchical, divide labor, and cut unused communication links. Furthermore, the division of labor and the rules that make the authority/production mode and its attendant structure effective for well-structured problems was found to interfere with the groups' ability to cope well with ill-structured problems.

Coordination may be defined as maintenance of a class of patterns, specified by temporal (e.g., before-after) or spatial (e.g., to the right of) relations among the operations of agents or facilities. A pattern is a set of relations. There may be more than one pattern or procedure that produces the same result. As a process, coordination is a means of directing the operation of units so that their joint behavior attains a specified goal with higher probability and at lower costs. If these units are human agents, there must also be a common expectation of reward.

The *gross reward* attributable to a particular coordination pattern can be measured by the difference between the expected reward if the component activities were combined randomly and the expected reward if these activities are coordinated as specified. The *new reward* is the gross reward minus the cost at which it has been obtained. This cost will vary with different types of organizations. Hence there may be unsuitable coordination patterns with a negative net reward. There may also be optimal patterns of coordination for which the expected net reward is larger than for all others.

Conversely, we may assume an "acceptable" level of service in terms of quality, reliability, and speed that requires the cooperation of several servers. The optimal organization achieves this coordination in such a way as to provide an acceptable level of service at lowest cost.

Coordination may be achieved by the unguided activity of individual servers among themselves. Each server or operator may search for some partner or partners whose skills or resources complement his or her own; the server may negotiate with each of them to fit together their time schedules, and time spent on this will leave the server less time for performing his or her actual work. A hierarchical organization may be able to supply this coordination of persons, operations, and resources at substantially less cost by coordinating the efforts of the first-level workers through a full-time second-level coordinator, and possibly the efforts of these coordinators will be coordinated at further levels above them. Wherever this is the case, cost-benefit considerations may tend to favor replacing an egalitarian one-level organization by a hierarchical type of two or more levels.

Coordination can be *negative*, by ensuring the absence of obstacles. An obvious example of this is a traffic policeman or a signal at a traffic intersection that regulates the flow of traffic into a definite time sequence—for example, east-west, east-north, west-south simultaneously; followed by east-south and west-north; then north-south, and so forth. This is to ensure that the drivers are kept out of each other's way.

Coordination can also be *positive*, by ensuring the presence of prerequisites for tasks requiring that subtasks be sequenced or of simultaneously performed tasks that have to be synchronized. In many cases these coordinations can be carried out by lateral communication alone, among first-level servers, for example. Sometimes it is more efficient or even necessary for a supervisory coordinator to communicate vertically with other servers or coordinators. For example, a long construction site on a highway at which there is just one lane open has two traffic regulators at each end who alternate in stopping traffic in one direction and then the other. A third coordinator may be needed to observe that traffic in one direction is much greater than traffic in the opposite direction. This third coordinator should have greater perspective, of the kind he could obtain from a control tower or a helicopter. This coordinator is then able to communicate vertically to the two traffic regulators, specifying the unequal intervals of traffic flow.

Hierarchies may arise as a consequence of communication as well. Even in a service organization providing services that require no coordination there is communication between service providers and clients and among the service providers. Some of the communication is task related. As discussed previously, much of it is of a socioemotional nature, to keep the group viable and maintain trust. We regard the time spent on such communication as necessary overhead for the time devoted to providing services directly to clients.

5.4 SHOULD HIERARCHICAL ORGANIZATIONS GROW TALLER?

The number of managerial levels and tallness or flatness have long been taken as two of several characteristics of organizational structure (Porter and Lawler, 1964). In a *tall* organization the number of persons directly supervised by each manager is small and there are many levels in the chain of command (Ghiselli and Siegel, 1972). Experimental studies of the effect of tallness or flatness on performance have been conducted, resulting in fruitful controversy over the best methodology to use (Carzo, 1963; Carzo and Yanouzas, 1967, 1969a, b, 1970; Hummon, 1970; Ghiselli and Siegel, 1972), but little formal modeling has been done.

In this section we propose a simple organizational model for the purpose of deriving the optimal number of hierarchical levels in an organization. If the optimal number minimizes the total cost of maintaining and operating this organization with adequate quality and responsiveness, will an increase in the service load cause the optimum number of levels to increase or decrease? The relevance of this question for decentralization theory is that the number of levels is one of the dimensions of decentralization. Among two organizations that are the same in regard to pluralization, dispersion, functional specialization, and other dimensions considered earlier in this book, differing only in the tallness of their hierarchies, the taller is more centralized because the bottom level of the hierarchy is the most decentralized. The ratio of decision points of this level—direct service level—to the decision points at all higher levels could be used as an index of decentralization.

The significance of this question derives from the secular trend for request loads to increase as populations to be served increase in size, educational attainments, and needs for service. The search for conditions under which growth or decline in tallness is favored by increased loads may provide useful insights to students and designers of organizations.

Our first attack yields results only for three situations, each characterized by special assumptions (for derivation see Appendix 5.1):

(a) *Additive Situations*: A substantial change in the request load for, and in the number of the hierarchic levels of, a service organization usually is associated with a change in its fixed costs. If this change can be accounted for as the result of the addition of two separate processes, one cost change associated with the change in load and another cost change associated with the change in the number of levels, the optimum number of such levels will tend to increase as the request load increases.

(b) *Directly Proportional Cost Changes*. If the fixed costs of a service organization change in direct proportion to the request load—which seems a possible but not necessarily a frequent situation—the optimum number of hierarchic levels will tend not to change at all, regardless of any changes in the load.

(c) *Faster-than-Linear Cost Changes*. If the fixed cost of a one-level service organization increases faster than linearly with changes in the request load, if adding another hierarchic level at some larger volume of requests level will lower somewhat the average but not change the rate of cost increase, and if also these same conditions hold for the addition of any further increments in request load at hierarchic levels, the resulting values for the optimum number of levels will tend to decrease for high request loads.

Under two of the three assumptions discussed thus far in this section, increases in request loads will tend to make optimal hierarchic service organizations taller or leave them unchanged. A possible trend toward fewer levels and flatter organizations in response to increasing loads might occur, however, if the average span of control in the organization should increase—perhaps due to an increasing uniformity in the requests—faster than the increase in the optimum number of service levels that rising request loads might otherwise produce.

5.5 A BASIS FOR CALCULATING THE OPTIMAL NUMBER OF HIERARCHICAL LEVELS: AN ILLUSTRATION

In Appendix 5.3 we derive explicit formulas or numbers for λ^*, the number of hierarchical levels that minimizes total cost. In this section we describe, discuss, and define some of the variables and assumptions. In the next section we will add special assumptions and parameters that enable us to derive analytically a formula for λ^*. In the subsequent sections, we drop these specializing assumptions, replacing them by others of a less restrictive nature that enables us to calculate λ^* under various conditions by computer.

Quite generally, we regard a service organization as processing an incoming stream of requests in five stages: sorting, diagnostic, load scheduling, performing service operations, and inspection or termination.

5.5.1 Stage 1: Sorting. In one version of the model we take all incoming requests for service to arrive at a stage 1 server, interpreted as a receptionist or gross-sorter whose task is to send each client to an appropriate server at stage 2. In a multilevel organization, there may be so many receptionists that some of them are supervised by other stage 1 servers or by supervisors responsible for more than one stage. We could assume that all incoming requests are treated as they arrive at the highest level of the stage 1 servers, or we could view them as distributing themselves according to which stage 1 server is free.

In a clinic, for example, those in need of health care services may call or arrive in person and contact the first available receptionist. That server may grossly classify the clients into, for example, emergency and nonemergency cases. Further, if there are several emergency rooms in the clinic—for example, a psychiatric and nonpsychiatric unit—the client may be referred to one of these. If the case is not judged to be an emergency, the server may have to elicit from the client enough of the client's need for service to decide which doctor to refer the patient to, where and when.

At this point we return to our model of the service organization as if it could be described by a response function specifying how its output is codetermined by an incoming request *and* a state of the world. When a client in a clinic presents him or herself with an implicit request for medical services and an explicit complaint, the client also presents him or herself with an observable condition or state of health. The clinic's response depends both on the request and that state. The sorter receives at least some information about that state, for example, the sorter notices the client's general appearance. This output may be (1) a general alarm (e.g., if the client is believed to have a highly contagious disease or to be uncontrollably sociopathological, homicidal); (2) no alarm at all; or (3) a local alerting message (to a few selected agents in the clinic).

The sorter functions at any time in one of three modes, as do all other agents. One mode is routine sorting. This involves recognition according to prespecified criteria and requires simple monitoring and the application of standard tests.

Another is dealing with anticipated problems. This also involves continuous monitoring of critical state and request variables and responding to anticipated contingencies according to prerecorded decision rules. Dealing with anticipated problems differs from routine sorting when there is a great variety of rarely encountered problems, even though the majority belong to a smaller number of problem classes than can be processed routinely. It may become more costly to *prepare* to sort and service a vast number of rare requests than to suffer the consequences of such unpreparedness, for example, poor service or delay.

A third mode is dealing with problems that were not, and perhaps could not have been, anticipated. There is no prerecorded plan of action or a program to generate one. The sorter recognizes such a problem only because it is either strikingly unusual and/or different from anything remembered. An extreme response would be to assume the worst and issue a general alarm. A more moderate response is to bide time and to treat the new problem with kindness, compassion, and caution.

The sorting function, broadly interpreted, includes solicitation and acceptance or orders in an industrial or business organization. In this sense, it includes selling and advertising. Ideally, creative selling and order procurement, for services as well as goods, means actively identifying clients' needs. This statement is based on the assumption that a salesman, by virtue of experience and training, can better identify a client's need than the client.

5.5.2 Stage 2: Diagnosis. Stage 2 servers are diagnosticians. Their task is to identify the client's need, analyze the request for service, and translate it into correspondences of operations that must be performed either simultaneously or sequentially in a prescribed order. In a clinic, the diagnosticians examine the client's request (com-

5.5 The Optimal Number of Hierarchical Levels / 131

plaint), probe his or her history to ascertain genetic, developmental, and environmental conditions that might be correlated with the request, and examine and test the client to ascertain signs, symptoms, and laboratory findings. They recommend a course of medical management, based on their understanding of probable causes.

The client's request has now been transformed into a request on the client's behalf, from a stage 2 server to servers at stage 4, for more specific operations or tasks. The servers in stage 4 are called operatives or doers. They may be the same people as the stage 2 servers, acting now in different roles. Thus, the diagnostician may double as a surgeon; having diagnosed a patient and recommended surgery, he may do it himself.

The optimal number of sorters and diagnosticians, even in the absence of hierarchies, is shown in Appendix 5.2 to increase with the square root of the load and the number of specialties.

5.5.3 Stage 3: Load Scheduling. The request from the diagnostician does not necessarily go directly to the operator. It goes to a load and sequence scheduler, a stage-3 server. The scheduler aims to balance idleness and congestion among all the servers (and associated equipment) in the organization, ideally so as to keep no facility idle (perhaps neither less nor more than 25 percent of the time to avoid intolerable variances or swings in waiting time) nor with a waiting line for its use. This scheduler also arranges for maintenance, replacements, rescheduling in case of breakdown, and so forth. In a clinic or hospital, for example, the load scheduler specifies which operatives are to perform the steps in pre- and postoperative care and the team to perform the surgery, as well as the exact time and place.

In practice, it may be a family physician in private practice whose receptionist does the gross sorting, while the physician takes responsibility for diagnosis and recommended treatment, and if a complex operation is indicated, may do part of the load scheduling by assembling a surgical team. Hospital officers arrange for scheduling appropriate facilities. Ideally, the client (i.e., patient) should be aware of available options among possible surgical teams and be sufficiently knowledgeable to choose wisely. The ultimate responsibility for accepting the overall service or response to his or her request is his or her own.

Assigning requests to servers according to a time schedule is another of the load scheduler's tasks. The sequence scheduler in a bookbindery must, for example, specify that bindery 5 should wait for printed sheets of book 2 to arrive from printer 3. Moreover, the same sequence scheduler may decide that the printed sheets for book 7 may be arriving in the same time period from printer 1 and, because of special marketing conditions, should be given higher priority. Sequence scheduling actually often is decentralized, although the total system benefits are not always clear.

5.5.4 Stage 4: Performing Service Operations.

A major reason for structuring a group of operatives into a hierarchy is to coordinate their joint activities so that they perform as a team according to the correspondences specified by a diagnostician. Small enough teams may coordinate themselves. Thus musical duets, trios, and sometimes even sextets do not require coordination, though an orchestra does. Similarly, all the players in a basketball team spend their time coordinating one another's actions, but in a football team it is necessary to assign responsibility for coordination to one player.

The request, together with all that has already been done to service it in stages 1 to 4, arrives at a controller/checker in stage 5. This person is responsible for putting the finishing touches on the service rendered and releasing the "response" for delivery to the client. In the case of a hospital, the response is the totality of the medical diagnosis-management-treatment through release from the hospital. It is this health care response package that has been delivered to the controller/checker.

There may be hierarchies within each stage. The load scheduler is in a sense above the operatives and even the diagnosticians. The controller checker may refer clients back to any of the other stages. At higher levels there are servers not easily classified into the five stages described so far, specifically managers and planners. There are several reasons for organizing these servers into more than one level. One is the need for coordination in tasks requiring the synchronized, cooperative behavior from several servers. The functional components of a computer system, for example, are controlled by a supervisory unit, usually in software form. A request, in this case a program waiting to be executed, calls for the operation of several parts of the system; some simultaneously, some in a carefully planned sequence. The supervisor must give advance notice as well as supply needed input data on each part and then signal to it when to start and when to cease operating as instructed. Because of limitations on memory and information processing speed a supervisor can reliably supervise only a fixed number of units.

Another is that a request may require the operation of a unit outside the control of the supervisor handling that request; if so, the request must be transferred to another, coordinated supervisor in midstream. If the need for such units was recognized at the outset (by a proper

5.6 Organizational Design / 133

diagnosis of the program and the recognition by the load scheduler that it required units beyond the control of one supervisor), the request would have been initially assigned to a higher-level supervisor who controls the lower-level supervisors.

One reason for hierarchizing operatives is the decreased cost due to time saved by substituting brief vertical communication (between a worker and the supervisor) for more prolonged horizontal communication (between a worker and peers or co-workers). Another is the possibility of error by a server or of a complaint by the client about a server's performance that should be settled by a more experienced or responsible server. Finally, greater experience is needed for dealing with certain requests or problems relating indirectly to requests; these may be highly aggregated situations calling for farsighted decisions of large scope, and affecting many servers in the organization.

5.5.5 Stage 5: Inspection and Termination. The last stage in servicing a request consists of checking that the service was properly performed, delivering it to the client to the client's satisfaction, accounting for it (e.g., bills rendered), and closing the case. Performance is evaluated according to professional standards to ensure that best available know-how and knowledge were brought to bear. It is also judged according to client satisfaction. If it is responsive to the client's request and meets his or her need without imposing unacceptable burdens on others, it is approved. If both these conditions are met, total response time becomes the primary performance measure. If either of these two conditions is not met, the request may be turned back to servers at an earlier stage, usually stage 4, but occasionally stages 3 and 2. If there is a conflict between client satisfaction and professional standards, the request may be sent to a higher-level inspector for conflict resolution.

5.6 ORGANIZATIONAL DESIGN

There is a voluminous literature on the relations between management and decentralization. A major reason that managers often give for centralizing is the cost savings and efficiencies they believe to ensue from standardization, economies of scale, concentration of resources, and so on. They consider these economies beneficial to the welfare of their organization. As mentioned previously, however, the economies of scale and other cost savings due to centralization are often illusory, for the cost of expensive and more clerical and professional staff often more than compensates for the reduced number of managers. But as Perrow (1970, 1972) has taught us, decentralization and increased bureaucratization often go together. Thus, the major "cost" of decentralization lies in the added effort required of managers to formulate and state objectives for their own tasks and for tasks to be delegated more clearly, giving the manager more autonomy, his or her own resources, authority, and so on. The greatest effort must go into operational specifications of expectations and credible sanctions to be used if these expectations are not met. Whether long-range planning, policy formulation, and overall control and evaluation should be centralized at the top—presumably to have a single source of authority, to effect smoother coordination, to standardize and maintain efficiency—is not so easily resolved (Ehrle, 1970). Decentralization in federal programs has been interpreted to mean placing responsibility for decisions and control at the level close to clients. It is feared that central headquarters could not plan and evaluate effectively if it were also involved in day-to-day program operations and that lower-level centers could not effectively and objectively plan and evaluate (Ink and Dean, 1970).

Planning may be viewed as shaping goals. It is also the creation of images to be shared by clients and members of the service organization about the kind of organization it is, would like to be, would like to be seen as, would like to become, and the kind of services it provides. A planner is knowledgeable about many diverse topics, from which he or she must be able to select with sensitivity, combine, and bring to bear. The planner's scope and time horizon are relatively large. This means he or she generally has a larger, faster, and better organized "memory" and processing capabilities; it also means that he or she processes data in a more highly aggregated and summarized form. The planner deals with forests rather than trees. These qualifications tend to place the planner at a rather high hierarchical level, either in a line or staff position.

If staff is to line as a legislative is to an executive body, planners are more likely to be in staff positions. An executive is more likely to carry out policies that he or she shaped, or that were formulated by *his* or *her* staff than by an independent planner. On the other hand, if a planner cannot create policies that go beyond what an executive is likely to do, the organization tends to become reactive or passive rather than boldly innovative and farsighted. Thus, planners should perhaps be in a structure that is not hierarchically connected to the managerial hierarchy, although there must be interdependencies.

Control and evaluation are major functions of management and require qualifications similar to those of planners. In addition, a man-

5.6 Organizational Design / 135

ager must be able to select, motivate, and reinforce a team of subordinates. The manager needs less imagination in shaping general policies and images than in efficiently carrying them out on a day-to-day basis.

Several processes promote the growth of hierarchies. If the capacity of an executive is too limited for the level he or she occupies, the number of errors (poorly treated clients) increases. The manager may be demoted, kicked upstairs, dismissed, or even get more subordinates or staff. If maintaining organizational stability and morale favors the promotion of persons, but not their demotion or dismissal, individuals competent at lower levels of the hierarchy may be promoted step by step to a level at which they are not competent, and they may stay there for long periods. This has been called the "Peter Principle" (Peter and Hull, 1969).

Conversely, competent higher-level servers can function as backups or troubleshooters. This gives rise to hierarchies because of limitations or imperfections. But we can also start at the top, with a manager whose load exceeds his or her capacity. This manager delegates downward. This gives rise to hierarchies because of rising loads. Nevertheless, two organization charts can have the same number of levels and one may be much more dispersed than the other.

In Figure 5.1 we summarize the picture of a five-stage multilevel service organization developed up to this point. Even this rather complex picture oversimplifies reality, but it is useful for helping us chart out the logical boundaries of our problem for helping us assign priorities to variables and decentralization. As we shall see, to analyze such models mathematically or even by computer, we must make further simplifications. The mathematical analysis is presented in Appendix 5.3, and only a nontechnical overview of its results can be given here in the text.

We calculated the degree of flatness that minimizes total cost when it ceases to pay to add just one more level to an organization with a given number of levels. We interpret decreases in the optimal number of levels as increases in the flatness and a movement toward decentralization. To obtain a cost formula that is sensitive to the effects of adding levels, we assumed that hierarchical levels allowed for vertical communication, which could be traded against horizontal communication. That is, the introduction of a supervisor would reduce the need for horizontal communication among those the supervisor supervises, thus enabling them to process more requests in the same time and decreasing the number of servers needed to handle the same request load. The resulting decrease in cost is partially offset by the increase in cost of adding the supervisor, and it would not pay to add the supervisor if, on

136 / *Hierarchical and Network Structures*

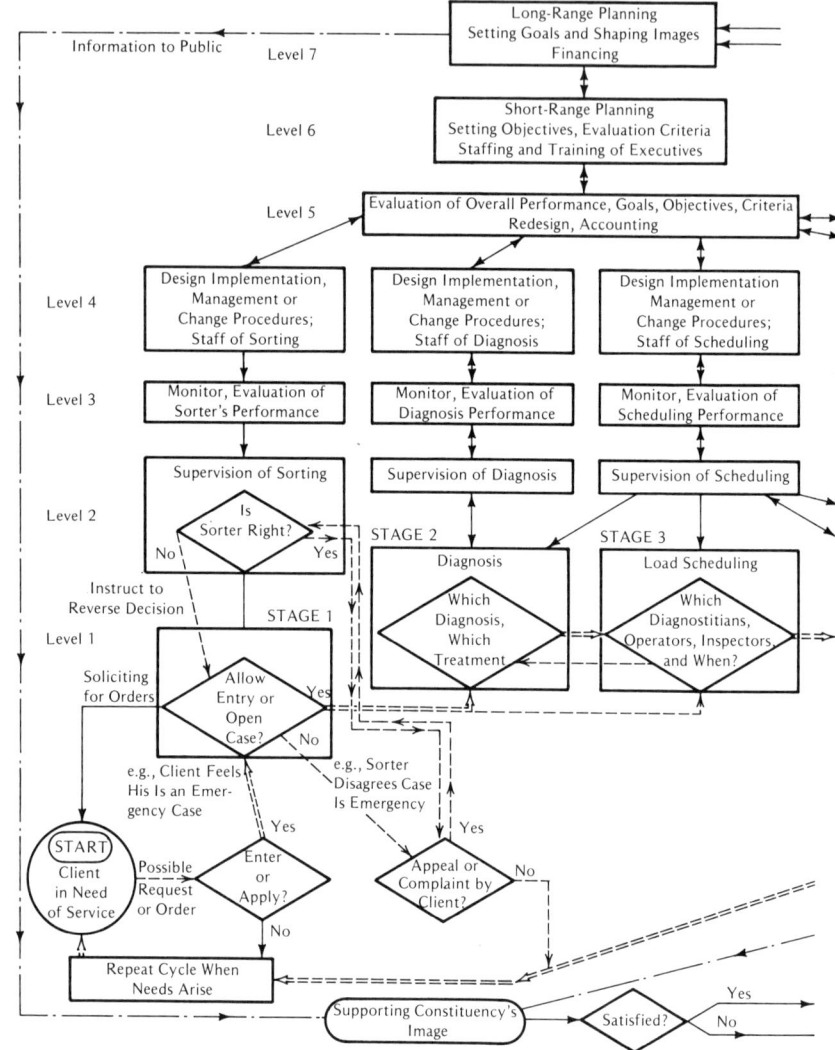

5.6 Organizational Design / 137

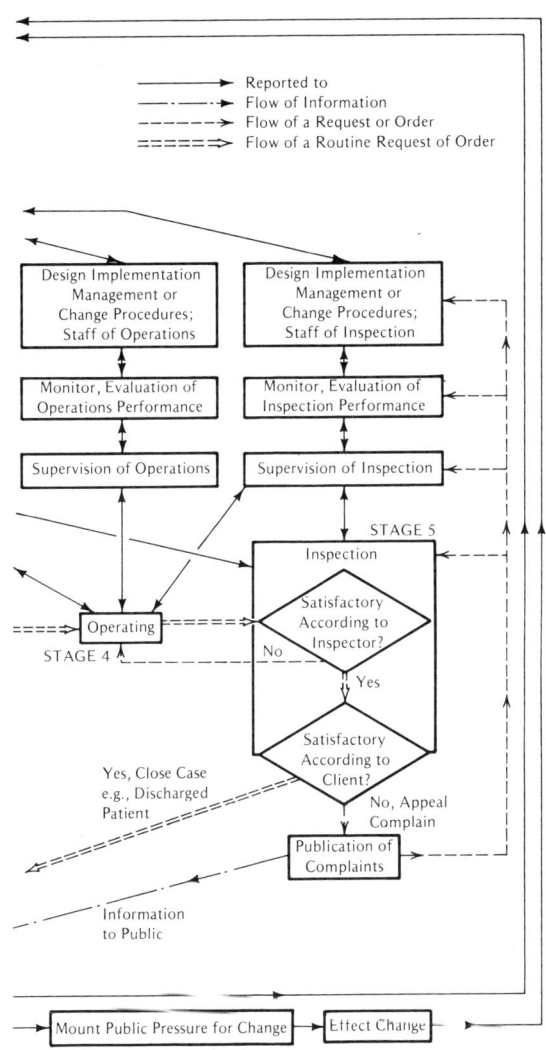

Figure 5.1. Functional sketch of a 5-stage, 7-level service organization.

balance, there were no savings. As we go up the hierarchy, the savings thus made possible get less and less, and the highest level at which it no longer pays to add a supervisor is the one we seek.

We find that it pays to keep tall organizations only if processing requests requires immensely more vertical than horizontal communication. This would hold in organizations servicing requests that are nonroutine and require a great deal of structuring into many levels of aggregation, such as a very extensive military campaign or a far-flung multinational nondiversified business in which there is great uncertainty and risk requiring the experience, broad perspective, and risk-taking of higher-level executives.

To account for tall organizations in the absence of such conditions, which we would call cost-ineffective from the viewpoint of the dimensions and values we took into account here, we would have to introduce the value that executives attach to power, control, authority, and so on, that go with higher-level positions. Moreover, if a tall organization is no longer cost-effective, though it once was, humanitarian and other considerations enter into the mechanisms whereby higher-level executives are kept or keep themselves in secure, well-paid, powerful, and entrenched positions. Some of those considerations are discussed in Chapter 7.

5.7 THE OPTIMUM NUMBER OF HIERARCHICAL LEVELS DETERMINED BY COMPUTER SIMULATION

In order to gain some insight into the factors influencing the flatness of a service organization, we constructed a computer program for calculating the total cost for various levels of flatness. A major determinant of the total operating cost is the total time it takes to service an average request. We took this to be the sum of three times.

The first, T^{sfl}, is the time an agent spends in communicating laterally with other servers at the same level or with him or herself by thinking or writing memos for his or her own use. We assumed that the time needed for this activity decreases if T^{ud} increases. Here, T^{ud} is the time an agent spends communicating vertically (up and down) with his or her superiors and subordinates. In Appendix 5.3 the following relation is derived:

$$T^{sfl} = 3/p_h - (p_v/p_h) T^{ud}.$$

T^{ud} is the second term in the total time to service a request.

The third is T^w, the time an agent spends in direct work to service a

5.7 Optimum Number Determined by Computer Simulation / 139

request. This was assumed to decrease as T^{sfl} or T^{ud} increases: the more time an agent spends on efficient vertical and horizontal or self-communication the less time is needed for direct work on a request, according to $T^W = 10 - 1/2T^{sfl} - 1/5T^{ud}$. Thus, given T^{ud}, p_h, and p_v, we can calculate the total time to service a request.

Underlying this calculation is the assumption that the probability, p_h, of an agent obtaining an item of information needed to service a client's request through lateral communication in a small time interval does not change in time and that these events occur independently in nonoverlapping time intervals. This implies that the agent obtains the needed information by time t with a probability of approximately $1 - e^{-p_h t}$ (a Poisson process). This enables us to interpret $1/p_h$ as the time it takes for that probability to increase from 0 to $1 - 1/e$ (about .63), and to interpret $1/p_v$ as a corresponding "half-life" of vertical communication. If this Poisson model holds at least approximately and if our time unit for vertical communication was 10 minutes, the likelihood of failure or nonsuccess within that period would be 37 percent; within 20 minutes it would be less than 14 percent, about 5 percent within half an hour, and less than 2 percent after 40 minutes. In most of the calculations we present $p_h = .9$ and $p_v = .1$. The model and the results are detailed in Appendix 5.4.

Empirical studies (e.g., Hage, Aiken, and Marrett, 1971) suggest that as organizational structure becomes more diversified because of functional specialization, these diverse specialists need to coordinate and therefore the volume of communication increases. Most of this increase is in horizontal communication, especially across departments at the same hierarchical levels. To the extent that superordinate managers specify job descriptions and expectations with greater clarity, the need for up and down communication decreases. The volume of communications, especially across departmental boundaries, increases as power is diffused throughout the organization. Most importantly, "as organizations have more and more of a sharp status pyramid, upward communication tends to be considerably inhibited just as it is when power is concentrated in the hands of a small elite."[2]

Many managers believe that sharp programming of all coordinative interactions is the best way to overcome the ills of bureaucracy that come with decentralization. This may not be true (Ehrle, 1970). Coordination can also be attained by two-way communication in all directions, with greater reliance on socialization than on the use of sanctions for social control.

5.7.1 The Value of Higher-Level Servers in Controlling Errors.
We now investigate the value of hierarchies for detecting and correcting errors in servicing requests. Let $(1 - E_{l,s})$ be the probability

that Agent $A_{l,s}$ at hierarchical level l and at stage s, where $l = 1, 2, \ldots,$ λ, $s = 1, 2, \ldots, 5$, services his or her requests correctly. For example, suppose that $A_{1,1}$ is a receptionist in a clinic having to sort incoming cases into emergency or nonemergency categories. $A_{1,1}$ may err by calling a nonemergency an emergency or by calling an emergency a nonemergency. In general, these error rates differ, but let us take them both to be $E_{1,1}$. Let us suppose, for now, that only the client is in a position to question such decisions while there is still time to reverse them and that the client does so by complaints or appeals. Though clients may err too and do not always speak up, complaint gathering retains its crucial importance for error reduction in hierarchies.

In practice, complaint gathering has turned out to be one of the main residual achievements of municipal decentralization. The importance of the *ombudsman* role soared after decentralization was started in the late 1960s. To be effective in complaint gathering, however, the existence of a center with this function must be known, visible, and easily accessible to would-be users. If easy access is taken to mean "within a five-minute walk" for Manhattan residents, there should be such a center every 10 blocks. That is far from the case, and even if it were, the existence and location of such a center are not widely known. A survey of 450 residents in three New York neighborhoods showed that only 11 to 26 percent of the respondents knew about their neighborhood action program, 23 to 33 percent about their community school boards, and 58 to 68 percent about their local health center (Yates, 1973).

If the organization is *error-sensitive*, in the sense that the cost of poor treatment is extremely high in comparison to the costs of maintaining the organization and the clients' time, and if the agents at level 1 made many errors in over half their cases, the most cost-effective organization would then be the one with the maximum number of hierarchical levels. That is, it pays to centralize; it costs less to maintain organizations with very incompetent agents at the bottom who are checked by more competent agents at other levels dealing with cases where errors are costly. As the competence of the bottom level agents increases, it pays to centralize less; the optimum number of levels goes to three, provided the error costs are still high.

Table 5.2 shows some suggestive results. It should also be compared with Tables 5.3 to 5.11, all of which show fixed costs, opportunity costs and the costs of poor treatment for varying values of E and the parameter settings shown in Table 5.1. Figure 5.2 shows graphically how the total cost varies with error rate. E for various values of λ, based on Table 5.2. For a given caseload the effect of different probabilities of error changes with the value of the time of clients as seen by compar-

Table 5.1. Parameters Used in Computer Simulations to Compute Costs in Varying Conditions

Table	δ	δ'	$E_1 = \epsilon$	E_2	$E_3\ldots$	$c(o)$	p_v	p_h	λ	B	C	T^{ud}	L	CE
5.2	.75	.05	$.05 \to .50$	.03	.01	5.0	.9	.1	10.0	0.5	0.2	8.0	10^3	10^4
5.3	.99	.10	$.05 \to .50$	$.03 \to .30$	$.01 \to .10$	5.0	.9	.1	10.0	0.5	0.2	8.0	10^3	10^4
5.4	.75	.05	$.05 \to .50$	$.03 \to .30$	$.01 \to .10$	5.0	.9	.1	10.0	0.5	0.2	8.0	10^3	10^4
5.5	.50	.02	$.05 \to .50$	$.03 \to .30$	$.01 \to .10$	5.0	.9	.1	10.0	0.5	0.2	8.0	10^3	10^4
5.6	.75	.05	.05	.03	.01	$5 \to 5\times10^5$	.1	.1	10.0	0.5	0.2	1.0	10^3	10^4
5.7	.75	.05	.05	.03	.01	$5 \to 5\times10^5$	.9	.1	10.0	0.5	0.2	8.0	10^3	10^4
5.8	.75	.05	.05	.03	.01	5.0	.9	.1	10.0	0.5	0.2	8.0	$10^3 \to 10^8$	10^4
5.9	.75	.05	.05	.03	.01	5.0	$.01 \to .90$	.1	10.0	0.5	0.2	8.0	10^3	10^4
5.10	.75	.05	.05	.03	.01	5.0	.9	.1	$1 \to 50$	$0.5 \to 5.0$	$0.0 \to 9.0$	8.0	10^3	10^4
5.11	.75	.05	.05	.03	.01	5.0	.9	.1	10.0	0.5	0.2	$0.8 \to 80$	10^3	10^4

Table 5.2. Effect of Error Rates at Level 1, on Total Cost ($\delta = .75$, $\delta' = .05$, $E_{2,s} = .03$, $E_{3...5,s} = .01$, $c(o) = 5.0$, $p_v = .9$, $p_h = .1$, $A = 10.0$, $B = .5$, $C = .2$, $V = 8.0$, $L = 1000$, $CL = \$10,000$)

			Costs		
$E_{1,s} = \epsilon$	λ	Fixed	Client Opportunity	Poor Treatment	Total
.05	1	9748	51,468	111,557	172,773
	2	9786	21,969	6120	* 37,875
	3	13,678	20,025	6066	39,769
	4	18,840	19,883	6063	44,785
	5	26,380	19,875	6062	52,265
.10	1	11,372	61,149	492,546	565,067
	2	9,786	24,409	23,224	* 57,419
	3	13,678	21,560	22,899	58,137
	4	18,840	21,352	22,881	63,073
	5	26,328	21,340	22,880	70,548
.15	1	11,372	70,885	1,200,218	1,282,475
	2	9786	26,915	50,529	87,230
	3	13,678	23,108	49,597	* 86,383
	4	18,840	22,830	49,545	91,214
	5	26,328	22,814	49,542	98,694
.25	1	12,997	86,126	3,563,493	3,662,615
	2	12,075	31,986	132,826	176,888
	3	13,678	26,140	129,277	* 169,095
	4	18,840	25,714	129,079	173,632
	5	26,328	25,690	129,068	181,085
.35	1	12,997	89,371	6,375,114	6,477,481
	2	14,272	36,895	247,600	298,768
	3	15,303	28,930	239,079	* 283,312
	4	20,464	28,349	238,608	287,849
	5	27,593	28,316	238,581	294,849
.50	1	11,372	87,839	9,058,222	9,146,060
	2	16,562	43,317	470,390	530,269
	3	17,562	32,377	449,202	* 499,071
	4	22,754	31,472	448,038	502,264
	5	30,242	31,426	447,972	509,640

Note: Asterisks refer to lowest cost.

ing Tables 5.2 and 5.4. It also varies with the costs of errors or failures in serving them and the importance and effectiveness of vertical communication, p_v, that is, of referrals to higher hierarchic levels for maintaining error rates at each level indicated.

A few findings may be pointed out:

1. In all cases, having more hierarchic levels will increase the fixed cost of the organization.

5.7 Optimum Number Determined by Computer Simulation / 143

2. As the number of hierarchic levels increases, with still uncongested vertical communication channels, the cost of the clients' waiting time declines, but the savings per level added become smaller.
3. The same is true of the cost to clients of errors in the service or treatment they receive.
4. The aggregate of all costs tends toward a minimum for organizations with two hierarchic levels when error probabilities are low, and for three-level organizations as error frequencies increase.
5. As caseloads increase by orders of magnitude beyond the 1000 cases per month, assumed in Table 5.2, the optimal numbers of hierarchic levels will increase, but the effects of increased error frequencies and error costs will continue to make their own contribution toward making the optimal organization taller.
6. If the value of the clients, their time, and their losses from service errors count for little, it may seem rational to have them served by a two-level, or in any case, by a relatively flat organization. Natives in a colony, the population of a country under military occupation, or minority members of a racist society are often subjected to the control of private soldiers and their sergeants and to similar low-level decision makers in the police, hospitals, and other services. If people in highly developed countries are considered more valuable, this should find expression, according to this model, in their being served by taller, relatively multilevel organizations and administrations permitting a ladder of appeals to higher hierarchic levels for revision and control.

Table 5.3 and the corresponding Figure 5.3 show the above conclusions to be sensitive to the values of δ and δ', the probabilities of clients appealing correct and incorrect decisions, respectively. Error-sensitive organizations benefit from having somewhat more cantankerous clients. As the error rate of agents at higher levels goes up, of course, the cost of poorly treated cases goes up, as expected.

Suppose that clients are very reluctant to appeal decisions. It seems safe to conclude from our analysis of the computer output that high appeal rates, despite the nuisance of an exaggerated rate of unjustified complaints, are desirable for servers and clients alike. This increases the desirability of some degree of hierarchy, and we turn next to the question of how much.

5.7.2 Effect of the Cost of Delay. The cost to the client of delay is most easily estimated by $c(0)$, the opportunity cost of a client's time, in dollars per hour. For the client in the waiting room of a clinic, this may

Table 5.3. Effect of Error Rates on Cost ($\delta = .99, \delta' = .10, c(o) = 5.0, p_v = .9, p_h = .1, A = 10.0, B = .5, C = .2, T^{ud} = 8.0, L = 1000, CE = \$10,000$)

					Costs		
$E_{1,s} = \epsilon$	$E_{2,s}$	$E_{3,\ldots,5,s}$	λ	Fixed	Client Opportunity	Poor Treatment	Total
.05	.03	.01	1	9748	51,468	111,557	172,773
			2	9786	23,678	9	*33,473
			3	13,678	20,839	9	34,526
			4	18,840	20,465	9	39,314
			5	26,328	20,425	9	46,762
.10	.06	.02	1	11,372	61,149	492,546	565,067
			2	9786	25,609	35	*35,430
			3	13,678	22,106	34	35,818
			4	18,840	21,525	34	40,398
			5	26,328	21,456	34	47,818
.15	.09	.03	1	11,372	70,885	1,200,218	1,282,475
			2	9786	27,544	77	37,407
			3	13,678	23,476	73	*37,227
			4	18,840	22,647	73	41,560
			5	26,328	22,543	73	48,943

.25	.15				3,563,493	3,662,615
		1	12,997	86,126	205	44,271
		2	12,648	31,418	188	*40,389
		3	13,678	26,523	186	44,119
		4	18,840	25,093	186	51,400
		5	26,328	24,886		
.35	.21				6,375,114	6,477,481
		1	12,997	89,371	387	48,325
		2	12,648	35,291	342	*43,995
		3	13,678	29,975	335	46,994
		4	18,840	27,820	334	54,132
		5	26,328	27,470		
.50	.30				9,058,222	9,146,060
		1	11,372	76,466	749	57,333
		2	15,510	41,074	622	54,090
		3	17,570	35,898	603	*51,912
		4	18,840	32,469	599	58,749
		5	26,328	31,822		

Note: Asterisks refer to lowest cost.

Table 5.4. Effect of Error on Cost ($\delta = .75$, $\delta' = .05$, $c(o) = 5.0$, $p_r = .9$, $p_h = .1$, $L = 1000$, $A = 10.0$, $B = 0.5$, $C = 0.2$, $T^{ut} = 8.0$, $CE = \$10,000$)

$E_{1,s} = \epsilon$	$E_{2,s}$	$E_{3...5,s}$	λ	Fixed	Client Opportunity	Poor Treatment	Total
.05	.03	.01	1	9748	51,468	111,557	172,773
			2	9786	21,969	6120	*37,875
			3	13,678	20,025	6066	40,769
			4	18,840	19,883	6063	44,785
			5	26,328	19,875	6062	52,265
.10	.06	.02	1	11,372	61,149	492,546	565,067
			2	9786	24,449	24,938	*59,174
			3	13,678	21,712	24,538	59,928
			4	18,840	21,445	24,513	64,798
			5	26,328	21,428	24,511	72,268
.15	.09	.03	1	11,372	70,885	1,200,218	1,282,475
			2	9786	27,045	57,210	94,041
			3	13,678	23,530	55,785	*92,992
			4	18,840	23,097	55,686	97,623
			5	26,328	23,067	55,679	105,073

.25	.15	.05	1	12,997	86,126	3,563,493	3,662,615
			2	12,075	32,459	165,645	210,179
			3	13,678	27,490	157,778	*198,946
			4	18,840	26,595	157,140	202,575
			5	26,328	26,519	157,086	209,933
.35	.21	.07	1	12,997	89,371	6,375,114	6,477,481
			2	14,272	37,911	339,556	391,740
			3	15,303	31,720	313,904	*360,927
			4	20,464	30,195	311,549	362,209
			5	27,953	30,044	311,318	369,315
.50	.30	.10	1	11,372	76,466	9,058,222	9,146,060
			2	16,562	45,313	745,679	807,554
			3	20,706	37,984	652,011	710,701
			4	22,754	35,266	642,150	*700,170
			5	30,232	34,940	640,984	706,167

Note: Asterisks refer to the lowest total cost.

Table 5.5. Effect of Error Rates on Total Cost ($\delta = .50$, $\delta' = .02$, $c(o) = 5$, $p_v = .90$, $p_h = .10$, $A = 10.0$, $B = 0.5$, $C = 0.2$, $L = 1000$, $T^{ua} = 8.0$)

					Costs		
$E_{1,s} = \epsilon$	$E_{2,s}$	$E_{3...5,s}$	λ	Fixed	Client Opportunity	Poor Treatment	Total
.05	.03	.01	1	9748	51,468	111,557	172,773
			2	9786	21,006	26,373	*57,166
			3	13,106	19,883	26,310	59,299
			4	18,267	19,844	26,308	64,419
			5	25,756	19,843	26,308	71,907
.10	.06	.02	1	11,372	61,149	492,546	565,067
			2	9786	23,968	113,292	*147,046
			3	13,678	22,136	112,684	148,498
			4	18,840	22,043	112,667	153,549
			5	26,328	22,040	112,666	161,034
.15	.09	.03	1	11,372	70,885	1,200,218	1,282,475
			2	11,410	27,175	274,345	312,930
			3	15,303	24,570	271,725	*311,597
			4	20,464	24,396	271,635	316,495
			5	27,953	24,390	271,632	323,975

.25	.15	.05	1	12,997	86,126	3,563,493	3,662,615
			2	13,700	34,016	888,805	936,521
			3	15,303	29,733	896,403	*914,438
			4	20,464	29,301	868,567	918,332
			5	27,953	29,282	868,529	925,764
.35	.21	.07	1	12,997	89,371	6,375,114	6,447,481
			2	13,700	40,805	2,051,799	2,106,303
			3	17,592	34,826	1,970,417	*2,022,835
			4	22,754	34,000	1,966,207	2,022,960
			5	30,242	33,955	1,965,980	2,030,177
.50	.30	.10	1	11,372	76,466	9,058,222	9,146,060
			2	17,614	49,057	5,462,533	5,529,204
			3	19,217	41,002	5,038,427	5,098,646
			4	24,379	39,382	5,011,581	*5,075,341
			5	31,867	39,272	5,009,761	5,080,900

Note: Asterisks refer to the lowest total cost.

150 / Hierarchical and Network Structures

Table 5.6. Varied Opportunity Cost to Client ($\delta = .75, \delta' = .05, p_v = .10, p_h = .10, L = 1000, A = 10.0, B = 0.5, C = 0.2, E_{1,s} = \epsilon = .05, E_{2,s} = .03, E_{3...5,s} = .01, T^{ud} = 1.0$)

			Costs		
c(o)	λ	Fixed	Client Opportunity	Poor Treatment	Total
5	1	9748	51,468	111,557	172,773
	2	12,610	47,593	6120	* 66,323
	3	16,502	47,827	6066	70,395
	4	21,664	47,840	6063	75,566
	5	29,152	47,841	6062	83,055
50	1	9748	514,682	111,557	635,986
	2	12,610	475,932	6120	* 494,662
	3	16,502	478,269	6066	500,837
	4	21,664	478,398	6063	506,124
	5	29,152	478,405	6062	513,620
500	1	9748	5,146,819	111,557	5,268,123
	2	12,610	4,759,320	6120	* 4,778,049
	3	16,502	4,782,688	6066	4,805,255
	4	21,664	4,783,975	6063	4,811,700
	5	29,152	5,784,044	6062	4,819,258
5000	1	9748	51,468,144	111,557	51,589,440
	2	12,610	47,593,184	6120	* 47,611,904
	3	16,502	47,826,832	6066	47,849,392
	4	21,664	47,839,648	6063	47,867,344
	5	29,152	47,840,304	6062	47,875,504
50,000	1	9748	514,681,344	111,557	514,802,432
	2	12,610	475,931,648	6120	* 475,950,080
	3	16,502	478,267,904	6066	478,290,176
	4	21,664	478,396,160	6063	478,423,552
	5	29,152	478,401,536	6062	478,436,352
500,000	1	9748	5,146,808,320	111,557	5,146,927,104
	2	12,610	4,759,310,336	6120	*4,759,326,720
	3	16,502	4,782,673,920	6066	4,782,694,400
	4	21,664	4,783,968,256	6063	4,783,992,832
	5	29,152	4,784,029,696	6062	4,784,062,464

Note: Asterisks refer to the lowest total cost.

5.7 Optimum Number Determined by Computer Simulation / 151

Table 5.7. Varied Opportunity Cost to Client ($\delta = .75, \delta' = .05, p_v = .90, p_h = .10, L = 1000, A = 10.0, B = 0.5, C = 02, E_{1,s} = \epsilon = .05, E_{2,5} = .03, E_{3...5,s} = .01, T^{ud} = 8.0$)

			Costs		
c(o)	λ	Fixed	Client Opportunity	Poor Treatment	Total
5	1	9748	51,458	111,557	172,773
	2	9786	21,969	6120	* 37,875
	3	13,678	20,025	6066	37,969
	4	18,840	19,833	6063	44,785
	5	26,328	19,875	6062	52,265
50	1	9748	514,682	111,557	635,986
	2	9786	219,691	6120	235,597
	3	13,678	200,248	6066	* 219,991
	4	18,840	198,830	6063	223,732
	5	26,328	198,749	6062	231,139
500	1	9748	5,146,819	111,557	5,268,123
	2	9786	2,196,909	6120	2,212,814
	3	13,678	2,002,470	6066	2,022,213
	4	18,840	1,988,293	6063	* 2,013,194
	5	26,328	1,987,481	6062	2,019,871
5,000	1	9748	51,468,144	111,557	51,589,440
	2	9786	21,969,088	6120	21,984,976
	3	13,678	20,024,688	6066	20,044,416
	4	18,840	19,882,928	6063	19,907,808
	5	26,328	19,874,784	6062	* 19,907,152
	6	38,047	19,874,304	6062	19,918,384
50,000	1	9748	514,681,344	111,557	514,802,432
	2	9786	219,691,152	6120	219,707,040
	3	13,678	200,247,824	6066	200,267,552
	4	18,840	198,830,032	6063	198,854,912
	5	26,328	198,749,152	6062	* 198,781,520
	6	38,047	198,744,528	6062	198,788,608
500,000	1	9748	5,146,808,320	111,557	5,146,927,104
	2	9786	2,196,911,360	6120	2,196,926,976
	3	13,678	2,002,477,824	6066	2,002,497,280
	4	18,840	1,988,299,008	6063	1,988,323,584
	5	26,328	1,987,490,304	6062	1,987,522,304
	6	38,047	1,987,443,200	6062	*1,987,486,976
	7	55,689	1,987,502,080	6062	1,987,502,080

Note: Asterisks refer to the lowest total cost.

Table 5.8 The Effect of Client Load on λ^*, the Optimal Number of Hierarchical Levels ($c(o) = 5.0$, $\delta = .75$, $\delta' = .05$, $E_{1,s} = .05$, $E_{2,s} = .03$, $E_3, \ldots, s, s = .01$, $\epsilon = .05$, $p_v = .90$, $p_h = .10$, $A = 10.0$, $B = 0.5$, $C = 0.2$, $T^{ud} = 8.0$)

Load	λ^*	Costs				
		Fixed	Client Opportunity	Poor Treatment	Total	Unit
1000	2	9786	21,969	6120	37,875	37.875
5000	3	38,936	100,124	30,328	169,388	33.877
50,000	4	349,854	994,150	303,130	1,647,133	32.942
500,000	4	3,436,024	9,941,499	3,031,298	16,408,821	32.817
5,000,000	5	34,308,848	99,374,416	30,312,032	163,995,296	32.799
50,000,000	6	342,982,912	993,720,320	303,120,896	1,639,824,128	32.796
100,000,000	6	685,944,320	1,987,442,944	606,240,512	3,279,627,776	32.796

5.7 Optimum Number Determined by Computer Simulation / 153

Table 5.9 Variation of ρ_v ($\delta = .75$, $\delta' = .05$, $L = 1000$, $\rho_h = .10$, $c(o) = 5.0$, $A = 10.0$, $B = 0.5$, $C = 0.2$, $E_{1,s} = \epsilon = .05$, $E_{2,5} = .03$, $E_{3...5,s} = .01$, $T^{ud} = 8.0$)

			Costs		
ρ_v	λ	Fixed	Client Opportunity	Poor Treatment	Total
.90	1	9748	51,468	111,557	172,773
	2	9786	21,969	6120	*37,875
	3	13,678	20,025	6066	39,769
	4	18,840	19,883	6063	44,785
	5	26,328	19,875	6062	52,265
.10	1	9748	51,468	111,557	172,773
	2	13,847	44,862	6120	*64,829
	3	17,740	44,863	6066	68,668
	4	22,901	44,860	6063	73,823
	5	30,390	44,859	6602	81,311
.05	1	9748	51,468	111,557	172,773
	2	15,472	49,284	6120	*70,877
	3	19,364	49,662	6066	75,091
	4	24,526	49,685	6063	80,273
	5	32,014	49,686	6062	87,763
.01	1	9748	51,468	111,557	172,773
	2	15,878	53,446	6120	*75,445
	3	19,770	54,178	6066	80,014
	4	24,932	54,226	6063	85,220
	5	32,420	54,229	6062	92,711

Note: Asterisks refer to the lowest total cost.

be the rate of pay that the client could be earning. If the client is bleeding profusely, however, it is the cost of not being attended to by someone who could save his or her life by stopping the bleeding. That cost, if the minutes spell the difference between life and death, could be the value of the client's life divided by the number of hours left if the bleeding is not stopped. Similar considerations hold for clients awaiting the services of fire or police departments or antiaircraft or antiballistic missile defenses. In Tables 5.6 and 5.7 we computed the optimal number of hierarchical levels and the total costs as $c(0)$ varies from \$5 to \$500,000 per hour. In Table 5.6, the value of p_v, the probability rate of success through vertical communication, was taken to be .1, and T^{ud}, the average vertical communication time per request, was 1 minute. The small p_v represents a situation in which relatively little knowledge is needed on the part of higher-level servers to deal

154 / Hierarchical and Network Structures

Table 5.10. Variation of A, B, C (coefficients for relating communication) ($\delta = .75, \delta' = .05, p_v = .90, p_h = .10, c(o) = 5, E_{1,s} = \epsilon = .05, E_{2,s} = .03, E_{3,\ldots,5,s} = .01, L = 1000, T^{ud} = 8.0$)

					Costs		
A	B	C	λ	Fixed	Client Opportunity	Poor Treatment	Total
10.0	0.5	0.2	1	9748	51,468	111,557	172,773
			2	9786	21,969	6120	*37,875
			3	13,678	20,025	6066	39,769
			4	18,840	19,883	6063	44,785
			5	26,328	19,875	6062	52,265
1.0	0.5	0.2	1	9748	46,927	111,557	168,232
			2	9786	15,134	6120	*31,040
			3	13,106	12,945	6066	32,116
			4	18,267	12,786	6063	37,116
			5	25,756	12,777	6062	44,595
20.0	0.5	0.2	1	13,403	66,606	111,557	191,566
			2	11,817	36,082	6120	*54,019
			3	15,709	34,216	6066	55,991
			4	20,870	34,079	6063	61,012
			5	28,359	34,071	6062	68,492
50.0	0.5	0.2	1	21,526	112,019	111,557	245,102
			2	19,940	78,420	6120	*104,480
			3	23,832	76,790	6066	106,687
			4	28,993	76,665	6063	111,721
			5	36,482	76,659	6062	119,203
10.0	0.05	0.2	1	9748	46,927	111,557	168,232
			2	11,817	26,840	6120	*44,777
			3	15,709	25,646	6066	47,421
			4	20,870	25,558	6063	52,491
			5	28,359	25,553	6062	59,974
10.0	5.0	0.2	1	9748	51,468	111,557	168,232
			2	9786	15,466	6120	*31,372
			3	13,106	12,968	6066	32,140
			4	18,267	12,787	6063	37,117
			5	25,756	12,777	6062	44,595
10.0	0.5	0.0	1	11,778	60,551	111,557	183,886
			2	9786	22,632	6120	*38,539
			3	13,678	20,072	6066	39,816
			4	18,840	19,886	6063	44,788
			5	26,328	19,875	6062	52,265
10.0	0.5	2.0	1	9748	46,927	111,557	168,232
			2	9786	21,637	6120	*37,544
			3	13,678	20,001	6066	39,745
			4	18,840	19,882	6063	44,784
			5	26,328	19,875	6062	52,265

5.7 Optimum Number Determined by Computer Simulation / 155

Table 5.10. (Continued)

					Costs		
A	B	C	λ	Fixed	Client Opportunity	Poor Treatment	Total
10.0	0.5	9.0	1	9748	46,927	111,557	168,232
			2	9786	21,637	6120	*37,544
			3	13,678	20,001	6066	39,745
			4	18,840	19,882	6063	44,784
			5	26,328	19,875	6062	52,265

Note: Asterisks refer to the lowest total cost.

with the situation. This might apply, for example, to breaking up of a street fight by the police. Note that only two levels of organization are optimal no matter how large $c(0)$ gets.

In Tables 5.3, 5.4, 5.5, p_v = .9, reflecting higher effectiveness of vertical communication, more knowledge is required from the higher-level agents. Also $T^{ud} = 8$. More time per request is spent on vertical communication. The optimal number of hierarchical levels now increases as the logarithm of $c(0)$, going up by 1 for each order of magnitude increase in the client's cost of delay. Such a situation is exemplified by defenses against nuclear attack. The conclusion, that a tall hierarchy should be in place for this complex task when the stakes are high, is also plausible in such an example.

5.7.3 Effect of the Input Load. A slightly modified version of the computer program was run to compute the optimum number of hierarchical levels for various values of L and to show how the associated unit cost varies as client load varies. The new program permits us to study client loads that are arbitrarily large while also analyzing structures with an arbitrarily large number of hierarchical levels. The results are shown in Table 5.8. The optimum number of hierarchical levels, λ^*, are shown in column 2. The client load per time unit is listed under "load" in column 1. Figure 5.4 shows a plot of λ^* versus load on a semilog scale. The data show that not only does λ^* increase with increasing load but, for the parameters specified, λ^* also increases by one level for approximately each increase of an order of magnitude in the parameter, that is, load.

The figures show that, as the load increases, unit cost decreases, but at a decreasing rate. A plot of the unit cost versus load is shown in

156 / Hierarchical and Network Structures

Table 5.11 Variation of Amount of Time Needed in Vertical Communication ($\delta = .75, \delta' = .05, p_v = .90, p_h = .10, c(o) = 5, A = 10.0, B = 0.5, C = 0.2, L = 1000, E_{1,s} = \epsilon = .05, E_{2,5} = .03, E_{3,..5,s} = .01$)

			Costs		
T^{ud}	λ	Fixed	Client Opportunity	Poor Treatment	Total
80	1	9,748	51,468	111,557	172,773
	2	48,929	109,117	6,120	*164,166
	3	55,111	114,580	6,066	175,756
	4	60,272	114,964	6,033	181,299
	5	67,761	114,986	6,062	188,809
8	1	9,748	51,468	111,577	172,773
	2	9,786	21,969	6,120	* 37,875
	3	13,678	20,025	6,066	39,769
	4	18,840	19,883	6,063	44,785
	5	26,328	19,875	6,062	52,265
4	1	9,748	51,468	111,557	172,773
	2	6,924	19,368	6,120	* 32,412
	3	10,816	17,202	6,066	34,084
	4	15,977	17,045	6,063	39,085
	5	23,466	17,036	6,062	46,564
2	1	9,748	51,468	111,557	172,773
	2	8,954	30,554	6,120	* 45,629
	3	12,847	29,339	6,066	48,252
	4	18,008	29,249	6,063	53,320
	5	25,497	29,244	6,062	60,803
.8	1	9,748	51,468	111,557	172,773
	2	10,985	41,012	6,120	* 58,117
	3	14,877	40,686	6,063	61,629
	4	20,039	40,659	6,063	66,761
	5	27,527	40,657	6,062	74,247

Note: Asterisks refer to the lowest total cost.

Figure 5.5. Unit cost decreases rapidly as the client load ranges from 1000 to 10,000, only to level off in the 10,000 to 100,000 range. Beyond that load level, it continues to decline slightly.

5.7.4 Effect of Vertical Communication Effectiveness.

If vertical communication is reasonably effective—that is, if p'_v, the probability rate of finding needed information through vertical communication, exceeds .1—and the cost of poorly treated cases is not enormous, two-level organizations cost least (see Table 5.9 of the appendix and Figure 5.6). As p_v becomes very small, the cost considerations alone

5.7 Optimum Number Determined by Computer Simulation / 157

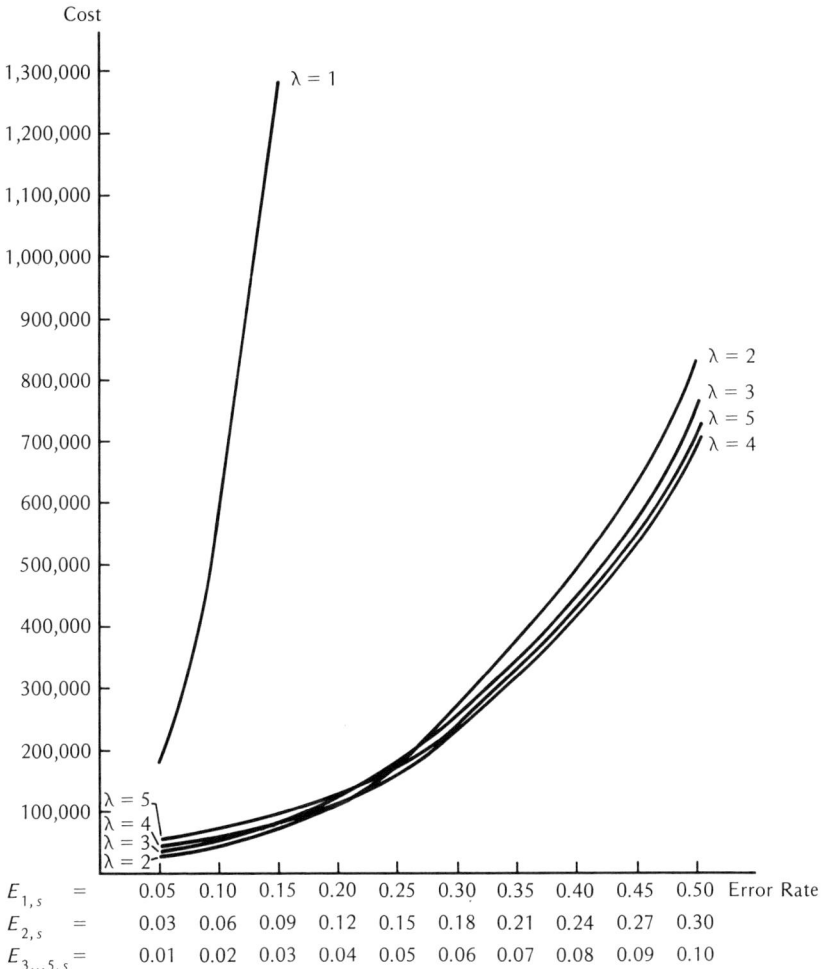

Figure 5.2. Total cost vs. error rates for a variable number of hierarchical levels.

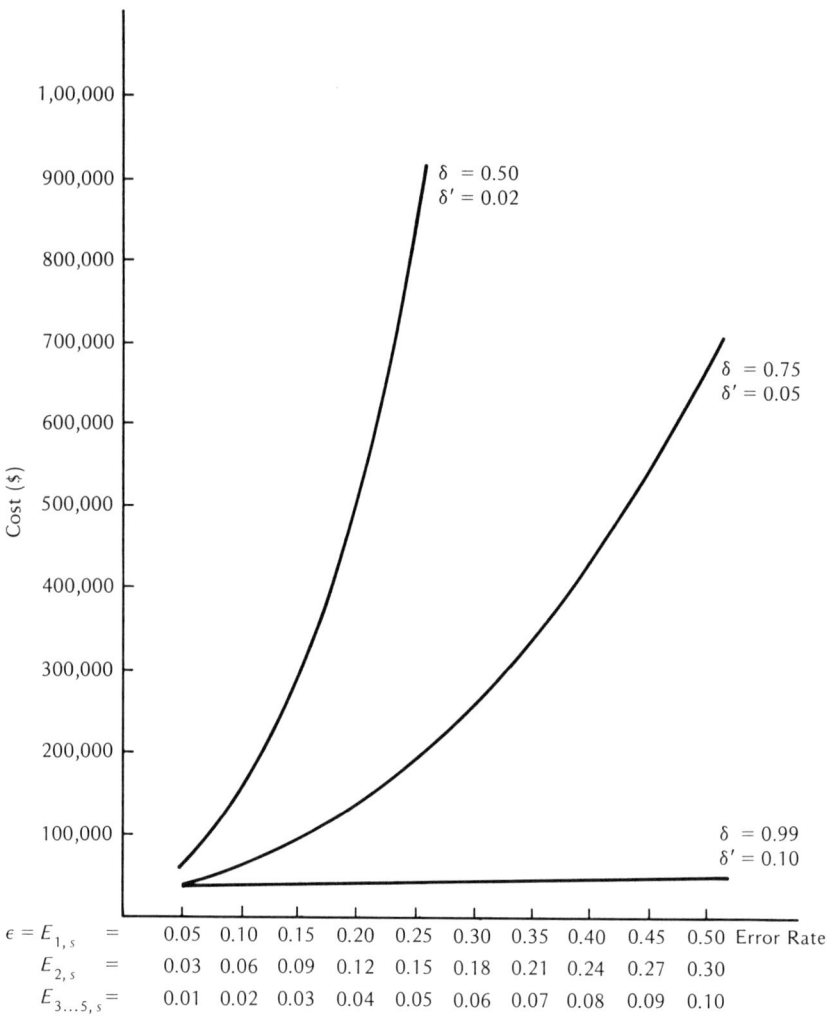

Figure 5.3. Optimum total cost vs. error rate for variable probabilities of client appeal.

5.7 Optimum Number Determined by Computer Simulation / 159

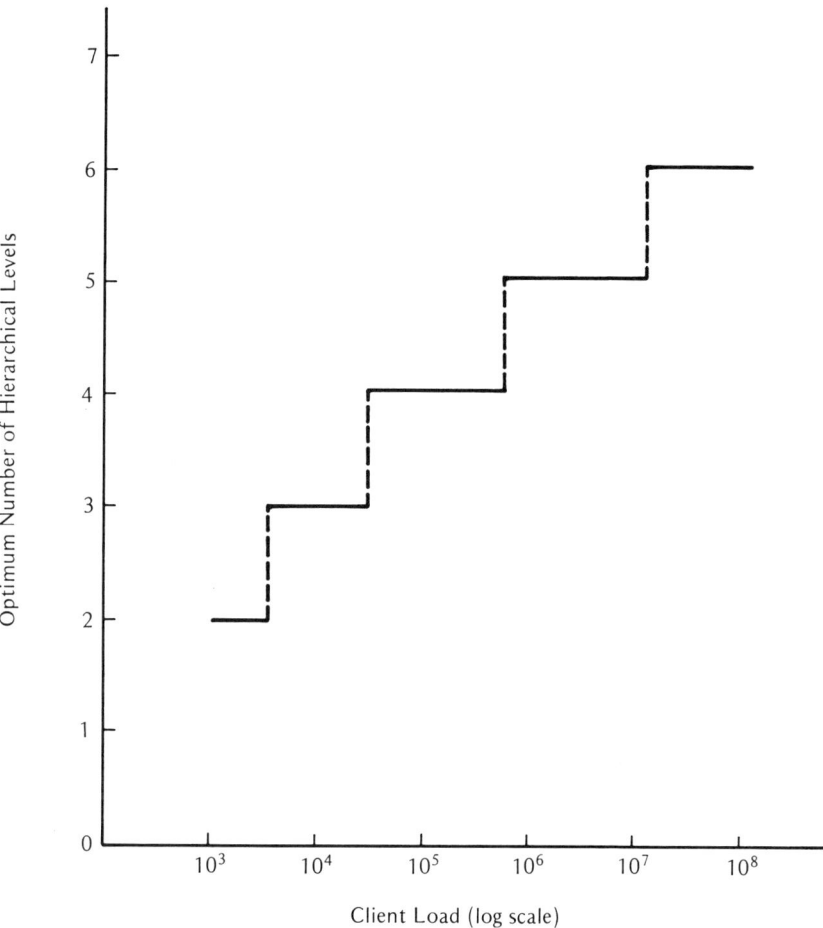

Figure 5.4. Optimum number of hierarchical levels vs. client load.

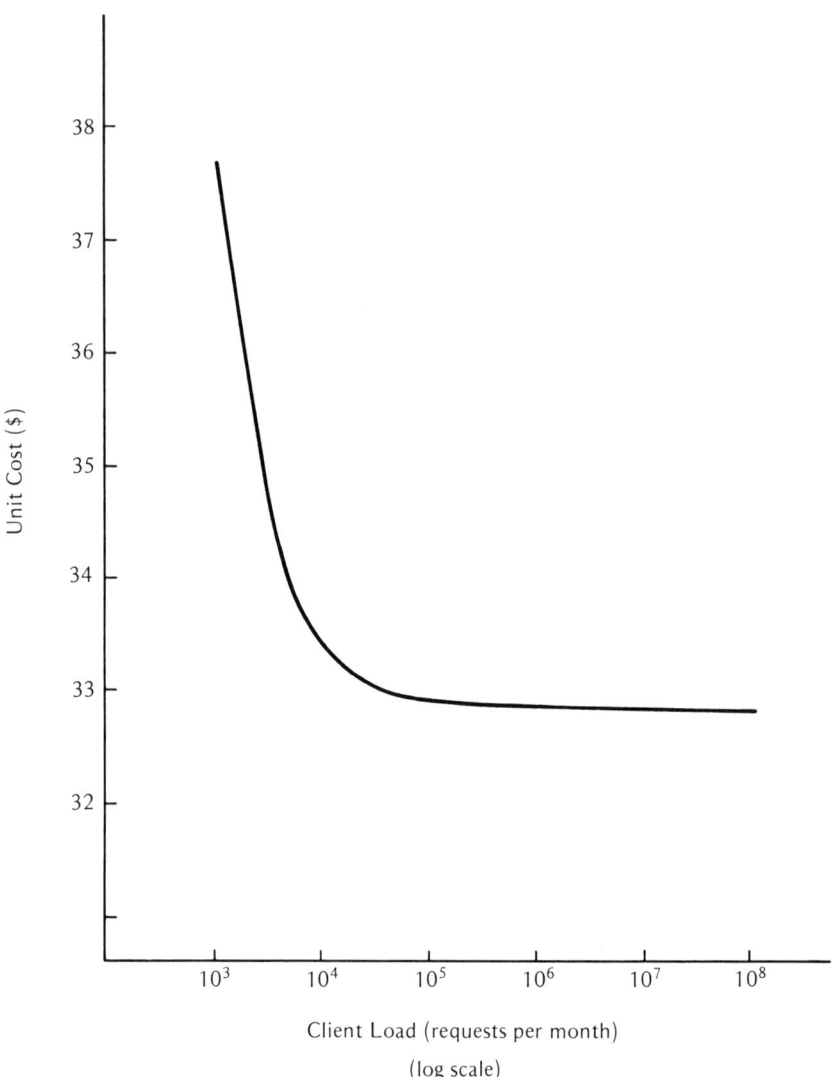

Figure 5.5. Optimal unit cost vs. client load.

5.7 Optimum Number Determined by Computer Simulation / 161

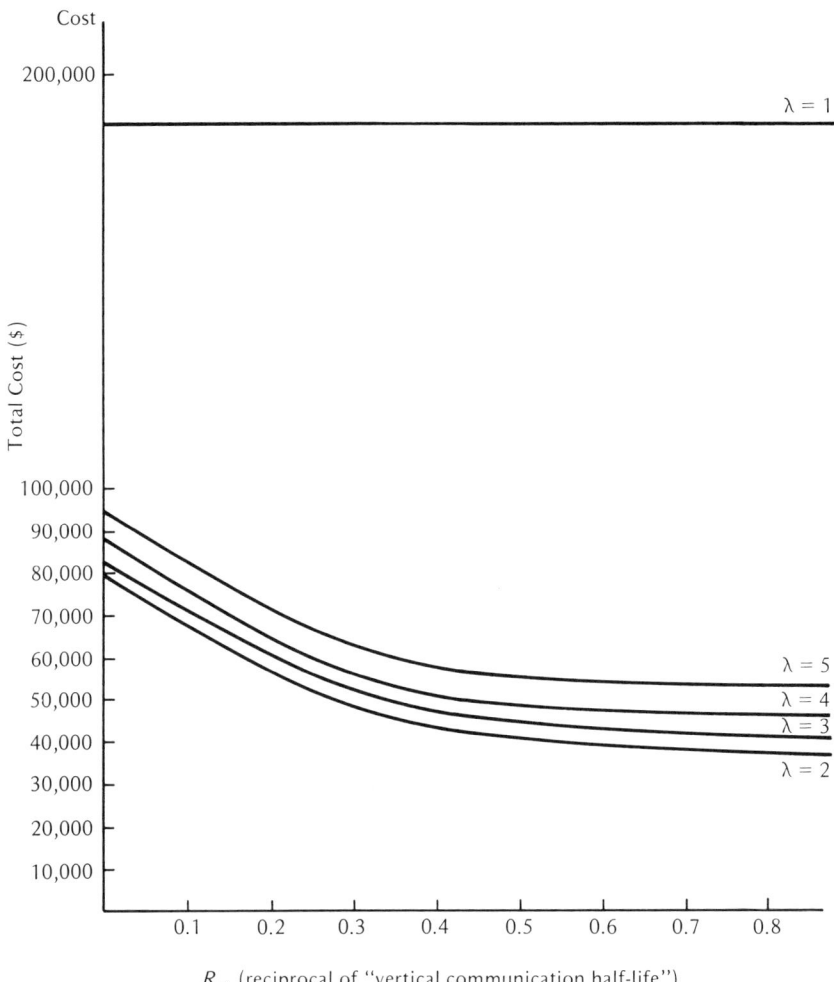

Figure 5.6. Total cost vs. effectiveness of vertical communication for variable flatness.

favor a one-level organization, but the cost of poorly treated cases may become too high. If the cost attached to such cases is moderately high, two-level organizations still seem least costly.

5.8 DEPENDENCY ON NATURE OF THE INPUT LOAD: SPAN OF CONTROL

So far we have avoided analysis of the incoming request stream upon the costs of organizations with varying numbers of hierarchical levels. We have made the obvious point that if all or most of the incoming requests were the same, a second-level server need spend little time in supervision; he or she could supervise more first-level servers (greater "span of control") and fewer second-level servers would be needed. Thus uniformity in the request stream favors broader, shallower, flatter—decentralized—organizations.

Uniform or not, if the incoming requests require much coordination, more higher-level servers are needed. The greater the number of servers per request that need to be coordinated, the greater T^{ud}. In the models we have analyzed so far, this does not greatly affect the optimum number of levels. The effect of fluctuations or deviations from uniformity in the number of servers per request that need to be coordinated, hence T^{ud}, may favor more hierarchical levels in that higher-level servers are required to attend to the rarer, more complex requests. This corresponds to the hypothesis that "the greater the degree of centralization, the higher the proportion of vertical task communication" (Hage et al., 1971, p. 861).

The span of control, in the model that we analyze by computer, becomes a random variable because the number of servers on any level depends not on L but on the expected load, EL, the mean of a random variable. This randomly varying load exceeds EL by the internally generated load, which is determined by the chances of errors being made, detected, appealed, corrected, and so on. On the whole, our considerations would lead us to suspect that secular trends favor increasing spans on control, up to the limits of human supervisory capacities, and that in turn may favor a trend toward fewer hierarchical levels or hierarchical decentralization.

If a higher-level server can get by with less supervisory time per subordinate, the time thus liberated need not be allocated to supervising more subordinates. Instead, it could be spent on longer-range planning. That becomes increasingly important when the nature of the input request load is shifting over time. Trends need to be analyzed;

future needs need to be sensed and anticipated; demands need to be created, shaped, projected, and aroused; the organization may have to be expanded, restructured, or restaffed. The span of control may not increase during such a period of change, and the number of hierarchical levels may remain unchanged. Decentralization is most likely in a period of little change that is well in hand, in which no planning is needed.

Decentralization may also be favored by a period of great uncertainty, in which no planning is possible. A decentralized organization may be able to render much better services in unanticipated and multiple crises than would a more centralized organization. Thus, if the nature of the request in the input stream is subject to seemingly random fluctuations, the most adaptable, flexible structure among generalist type of servers may be best.

The futuristic vision of rapid transformations from one structure into another that is better adapted to the client's needs may not only become realistic but also necessary. The flatness of organizations thus could vary with time, fluctuating in response to needs. The responses must neither lag too much nor too little. Nor must there be a response to each wiggle in the clients' request stream. Moreover, these fluctuations are probably superimposed on a longer-term drift toward greater flatness or hierarchical decentralization.

5.9 DECENTRALIZATION AND INNOVATION

Invention means finding a way to do something new, or a new way to do something old. In either case it implies some new combination of resources and operations discovered most often by one or a few persons at a time through a combination and selection process. *Innovation* is a change of habits by many people, such that an invention is being applied in practice on a relatively large scale. Inventions can be copied or imported, but innovations must be adopted and learned by people who are to utilize them.

What are the effects of an increase in decentralization on an organization's capabilities to innovate? As a first approximation, we may consider that decentralized organizations should have more intake channels or contact points with the clients, localities, or functions they serve and more responsibility, time, and resources at their lowest hierarchical levels to respond to the experiences and messages that may be found there. Moderate or "approximate" innovations that require only small cognitive steps and small changes of habits may become more probable, therefore, as an organization becomes more decentralized. More radical or cognitively remote innovations, requiring larger cognitive steps or longer sequences of cognitive efforts and larger changes of habits, may require more concentrated allocations of time, memories, cognitive capabilities, and material resources. They may be more likely, therefore, to occur in taller and more centralized organizations. In industry, more innovations have come from the higher levels of management and from special research laboratories than from employees' suggestion boxes. Similarly, the innovating governments of Europe in the sixteenth to eighteenth centuries tended to be more centralized than their feudal predecessors.

A second look may modify this simple view. Both approximate and remote innovations are needed. The few experts who know how to make shoes must pay attention both to the many "experts" who know where their own shoe pinches and to the very few experts who may discover new ways to make better shoes and substitutes for leather. Our task then becomes that of seeking some viable balance between centralization and decentralization in an organization that needs to innovate.

A second consideration involves the distribution of *learning resources*. Innovations are more likely to occur in systems with larger absolute and relative amounts of uncommitted resources, that is, resources that though not necessarily idle are quickly available for a large range of possible recommitments. These uncommitted resources correspond to what has been called "organizational slack" (Cyert and March, 1963). This principle should hold for tangible resources, such as capital, labor, and land, as well as for human knowledge and skills, both at the individual and group levels, and for the resources of organizations. All such uncommitted resources are potential resources for social learning, which includes learning to accept innovations and to act in accordance with them.

Innovations, therefore, will be promoted best by adjusting the degree and kinds of decentralization. This includes selecting the appropriate number of hierarchic levels. It also includes the distribution of tasks and resources among levels in such a way that the largest amounts of recommittable resources will be allocated to those points in the organization at which new needs of clients (and of the organization) are most likely to be reported and received. Linking response capabilities as effectively as possible to need perceptions should increase the probability of timely, innovative, and relevant responses.

5.10 CONCLUDING REMARKS ON FLATNESS AS AN ASPECT OF DECENTRALIZATION

The models we have analyzed in some detail are but a small sample of a great variety of other models of hierarchies that we have or could have begun to develop. For example, we could have replaced the assumption that the time for horizontal communication needed to service a request decreases *linearly* with the time spent on vertical communication by the assumption that it decreases *inversely* or as a negative exponential. This would have led to variants of the model we analyzed. We doubt that these variants would have altered the qualitative conclusions about conditions favoring flatness.

We also could have introduced a large number of additional variables to capture the complexity of real organizations more fully. For example, "difficulty of coordination" could have been defined and assumed to increase with the distance from the top of the hierarchy; clearly, "distance from the rank and file of the organization" decreases with distance from the top, and the point where these two oppositely sloped curves intersect could be interpreted as a "point of maximum vulnerability." "Job satisfaction" could have been introduced, as could findings stating that it increases with a person's authority and influence with the hierarchy (Tannenbaum, 1974), that it is negatively related to education, and so on. The relation between flatness and "alienation" could have been explored; presumably the bottom-level servers are less alienated in a flat than in a tall structure (Furniss, 1974).

In summarizing our general conclusions regarding flatness as an aspect of decentralization, we note that tallness does not necessarily imply steepness of an organizational pyramid. Promotion possibilities for executives increase with steepness, not just tallness. A taller and steeper organization provides more opportunities for recruiting, training, and testing of executives and managers. This increases the pool of managerial talent from which to draw for the higher-level positions. However, the taller and steeper the pyramid, the more remote lower-level servers see themselves from the top and the greater their feelings of alienation and powerlessness. There is also likely to be a high turnover at the higher levels, leading to instability when it becomes too high.

Executives are expected to make decisions. If they make unwise decisions, which is often difficult to ascertain and is usually evaluated only long after the decision is made, they might be given another chance. If they make no decisions, they are removed. One of the important questions in determining organizational structures is their effect on the wisdom of the decisions made (Deutsch and Meadow, 1961).

In very tall and steep hierarchies, relatively incompetent supervisors can supervise one or two subordinates. It would take a more competent manager to supervise a large number. Thus, we might expect to find more incompetent managers in tall and steep hierarchies than in flat ones. The capacity or span of control of a manager can be increased by relaxing the standards of control, allowing the manager to sample reports from subordinates or by staff and technological aids that amplify his or her performance.

On the whole, our analyses in this chapter suggest that the dominant trends of current and future technology will tend to favor greater flatness as an aspect of decentralization.

Chapter 6

Delegation and Control

6.0 INTRODUCTION

It has become customary to distinguish between administrative and political decentralization. The latter means giving more power to citizens, and it will be discussed in the next two chapters. Administrative decentralization, the focus of this chapter, means delegation of authority to command and to control, generally to servers who are closer to the clients.

Administrative decentralization refers to both a condition and to a process (Bresnick, 1973). As a process, it is likely to effect changes in ways of measuring services rendered—for example, the number of properly treated clients of a health service or the number of complaints. It may also change ways of measuring resources made available for service, such as the number of operational garbage trucks (Yin, 1972). As a condition, administrative decentralization is a property of organizational structure, relating to the distribution of capacities. We will examine administrative decentralization both as a process and as a condition, with special stress on the relation between these two ways of viewing it.

In the literature of organization theory, which deals with decentralization as a condition, the notions of delegation and span of control occupy central roles (Urwick, 1956; March and Simon, 1958; Blau and Scott, 1962; Etzioni, 1961). Organization theorists (e.g., Selznick, 1964) have long distinguished between formal and informal organization. *Formal organization* is a structure for systematically ordering positions and duties that define a chain of command and bring about administrative integration of specialized functions.

Delegation is viewed as the central relation in this structure, one that requires continuous elaboration of formal mechanisms for coordination and control. *Control* refers to circuits of communication channels in which signals are transmitted downward in an authority hierarchy. The purpose of such signaling is to coordinate or govern the behavior of subordinate agents and to feed back information upward about their results. Control, thus, is also based on communication of messages transmitted upward in the same hierarchy about the state of the world and activities of the controller's subordinates.

The channels of communication and control that are actually used are part of the *informal organization*. This reflects the spontaneous efforts of individuals or clusters of individuals to control the conditions of their existence. It need not coincide with the formal structure. Actual delegation generates centers of interest and depends on loyalties. Command over the responses of individuals requires communication and persuasion in the context of such interests and loyalties.

Control circuits ordinarily carry negative feedback signals. They produce effects that oppose or reverse the current behavior of the system whenever it moves away from a goal relationship to the outside world in such a way as to minimize the system's inner disequilibrium.

Often a control circuit then includes a specific *regulatory link* or *setting*, such as the temperature setting of a thermostat or the course setting of an automatic pilot, by which, within some limits, this goal relationship can be set or changed. The feedback circuit may then control the behavior of the system. But the regulatory link controls the setting of the goal. Through it, the behavior of the control circuit and the system is controlled, and limited goal changes are possible.

In man-made control systems, such regulatory links permit the system to be governed from outside by its human users. Whoever controls the regulatory link controls much of the behavior of the system. In biological systems as well as in sovereign states, by contrast, the goal-setting function most often is exercised autonomously, or it is even scattered among several links or stages of the control circuit.

In more complex control systems, both man-made or biological, the processes of goal setting and goal seeking may be modified by stored information recalled from *memory*, often in dissociated and/or recombined forms. In those cases, the behavior of a system will be controlled by whoever controls the storing and recall of information in such a memory and/or the processes of dissociation and recombination of information within it. The more concentrated the regulatory, goal-setting links and memory facilities of a system, the more concentrated its structure of control will be.

Tightly managed organizations, with control exercised from the top down, would be considered centralized. However, the demand for control from the top hierarchy leads to increased delegation of authority, according to organizational sociologists. It increases the amount of training in specialized competences, and thus subordinates can deal better with a small number of problems. But delegation also has dysfunctional consequences for achieving the goal of the organization. It increases the fragmentation of interests, with resulting departmentalization and greater commitment and loyalty to subunit goals than the overall goal.

Organizations in which some or all of those who are substantially affected participate in decision making and control are more decentralized. A building with a single thermostat to control the temperature of all rooms has a centralized heating system. Delegation is a shift from the central thermostat to a separate thermostat in each room.

Delegation will increase the costs of additional equipment, for example, more thermostats and/or memory registers and recall facilities. It may also improve responsiveness to local variations in intake at the same time that it may increase overall inadequacies in performance. In a centralized school, all students may be evaluated by the headmaster. Delegating this task to the homeroom teachers adds to their burdens. Hence more of them may be needed if the same teaching services are to be provided. That increases costs. But the evaluation will be based on more intimate contact—closer communication links—between the evaluators and the students, making this service more responsive. On the other hand, it will be less uniform and there is some risk that less capable homeroom teachers will evaluate less competently than the headmaster.

An overall gain of delegation is the value of the delegators' time that it frees. It enables the organization, as a whole, to perform functions and services it could not do before in addition to performing previous functions more efficiently by decreasing costs and/or error rates.

The problem of primary concern in this chapter is to determine how far delegation should proceed. We consider it desirable to delegate until the costs of more equipment transferred downward and inadequate overall performance begin to exceed the value of increased responsiveness and the value of the time liberated for higher-level delegators.

This problem arises in administrative decentralization of schools, for example. For school policy governance, it has been proposed (Havighurst, 1971) to delegate substantial responsibility to local community groups. Advisory school community councils were to be organized by school principals, with members named by the PTA (Parent-Teacher Association) and other parent and community groups. Funds for development, operation, and supervision of educational programs that do not violate constraints were to be allocated. A basis for evaluating such proposals, however, does not exist.

6.1 CONTROL, DELEGATION, AND PARTICIPATION: THE NOTION OF A RESPONSE MACHINE

To obtain a clearer conceptualization of "delegation" and "control," it is useful to reconsider a service organization modeled as an "if-then" machine, M as in section 1.3.7. Inputs or requests to M are responded to with outputs or responses. Inputs must be recognized and sorted into categories. This requires storage of either data about previous inputs or of programs that regenerate them so that the similarities and differences between two inputs can be determined. Generating outputs requires that decisions be made. Delegation of resources is the increase in response variety of each of the service units and the decrease in request variety for each of the service districts or constituencies (Ashby, 1952).

We regard an organization from two points of view. First, we see it as a single functional unit, M, immersed in an environment, E. M and E together constitute our universe of discourse, the "world." At any time, this world is in some state, s, a member of a very large set of possible states. A state can be described by a multitude of variables. The organization senses certain aspects of such states and may take actions aimed at *changing them*. Each state has a certain utility to the "world," which takes account of both its utility to individual clients, who pass between E and M, and its utility to M and E more generally. It is M's task to analyze each state and determine an output that maximizes the total net utility of the next state thus codetermined by the current state and M's action within the allowed constraints.

M is an "if-then" machine. If the condition of the "world" is s, then M responds with service, r, according to a function characterized by the set of all such s-r input-output pairs. Inputs or requests for service may be analyzed into subrequests. Thus the surgeon's client, having made an appointment, presents himself or herself together with a possible complaint. His or her presence, a complaint, or a presenting symptom

6.1 Control, Delegation, and Participation / 171

and X-rays may be four components of the request, and they are related in that each refers to the other three. Subrequests may also be related to subservices.

Unless all these relations are satisfied, it may not be possible to render services in a way that is appropriate and satisfactory for s. A coordinator, therefore, is supplied with a list of subservices, subrequests, and explicit relations that are required to hold. The coordinator must first interpret the relation so that he or she can specify some operations to be performed in order to check if the relation is satisfied. The relation might be specified by: "Anesthesia and opening the chest to reach a cyst on the lung is necessary for adequate removal (r) in response to need (s)." Suppose that surgery were so specialized that one specialist was responsible for only anesthesia, another only for incisions, yet another for retractions, and so on. A coordinator would then have to see to it that both an anesthetist and two surgeons are available to work on the same client at the same time and that their tasks are ordered according to the situation.

Secondly, we see M as a communication and control net of agents or submachines, denoted by A. The submachines perform more specialized operations and certain relations must hold among certain outputs and inputs. One such relation is that specified operations by certain submachines must be completed before the functioning of certain other submachines can begin. Another relation specifies which submachines must operate simultaneously. These component submachines or participating agents are classified into sorters, diagnosticians, schedulers, operators, checkers, coordinators, strategists, and managers. Like M itself, each agent is attuned to receive some of the information about the state. A particular sorter, for example, may be responsible for monitoring seismic signals from a particular area, the heart rate of a patient, or the deployment of troops in a particular sector. The output may be (1) *a general alarm*, (2) *no alarm at all*, or (3) *a local alerting message*. The latter would be accompanied by the selection of one or more agents in M to be alerted, a tentative judgment of significance and complexity, and a message that is a filtered version of the sorter's inputs to be passed on.

6.1.1 The Sorter's Problem. A sorter does three things. First, he or she sorts. This means recognition according to prespecified criteria and involving no further information processing. Second, he or she deals with anticipated problems. This involves continuous, periodic, or random sampling of selected attributes of the state: the monitoring of indicators or crucial variables. Each possible value of these indicators is anticipated, and prerecorded decision procedure specifies how the agent is to respond in every anticipated contingency. Third, he or she deals with critical situations that are unanticipated. There is a prerecorded plan of action. The only two characteristics by which the sensor-sorter "recognizes" such a state is that it is strikingly unusual, different from anything familiar. A conservative strategy is to assume such situations to be dangerous until evidence to the contrary has been obtained. The sorter issues a general alarm. One possible response is a standard "panic reaction" or general mobilization designed to cope with "any" contingency. This may, in fact, be irrelevant and inappropriate to the situation that occurred, but it might buy the time needed for a more accurate assessment and formation of a novel response strategy. The optimal strategy is probably characterized by "kindness and caution."

A continuum rather than a sharp boundary exists between situations that are predictable and those that are not. The essence of the transition between these two types of states lies in the notion of a class of states. Information about states received by agents is incomplete and not 100 percent accurate. It is, in principle, impossible for an agent to be sure that the exact state that was encountered once has recurred.[1]

A sorter may select a diagnostician and/or other agents to whom to send an alerting message. A recipient either takes the responsibility to respond, transfers it to another agent, or does neither. This procedure is repeated until the state changes and the process repeats, starting with the new state. If all goes well in the short run, the new state will be as much of an improvement, that is, an increase in utility[2] over the previous one, as is possible, and it will have been the result of a response designed to bring about the state. If all goes well in the long run, the cumulated sum of utilities of all the states encountered is as close to the maximum as it could be.

The more decisions the sorter has to make and the larger the number of alternatives, the greater is the required information-processing and storage capacity. If storage or processing capacity is inadequate and the agent does not refer the decision to a qualified decision maker, the agent is likely to err or make an inadequate decision. If the agent could and should make the decision because he or she is neither over- nor underqualified, the agent can still err by referring it to someone else inappropriately.

Each decision maker requires material facilities to store and process the information necessary to fulfill the task adequately. To keep the discussion simple, we shall refer henceforth only to facilities for storage or memory, leaving the questions of information-processing capacity for a separate study. In a hierarchical organization, we then ask, how should memory capacity best be distributed among its several levels?

To be *responsible* is to be subject to sanctions for the outcome of one's actions and decisions. Usually an agent subject to sanctions for the outcome of a decision is also supposed to have had some causal influence over it, that is, some power to make this particular outcome more or less probable.

If each agent serves in many roles, they all can coordinate the schedule themselves up to a point at which the load is too great. We would call the situation short of this limit completely *decentralized* with respect to hierarchies. As the load grows, such a decentralized organization would either begin to function chaotically, begin to form a hierarchical structure, or fragment into smaller and less completely decentralized organizations, each dealing with a share of the load. Possibly these fragments resulting from the third course may not be entirely independent but can collectively coordinate and schedule themselves as well. Thus, the same overall degree of partial decentralization—estimated in accordance with the procedure outlined in Chapter 2—could be nearly maintained even if the load increases, though the number of hierarchical levels increases. Here, a set of decentralized "fragments" are themselves units in a larger decentralized grouping of such units. The larger group may, once again, be viewed as units in yet larger decentralized aggregates.

An organization is *delegationally decentralized* to the extent that any of a large number of low-level agents could deal adequately with any problem. In a tight organization, by contrast, each decision would be channeled to just one agent who had exclusive jurisdiction to make it. In a highly centralized organization, this exclusive agent would be at a high level in the hierarchy. Clearly, a decentralized organization is more redundant and hence more costly, but it is less vulnerable to error and fluctuations in load.

6.1.2 The Policymakers' Problems. The entire discussion up to now dealt with requests for short-run service initiated by clients, but not with longer-range policy questions. These may be initiated by agents at higher levels of the organization. Such policies may involve other agents and clients who may or may not participate in the relevant decisions.

We consider three kinds of participation: (1) other agents are informed but not consulted;[3] (2) other agents are invited to advise as well; (3) other agents can vote and share in making the decision with some degree of weight attributable to their contribution.

174 / Delegation and Control

An agent can participate in a decision if he or she is responsible for the decision or for the information that is necessary for it. This includes the possibility of control or delegation but not referral. An organization is *participationally decentralized* if the information input channels and/or the decision input channels are numerous. This will be analyzed in greater detail later in this book. An agent can contribute general informational input or specific decisional input. The latter is authoritative in the sense that it represents a share in the authority of the decision-making body.

Extreme decentralization of memory and input channels may result in an overfragmented organization, that is, an organization incapable of action, or no organization at all. In such cases, the cost of providing services at a specified performance level may be very high. In compensation, each client may have his or her own highly responsive and custom-tailored service organization.

Extreme centralization of memories and input channels may result in a rigid organization, capable of performing well only for certain clients and services. While the costs of providing services at the same specified performance level as in the extremely decentralized case is lower, such an organization may not be as responsive to the needs of all its clients.

6.2 ORGANIZATIONAL PATTERN MAINTENANCE: NATURAL CONTROL MECHANISMS SHAPE STRUCTURE

Before studying normative questions of how to design and change organizations toward or away from decentralization according to rational criteria, we wish to examine some of the existing mechanisms that maintain organizational structures as they are. How a large organization best controls its activities or solves its problems may depend on the incentives to managers for doing what will optimize the net worth of the organization.

Arrow (1964) has formulated the problem as follows. The organization tries to maximize an objective function, that is, achieve a set of goals common to its members; each of the members has objectives of his or her own, each member can make decisions within a certain scope constrained by the decisions of others and the organization's external environment, and communicate some, but not all, of his or her observations about the workings of the organization.

How do the members manage to act according to operating rules and to persuade others to act in accordance with these rules so as to

6.2 Organizational Pattern Maintenance / 175

maximize the organization's objective function? The literature on administrative decentralization has recently become very large and it is expanding quickly (Furniss, 1974). It has been applied to large corporations, a variety of municipal service organizations, legislatures, economic systems, and so on. Business corporations have been concerned with this issue since at least the major steps toward decentralization taken by General Motors and IBM (Rubenstein, 1964). Nonetheless, some top-level businessmen have continued to think that orders must arrive and be enforced from above.

Lower-level managers are expected to provide higher levels with information needed to detect violation of orders and other input to top-level decision making. Yet, they face a dilemma. Channeling up all the information is costly to the sender, not only in effort and time but also in risking actions counter to his or her interest, and it may swamp the upper-level manager enough to impede his or her decision making. (On this last point, see Simon, in Greenberger, 1962). On the other hand, withholding information from the top incurs the risk of poor decisions. This is against the common interest. It is increasingly recognized that managers down the line and close to the clients know more about their scope of activity than higher officials. This has led to greater freedom for initiatives to the manager down the line, especially since the manager's successes and failures are more visible to the top. (For a mathematical approach to delegation, see Appendix 6.1.)

The central problem of organizational control can be formulated as follows, in an idealized example. Suppose that an organization exists for the purpose of maintaining the flow of gases in a pipe network without mishap, which means that the state of the gases must be known at various points and times. Several managers must occasionally make decisions, such as turning valves and changing settings, based on their education and experience, for the system to work normally. Each manager has incomplete and uncertain knowledge about the state of the system at all times, but the manager may request information, at a cost, from observers stationed at various points. This removes some of the uncertainty and decreases the risk of making a wrong decision. A manager may also communicate information he or she has obtained to other managers. If this internal communication system does not maintain normal gas flow, it may be due to poor execution of decision rules by individual managers. It may also be due to the inability of some managers to persuade others to act according to good decision rules. Appropriate corrections can be made until a structure that is stably self-regulating emerges.

There are, of course, varying degrees of conflict of interest between higher and lower officials. Such conflicts arise, in part, from sociocultural and behavioral factors and from factors relating to the objectives of the organization.

It is tempting to try to apply economic theory by attaching a (transfer) price to all costly transactions in order to provide incentives. The control problem then becomes finding appropriate prices so that suboptimization by each manager leads to optimization of the organization's objective function. Arrow (1964, 1974), however, has pointed out four severe limitations to applying a price system. One of these lies in the use of price for persuading others to follow decision rules. Suppose that a manager M gets payments from a higher-ranking executive, such as the company president, P that are proportional to how well he or she does (e.g., his or her profits). If P pays an amount equal to the value of M's services, then M has considerable incentive, but takes most of the risks. M would do this if the risks and uncertainties are not enormous or if his or her knowledge about the decisions in the scope of the job is vast. If the uncertainties are great and P's more general wisdom and experience in making decisions in the face of uncertainty are called for, P may pay less and thus M has less incentive. A price system, whether through a market mechanism or as a control mechanism, introduces some centralization. Moreover, for reasons of the coupling between P and M, as described above, with P being better versed to cope with uncertainty and take risks than the lower official M, there appears to be a limit to the degree of administrative decentralization. This assumes, of course, that price is a primary determinant of incentive. Propensity to take risks could, for some people, be an incentive in its own right, even if the stakes are low.

According to a "contingency theory" of Lawrence and Lorsch (1969), if the environment of a large organization is relatively dynamic and uncertain with unpredictable fluctuations in highly competitive markets and unanticipated developments in technology, an administratively decentralized structure leads to greater organizational effectiveness. If the environment is stable, a centralized structure is more effective according to that theory. It seems to us that it is not so much the extent to which the environment is static or dynamic that matters. More important is whether our collective wisdom is such that we can cope with the uncertainty by mobilizing and motivating a team of experts such as M above or whether we must let a risk taker such as P stick his or her neck out. If the environment is such that we do not have or cannot mobilize the know-how to cope with it, then we are likely to centralize.

Boseman and Jones (1974) developed an index of decentralization and one of organizational effectiveness in order to test the "contingency theory" in the face of a challenge from a test by Negandhi and

6.2 Organizational Pattern Maintenance / 177

Reimann (1972). In doing this, they considered two aspects of effectiveness: behavioral, composed of seven three-point scales, such as employee job satisfaction, absenteeism, and turnover; and economic, namely, percentage of increase in sales. Applying this index to 20 firms in competitive and noncompetitive markets, they concluded that in noncompetitive markets firms with a low decentralization index have a low *economic* effectiveness index consistent with the "contingency theory," though they have a high *behavioral* effectiveness index, as found by Negandhi and Reimann in their study of firms in India. It is by no means evident from such studies whether the "noncompetitive" market was such that the economically "ineffective" decentralized firms had no people to cope within either the competitive or the noncompetitive market while the effective and centralized firms did.

Among the problems of decentralized decision making the issue of resource allocation decisions has served as a prototype (Trinkl, 1973). The question is to explain how a central decision maker can persuade subordinates with autonomy for making decisions in their own spheres to arrive at a "best" allocation of programs within their spheres. Numerous mathematical models of resource allocation in decentralized organizations have been published (e.g., see Ruefli, 1971, for a model that assumes no global objective function as such and that replaced optimizing by satisficing, which means settling for a prespecified level of aspiration, and by a three-level model, Ackerman, 1970, concluding that there is greater decentralization in diversified than in vertically integrated corporations). Most of these models deal with optimization or suboptimization of assumed objective functions, as is customary in economics. Such objective functions, however, can seldom be specified, even inexactly, for noneconomic organizations, such as those providing various municipal services. For these organizations, often the level of policy outputs is a suitable output measure of effectiveness.

A high level of policy output is achieved through considerable coordination in planned transportation, land use, and so on. Los Angeles is said to produce a low level of policy output while Chicago is high, with Detroit and many other cities in between (Banfield, 1965). Several studies such as these suggest that centralization furthers higher levels of policy output. Several other studies, however, led to the opposite conclusion (Clark, 1968; Aiken and Mott, 1970). To resolve the contradiction, Clark (1972) proposed the notion of a public good as one that is not privately consumed or produced, such as air and water. For such goods and services, the more decentralized, the lower the organization's policy output levels. "For separable goods and services, the more decentralized the decision making structure, the higher the level of outputs."[4]

6.3 ORGANIZATION DESIGN: HOW SHOULD DECISION MAKING AND MEMORIES BE DISTRIBUTED OVER LEVELS?

We have interpreted delegation to mean the redistribution of memory throughout an organization. By memory we do not mean storage capacity but how much the agent occupying a position knows. This reflects the agent's educational background as well as experience, intelligence, specialized expertise, and, above all, ability to organize and use it. Historic memory is particularly important for policymakers at higher levels. For example, many of America's foreign policy elites, trained at Harvard, Yale, and Princeton, as well as the American public have no effective political and historic memories going back before the eighteenth century into the more than a thousand years of the world's nonhegemonic history (from 400 A.D. to 1840).

We now define the memories and numbers of agents at higher levels in the hierarchy in order to derive an expression for the utility of all these resources. We then ask how the memory allocations should be distributed to maximize the utility. Memory that is concentrated more toward the lower levels characterizes an organization in which decision making is delegated. The ratio of memory allocations at two levels can be interpreted as the delegational aspect of decentralization.

In Appendix 6.2, we present and analyze a model in which a bottom-level server services a request by relying on his or her own memory (containing, in accessible form, the server's codified experience, knowledge, etc.) or by referring the request to a superior with a larger memory. An expression for net utility was derived from considerations about the benefits from appropriate upward referral opposed to the costs of providing such backup. This expression was used to derive a ratio of the subordinate's to the supervisor's memory sizes that maximizes the net utility.

The optimal ratio is a simple measure of delegational decentralization. If it is 0, all the memory is concentrated in the supervisor, suggesting a centralized distribution. If it is 1, the memory is evenly spread over supervisor and subordinate, suggesting a decentralized structure. We found the optimal ratio to increase with increasing request loads up to a point of diminishing returns, after which the ratio levels off to the ratio of the subordinate's to the supervisor's wage rates; a trend toward equalizing pay over levels would increase the upper limit of the memory ratio, favoring delegational decentralization. It is also favored as the client's utility for the service increases but is disfavored by increases in the client's opportunity costs for the service.

These models also enabled us to derive an optimal ratio for the number of servers at the subordinate to the supervisory levels. This is the average span of control, which we found to vary—if other conditions remain equal—as the square of the client's utility for the service and as the square of the load. Trends toward higher loads and more useful services would thus favor broader or flatter, more decentralized structures.

6.3.1 Preemption and Exclusiveness. One of the most conspicuous factors reducing control of a facility, or access to a service point, is its partial or complete preemption by another actor or user. If two persons try to use the same limited facility simultaneously, they are apt to reduce the amount of effective control enjoyed by each. If they must use it in succession, they may burden one another with waiting times, uncertainty about priorities and liability for damage or misuse, and with costs of readjusting or resetting the facility for the specific needs of each user.

All such costs tend to operate in a direction opposite to the capital economies of sharing, and they tend to promote a desire for *exclusiveness* of use or access for each user. Such operational exclusiveness is often defined as privacy, ownership, or privilege in particular cultures and ideologies. Thus a wide dispersion of the ownership of capital and of decision making by a large number of individual producers and consumers sometimes has been perceived as decentralization, particularly when the invisible hand of some automatic market mechanism was expected to keep the costs of coordination low and to generate a high probability of rewarding outcomes for all.

Where these assumptions proved untenable because ownership became concentrated, coordination through automatic markets failed and special mechanisms of distribution and control had to be sought. These most often were of a more political, bureaucratic, and centralized character, whether in the form of large private corporations in conjunction with large public welfare bureaucracies or in the form of centrally planned collectivistic institutions, such as in the Communist-ruled countries.

The expression for the total utility, therefore, should contain an added term that expresses how much the client or agent values ownership and control of a system or subsystem. If this greatly exceeds how much the client values improved quality of service, then a kind of decentralization, consisting of many stand-alone units, is implied. This is particularly useful where little or no coordination in the use of such facilities is needed and capital costs are moderate or low. Bathtubs, automobiles, telephones, and toothbrushes are obvious examples. If capital costs and coordination needs are high, then the largest group of users or agents who agree that the predictability, accessibility, responsiveness, and quality of a given system meets their requirements should agree to share such a system rather than maintain their own.

6.3.2 Further Policy Considerations. One of the most important benefits of a library network organized into the kind of hierarchy we considered is that certain processing functions can be pooled. Thus, the values of some parameters, such as the one denoting utility in Appendix 6.2, would be increased to indicate the added benefits of coordinated processing done by dedicated professionals. The number of agents at the bottom level will decrease because fewer agents will be needed there to keep up with a given load. Of course, if the centralized processing is done at a higher level, the number of agents at that level must increase to accommodate the load of incoming items that are to update the various stores.

In general, concentrating capital resources improves quality and increases net utility. Thus, if the network is to utilize its potential for coordinating certain functions that can be shared, it should centralize to increase utility from this point of view.

While a number of considerations like the above favor centralization, there are others that favor decentralization. Effective control has a certain utility for its own sake. Some users would prefer a small, poorly cataloged and maintained collection of their own to the larger, better organized resources of larger libraries. Presumably what they cherish is predictability, accessibility, and responsiveness. These performance characteristics are measurable in terms of expected delay times and probabilities of success. Persons are more likely to be reinforced by experience from a system over which they have a high degree of control and a high degree of perceived predictability, accessibility, and responsiveness. This feeling may not correspond to reality, but it may govern their demands and account for some of the high degree of decentralization that is observed.[5]

If the utility of effective control for its own sake is ignored and the request load is the most influential variable on the optimal distribution of storage, the trend for the load to increase favors decentralization. If clients increasingly value speed and predictability of access so highly that they would forego the larger, concentrated resources of a system they must share with others, this favors decentralization even more. The tradeoff between the clients' need for certainty or predictability and quality of service together with the similar tradeoffs from the viewpoint at each level are probably the primary determinants of the desirable degree of decentralization in a client-centered service organization.

6.4 ORGANIZATIONAL CHANGE: WHEN DOES IT PAY TO SHIFT MEMORY DOWNWARD?

Delegation can be interpreted as a process of changing jurisdictions over requests to be serviced. *Jurdisdiction* is a name for the intended or formal allocation of classes of service cases to particular actors and levels in an organization. Its material counterpart consists in an ensemble of intake and communication channels, storage facilities for memory and recall of information, and facilities for information processing and decision making needed to cope with these cases to an adequate degree. It is these facilities and their functioning that make jurisdiction real; without them, it remains a pretense.

The allocation of these facilities among the different levels of a hierarchical organization is implied at any time in the design of an organization. Reallocating responsibility for certain requests to another service station can be done in two ways. The first is to staff the service station by a server with appropriate training and experience, that is, with what we have called memory. Having chosen the organizational structure, it is necessary to allocate specific responsibilities and authorities between headquarters and local units, plan the relations among them, and find and assign the best people available for the positions thus created (Smith, 1958, p. 157). Rather than staffing these slots by recruitment from outside the organization, which the previous section may be interpreted as dealing with, we consider a fully staffed organization and analyze the effect of transfers of staff and/or equipment within the organization. In this section we analyze some special cases of these patterns. The second pattern of reallocating responsibilities is to refer individual requests to various existing servers in the organization. This method is analyzed in the following section.

The simplest case to study is a two-level organization. For our present purpose, we need not distinguish among various stages, or take account of the other dimensions of decentralization considered so far. The key variable of interest is M_l, the number of chunks of memory characterizing the service capability of a server at level l. That is $b_l m$ in the notation of Appendix 6.2. A chunk is a string of bits that fit together as would a valuable record in the server's external files or library; the equivalent inside the servers's mind is a useful statement about how to act wisely, derived from years of accumulated experience and education and processed in association with other chunks by trained intelligence. In Appendix 6.3, we present a model enabling us to find conditions under which it pays to increase memory at the bottom level.

6.4.1 Conservative Downward Transfer of Memory. Let m be a number of bytes of memory, to be calculated, that are transferred downward from M_2 to M_1. Let L be the total input load, with L_i being the load at level i, i = 1, 2, and

$$L = L_1 + L_2$$

We now wish to compare cost C of such an organization with the cost C' that results if M_2 is replaced by $M_2 - m$ and M_1 by $M_1 + m$. We seek conditions under which $C' \leq C$ and the value of m that minimizes C'. We find that it pays to delegate if M_2 is large. This expression, as well as an expression for m, is derived in Appendix 6.4.

6.4.2 Including Conservative Shifts of Load. We repeat the above calculation, but we increase each bottom-level agent's load by fm requests per hour. Here f is the rate, in requests per hour per byte, at which his or her load is increased. This is to be calculated along with the amount of memory to be transferred. Thus, L_2 is replaced by $L_2 - fm$ and L_1 by $L_1 + fm$. Minimizing the expression[6] for the total cost gives a surprisingly simple result for m. It is

$$m = (M_2 - M_1)/2$$

The formula for f is more complex, and it is positive only when the load on the bottom-level servers should be more than half the total load, and the expected cost of the cases they treat poorly should be less than the cost of storage and retrieval.[7] The interesting result is the expression for m. It asserts that if the memory at level 2 exceeds that at level 1, which would normally be the case, then it pays most to transfer down half of the difference. Thus, if $M_2 = 2M_1$, a shift to equalize the two memories should occur. If $M_2 = 3M_1$, then $(3M_1 - M_1)/2 = M_1$ bytes should be shifted down, making $M_2 = M_1$ again.

The most cost-effective procedure appears to be to shift so as to equalize the memories of both levels if the cost of poorly treated cases is the same at both levels.

6.5 WHEN DOES IT PAY TO REFER REQUESTS DOWNWARD?

The analysis of referral networks has received some attention in the literature (Kochen and Donohue, 1976), but it has not been related to the study of decentralization and delegation. The particular idea on which the present analysis is based is that it does not pay to refer a request to a subordinate if explaining it to the subordinate takes at least as long as doing it oneself.

We find, by carrying out the analysis shown in Appendix 6.5, that it never pays to delegate downward more than one level at a time and that it pays to do this when the time to explain to a subordinate what must be done is no greater than the time to do it by oneself divided by the number of hierarchical levels.

6.6 OVERALL CONSIDERATIONS

Our analytic considerations[a] have led us once again to the subsidiarity principle, which recommends that, whenever possible, decisions should be delegated downward to the lowest level where they can be adequately made. But the implications go beyond this principle, which in itself proposes no change in the distribution of resources. Rather, they suggest a shift toward greater equality in the distribution of the resources (i.e., memories that cumulate, organize, and make available experience, judgment, and knowledge) needed to make such decisions. In other words, forces that favor minimization of total costs to society, and to the clients of service organizations in particular, tend to favor delegational decentralization not only in terms of jurisdiction but also of resources.

A number of moves toward administrative decentralization have actually been made in American municipal governments since the middle of the twentieth century. This meant primarily an expansion of management at the district or neighborhood levels or attempts at delegating decision-making responsibilities to district officers. In the literature this has been called "*devolution.*" It sometimes also meant the assignment of additional activities to civil servants operating in neighborhoods (Nordlinger, 1972). Have such shifts actually occurred? In New York City, of five municipal agencies in which such delegation was planned, only one showed a major shift in a management function, and this shift was in interagency communication (Yin, Hearn, and Meinetz, 1974). Central headquarters retained major decision-making responsibilities for such functions as budget and personnel allocations, priority setting, and information gathering.

The initial aims of decentralization in New York in 1971 were to improve service delivery. The idea was to integrate services horizontally at the same time that responsibilities were delegated vertically. Each sanitation superintendent, police precinct captain, or parks foreman was to have enough power to act autonomously within his or her own agency as if this person were the commissioner for his or her own neighborhood. At the same time district boundaries were to be aligned so that all agencies served the same set of districts, with coordination of the agencies' activities.

While horizontal interagency communication and coordination increased as of 1973-1974, little delegational decentralization was found. This may have been due to lack of sufficient power at the district level. Our analysis would lead us to suggest that the total costs to society of delegational decentralization would have been less than those that actually resulted. The financial condition of New York City in 1974 would tend to support this suggestion. If a district manager were not given or did not have enough power to effect delegational decentralization, then it occurred at a cost. Similar considerations have been published in studies based in other cities and other services (e.g., Ardell, 1972; Macy, 1970).

The recommendation of the New York study to reverse the two phases in decentralization strategies and develop organized citizen participation first, with delegation second, leads into the next chapter in which we examine the concept and effects of participation in more detail.

Chapter 7

Decentralization and Political Power

7.0 INTRODUCTION

All service systems need social and political power. They need it to overcome obstacles, reach clients, maintain open channels of communication and transactions, mobilize and deploy resources, win compliance and support, and keep their own organization viable against disturbance and destruction. They need power as an instrument to perform these and similar tasks and generally to perform the class of services to which they are committed.

But such systems also may be organized and structured so as to pursue increases in their own power as an end in itself. Often, the motive for centralizing is primarily someone's urge to maintain or increase power. Machiavelli suggested centralization as positive and decentralization as negative reinforcement for a ruling prince.

In discussing the relations between decentralization and power, it is useful to distinguish between power to compel and power to prevent or deter. To compel people to pay taxes, more power, and hence often a centralized organization, will be necessary. Merely to deter people, for example, from theft, a more decentralized form of power may suffice.

Service systems also can be influenced by outside power, and they in turn are likely to impinge upon the distribution of power and other

186 / *Decentralization and Political Power*

values among the various groups, organizations, strata, and classes of the society in which they operate.

Power needs to be supplemented by other mechanisms that prevail in a service organization. Mechanisms that keep the organization together are market mechanisms, habitual compliance supplemented only by coercion, and cooperative mutuality and voluntary collaboration, as in the case of charity. Different service organizations employ different mixtures of these mechanisms.

As service systems seek power, influence power, and are influenced by it, their components, subsystems, and personnel do the same. They, too, may limit themselves to the power they need to fulfill their service functions. They may seek power for other purposes or as a value in itself. And they, too, may have an impact on the distribution of power within and outside the service system.

What is the nature of this power that is so pervasive in almost all service situations? We shall first discuss the general concept of power and, after that, the ways in which patterns of power and patterns of decentralization affect each other.

7.1 POWER: CLARIFICATION OF THE CONCEPT

7.1.1 Based on Compliance. Power can be seen as a limited asymmetrical two-way relationship between human actors. The simplest notion of political power defines it as the *probability to prevail* in a conflict. The notion of "prevailing" implies, in turn, that each of the clashing sides or parties has a program of its own that, if executed, would be partly incompatible with that of the adversary. *"To prevail,"* therefore, means to continue carrying out one's own program and overriding one's rival when execution of both programs is impossible. If an actor has already become committed to a program but has not yet carried it out completely, the not-yet-executed rest of such an already adopted program may be called the *intention* of the actor who has become committed to it (Miller and Chomsky, 1963, p. 486).

To define this concept further, consider two power holders whom we call *controller* and *respondent,* each committed to his or her own program, respectively. By a *program* we mean an imagined or recorded sequence of actions governed by "if-then" rules to be carried out, one at a time, until a final act takes place, according to a stopping rule (Miller, Galanter, and Pribram, 1960; Miller and Chomsky, 1963). The level of specificity and precision with which these actions and rules are

7.1 Power: Clarification of the Concept / 187

prerecorded varies greatly and is constantly subject to change. Underlying a program is a set of beliefs implying that execution of the program will lead the power holder who is committed to the program to a state he or she greatly prefers to his or her present state (Kochen, 1971b).

By the *will* of the controller or of the respondent, we mean the fixing of that intention by filtering out all messages incompatible with it after it has been formed (Deutsch, 1963; 1974).

A person has total power over another if, whenever the controller and respondent each specify different actions at the same time, the action specified by the controller is taken, but only after the respondent knows the controller's intention and will. The respondent may know this very directly from the controller's acts that force compliance by superior strength, or less directly from the respondent's voluntary anticipation of the controller's perceived power and will (Morgenthau, 1948; Friedrich, 1963). In intraspecies animal contests where the prize is often reproductive advantage, sheer force is seldom used. Displays that signal which contestant intends to endure longer are common (Smith, 1974).

7.1.2 Based on Control. This notion of power is similar to Dahl's (1968) and it is used in discussions of decentralization (e.g., Nordlinger, 1972). Here, the controller has "power" over the respondent if the controller "controls" the latter's behavior or evokes certain responses from him or her, while the respondent does not control the controller's behavior in that sense. This kind of dependence has been interpreted as a version of causality, though a correlation analysis may be more appropriate. The latter would treat the controller's behavior as a random variable (e.g., the amount of insulin recommended for a randomly chosen patient) that is expressed as a function of such other random variables as the larger environment of the controller and respondent, the controller's past behavior, the respondent's past behavior, the interaction of the controller and the respondent in the past, and a pure noise factor. If the controller's behavior is assumed to be a *linear* function of such other factors, one can determine how much of the variance in the controller's behavior is accounted for by each of these factors and obtain the extent of the respondent's dependence on the controller, the autonomy of each, and the extent of their interdependence. The controller's power over the respondent is then the extent to which the latter's behavior is accounted for by the controller's or by their interaction. Conversely, the respondent's power over the controller is the extent to which the latter's behavior is accounted for by the respondent's or by their interaction. Presumably, the controller's power over the respondent is, in general, not equal to the respondent's power over the controller.

This adaptation of Dahl's notion of power can be viewed as a refinement of the notion based on intention and will. We describe the controller's behavior by a program P_C. This is a function that assigns to time t an action $P_C(t)$ by C (the controller). Then we can restate the preceding discussion in terms of the conditional probability, $P_C(t)$ = Prob $(P_C(t)/F)$, and similarly for $P_R(t)$, where F stands for conditions specified by values of the various factors believed to "determine" or "cause" or "control" $P_C(t)$ and $P_R(t)$. Since our discussion of the "control" version of power included in the interaction between the respondent and the controller in general terms, we may interpret it to include the communication of intention and will from the controller and the respondent and vice versa.

7.1.3 The Limited Asymmetry of Power. If the controller's behavior were accounted for by the respondent's behavior to the same extent that the respondent's behavior is accounted for by the controller's, there would be no reason to call them "controller" and "respondent." A genuine power relationship is, however, asymmetrical. The extent to which the respondent's behavior is accounted for by the common environment is less than the extent to which the controller's behavior is accounted for by that environment. The part of the respondent's behavior devoted to transactions with the controller is larger than that of the controller. The extent to which the respondent's behavior is autonomous—accounted for by his or her own past behavior—is, in general, less than the corresponding extent for the controller.

Thus, the controller devotes only a relatively small fraction of his or her time and energy to dealing with the respondent, while the latter must allocate to the same transactions a substantially larger portion of his or her time and energy. If the ratio of the controller's power over the respondent to the respondent's power over the controller exceeds 1, generally, so will the ratio of the controller's autonomy to the respondent's autonomy.

The asymmetry is limited, however. The relationship is not entirely one way. The respondent does control the controller's behavior to some extent. The controller must commit some of his or her time and energy to maintaining power over the respondent.

Finally, both the controller and the respondent are subject to the power of third actors in their environment, albeit to different degrees; and even their autonomous actions include the effects of random errors that they cannot control, although again to different extents.

7.1.4 Gross vs. Net Power. The gross power of the controller is the total amount of behavioral change that he or she can impose directly on the respondent. But since the controller in turn is subject to some direct power exercised by the respondent, the *net power* of the controller over the respondent is the difference between the two gross powers operating in opposite directions. The corresponding net power of the respondent and the controller is the same difference but with a negative sign. These calculations assume, to be sure, that 1 percent of the controller's output is equivalent to 1 percent of the respondent's, since we are here comparing only the percentage changes that each actor can impose on the repertory of behaviors available to the other. From the point of view of a third party, of course, every 1-percent change in the extent of, say, the controller's repertory may be twice or several times more important than any such 1-percent change in the ensemble of actions available to the respondent.

7.1.5 The Power of Third Parties and the Environment. As long as we think of power only as a relation between the two parties, we are likely to overlook another set of relationships that may be equally or more important to each of them—namely, their relationships with any and all third-party actors and with the larger social and political environment. Shifts in relative power between two German democratic legislators were not the most important thing that happened to them in early 1933 when Hitler took power in Germany. Nor would a quarrel about a disputed cabin assignment have proved to be the most important problem for two passengers of the *Titanic* when it struck an iceberg and sank with many victims in 1913. Similarly moot might be the question of which of two great powers could "prevail" in nuclear warfare.

In terms of game theory, power contests are too often seen as zero-sum games between two parties, instead of more realistically as a variable sum game in which both rivals can also win or lose against a third party, which may be called "the bank," or "fate," "nature," or "the environment" (Rapoport, 1960, pp. 166–179; Rapoport and Chammah, 1965, pp. 9–30).

Beyond Dahl's notion, referred to above, power relations may go beyond the circle of intrahuman affairs. The amounts, gains, and losses in the "power over nature" exercised by human actors remains meaningful in political and social science. Increases in the power of the environment over an actor can be measured operationally in terms of the increase of that portion of the actor's behavior that can be predicted simply from a knowledge of his or her environment, somewhat as the course of a piece of driftwood can be predicted from knowledge of the stream. Conversely, an increase of an actor's power over the environment could be at least estimated in terms of percentage increases in the domain and scope of the actor's repertory of behavior, taking his or her earlier, narrower repertory as a base.

Thus it is possible for an actor respondent to remain subordinate to the power of the controller, while at the same time greatly increasing his or her power over the tangible environment. The American colonies during much of the eighteenth century increased their power over the New World while still remaining subject to British power. Another way of describing the class of such situations is to say that the American colonies between 1725 and 1775 grew only moderately in actual power vis-à-vis Britain. But they increased greatly in power resources and hence in the potential power available to them—a potential that they then turned to an ever greater extent into actuality from 1775 onward.

Such power resources were then, and are now, a distinct fundamental dimension of power—but not the only one. In the context of a game theoretic formulation, the power of someone in a legislative body or committee has been defined as this person's chance of being pivotal, that is, critical to the success of a winning coalition (Shapley and Shubik, 1954; Riker, 1962). This does not take into account prestige or moral influence. But it does make possible the calculation of how often this person is pivotal and analysis of the distribution of power. Any scheme for distributing power either leads to this measure of power or to logical inconsistency.

7.1.6 Power vs. Authority. The discussion of power so far has dealt with it as if one person were controlling others and his or her ability to get them to comply with his or her will were an end in its own right. But a person exercises power not *solely* for the joy of controlling or imposing his or her will upon others: a person also wants to attain certain ends—noble or base—and usually *needs* the help of others to attain these ends. He also may not *trust* others to perform certain needed tasks as well as or the way he believes they must be done unless he controls their performance. If one person attains an end without the help of others that another person attains only by imposing his or her will on others, their substantive power in respect to that end will be as equal or different as their probabilities of success, even though the second person may have greater political power over other people.

Authority is primarily a property of sources of messages in relation to certain receivers. It gives such sources greater weight in the decision processes of these receivers, to some extent, regardless of the content of these messages. They might be given lesser weight if they came from another, less "authoritative" source. Shakespeare's King Lear remarks that a dog's bark is taken more seriously when the dog is a watchdog: "a dog is obeyed in office"—that is, in an authority role.

The controller has authority over the respondent for the attainment of his or her intended goal if the controller is *allowed* to execute a class of programs including P_C and *disallowed* to execute programs in another class. This authority is legitimized by a third party that may include the respondent. Thus, if the controller exerts power over the respondent with the respondent's consent, the controller may still have authority, but not from the respondent. Finally, the controller may have such authority, not in the eyes of the respondent, but in those of some third party X.

Power and authority may be independent, though a powerful person can sometimes secure, or seem to secure, authority better than one who is powerless. The idea of consent and allowing someone to execute a program is rooted in the idea of freedom and free will. If the respondent *says* that he or she consents to the controller's control or to subordinate his or her will to the controller's because the controller coerces the respondent to say this by threats of sanctions supported by the controller's powerful resources, then the respondent may not have given his or her consent freely. In that case, the controller does not have authority over the respondent from the respondent; it is not legitimate power. On the other hand, the boundary between consent that is given freely and consent given under shades of subtle coercion is quite fuzzy. The controller may manipulate the respondent's fears deviously to persuade the respondent that he or she is consenting freely, and such manipulative skills are part of the controller's power.

A different operational test of authority consists of the association of either the source or the content of a message with the internally held notions of "right" and "wrong" of its recipient. The latter has learned these notions earlier, most often in childhood, and they have become part of the recipient's personality. Freud called them the superego; earlier writers often spoke of conscience, which, as an ancient Greek sophist remarked, determines our actions when we believe that nobody is watching us. Acting contrary to such authoritative orders would then mean to violate one's conscience or superego, and it would be likely to be followed by painful internal self-punishment or intrapsychic conflict.

A major leverage for ensuring a concordance between power and authority derives from the resources and support necessary to maintain power. It is those who supply these resources who can legitimize power. Yet, power usually cannot control all kinds of resources. To execute some steps in a program requires a psychic commitment, and people's minds are so complex and combinatorial that they cannot be controlled completely and dependably from the outside over longer periods of time (Deutsch, 1966). Major programs in large organizations seldom get carried out unless there is consensus and commitment among the key people. Otherwise, such key people can undermine or sabotage the entire program. It is such a core of key people who legitimize their superior's power. Their commitment to a common cause is the most precious resource that a power holder cannot always control.

Arrow (1974) has argued that authority gives an organization its ability to make better judgments about how to allocate limited resources than do its individual members. An organization can collect and sift information in a way that takes into account the social effects of individuals' action, either through consensus—that is, any reasonable and accepted means of aggregating individual interests—or by authority. Consensus requires agreement on a level above the level of short-term self-interest of individuals. When that does not occur, "convergent expectations" cause individuals to accept authority to provide information and decisions for collective action that enables individuals to more fully realize their basic values, despite divergent tastes and moods.

Decentralization has been distinguished from "deconcentration" (where decisions are made centrally but their implementation is dispersed and delegated) by stressing that agents are primarily directed by, and responsible to, the political subsystem of the agents (Lundquist, 1972). Politics has been defined as the authoritative allocation of value (Easton, 1965), and this definition has been applied to administrative control. In our view, decentralization allocates more than value. It reallocates time, attention, service capabilities, participation, location, specialization, input and output channels, power, control, responsibility, and authority. This reallocation process is authorized by someone at the same time that it shifts authority from some groups to others. Theories of authority may be usefully related to the further elaboration of decentralization as governed by the authoritative reallocation of authority among other values.

7.1.7 Authority vs. Autonomy. Commands sent over a control path and messages transmitted through a communication channel are, or should be, acknowledged, interpreted, evaluated, and possibly acted upon. Evaluation requires checking the authenticity of the transmission and the reliability of the source as well as its authority to issue that command or communication. Finding that a sender is authorized to send a message does not automatically "obligate" the receiver to obey or believe its content regardless of the receiver's own evaluation of that content. The order to enforce affirmative action, to ensure that there is at least one woman and minority member in every list of candidates for an open position, may come from the head of the organization, but biased recipients of that order usually can find ways to subvert it if they wish.

Of course there are several mechanisms that keep authority and power together. (1) Recipients of a message may not have the ambition, energy, interest, intelligence, and background to question it. (2) Those with authority build up a good track record of having sent useful, reliable messages and wise orders most of the time, and recipients have come to trust them. Thus, under stable conditions, the authority of a person tends to adjust itself according to this person's record in the "memories" of other persons. (3) Obeying the orders or accepting the word of an esteemed authority reinforces the recipient by making the recipient feel secure, while the opposite leads to fear or guilt.

Nonetheless, as discussed earlier, every person's behavior is to some degree autonomous. Autonomy, like authority or power, may become a value in its own right. Complying with authority reduces the costs of checking the content of orders and communications but increases the expected cost of error. Since there may be more than one authority, it also increases costs if there are inconsistencies among messages with the resulting confusion and dilemmas.

7.1.8 Power and Responsibility. A person (respondent) is responsible to another person (controller) to attain an intended goal by the execution of a program P_R if: (1) the controller expects the respondent to carry out P_R; and/or (2) provides positive reinforcement to the respondent for carrying it out; and (3) negative reinforcement for failure to execute P_R or for carrying out certain other programs. The controller also specifies limits on what kinds of actions in the respondent's program the controller will tolerate. One mechanism by which the respondent manifests his or her responsibility to the controller is that of *guilt*. We may view the respondent's feeling of guilt as the expectation of undelivered deprivations or sanctions due to faults or errors by the respondent in executing the expected program.

It is possible for the respondent to be responsible for a program to the controller without having the power (e.g., without adequate resources) and without the authority to carry it out. This would place the respondent in a double bind: the respondent is frustrated if he or she tries to carry out the program, for he or she cannot and may not do so, but he or she is punished for not trying to carry it out. To escape this dilemma, the respondent may try to replace this program by one he or she can and may execute, with a slight shift in definition of responsibility. The respondent needs a certain amount of strength or power to do this. Lacking this may lead to progressive loss of psychic integrity.

The importance of who interprets and perceives responsibility, authority, and power, as well as the differences between such interpretations, becomes apparent now. First, we need to distinguish between what the controller expects of the respondent and what the controller *says* he or she expects of the respondent. Secondly, we should distinguish between the above two and what the respondent thinks the controller expects of the respondent. Finally, all three may differ from what the respondent expects of him or herself, from what the respondent thinks he or she should do. The respondent, as well as the controller, may or may not be aware of such differences. Nonawareness may be the cause of malaise that is very prevalent in organizations. Awareness may lead to planned conflict and confrontations, resolved by escape, negotiation, surrender, or victory.

Ideally, if a person is given responsibility, there is an appropriate degree of power and authority that this person should also have if the intended goal is to be reached. Table 7.1 shows the consequences of various combinations.

7.1.9 Power and Influence. Power and influence are both key concepts of political science and vital to any political analysis of decentralization. Power and influence are nearly identical concepts. The controller influences the respondent by *persuading* the respondent to follow the controller's program, to voluntarily *agree* with the controller's suggestions for action. The controller negotiates with and explains to the respondent, in the context of cooperative rather than an adversary relation. Influence is based on persuasion, explicit or im-

Table 7.1. Consequences of Various Combinations of Power, Authority, and Responsibility

Power	Authority	Responsibility	
Too little	Too little	(Too much)	Double-bind, breakdown
(Too much)	Too little	Too little	Legitimized wantoness, ruthlessness
Too little	(Too much)	Too little	Pompousness
Too much	Too much	(Too little)	Tyranny
(Too little)	Too much	Too much	Disillusionment
Too much	(Too little)	Too much	Illegitimate effectiveness

plied. It always involves the mobilizing by the influencer or controller of some memories and values of the respondent himself or herself, so that one part of the target individual's or group's decision system will be pitted against another part. Influence applies to people connected by all kinds of biological or human bonds: symbiotic, parasitic, affective, adversary, and so on. Power applies mainly to people in a relation of actual or potential contestants, or of the victor-vanquished type.

Energy-wasting power struggles often occur among people who fear that there are not resources to meet their need or greed as well as everyone else's. They occur even more often because some power seekers have, as a personality trait, a need to dominate. If they find, as their partners, people with a complementary need to be dominated, a stable lock-in nonconflict situation may take place, even if it is sociopathological. Both in power struggles and such dominance-submission hierarchies or communes, energy often is diverted from where it could be more creatively applied.

Influence, on the other hand, is often the currency that makes social processes work toward helping people attain what they value. Intellectual influences nourish and structure the growth of knowledge. Friendships help people obtain jobs, hearings from people in power, votes, advice, and so forth. "It is not what you know but whom you know that helps you succeed" is not all pejorative. People with great wisdom often also know and are known by a great variety of people. Among these are also included people with even greater wisdom.

7.2 ASPECTS OF POWER

The following eight features should be specified when a person's power is described.

7.2.1 Means of Power or Resources. These are devices that can be used to produce positive or negative sanctions—that is, rewards or penalties for other actors. They include material facilities and supplies, such as arms, food, and productive installations; numbers of supporters, such as partisans, voters, soldiers, officials, and employees; social and economic facilities, such as property, gold, money, and credit; and intangible but observable assets, such as knowledge, goodwill, skill, motivations, and loyalties of both the actors and their supporters (Morgenthau, 1948, 1973; Knorr, 1957, 1973). They also include the kind of psychic commitments previously mentioned. The power resources of a service agency include its equipment and personnel, skills and knowledge of the latter, and the reserve resources that the agency can call upon in case of need.

7.2.2 Base and Scope Values. This is a value system for ordering and ranking the outcomes controlled by the controller, but needed or desired by the respondent. Such valued outcomes have been classified under eight headings that can be listed roughly in declining order of competitiveness: deference, rectitude, power, wealth, well-being, affection, skill, and enlightenment (Lasswell and Kaplan, 1950; Deutsch, 1966, 1970; Gurr, 1970). There are at least three other ways of categorizing values. One, from Maslow (1954), lists five categories: self-actualization; materialism (including prestige); belongingness; security; survival. Another, from Foa (1971), lists: money; goods; status; love; services; information.

If the respondent is, or feels, deficient in any of these values, and if the controller controls some possible supply of them, then the respondent may be motivated to give up to the controller some units of another set of values that the controller controls. We call that second set a *scope value*. By means of controlling base value i, the controller has power over the respondent in regard to scope value j. Any of the eight value categories can function either as a base value or as a scope value.

The result is a network of quasi-exchange relationships, based on the specific relative deficiencies of the respondent and the corresponding specific relative kinds of affluence of the controller. Thus, a rich individual lacking prestige may purchase directly or indirectly some title, rank, or other element of respect and deference; or an actor or organization, deficient in legitimacy, may use power or wealth in order to earn or otherwise acquire greater rectitude, or at least its appearance. The base value and scope values controlled by a service agency, vis-à-vis its clients, depend critically upon their needs and deficiencies; but its power and prestige vis-à-vis other agencies may be greater if its clients are more powerful.

7.2.3 Weight of Power. This has been discussed already; it is the change in the probability of an outcome, caused by or associated with, some actual or anticipated behavior of the controller. If the weight of power of the controller over the respondent is greater, the more improbable the compliant behavior of the respondent would have been without the controller's actual or anticipated intervention. If the weight of power of a service agency is limited, it can expect compliance from its clients in the main only in regard to things they were likely to do anyway. Commands that run counter to strong habits or desires of people require a great weight of power for influence by those who utter them, or else they are likely to be evaded or disobeyed. Thus the order of the government of India in 1976 to certain categories of persons, such as government officials, to limit the number of their children or accept either sterilization or various penalties seemed to require a greater weight of power—and to imply a greater capacity to cope with losses of political support—than the government proved able to sustain; and the 1977 elections brought about its fall.

7.2.4 Domain of Power. This has several subaspects. One is the set of persons over whom one can exercise power. Examples are the subordinates of a bureaucrat, the subjects of a state, and to some extent the clients of a service agency, insofar as it exercises markedly greater power over them than any power they have over the behavior and structure of the agency.

Another subaspect of the domain of the controller may be the geographic area over which the controller's power extends. In legal terms, the formal power of a ruler or an agency is uniform across the entire area covered by the ruler's or agency's jurisdiction. In actual terms, however, power tends to diminish with geographical and social distance, as do most transactional relationships, so that some analysts have spoken of a "loss of strength gradient" (Boulding, 1962).

Yet another subaspect of power domain is the set of intended goals requiring the execution of complex programs, vast resources, vast authorization, great responsibilities, and so on, that the controller is able to accomplish.

7.2.5 Scope of Power. This is the set of aspects of behavior of the respondent in regard to which the controller is likely to be obeyed. Highly specialized service agencies, such as survival units, are limited in the scope of their power; functionally diffuse agencies with more general competence or jurisdiction, such as governments, have a wide scope of power. The scope can be defined as a subset of the functional spaces defined in Chapter 3.

The controllable scope is related by the means or resources available to the power holder; the greater these means, the greater the power holder's scope. It would decrease, however, as the domain of power increases. The more people over whom the controller holds power, the more difficult it would be for the controller to maintain that power if these people vary greatly in their competencies.

7.2.6 Range of Power. This is the difference between the extreme positive and negative sanctions—that is, between the highest reward and the worst penalty—that the controller can deliver to the respondent, or credibly promise the respondent. This notion assumes that these sanctions can be arranged on an interval scale, or that such a ratio scale can be computed for them by a method proposed by Von Neumann and Morgenstern (1947). The range of power depends in large part on the means or resources that the controller can devote to its production. In turn, increases in the range may produce increases in the weight of power, but the relationship between these may depend in part on contingencies, such as the susceptibilities of the respondent to threats and promises. In addition, extreme sanctions applied to the respondent may have a positive or negative effect on the behavior of third-party actors in the political environment; thus extreme penalties threatened or inflicted upon the respondent may arouse sympathies and allies for the respondent, actually decreasing the weight of the controller's power over the respondent, while increasing its cost to the controller.

7.2.7 Exclusiveness of Power. This is the probability of the controller's *not* having to share with any third-party actor any decisions about severe sanctions offered to or imposed on the respondent. Together with the means and the range of the controller's power over the respondent, this exclusiveness contributes to the weight of the controller's power.

7.2.8 The Viability of Power. This is the probability of a power relationship or power pattern to survive across time and processes of external or internal change. Will power persist and grow among a particular group of actors over some relevant span of time, or will it stagnate or disintegrate? This dimension is distinct from the amount of power resources of an actor, and from the domain and weight of the actor's power at a particular moment; it can sometimes prove far more important. "How strong is this organization?" is one good question. "How likely is it to last?" may sometimes be an even better one. This point is further discussed in a later section of this chapter.

7.3 THE DISTRIBUTION OF POWER AND DECENTRALIZATION

Power may be concentrated or it may be scattered and diffused. Of two organizations that are alike along all the other dimensions of decentralization except for the distribution of power, we call *less centralized* the one in which power is *less concentrated*. The degree of

7.3 The Distribution of Power and Decentralization / 199

power diffusion thus affects the overall degree of decentralization and is in turn affected by it.

Normally, in an organization the agents at the higher hierarchical levels have greater means, more base values, larger weights, ranges, and exclusiveness of power than do their counterparts at lower levels in the hierarchy. Occasionally, a lower-level agent will show promise of ranking highly on all these aspects of power. This agent is likely to be promoted. Occasionally, too—perhaps less frequently—an agent at a high level does not rank highly on all these power attributes, either because the agent was promoted by mistake or the agent's powers waned with age, disuse, and so on. Except for such anomalies, power ought to be distributed in an organization in a way that somewhat parallels the hierarchy, $n_1, n_2, \ldots, n_\lambda$, or the salary scale, $c_1, c_2, \ldots, c_\lambda$.

If a disfavored group or class is weak on the average across the aggregate domain of a service system, but strong in some smaller region, it should gain from decentralization; and a favored group, predominant on the average but weak in some localities, should gain from policies of centralization and amalgamation. As a group over time shifts from one of these conditions to the other, its attitudes toward decentralization are likely to reverse. Weak reformers, like weak conservatives, often settle for local strongholds at least temporarily; whereas powerful reformers, like powerful conservatives, often prefer to centralize.

Thus in the United States, elite groups in metropolitan areas often have been weak in voting powers for taxes. They have favored the decentralization of local taxes and services in the direction of suburban autonomy. The same upper-middle-class strata were more influential in the field of education. They have favored centralized systems of citywide school administration that subordinated the schools in poor and/or racial minority neighborhoods to white middle-class supervision and standards.

The major efforts needed to eliminate the vast inequities pervading America's school resource distribution system (Guthrie, 1972) could go either in the direction of centralization or decentralization. As the poorer strata and the minorities gained greater power in the central cities, they demanded school and police decentralization, and through it, greater powers for their own neighborhoods. When the former "underdogs" acquired still greater power at the metropolitan, state, or federal level, they tended to become centralizers; and the formerly privileged groups now demanded decentralization, local autonomy, and the neighborhood school. In this shifting power struggle, the considerations for a service system that would provide better schools for all the children of whatever class and race often was obscured.

On a national and international level, white farmers in Rhodesia—forming only 5 percent of the population—proclaimed their loyalty to the British Crown, as long as the empire seemed associated with white supremacy; when Britain accepted nonwhite majority rule in India, Pakistan, and many parts of Black Africa, their loyalties became reversed; and in 1964 they declared their secession from the British connection. By 1978, when the separate state no longer seemed capable of securing power for the white minority as a class and racial group, some of these people had once more to look for a level of political affiliation that might satisfy their privileges in the midst of a 95-percent black majority and on a continent where by then black governments had come to predominate. Only when and where power needs are less desperate and urgent is it likely that consideration of humane, responsive, and cost-effective government will once again become a focus of political attention.

7.4 THE CONSERVATION OF POWER

It is widely believed that power gained by one person in an organization is power taken from another. Power is thus perceived as something like a fixed and limited resource in the organization, as if the sum of the powers of all people in it remains constant even if there are shifts among the people themselves. Power, thus perceived as a limited and coveted quantity, may come to be valued as an end in itself. Such perceptions may account for many of history's most intense conflicts.

Influence, treated as a synonym for power, has been viewed as the manifestation of political transactions in a formal organization. Power raises and their effects have been viewed as comparable to wage raises (Lammers, 1967). But if the total amount of power is a more effective predictor of organizational productivity and morale than hierarchical power distributions, the notion of fixed power is more appropriately replaced by one of expanding power (Kerr, 1954; Likert, 1961; Tannenbaum, 1962).

The struggle between the Palestinians and the Israelis, both of whom claim legitimate rights to the same land, is over political control or power. The conflict in 1976–1977, between Rhodesian whites holding out for at least two more years of white minority rule and blacks insisting on black majority rule in at most 12 months, was one of power. Quarrels among spouses are more often about whose will is to prevail than what is in the best interest of either or both; they are power struggles. One must prevail and the other must give in. This is the notion of the zero-sum game, or fixed-sum game, referred to above. But is this conception correct?

7.5 EFFECTS OF DECENTRALIZATION ON POWER AND VICE VERSA

Centralization can help the moderately powerful to maintain or increase their power. They do this by concentrating resources, decision making, supervision, and control. Decentralization, by dispersing resources, tends to dilute the power of the strongest. Excessive decentralization may scatter power until the service-providing units are fragmented to the point that none has sufficient strength to render adequate service.

Decentralization is in the interest of both the very weak and the locally very strong. Centralization, on the other hand, favors those in between or those in transition. According to Brzezinski, "the increased flow of information and more efficient techniques of coordination need not necessarily prompt greater concentration of power"; and "greater devotion of authority and responsibility to the lower levels of government and society" is thus made possible (Brzezinski, 1967).

On occasion decentralization has been identified with federalism (Ostrom, 1973). Federalism is said to be characterized by the sharing of functions and mutual interaction among bureaus (Haider, 1971). Woodrow Wilson felt that the more power is divided, the more irresponsible it becomes, and that the American system of government was becoming less federal and more unitary or centralized. Riker (1964) has defined federalism as a bargain between prospective national leaders and officials of constituent governments for the purpose of aggregating territory, the better to lay taxes and raise armies. Note the similarity of this definition to a definition of centralization/decentralization as "the territorial and/or functional distribution of power" (Lasswell and Kaplan, 1950). A unitary state is one in which the rule is centralized; a federal state is decentralized territorially. Ostrom takes exception to the case against federalism as something close to racism by characterizing it as rich in overlapping jurisdictions with substantial autonomy among jurisdictions, substantial degrees of democratic control within jurisdictions, and subject to an enforceable system of constitutional law. Too high a degree of federalism would involve excessive costs of decision making for small isolated communities.

The federal system stresses *shared* functions among segments of government that depend on one another. According to Haider (1971), its principal feature is the mutual interaction of national, state, and local governments to solve problems of increasing scope and complexity. There is a trend toward greater authority for the chief executives (governors, mayors, county chiefs), and also toward greater sharing in financing and administration of municipal functions at higher levels, such as county, metropolitan, state, and federal levels. Decentralization is taking place in cities not so much by formal transfers of authority as by negotiated agreements, flexible bargaining, and accommodations to pressures from mayors and organized community groups.

In our own view, some general inferences may be proposed for further investigation. If other things remain unchanged, the total amount of power in a system is likely to increase as communication channels and feedback circuits are made shorter and delays and congestion are reduced, such as in a decentralized system.

Kaufman (1963, p. 12) has suggested that the "chief single index of centralization" is the control held exclusively by central authorities in an organization. This control extends to the appointment and dismissal of employees in a business organization, as well as to the determination of conditions of employment. From the viewpoint of the employees:

> Organizations are considered decentralized when persons who occupy the formal positions of leadership are seriously restricted in these respects, and when, as a consequence, nominal subordinates owe the leaders little in the way of gratitude and are relatively immune to leadership sanctions.

In the case of service agencies, the sanctions extend beyond the employees to the clients.

Decentralization reduces the range and weight of power within the agency that may be applied by its top echelon, but it may increase the power of the agency as a whole, vis-à-vis its larger environment. Precision and control of execution and the related dimension of stability of intent are two dimensions of power that are apt to increase by decentralization. Each of the four stages of the power process are affected by these changes.

In the first stage, recognition of the object of power is circumscribed by policies of decentralization. The domain of power is restricted. However, this limitation in domain allows expansion in scope. While an orthodontist at a clinic sees fewer patients than a dentist, he or she may tend to more teeth and provide more extensive dental care, including long-range or preventive attention. The responsiveness of an agency depends on this ability to augment or adjust the scope of power exercised as pressures rise.

7.5 Effects of Decentralization on Power / 203

When we come to the recognition of a goal and formulation of a plan of action in the power process, we again see the consequences of Kaufman's observation that, in a decentralized context, intraorganizational authority is restricted and gratitude less compulsory. This will affect the extent of planning and likelihood that ambitious plans will be undertaken, for the freedom to exercise authority is restricted, as well as its expected reward.

The execution stage of the power process is the stage most affected by reductions in domain, weight, resources, or scope. Since it is not possible to administer grandiose sanctions, neither is it likely that very high costs will be incurred. Whereas bureaucracies accomplish whatever business they are about through the exercise of power, a local coordinator of activities (such as a traffic light) accomplishes its tasks through authority. The role of coordinator of affairs need not necessarily become one of manipulator or controller. Certainly there is no technological necessity for this, as has been demonstrated in the preceding chapters.

The final stage of the power process, as outlined above, is the appraisal of the effects of power, and it is the core of the argument used by many advocates of decentralization. With the domain reduced, the accessibility of power is supposed to be greater; the social distance from top to bottom of the hierarchy is supposed to be smaller than in a centralized arrangement. The informational distance between agents and clients is supposed to be reduced. Where this actually is the case, this reduction provides greater possibility for review by the public and appraisal of execution of policies. This is one aspect of responsiveness. Since the overall power of the system rests with its ability to accomplish what it sets out to do, we can see that this becomes more feasible as the acceptability of its policies increases. In other words, decentralization presents an avenue by which power can be made more legitimate and converted to authority.

The real power of the decentralized system lies in its ability to adapt and adjust to circumstances. While this seemingly derives from the material resources at its disposal, it does not provide a clear indicator of power. The real indicator of power is the system's ability to maintain itself in the face of other processes, have its way in cases of conflict, and retain a high probability of reaching its goals. This derives from the ability of the system to avoid useless expenditure of effort, at the same time managing to respond effectively when the need arises.

Such adaptability, as well as capacity for initiative and innovation, depends in large degree on combinatorial processes and on the critical selection of their results. Decentralized organizations in which each component rigidly defends its "own" jurisdiction and resources may become nearly incapable of producing any relevant new combinations. Only a high degree of *learning capacity*—the ability to change routines of behavior and to reallocate resources and facilities (Deutsch, 1975)—is likely to keep a decentralized organization adaptive, viable, and innovative.

7.6 CONCLUSIONS

As part of our stated aim in the preface, we hope to provide the reader with some clear ideas concerning decentralization. These concepts map out the realm of the possible in technological and economic terms and culminate in political implications. Let us review some of the conclusions of previous chapters to see their political relevance.

First, we found that *technological trends favor pluralization* of facilities. As mentioned above, this suggests a limited domain for each agency with concomitant shifts in power. This is modified somewhat by considering the dispersion of these agencies. We found that the number was affected by spatial unevenness of request load. Small pockets of population cannot support effective decentralization.

Similarly, when considering informational distance, we found that a system in which information is shared produces, predictably, a smaller need for pluralized communication facilities. So a common ideology or inclination to communicate imposes constraints on the proliferation of facilities. At any rate, the *domain* is restricted.

This does not preclude augmentation of *scope*, however. In fact we found that *domain gives way to scope*, once functional specialization is considered. This is one of the major conclusions of this book. We found that there are tradeoffs along the various dimensions of power. Thus, for example, congestion is not simply abolished by pluralization of facilities; it is moved to a higher level. Where previously we had problems of waiting lines, we now have problems of overloaded telephone exchanges.

One recurrent theme in the literature on decentralization is dynamic tension described as present in decentralized systems. Individual decision units have a tendency to develop incompatibilities with one another so that concerted action becomes difficult or impossible. In the face of urgent problems that demand speedy decisions, this could prove problematic without a strong central authority to decide on distribution of facilities and funds. Furthermore, inequality of power in decentralized settings may result in a power monopoly by local potentates, as was the case in English local government in the last century. The only check to the development of such a local power monopoly is the mediating power of some central authority—one that can intervene if necessary. So there exists a strong tension between the growth of regional autonomy and the need for the central power of arbitration.

In a similar view Fesler (1965) points out that language dichotomizes centralization versus decentralization. Actually, power considerations are complex and difficult to measure, especially in one dimension and in polar terms. We are dealing not with a static object but a dynamic process with ubiquitous tensions. A regime may appear extremely decentralized from one perspective, only because it is highly centralized from another. Local differences are overriden in centralized systems so that some overall policy emerges—whereas the patchwork of decentralization may be a source of incessant conflict. It may preclude the making of any decisions that affect several decentralized entities (e.g., in resource allocation). In the face of urgent problems, this "decisionlessness" may be detrimental to all. Hence a balance is required between central power of arbitration and local pressure.

Fesler states that small decentralized political entities tend to ossify. In England in the eighteenth century, self-government placed power and responsibility in the hands of local potentates, effectively eliminating popular control, despite its theoretical existence in the law books. Possibly, only large-scale solidarity can oppose this type of power imbalance in local regions, that is, central power required to moderate local money barons, warlords, and so on. His findings accord well with our stress on learning capacity, as set forth in the preceding section.

Administrative decentralization may be nullified by functional centralization necessitating reliance on information provided by a few "experts," for example, monied interests, exemplified by corporation executives who find their way onto congressional committees time and again because of their experience and capacity to exercise power. Thus central authority sometimes allows constituents to vote freely on agenda items that they have no power to alter because only the expert has the means to draw up the agenda.

Conditioning further nullifies the effects of administrative decentralization. In fact decentralization "works" where the decisions of local administrators are fairly predictable and conform with overall policy.

As Carl Friedrich (1963, p. 667) puts it:

...it is essential that decentralizing patterns of the distribution of power be considered as dynamic, rather than static, as continually evolving and oscillating between greater unity and diversity. . . .

Giving due weight to these considerations, we still find no support for the cynical view that centralization and decentralization depend wholly on the power of those interested in one or the other of these arrangements. Polemarchus of Plato's *Republic* already expressed the view that there was little more to society than naked power. Even earlier, Thucydides, in the Peloponnesian War, recounts how an Athenian ambassador tells the people of Melos that in reality, "the strong do what they can and the weak suffer what they must."

Decentralization in itself will not always help the strong or the weak, or one social class or another. If industrial wage earners or the poor need swift and concentrated action, it may serve them well to centralize their efforts. But where and when they mainly need to maintain or renew their motivation and strength, decentralization may benefit them more. Conversely, privileged groups may benefit from centralization when their interests require quick and massive action, and they will do better with decentralization if a broad network of privileges is to be maintained over a long time and in many places. Hence, big northern U.S. businesses in the late nineteenth century learned to concentrate capital resources while southern conservatives or elites tenaciously defended their privileges by stressing states' rights and decentralization. Mao Tse-Tung urged his followers in the Chinese civil war to fight concentrated battles when they were strong, but to resort to guerilla warfare when they were not.

If it is important to concentrate *existing* resources at a particular spot and time, then it pays to centralize. If it is important to *create* power and resources or to continually renew them, then decentralization is likely to be better. Military history suggests that concentration of forces wins battles, but that widely based support and broad coalitions win wars.

Something similar may apply to information. Centralization may help to unify executive commands and give adequate backing to a few large projects, but decentralization may be more conducive to a wide variety of new discoveries and innovations. Perhaps the optimum balance between centralization and decentralization can be described in terms of a rank-size distribution, which in turn will vary for each class of tasks with the distribution of the most important tasks to be accomplished at a given time and place.

Chapter 8

Political Values: Participation and Equality

8.0 INTRODUCTION

A service organization interacts with many classes of participants: clients, beneficiaries, sponsors, employees, and members of the communities to which the organization belongs. They may participate in decisions and in restructuring the organization.

We discuss the role of these various participant classes by analyzing the concept of participation, which is identified as an aspect of decentralization. Then we discuss the political aspects of the various objects of our study. The probable consequences of greater participation are explored to determine which degree of participation is optimal.

8.1 POLITICAL BACKGROUND

The political theory underlying this book assumes that modern governments retain "their just powers by the consent of the governed." Hence, their legitimacy (authority) and power will depend on their ability to respond adequately to the popular demands made upon them.

We assume that ethnic, linguistic, cultural, and social uniformity facilitates centralization. According to traditional theory, strong centralization under nonuniform conditions usually would be more difficult. But centralization and decentralization coexist in many societies. The family may be decentralized but the political system may be centralized; the economy may be decentralized and the churches centralized.

We examine conditions under which participational decentralization of service organizations is preferable from the viewpoint of rationality or cost-effectiveness. Our normative statements as to what would be best, or what should be done, are formulated first and foremost from the viewpoint of the subjects or clients. But they are expected to include the interest of the community in ensuring adequate service at low cost. They also include the interest of the leaders or rulers, insofar as their power in the long run depends on their capacity to respond to the demands made upon them quickly enough and adequately enough to retain their political support.

Much of the well-known political and social theory on centralization and decentralization implies that centralization is preferable on the grounds of efficiency and that modern technology, with its jet aircraft and electronic communication, has increased the pressures toward centralization. Ellul (1954, 1965), for example, asserted that "the major impetus for centralization is the inevitable result of the conjunction of technology, modern organization, and the state." Some theories also assert, however, that decentralization is better suited to protect the values of democracy, liberty, and popular participation in decision making. "Centralization is evaluated as a negative, dehumanizing trend, at least for those who value the political participation of individual citizens. Almost in reaction, decentralization has taken on an increasingly positive meaning" (Hart, 1972, p. 604). Some theorists point out that these different views balance to some extent and that the optimal point on some more or less continuous centralization-decentralization scale must be discovered in each case; they give little further indication as to how these discoveries are to be made.

8.2 THE CONCEPT OF DECISIONAL PARTICIPATION

To define decisional participation operationally, we analyze the notion into three parts according to what the client participates in: (1) performance of the service; (2) decisions affecting the client personally; (3) service to third parties. The first two dimensions relate to the notion of autonomy (Deutsch, 1966a). The last is often strongly related to power (Lasswell and Kaplan, 1950).

8.2 The Concept of Decisional Participation / 209

The most obvious kind of participation by clients in a service is to perform the service themselves. A person can request a barber to shave him or he can shave himself. If he participates to the extreme extent of doing it himself, he still may utilize equipment that requires services, such as occasional repair, cleaning, or repurchase of the shaving apparatus. The surgeon's client must participate in the service, but the client cannot operate on him or herself. At the other extreme on the scale of participation in performing the service is the automobile owner who brings his or her car for servicing without making any contribution to the performance of the service, except paying for it. We propose to measure the degree of participation along this dimension by the *fraction of the total man-hours used to perform the needed service that are contributed by the client.*

Participation by clients in making *decisions* that affect them differs from participation in performing the service. Whether or not to have a surgeon perform a surgical operation is largely the client's decision. The surgeon may recommend it and may supply the patient with all the estimated risks, facts, and arguments enabling the patient to make a wise decision. If the patient is unconscious or otherwise unable to make a decision, the surgeon may take the decision upon him or herself in order to save the client's life. Generally, however, the patient or the patient's family is supposed to give informed consent and bear the responsibility for the decision.

The extent to which a client participates in a decision that concerns the client directly might be measured by the fraction of the total time spent on making the decision that is spent in direct communication with the client. For example, if the client is a prisoner before a 10-person parole board who consider for 30 minutes whether to release the prisoner, of which the prisoner spends 20 minutes in their presence, then the extent of participation is 20/30. Another, better way of measuring the extent of participation is to take the fraction of the prisoner's share in a vote. Thus, if the prisoner could vote on his or her release, and each person gets one vote, the extent of participation would be 1/11. If the decision were determined by the amount of bail that could be raised, then the extent of participation is the fraction of the required bail that the prisoner could raise.

The client who participates to a large extent in decisions or performance of services to meet his or her needs has a great deal of autonomy. Autonomous but incompetent clients are likely to suffer more than they benefit. Giving both prisoners in a prisoner's dilemma complete autonomy of deciding whether or not to cooperate may also cost both of them more than they gain, but for a different reason. Both gain only if they negotiate and agree on a compromise, with each giving up some autonomy in his or her own decision (see Figure 8.1).

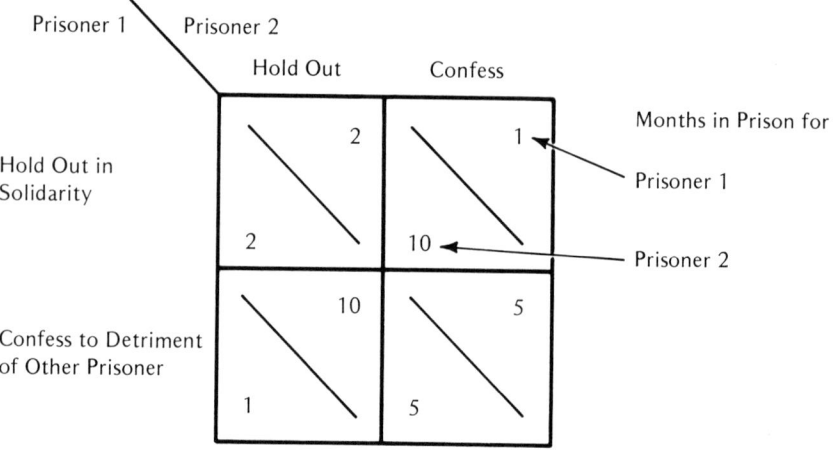

Figure 8.1. A prisoner's dilemma.

Any of the parties may also participate in performing a service for another client. It is clear how sponsors participate. But clients can participate in this way too. Passengers in a multicar collision are all clients of first-aid services, and some of them may participate in providing first aid to others. To some extent, each client is also a service provider. For some functions a given person is primarily a client, while for other functions this person is primarily a server. For some functions, the client serves primarily him or herself.

8.3 PARTICIPATION IN ORGANIZATIONAL REDESIGN

To participate in redesigning an organization is to exert far more influence than merely to participate in decision making within it. An organization in which more members have a greater say in defining job responsibilities and specifying which job slot reports to which other one and who is to fill them is more decentralized than one in which such decisions are all made at the top.

Neither man-hours spent in contributing to service nor voting strength in making service-related decisions affect the structure and staffing of an organization. If clients participate in the design of the organization, responsiveness to their interests and concerns is most likely to be affected. If the parents of children attending the school of a predominantly black community voice their opinion and exert pressure for black teachers and an administrative structure that enables the parents to intervene even in minor decisions, they are more likely to get actions that they prescribed and by people accountable to them. If the parents find that they are not speaking with a unified voice and that they lack a certain expertise, energy, and commitment, the importance of which they had not realized, they may find themselves dissatisfied with the organization they helped design. The teachers, too, are likely to be unhappy, and the children may not get a good education.

A plausible measure of participation in organizational design is the extent of public pressure that is brought to bear, measured by mail, telegrams, and telephone calls of a number and nature that would cause recipients to fear threats of boycott, loss of votes, and so on. The organizational structure that emerges in response to such pressure may be high in responsiveness as judged by the clients.

8.4 VALUE ASPECTS

Values can be assigned to at least four components: the clients; the servers; the services; and the serving organizations. As mentioned previously, there are also beneficiaries who may be none of these, such as the as yet unborn for a genetic counseling program or children for insurance services. There are also sponsors, whose values may or may not be identified with those of the serving organization, the clients, or the beneficiaries. Then there are also external constituents who are affected very indirectly, through "externalities" such as pollution, and whose values may differ from all the aforementioned.

Values can be assigned to each of these components from the viewpoint of each of the others. For the most part we are concerned with the value assigned by the client. The value a client assigns to *service* may depend on whether the service does or does not necessarily include the client's active participation.

The value a client assigns to other clients depends on this client's judgment of the client's capabilities, on an estimate of human worth and on a concern for viability. This value usually implies how much the client values active participation in terms of the training, experience, and confidence building this provides him or her.

We have already considered a parameter that measures the value of a client's time as judged by the client. It is R, the amount the client is willing to pay for a service of a certain kind characterized by a one-hour response time. (We have also used c'_{wa} or $c(o)$, the opportunity cost of a client's time lost in waiting.) If R is high, the client is not willing to wait long for delivery of the service and rather would forego the other goods and services that could be purchased by the increased expenditure. We should distinguish the case in which the client needs the response rapidly because it is a prerequisite either to a next step the client must take or for an urgent deadline from the case in which the client considers waiting for the response a poor use of his or her time. In the latter case, the client could improve the utilization of the waiting time by receiving the response at the site of work or scheduling his or her time so that he or she allocates to the waiting periods tasks that can readily be done then.

The value a client assigns to servers depends on the client's attitudes and general knowledge. Certain servers, especially in the healing arts and law enforcement, have commanded a certain respect, deference, and awe since the days of medicine men, voodooists, and tribal chieftains. Physicians, priests, and policemen are still feared and valued, but this feeling is declining as their clients become increasingly knowledgeable and participate in the service.

The value a client assigns to the services and the service organizations depends on the client's images of them. If the users of a library do not expect to find the books they want in it, they will not value the services of that library very highly; they may use it little, which could reinforce their belief, right or wrong; they may not vote for increased taxes to support libraries. Value is not necessarily expressed by how much a client is willing to pay. If a service is free, some clients may suspect that it is worthless, while others may believe that "the best things in life are free." This would call into question Downs's "law" of free goods, "Requests for free services always rise to meet the capacity of the producing agency" (Downs, 1967, p. 188), or the "law" that "Organizations that cannot charge money for their services *must* develop non-monetary costs to impose on their clients as a means of rationing their output."

The value that servers assign to clients will, in general, differ from the value that clients assign to clients. Some physicians, lawyers, and civil servants treat their clients as cases rather than as entire persons, and there are businessmen to whom the value of a client is the worth of the client's account. Possibly, how clients value themselves may be positively correlated with how servers value clients, and we would expect a high value to favor decentralization.

Servers value other servers according to whether they see them as colleagues, threatening competitors, judges, or friends. Until recently, physicians valued one another to an extent that precluded one from testifying against another in malpractice suits. Servers in the same service organization tend to value one another highly when there is high morale among the employees.

One reason that large industrial corporations sometimes decide in favor of decentralization is that it gives a greater number of potential executives a chance to develop and demonstrate their abilities. Not only does the increased participation by talented decision makers improve the corporation's performance, but it also increases the chances of bringing out and developing the greatest competence. Thus, there is also a value assigned to each server or bureaucratic agent. Many bureaucrats would value active participation by clients negatively with regard to the values assigned to the servers.

The serving organization may be regarded as a set of roles in which a role is a configuration of expectations (Barnard, 1938). Thus, the army is a service organization with an existence quite apart from the bodies that fill, at any time, the roles within it. The organization is assigned a value in its own right. It usually values active participation by clients negatively.

We can now visualize a table in which the values of *service, client, server,* and *organization* are compared. In one cell, for example, the value of the service greatly exceeds that of the server. That is, the servers are expendable, as long as the service remains. If a service is requested repeatedly, it then becomes more important than the server, as in a termite society in which the individuals are dispensed with. If a variety of services is called for, the servers are more important.

In the case where the client participates in the service to the extent of doing it him or herself, it is the equipment that is compared with its use for importance. If the function exceeds that of the instrument in importance, the instruments are disposable, such as syringes for mass immunization or Kleenex tissues. In the reverse situation, the instrument, or the server, tends to persist.

In another cell, the value of the client greatly exceeds all other values. This means that everything except the client would be expendable. This may hold at one time for one client but not to the same degree for another. They negotiate, form social contacts, and agree that perhaps everything but them is expendable.

Another possibility is that the value of the server greatly exceeds that of the organization. The army, but not the soldiers in it, is expendable in this case. Conversely, the value of the organization may greatly exceed that of the servers. That is the usual case for armies. Such organizations may become self-perpetuating. They may not perform adequately and still be, or on the positive side, they may perform a sequence of services. Thus, when the "March of Dimes" in 1960 was no longer needed for the conquest of polio, for which the organization was created, it continued to collect dimes but spent the funds for other worthy medical causes.

Some people value control positively for its own sake, particularly if the opportunity cost of their time is low, and some people value it negatively, especially when the opportunity cost of their time is high. Such opportunity costs of time spent on participation vary with income, social status, age, lifestyle, personality, and so on, but differently from the satisfactions that participation brings to individuals. Thus, increased participation may shift rewards from some individuals to others.

In a centralized organization each person is assumed to be content to confine his or her energies to an assigned task. That generally requires some participation in the rest of the operation. A few people try to avoid even that. Some people demand extra compensation for extra participation or involvement. But a few need to extend their personalities by controlling others, not for their instrumentality but as an end in itself. Changes in a person's responsibility often lead to changes in this person's self-concept. If an organizational incumbent, particularly one with a sense of mission, as in education, for example, is about to lose responsibility for certain decisions, this person is likely to fear such a change as a threat to his or her self-image. These fears generate some of the greatest barriers to decentralization. A necessary condition for the success of decentralization is the presence of enough people with strong, secure self-images who can adapt to change and an organization that can operate democratically, from "a base of liberal optimism about the capacity of people to learn from experience" (Clear, 1970).

8.5 THE PROBABLE CONSEQUENCES OF PARTICIPATION

In the literature on school decentralization (e.g., Clear, 1970), the basic problem is sometimes seen as defining decision-making areas to be delegated to local units for control. A "sovereign" local community might expect to have a voice in the selection and retention of local administrators, teachers, and instructional materials. In both the literature on decentralization in schools and local governments

8.5 The Probable Consequences of Participation / 215

(Richards, 1956), a pattern emerges whereby there is first a concern with the failure of centralization. This is followed by a growth of delegation of certain functions from the central organization (e.g., city councils) to local groups (e.g., district councils). Then comes concern about the failure of decentralization because of the inability of smaller, local districts to carry out delegated responsibilities in a satisfactory way. This is followed by moves toward multifunctional regional councils (e.g., Ardell, 1972) on the grounds that these organizations are more accountable and representative than special interest groups, provide for comprehensive rather than specialized planning, and encourage debate and participation by a wider public.

Within limits, participation by the clients often improves a service. The fact that talking human patients can participate in the service rendered to them by physicians makes the service better than the service rendered by veterinarians. The conversational interactions discussed in Chapter 4 contribute in essential ways to the quality of a service, and this obviously involves client participation. It is now well known that students learn better by active participation in the learning process than through passive activities such as listening to lectures or reading books. This is most evident in learning languages and skills.

While increasing the extent of the clients' participation in performing services generally increases their perception of the value of the service, there is a limit beyond which increasing the extent of participation is counterproductive for some services. The cliché, "too many cooks spoil the broth," suggests what is involved.

Technological progress favors increasing participation by clients in services to them. It favors the trend toward self-service and decentralization from this point of view. Cafeterias, self-service laundries, electric shavers, and do-it-yourself kits are all examples of this trend. There are, of course, evident limitations that no technological advance is likely to exceed. Do-it-yourself dentistry and surgery remain implausible.

Increasing client participation also increases the value of the server as well as the value of the client. To servers above a certain level of competence, client participation may take the form of positive reinforcement. This helps them learn and further improve their ability as servers. If client participation is time-saving rather than time-consuming, it may enable them to increase the number of clients they can serve per unit time. Of course, if a barber's clients increasingly tend to shave themselves, the barber may lose his or her skill in shaving them, and thus there are limits to the optimal degree of participation from this point of view too. From a cost-benefit viewpoint, the forces of technological progress and increasing demand, which favor increasing the upper limit of optimal participation, should cause the supply of servers for old services to decrease, if their value is to stay fixed or increase, but should also encourage the development of new services.

The value of clients may be raised when they participate to a greater extent if it bolsters their self-confidence, improves their skills, and increases their autonomy, to which they may assign a high value in its own right. The value of clients to themselves is largely determined by the value they assign to such attributes as autonomy and the extent to which they judge they possess them. To the server, the organization, the sponsor, and other constituents, a person's value may be estimated by an impersonal yardstick and they may regard the client or beneficiary expendable at *some* price. We do not consider this nonhumanistic point of view, though it is a logical consequence of unimaginatively applying cost-benefit analysis to such problems as environmental quality control and energy production.

Increasing participation by clients could also increase the value of an organization by making it more adaptive and viable. By bringing decision making to lower levels in the organization (levels 0 for clients and 1 for bottom-level servers), decentralization through increased participation improves the organization. Its capacity to process more information could also be increased through automated, formal information systems that update files and reduce time between planning sessions. This moves decision making up. It could favor centralization, depending on relative costs (Galbraith, 1970). While the costs of the hardware and software aspects of automated information systems are decreasing, their organizational aspects are becoming more costly as they become predominant in importance. Moreover, as Wildavsky (1976) has pointed out, they are no substitute for policy analysis. It is an open question whether, on balance, cost-effectiveness of service organizations is favored by increased or decreased participational decentralization. We conjecture that it is the former.

Many of the above arguments also apply to the participation of clients in decisions that affect them. All these arguments have assumed that the service, server, client, and organization each had a level of soundness and competence exceeding a generally accepted standard. If a client's competence is below that level, the value of all these factors goes down. Parents and students who lack elementary skills such as reading, and whose orientation to what knowledge exists and its uses is below some minimum, are harmed more than they are helped by increased participation in the decision-making process.

When it comes to participation in decision making, competence is an even more critical determinant of whether increased participation

8.5 The Probable Consequences of Participation / 217

increases the value of the service, the client, the server, and the organization. Setting standards, judging the abilities of various people relative to these standards, and enforcing rules to prevent those judged from failing to meet minimal standards are all performed by special servers. Who decides to place and maintain these servers in those sensitive positions, and to what extent should the clients participate in those basic hiring/firing decisions? Judging the competence of a formulator, interpreter, and enforcer of standards requires competencies that differ from those being judged. Such values as honesty, resourcefulness, creativity, and so on, are more important than knowledge or special skills. The larger the number and variety of clients who participate in such decisions, the more errors in the latter kind of judgment are likely to cancel one another. As Lincoln put it, "You can fool some of the people some of the time, but not all (most) of the people all (most) of the time." There is some safety in numbers and in increased participation in decision making. But it comes at a cost.

If making a decision requires checking with many participants, at least two dangers arise. First, there may be intolerable delays. Second, the decision may not get made at all if all the latent conflicts are brought to the surface and not resolved. Conflicts that are minor or that could have been safely left covert can be exaggerated beyond their merits and divert attention from important issues. Unnecessary and uncreative tensions may drain energy from the task of constructive decision making. The frustrations of delayed or stillborn decision making offset the value of greater participation. All these costs limit how much participation is useful.

As technology and demands advance, particularly in educating clients of all classes, more and more people are likely to meet minimum standards even while these standards are rising. These trends would seem to raise the values of participation more than they raise the costs, thus shifting the optimum degree of participation upward, toward greater decentralization.

The entire set of arguments apply with even greater force to participation by clients in service or decisions affecting third parties. Each client's striving for autonomy manifests itself in a condition governed by self-interest. The limiting factor is the need to resolve the inevitable conflicts of interest and values. The striving for power, in the sense of participating in service to and decisions affecting others, may increase the value of the service, clients, servers, and organization only in a condition where some clients prefer to have decisions affecting them made by others. If each person had an equal desire for considerable autonomy, then this condition would not prevail. If, however, we were to live in a world of decreasing equality, where only the educated get

218 / *Political Values: Participation and Equality*

more educated, more people might want others to make decisions affecting them and provide services for them. This would tend to decrease the degree of participation in making such decisions, only up to the point where the stresses due to the underlying inequalities become too great.

As modern communication technologies make people more aware of inequities and gaps, people tend to act to decrease these gaps. This would tend to increase the upper limit of desirable participation of both kinds.

8.6 IMPACTS OF TRENDS IN TECHNOLOGY, SOCIETY, CULTURE, ECONOMICS, AND POLITICS

Technological changes have occurred in the second half of the twentieth century that are equal to major events in the long evolutionary history of life on earth. Communication and computer technologies have increased in capacity and speed by nearly a factor of a million in a few decades with a prevalent trend toward networks of distributed information capacities accessible to a vastly greater number of people. Electronic voting, for example, is technologically feasible and can greatly increase public participation in politics. Whether this is, on balance, a benefit or a cost to society as a whole is as yet unclear.

What is critical is not just participation by a wider public, but participation by an enlightened public in large enough numbers. Technology promises improvements in the levels of public debate and in knowledge and understanding of issues and candidates as well. The power to control outcomes of political processes with increased participation may thus shift to those who control the quality and flow of information. Expert or advanced scientific knowledge cannot be readily packaged for utilization by the average voter. Nor is every person equally receptive to, or capable of, utilizing the same package. Speedy electronic votes about guilt or innocence in the heat of instant outrage stimulated by a crime televised as it occurred could be a disservice to the cause of justice. Similar objections could be raised to electronic voting on issues that threaten vested interests who present the voters with biased information.

Computerized accounting, electronic funds transfer, communications-command-control for early warning and management of crises, and numerous other present or near-future uses of technology are likely to change patterns of participation in major ways.

8.6 Impacts of Trends / 219

Technologies are offering great increases in efficiency. They are permitting us to perform functions we could not do or would not have thought of doing before. And they may within the next two decades cause us to change our lifestyles, as did the car, the telephone, and television. At the same time that costs of human labor are increasing, the costs of using technology are decreasing. This makes the use of technologies more widely available.

Yet, people at higher organizational levels prefer to talk face to face rather than communicating by writing or through computer terminals. While previously disadvantaged people prefer using technological media to direct human contact, saying that for the first time they feel that they are treated like everyone else, their more privileged colleagues view having to deal with a machine rather than a person as a demotion that is degrading or dehumanizing. Thus, successful and upward-mobile white nurses, teachers, librarians, and students often resist or fear the use of computers while their black counterparts are often eager to do so. Physicians, lawyers, and business executives are more likely to delegate direct use of a computer terminal to a staff assistant than do it themselves.

Community participation in school planning is a relatively recent notion (Murphy, 1972). In one trial of this idea by a group of architects, the first step was to generate views and counterviews and to establish credibility for further progress. Then, programs, aspirations, constraints, and directions were abstractly formulated. Subsequently, several study schemes were produced, and an "architectural-community solution" emerged. In this case, all the interested members of the community participated in the architectural design of a school.

There is also increasing participation in the medical services industry. It is being transformed into a "health-releasing process." Consumer participation is ministering to an ailing sick-care industry (Howard, 1972). Neighborhood health centers were to be organized with "maximum feasible participation" according to the mandate of the Office of Economic Opportunity's Community Action Agency. At least half the members of an advisory council to such a center had to be community residents. The governing boards that exercise direct power have, however, become less consumer oriented. Nevertheless, the neighborhood health centers can help the poor to gain power (Feingold, 1970) where they become entrenched and new forces enter into conflict. From this battleground, important decentralization policies eventually may emerge.

In government, too, citizen participation in both decision making and organizational redesign has been explored. This was largely in response to a wave of riots in 1967, indicative of the failure of public programs to reach large, alienated masses of disadvantaged people in inner cities. If a solution could not be found within the structure of this office, changes were made in the structure. Access by the citizens to the government bureaucracy, response time, and responsiveness were seen as key variables. Eventually, the governor of the state involved withdrew his investment and attention and brought about the experiment's demise. An advocacy program had, however, been initiated and stabilized and proved that the government could listen and become more responsive (Vosburgh and Hyman, 1973).

Though participation in organizational redesign is a rare occurrence—and in original organizational design even more so—it has far-reaching consequences when it does occur. South Africa and Rhodesia in the mid-1970s were willing to grant African blacks some participation in decision making but not in organizational redesign. Pressures toward that kind of participation foment revolutions and in this way may reverse the course of an organization along all the other dimensions of decentralization.

There are still vast inequities, however, that thwart fuller participation. In U.S. schools, for example, expenditures per pupil varied in 1970-1971 from $489 in Alabama to $1429 in Alaska (Guthrie, 1972). These serious problems of equity could be somewhat redressed by distributing budgets and resources differently. This would probably require shifts in the locus of control in the budget, and this requires participation in organizational redesign. There are also great inequities in voters' participation in elections that might bring about such shifts, and these are correlated with income distributions. People in the top 33 percent of U.S. income brackets, for example, voted 85 percent of the time, while those in the bottom third voted less than 35 percent of the time (Lane, 1952, p. 49; Verba and Nie, 1972, pp. 31-37, 132; Deutsch, 1974, pp. 274-276).

In a world that is reaching the limits of certain physical resources and probably leveling off in population as well, will the rich continue to get richer while the poor get relatively poorer? This may continue for a while.[1] In the longer run, however, the gap may decline either because the poorest will not survive or because more people, including the poor, will have increasingly more influence in the economic processes that govern returns on investments by the rich. The greater participation by more people, including the poor, will then lessen the gap. The decreased gap will, in turn, increase the number of participants.

One of the most important benefits of, and reasons for, participational decentralization is to alleviate the feelings of powerlessness, bitterness, frustration, and alienation that has become evident in the United States (Bauer, 1969; Ferkiss, 1969; Roszak, 1969; White, 1971).

8.6 Impacts of Trends / 221

This is probably true for other countries as well, possibly to a much greater extent. A major reason for this is that people have come to expect more and thus experience greater disillusionment when they realize the difficulty of realizing raised expectations. They have come to expect more, partly because there is more to be expected and partly because of their greater awareness.

According to Wolin (1960), politics are interfering less and less in the smooth operation of large organizations, which are no longer governed by people, but by principles. He claims that a meritocracy has arisen in which scientist-technicians collaborate with administrators and where rationality and technical expertise predominate. This escape from the sordid reality of politics, with its futility and the conflicts of naked strength, into rational, bureaucratized organization has, according to Wolin, lessened people's sense of solidarity, security, and certainty. Shifting the focus from people to organizations as objects of concern has deepened our sense of loneliness and need to fit or belong, our resentment against being twisted into conformity. Referring to Selznick, Wolin says " 'participation is prescribed only when there is a problem of cohesion' and should not interfere with 'the freedom of the leadership to deploy its resources'."

This simplistic view may be questioned, especially a decade after it was expressed, on the grounds that politics pervades even the most rational and efficient scientifically managed organization. Some contemporary thinkers go so far as to assert that a good manager can manage anything. Who gets to be a manager and the art of managing is very much a matter of politics. Insofar as few of us have the talents, opportunities, and whatever else it takes to become and remain managers, the rest of us are either managed or outside the management system. That may be one major reason for our sense of powerlessness or alienation.

These feelings of helplessness must be incorporated into the total cost, even if it is not strictly commensurable with costs used to measure efficiency and effectiveness. "The greatest challenge to public administrators operating within a participatory environment will be identifying and balancing citizen needs and demands against the potentially conflicting demands and socio-emotional needs of public employees, elected officials and administrative supervisors" (Herbert, 1972, p. 623).

The predictions made by Kaufman (1969) have, on the whole, come to pass. Concessions were made to the demand for greater local influence on public programs. Territorial officers with some authority over field personnel in functional agencies were established. Differences in human and financial resources soon generated disparities among the diverse small units. Some units encountered disaster in competition with others. This led to demands for central intervention to restore equality, balance, and concerted action. The predicted result is an oscillation between centralization and decentralization.

We can suggest at least one relation that may have a major influence on the course of these oscillations. It is the ratio between the costs or disutilities of participation, such as voting or attending meetings, and the direct perceived benefits or utilities attained by individuals through these activities. With growing affluence and costs of time as well as the complexity and opacity of many social and political processes, this ratio tends to decline, resulting in the well-known patterns of mass abstentionism and apathy among many voters in highly developed countries and highly educated groups such as university students. In many cases, this trend may override or greatly modify the tendencies toward growing decentralization and participation, discussed earlier in this chapter.

Chapter 9

Conclusions and Perspectives

9.0 INTRODUCTION

Our book has a relatively specific focus: the cost-benefit ratio of service systems. But its intellectual and motivational background has been much broader.

In this study of decentralization we have tried to create a more comprehensive, coherent, and clearer image of how responsive relations among people can be attained and maintained. We have asked what conditions in each service system will benefit society as a whole. Our inquiry has necessarily been intellectual and normative, or else we could have contributed little beyond saying that people organize themselves according to the distribution of power and control.

An alternative (descriptive) approach would have been to describe and explain the changing patterns of centralization and decentralization through the dynamics of power shifts due to both endogenous and exogenous factors. Yet another (ideological) approach would have been to view decentralization as a cherished value in its own right, nearly synonymous with slogans such as "self-determination," "democratization," "citizen participation," and "representativeness." We chose our analytical normative approach because it seemed to shed the most light on the more precise meaning of the basic concepts, the limits of what is logically possible or impossible, and the ideal conditions against which to compare present concepts.

We have focused our analysis on the responsiveness of relations between two (or more) people with one in the role of service provider and the other in the role of service recipient or client, because the analysis of responsive relations within an arbitrary set of people is still almost untractable. We stressed the study of service organizations rather than other groupings of people or individual servers because that is where steps toward or away from decentralization are most possible and under active consideration. More importantly, many social scientists see the next societal stage into which we are evolving as a technology-based service society (Bell, 1973).

Throughout our analysis our concern has been primarily with the client and the responsiveness of services to the client's needs. Indeed the roles of clients and servers often become reversed. Even more, the right organizational structure in our service organizations may hold a part of the secret for what enables society as a whole to exhibit emergent qualities that go far beyond the mere cumulation of all the individuals' successes in problem solving and self-actualization, much as the functioning of a brain goes beyond the successful functioning of its component neurons.

Our more specific question was what degree of decentralization, as a property of such an organization, is optimal, and whether that optimum tends toward greater or less decentralization with the dominant trends of our times.

In what follows, we first revisit the definitions of the decentralization concept and its relation to use by managers. Next, we summarize the various conditions that we have found to favor decentralization. Then we discuss the relation of our conclusion to the beliefs of those "decentralists" for whom decentralism is a value in its own right. Finally, we present our overall views about the likely and desirable changes in the organizational structure of a service society and present some recommendations to managers, planners, and researchers interested in furthering the research we have begun.

9.1 THE CONCEPT OF DECENTRALIZATION RECONSIDERED

In general, we are trying to move the question of centralization versus decentralization from its ideological form of "either-or" to the more nearly scientific form of "how much?" and "under what conditions?" For this purpose, however, we must first make clear how much of what. We stress that it is but one property of organizational structure. The degree of orderliness (negentropy) may be another property of organizational structure at the same level as decentralization, and there may be other such dimensions.[1]

In this case, there are also properties of organizational structure at levels that are subordinate to that of decentralization, such as pluralization, dispersion, and the other six dimensions we have analyzed. This notion is illustrated in Figure 9.1.

Since we have regarded decentralization to have at least eight important aspects, it is not reasonable to expect a single, simple-minded dichotomy, such as the phrase "centralization-decentralization" might suggest. Yet scales for the extent of decentralization have been used and we have also spoken of an optimal degree of decentralization, even when we meant only delegational, hierarchical, or participational decentralization.

In what follows, we discuss the possibility of combining our eight aspects of decentralization into a single overall index of decentralization. We compare this with such indexes proposed in the literature. We then discuss how the eight dimensions interact and act in combination in response to trends such as increasing loads. We finally discuss how the concept is likely to be used in practice.

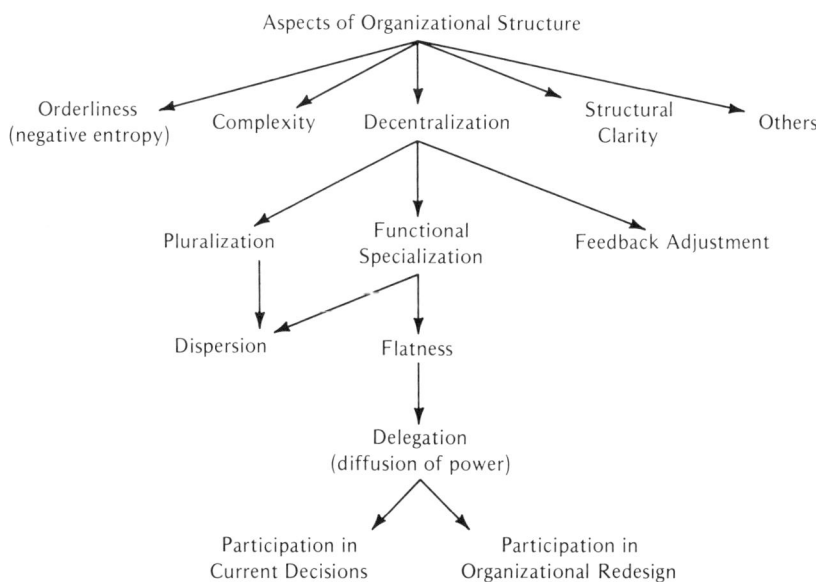

Figure 9.1. Our concepts of decentralization and organizational structure.

9.1.1 Scaling Decentralization: A Partial Ordering Along the Eight Dimensions.

A scale along which to measure the extent to which a service organization is decentralized would have many uses. But because we have considered "decentralization" to have at least eight attributes, not all of which are commensurable or independent, it is unreasonable to expect a single ratio scale. The best we might hope for is a partial ordering among the numerous possible combinations of values along our eight dimensions.

The simplest way to display these combinatorial possibilities is to consider two extreme possibilities for each dimension. Thus, an organization can be pluralized, or not, dispersed, or not, functionally specialized, or not, offer many feedback cycles or few, have many hierarchical levels or few, delegate decisions to a large extent or little, allow a great deal or little client-citizen participation in decision making, and provide for much or little participatory organization redesign. Altogether, there are 2^8 or 256 combinations of organizations varying along eight dimensions as shown in Figure 9.2.

To introduce further order and perspective into this set of 256 combinations, we evaluated our eight dimensions of decentralization for their importance as an aspect of decentralization. To each of the eight dimensions we assigned a priority, from 1 to 8, with which we judged it to be:

1. Of value or importance to *clients* in a decentralization decision
2. *Frequently* used in deciding on whether or not to decentralize
3. *Indispensable* for such decisions; how sensitive a decentralization decision would be to nonconsideration of that dimension
4. Of value or importance to the *community* in a decentralization decision
5. Low in risk of errors or in the *uncertainties* under which decentralization decisions are made
6. Of value or importance to the servers or *staff* of a service organization in a decentralization decision
7. Technically *efficient* or sensitive to technological advances
8. Sensitive to *costs*

For example, we felt that pluralization was most sensitive to costs, for doubling the number of stations doubles the fixed costs if we disregard economies of scale for capital goods. Dispersion was second most sensitive to cost, and delegation was least sensitive to cost. A certain number of responsibilities can be delegated downward without promising or giving raises to the delegate.

To take another example, we felt that dispersion was of greatest value to clients of a service organization because the close proximity of

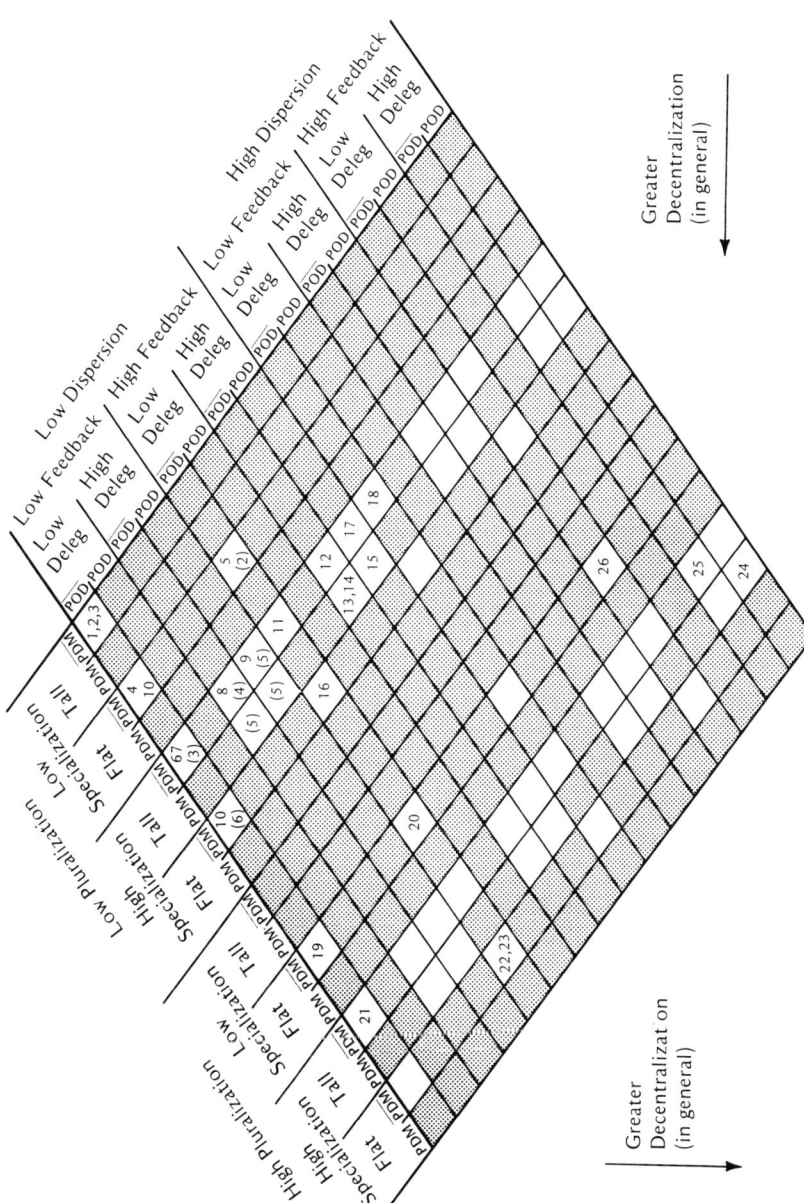

Figure 9.2. An ordering of structures on the eight dimensions of decentralization.

the service station was most important to them, with feedback of second most importance and flatness of the organizational structure least important.

If we combine the priorities assigned to the eight dimensions according to these eight criteria, we obtain the following list in order of decreasing priority, with each dimension of decentralization labeled so that high values correspond to decentralization and low values correspond to centralization (see Table 9.1).

Indeed, the eight aspects of decentralization are not mutually independent and calling them "dimensions" could sometimes be misleading. The interdependence among the eight aspects can already be described from logical considerations alone. High dispersion cannot, for example, co-occur with no pluralization or specialization. Delegation, at least vertically, cannot occur in a flat structure. Figure 9.1 shows some of these logical dependencies, with a relation indicated by an arrow, $A \to B$, to be read as "A determines B" or "B depends on A" or "we cannot have a high degree of B in the total absence of A."

Only feedback appears to be entirely independent of the other seven aspects. Pluralization and feedback seem to be independent. Participation is not possible unless there is some delegation, at least implicitly, of responsibility, authority, or power to the participants. Without some degree of functional specialization we would have no hierarchies, no delegation, and no participation in decision making.

With an extreme interpretation of the eight aspects of decentralization, we can eliminate most of the 256 combinations of highs and lows, in particular, by interpreting "low" to mean total absence. We have

Table 9.1. Eight Aspects of Decentralization

Priority Aspect of Decentralization	Measured by	Chapter in Which Discussed
1. Pluralization	Number of stations or agents	2
2. Dispersion	Average spread over space	2
3. Specialization	Number of functional specialties	3
4. Feedback	Number of conversational passes	4
5. Flatness	1/number of hierarchical levels	5
6. Delegation	Ratio of memory at bottom to higher levels	6
7. Participation in decision making	Fraction of people participating	8
8. Participation in organizational redesign	Fraction of people participating	8

9.1 The Concept of Decentralization Reconsidered / 229

organized these into the 16 × 16 table shown in Figure 9.2, in which the cells corresponding to "impossible" combinations are shaded. We call a structure most centralized if it is low on all the eight aspects of decentralization, and we call it least centralized or most decentralized if it is high on all eight.

In Table 9.2 we list a sample of examples of service organizations that correspond to the numbers inside some of the cells. In the table these are ranked roughly in order of decreasing overall decentralization. But this is only a general impression, as are the rows and columns of Figure 9.2, because of the various tradeoffs among combinations of attributes. The basis for the ordering in Table 9.1 is the lexicographic or counting sequence of the binary numbers representing each structure. This is also displayed in Figure 9.3.

Here, six of the eight aspects are reduced to three; impossible combinations ruled out by Figure 9.1 have been eliminated. Horizontally, we see all four possible high-low combinations of pluralization and dispersion. Vertically we see all three possible high-low combinations of specialization and flatness. (Nonspecialized and tall are ruled out.) In the third dimension we see three possible high-low combinations of delegation and participation in decision making or organizational redesign or both. To represent feedback that may be present or absent (high or low) for each of the above 19 structures, we underlined the numbers; these numbers refer to the ordering according to the binary representation, indicated by the numbers in parentheses (1) . . . (9) in Table 9.2 corresponding to items 4 to 9 and 16. The next possible binary number would be 01001000, but that violates Figure 9.1 because it calls for high dispersion without either pluralization or specialization. This also holds for 01011000. But after these two we can have the binary numbers corresponding to (3) − (9) in Table 9.2 with 01 in place of 00 for the first two binary digits. With 10 and 11 in those places instead of 00, we can have all 10, resulting in 19 cubes or 38 binary patterns. The ordering according to the binary numbers in Table 9.2 is also shown by numbers in parentheses in Figure 9.2.

The ordering is shown by the path on top of the drawing in Figure 9.3.

For a few of the entries, particularly countries and political entities, we use three rather than just two values of each of our eight aspects: high, medium, and low. To explain these assignments consider two cases in more detail. The first is the organization of data-processing services. This covers entries 8, 17, 20, 29, and 37 in Table 9.2. The second is the organization of the U.S. Federal Court System, entry 30.

Distributed or decentralized processing generally means that each geographic or functional entity has its own independent computer.

Table 9.2. Examples of Feasible Structures with Varying Degree of Decentralization

Name	Pluralization	Dispersion	Specialization	Responsiveness	Flatness	Delegation	Participation in Decision Making by Staff or Clients	Participation in Organizational Design by Staff or Clients	Binary Pattern	
1. Mohammed	Lo	Lo	Lo	Lo	Lo	Lo	Lo	Lo	00000000	Violates Figure 9.2 and Table 9.1 because of tall hierarchy without specialization
2. Byzantine Emperor and Church-head[a]	Lo	Lo	Lo	Lo	Lo (tall)	Lo	Lo	Lo	00000000	
3. Christ	Lo	Lo	Lo	Lo	Lo	Lo	Lo	Lo	01000000	
4. Oracle	Lo	Lo	Lo	Lo	Hi (flat)	Hi	Lo	Lo	00001000 (1)	First structure allowed by Figure 9.2
5. One Information and Referral Center	Lo	Lo	Lo	Hi	Hi	Lo	Lo	Lo	00011000 (2)	Second allowable structure
										More dec. than Ex. 4
6. Emperor or Pope in Medieval Western Europe	Lo	Lo	Hi	Lo	Lo (tall)	Lo	Lo	Lo	00100000 (3)	Trades specializ. vs. feedback and flatness
7. German Nazi Party	Lo	Lo	Hi	Lo	Lo (tall)	Lo	Lo	Lo	00100000 (3)	
8. Special Purpose, Batch-processing Computing Center	Lo	Lo	Hi	Lo	Lo	Hi	Lo	Lo	00100100 (4)	More dec. than Ex. 6
9. Authoritative Expert with High-level assistant Hired by Client	Lo	Lo	Hi	Lo	Lo	Hi	Lo	Hi	00100101 (5)	For example, specialized physician-nurse team
10. A Technician	Lo	Lo	Hi	Hi	Hi	Lo	Lo	Lo	00101000 (6)	For example, automobile mechanic
11. French Government	Lo	Lo	Hi	Hi	Lo	Lo	Lo	Lo	00110000 (7)	

#	Item							Code		Notes
12.	Independent Management Consulting Firm	Lo	Lo	Hi	Lo	Hi	Lo	00110100 (8)	Lo	
13.	Research Institute	Lo	Lo	Hi	Lo	Hi	Hi	00110110 (9)	Lo	
14.	A Municipal Government	Lo	Lo	Med	Hi	Lo	Hi	001x0110	Lo	
15.	Consulting Firm with Clients as Partners	Lo	Lo	Hi	Hi	Lo	Hi	00110111	Hi	
16.	Academic Department Run by a Secretary	Lo	Lo	Hi	Hi	Hi	Lo	00111000 (10)	Lo	
17.	Special Purpose, Time-sharing Computing Center	Lo	Lo	Hi	Hi	Med	Hi	0011x100	Lo	
18.	U.S. Army	Lo	Med	Med	Lo	Lo	Lo	0xx00000	Lo	
19.	Battery of Identical Vending Machines	Hi	Lo	Lo	Lo	Hi	Lo	10001000	Lo	
20.	General Purpose Time-sharing Computer Center with Terminal in One Place	Hi	Lo	Lo	Hi	Med	Lo	1001x000	Lo	
21.	Battery of Diverse Vending Machines	Hi	Lo	Hi	Lo	Hi	Lo	10101000	Lo	Also drinking fountains
22.	Private Clinic	Hi	Lo	Hi	Hi	Lo	Hi	10110100	Lo	
23.	Football Team	Hi	Lo	Hi	Hi	Med	Med	1011xxx0	Lo	
24.	U.S. Congress	Hi	Med	Hi	Hi	Med	Hi	1x11xx11	Hi	
25.	Swiss Federation	Hi	Med	Med	Hi	Med	Med	1xx1x1xx	Med	
26.	A Fleet of Taxis	Hi	Hi	Lo	Med	Hi	Lo	110x1000	Lo	
27.	Physician in General Practice	Hi	Hi	Lo	Med	Hi	Lo	110x1000	Lo	
28.	Fleet of Roving Ambulances	Hi	Hi	Lo	Hi	Hi	Lo	11011000	Lo	
29.	Set of Programmable Pocket Calculators	Hi	Hi	Med	Lo	Med	Hi	11x0x110	Lo	
30.	U.S. Federal Court System	Hi	Hi	Hi	Med	Med	Med	11xxxxx0	Lo	

Table 9.2. (Continued)

Name	Plural-ization	Disper-sion	Special-ization	Respon-siveness	Flatness	Dele-gation	Partici-pation in Decision Making by Staff or Clients	Partici-pation in Organi-zational Design by Staff or Clients	Binary Pattern	
31. Tax Collection Agencies	Hi	Hi	Hi	Lo	Lo	Lo	Lo	Lo	11100000	
32. System of Hospitals	Hi	Hi	Hi	Med	Lo	Lo	Lo	Lo	111x0000	
33. A Municipal Fire Department	Hi	Hi	Hi	Hi	Lo	Med	Lo	Lo	1110x00	
34. A Municipal Police Department	Hi	Hi	Hi	Hi	Lo	Hi	Med	Lo	111101x0	
35. A Set of Intelligent Terminals	Hi	Hi	Hi	Hi	Lo	Hi	Hi	Lo	11110110	
36. Families or Households	Hi	Hi	Hi	Hi	Med	Med	Med	Med	1111xxxx	
37. Network of Minicomputers	Hi	Hi	Hi	Hi	Med	Hi	Hi	Lo	1111x110	
38. Set of Neighborhood Clinics	Hi	Hi	Hi	Hi	Hi	Lo	Lo	Lo	11111000	
39. U.S. University System	Hi	Hi	Hi	Hi	Hi	Lo	Lo	Lo	11111000	Violates Figure 9.1 because of delegation in a flat structure
40. Network of Friendships, Acquaintances, Peers	Hi	Hi	Hi	Hi	Hi	Hi	Hi	Hi	11111111	

Note: Hi means a large extent of each dimension.
Note: Med or x means moderate extent.
Note: Lo means very little or nothing of that dimension.

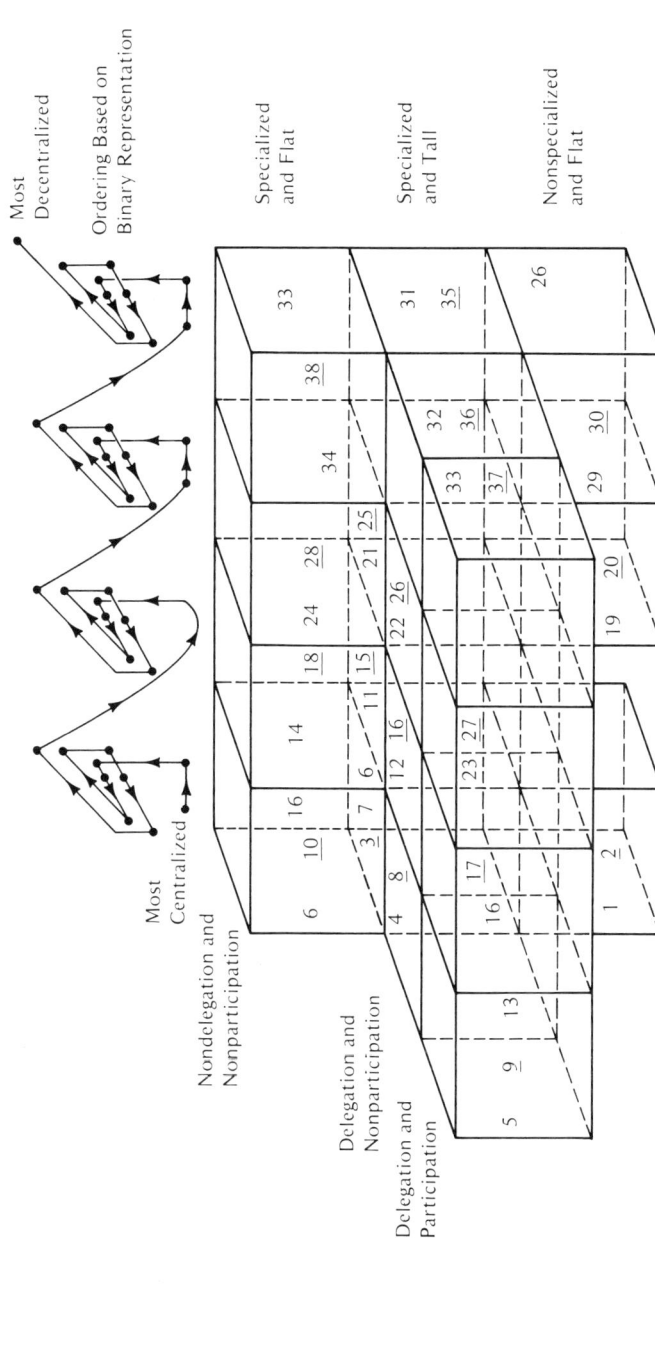

Figure 9.3. Display and ordering structures by degree of decentralization.

234 / Conclusions and Perspectives

Each installation is an independent operation from an organizational viewpoint. When large central processing units became widely available, top management sought in centralized processing a means of regaining corporate control and standards, of obtaining needed information and economies of scale that distributed processing did not provide. The arguments that are most often given (Hannan and Fried, 1977) in favor of centralizing a computer installation are: some decentralized minicomputers have unused capacity that is wasted, while others are so overloaded as to require costly upgrading or servicing; in a single large installation, fixed overhead costs, such as floor space and air conditioning, cost less than the equivalent items for distributed facilities with the same total capacity; large centers require fewer managers, staff, and support personnel; large computers, which until recently had higher internal processing speeds and larger main memories, may provide lower unit cost and make possible a larger variety of high-level languages, the use of hierarchically structured files and large scientific computations, and the use of large data bases that are not feasible with minicomputers. The quality of people attracted to larger centers is often greater than those working on smaller stand-alone facilities, where there is often a faster turnover of personnel. Centralized processing has been felt to provide recognition of corporate needs, economies of scale, standardization of procedures, consolidation of technical resources, and consistent and secure data.

Yet decentralized or distributed computing has many advantages. The analysts are more responsive to the users and their needs. The computer costs are more visible and readily controlled because users are accountable for them and project managers are directly accountable to users. The possible conflicts between divisional analysts and central programmers may not conform to organizationwide standards, may not fit well into overall corporate guidelines and priorities, but in the long run, they may contribute to the viability of the total organization. Decentralized processing is felt to provide recognition of local or functional needs, lower incremental costs, system tailorability, responsive technical resources, and accessible data.

As the cost of processing, storage, and soon thereafter communication channels continue to decrease until they are no longer limiting factors, the use of intelligent terminals, networks with distributed processing, input, control, and remote job entry all combined will become widely available. The resulting system will be characterized by: high degrees of pluralization (items 20, 29, 37), in that there may be a processor and memory in every terminal; high dispersion (items 29, 37), with terminals as ubiquitous as home television sets or telephones (possibly programmable hand-held calculators (item 29) can

9.1 The Concept of Decentralization Reconsidered / 235

permit their users to insert tapes into remote entry stations and pick up output there as well); and high specialization (item 37), in that some computers in the network would be tailored to do only Fortran with exceptional efficiency, while others would excel only in another programming language, and so on. It (item 37) would have very high feedback capabilities through time sharing, but it may have a tall hierarchy of supervisory levels, especially since many of the intelligent terminals will have considerable processing and storage capabilities. Participation in decision making may increase only later; it is already in evidence among the networks of highly creative and interactive computer scientists in artificial intelligence (Levinthal et al., 1975) and in computer conferencing (item 37). Participation in organizational redesign may come about only much later.

Mathematical models to help in the design of distributed information systems are being developed by Bucci and Streeter (1976) but are not yet sufficiently advanced to deal with complexity to provide reliable guidance to designers.

In 1967 it was held that computers would have but little impact on management (Dearden, 1967). It was thought that the trends toward decentralization of large corporations during the 25 years preceding 1967 would be reversed by information technology. This was two years after the Digital Equipment Corporation introduced the first mass-produced minicomputer. At a cost of a few thousand dollars such a device can be dedicated to a single task such as keeping track of equipment orders, running a laboratory experiment, controlling a machine, or making out a payroll. By 1973, however, "the day of the large general-purpose, single-facility computer center may be ending for many educational and research institutions" (Greenberger, 1973a). Shifts toward national resource sharing by means of networks were predicted (Greenberger et al., 1973b). By 1977, even the biggest and best managed enterprises, the Bell Telephone Labs, led the way in replacing large data-processing systems by a large number of minicomputers (Klein, 1977). The volume of sales for the Digital Equipment Corporation had climbed to the billion-dollar mark.

Even in 1968, polymorphic and distributed computing were widely used ideas. To nurture the development of an information service industry, improvements in the effectiveness of the free enterprise system were analyzed (Dennis, 1968). Yet, "the establishment of a central authority is strongly recommended even in decentralized operations," because this is a good way of resolving data-processing problems that are common to many groups (Auerbach, 1976).

As a second example, consider the federal court system of the United States. In terms of both pluralization and dispersion, this system ranks

236 / Conclusions and Perspectives

high because of the nation being divided into U.S. District and Appellate Court districts. This system provides for modest functional specialization. While special courts do exist for claims regarding such things as taxes and patents, district courts will take cases regardless of the nature of the case so long as it falls under federal jurisdiction. In terms of relative flatness of the organizational hierarchy, the system is characterized by a moderate amount. The federal court system is composed of District, Appellate, and Supreme Courts with the Appellate Courts possessing the power to overrule district courts and the Supreme Court having the same power over the appellate courts. The number of feedback cycles that exist in this system is medium. Lower-court judges will typically closely watch attempts to overturn their decisions in the higher-level courts. Supreme court justices are known to study public opinion polls as one aspect in their attempt to make a decision in the interpretation of the infinite ambiguity of laws. Yet they keep "clients" waiting for long periods. The lower courts have been granted the authority to make decisions on the cases presented before them, indicating a moderate degree of delegation.

In so doing, the lower courts are also granted the right to participate in decision making. However, the ability of judges at any level to participate in organizational redesign is fairly low. The procedure for the Constitution does not formally grant any more power to the courts to participate in organizational redesign than it does to any other group.

9.1.2 Interactions Among the Eight Aspects. In the preceding chapters we have generally analyzed just a few aspects at a time, and we have treated the other aspects as remaining fixed. Thus, in Chapter 6 we calculated the degree of delegation that minimizes total cost, without taking account of the other aspects. When we computed the degree of pluralization (number of identical facilities to be deployed over a linear strip with uniform demand), we assumed an optimal pattern of dispersion for any degree of pluralization. It followed that dispersion does not vary with pluralization: if we measure dispersion by the average distance between one of n facilities that are equally spaced along a D-mile line to the center of the line, then dispersion is $D/4$ for n even and $D^2(1 - 1/n^2)/4$ for n odd, where n is the degree of pluralization. When we calculated the flatness that minimizes total cost, we assumed a degree of pluralization (n) at each level that was just necessary to handle the load. Thus, if load stays fixed and we change flatness, the degree of pluralization at each level may change.

In Chapter 3 we did compute both the degrees of pluralization and functional specialization that simultaneously minimize total cost. To investigate the effect of more than two variables, each of which can be independently selected to minimize total cost, is quite difficult, and it is left for future investigation.

A promising approach that we have not yet used is to use a service production function. As before, we characterize a service organization by six sets: clients' service providers; Euclidean space in which persons and equipment are located; functional specialties; documentary files necessary to record the organization's policies and affairs; devices or equipment. A service production function transforms an input, such as m, the number of person-hours needed to render a specified service, into an output such as the rendering of services with probability of success p, and utility u. Elsewhere (Kochen and Deutsch, 1979), we use a simplified model to derive the number of service providers n, each costing c dollars per hour, so as to maximize expected net utility. We find that n increases with m and u but decreases with p and c. Interpreting n as the desired degree of distributedness or decentralization, this means that longer times to service requests (because they are becoming more complex), increases in utility of service, decreases in cost per service provided and decreases in probabilities of success (which may vary inversely with difficulty) favor decentralization.

Our first aspect of decentralization, pluralization, corresponds to the distribution of the total number of available person-hours over the service providers. If all m needed hours are concentrated on one ($n = 1$) provider—we have extreme centralization. At the other extreme, the m needed hours are evenly spread over the n providers.

Dispersion can be interpreted as a mapping from the set of devices into the set of locations, or the assignment of a site to each item. This distribution, too, can vary from one that is very concentrated with all items close together to one that is widely dispersed. The same comments apply to documents and the work stations of service providers.

Functional distributedness can be interpreted as the spread in the mapping of the set of service providers into the set of functional specialties. Included among the set of specialties are elements that are unions of specialties, and providers who are assigned to a union of many sub-specialties correspond to generalists. In a functionally centralized service, all providers would be assigned to the same "specialty," i.e., they would all be generalists. If each provider were a specialist who spends *all* his time in a sub-sub-specialty, the service would be centralized in a different sense.

Hierarchical flatness can be interpreted as a mapping of the total funding into the set of service providers that is uniform: an equal share for everyone. If all the funds are under the control of the person in charge, who allocates portions to subordinates who, in turn, do the same, we have a tall, centralized hierarchy.

Delegation involves the distribution of the total knowledge (in bits or bytes) required to render adequate service over the providers. If it is all concentrated in one person, we have a delegationally centralized service. In the other extreme, where knowledge is distributed uniformly, there are variations from the case where everyone knows the same thing, which may be insufficient to service rare and complex cases, to where everyone has unique knowledge that just complements everyone else's. The latter situation would require an information and referral network, and if it is large, coordinators and linkers are required.

The degree of feedback, which was one of our eight aspects, can be interpreted by the distribution of the total number of hours needed for communication over both the clients and service providers. If all these hours are used up by the providers communicating with one another, no time is left for communicating with clients, and this aspect of the service is centralized. If it is all distributed over the clients, this aspect is decentralized.

Participation, the last aspect we considered, can be regarded as a distribution of the number of decisions made per month over both providers and clients. If it is all concentrated in one person, we have a participationally centralized structure.

Each of the eight distributions mentioned above can be characterized by parameters. If, for example, one could be represented as a Normal distribution, two parameters (interpreted as its mean and variance) would suffice. A production function relating input to output variables could then be used to derive an expression for the net utility in terms of these structured parameters. It may then be possible to find regions in parameter space that correspond to minimum net utility, subject to various constraints.

9.2 SUMMARY OF CONDITIONS FAVORING DECENTRALIZATION

We started our analysis with the following assumptions:

1. Some values, such as the desirability of highly responsive links between the providers and recipients of human services, are shared by nearly all members of society.
2. When people organize their activities to provide services, the total cost to society, including all hidden costs and everyone affected, should be least.

9.2 Summary of Conditions Favoring Decentralization / 239

3. All people should settle for, and have available, no less than the best services available to which they are entitled, because of their need and their ability to reciprocate in some form.
4. Provision of services will occupy an increasing fraction of our labor force, and postindustrial or highly informed society will be an increasingly technology-based service society.
5. Population, levels of education and production, standards of living, and hence demands for service will all increase up to a limit.
6. The development of technologies has already passed certain irreversible major turning points, but its impact on society is yet to come and will effect major changes in lifestyle, including demands for a greater sense of community, higher levels of consciousness, and greater sensitivity and concern for the human condition. Only the cost of human labor and the value of people's time will be limiting factors, despite the possibility that certain natural resources will be depleted.
7. To survive, institutions will have to adapt more rapidly in their capacities for coping with a large variety of increasingly complex problems, facing them at a higher rate of decisions per unit of time.
8. Knowledge will continue to grow, as will the number of special disciplines.

We submit that these assumptions are plausible. From them we derive a number of conclusions about what degree of decentralization would satisfy all of them and how that optimal degree is likely to change. Most of these conclusions did not violate our intuition or sense of what was reasonable—but some of the conclusions forced us to revise our preconceived intuitions.

9.2.1 Effects of Load on Size. Increase in the request load, L, increased all our eight aspects of decentralization except flatness, feedback, and participation. As loads increase, the size of service organizations to service them increases unless technologies can amplify the capacities of individual servers so that the same number of servers can deal with expanding loads. As the number of servers in an organization increases, so does the number of levels because of the increasing need for coordination and control, up to a limit. When that limit is reached, organizations may split, divide, and form larger organizations, much as cells divide to form larger assemblies, with increasing size, and therefore the servers within the organization most directly in contact with the client may not have less time to spend with clients, and there will be no resulting decreases in feedback and participation by both clients and the servers in direct contact with them.

9.2.2 Decentralization, Standardization, and Participation. An argument in favor of centralization that is frequently expressed by corporation executives is that it abets standardization and the resulting gains in efficiency. In the first place, standardization is not a universal net benefit. There is considerable diversity of opinion, for example, about the virtues of standardized housing, clothes, and food. A major determinant of the quality of life is variety of options among which clients can choose to express their individual and diverse values, tastes, and interests. But as the number of options grows ever larger, the marginal utility of adding still more options will decline, while their costs of production, and even the client's costs of choosing between them, may increase, bringing the rational increase of options to a halt near some relative optimum.

Second, standardization may be imposed upon clients by a centralized management without the input of clients, thus incurring the risk of displeasing most of them. For example, the new transaction network service (TNS) developed by AT&T may result in the de facto establishment of standards for electronic funds transfer (EFT) without input from users or competitors of AT&T. AT&T executives may not intend to dictate exclusive use of TNS and may claim to offer but one alternative; however, if it is developed, marketed, and serviced by AT&T, which reflects the rather centralized nature of the telecommunication industry, this may lead to an inadvertent misuse of standards.

Third, when standardization is not in the interest of a key firm in a centralized industry, this may result in a delay of standardization contrary to the interests of clients and other participants. An example of this is IBM's silence on standards proposed by the Electronic Industries Association for interoperability between older and newer data communication interfaces.

The existence of centralization in a number of American industries, interpreted as a concentration of power, had been recognized by the late Senator Philip A. Hart. Arguing that "too much power with too few endangers the public interest," Hart introduced an industrial reorganization act. It would have affected seven major U.S. industries, including computers and communications. Though that bill never gained enough support to pass, it did lead to support for antitrust legislation.

9.2.3 Effects of Experience and Delegation. As human needs require more complex services for their satisfaction, servers with more experience are needed. Even bottom-level servers would have to have more experience. As argued in Chapter 6, increases in load requiring more experienced servers favor shifting memory or experience to lower levels, thus slightly equalizing the distribution of the capabilities and experience over the vertical levels. This would favor increased flatness as well as all the other aspects of decentralization. At the same time, major new capabilities, so long as they are still scarce and costly, might first have to be installed centrally and near the top, with wider delegation and dispersion following later, as this "generation" of capabilities or equipment becomes more plentiful and cheaper.

9.2.4 Need for Opportunities to Train Executives. Outstanding executives are very hard to recruit, train, and keep. Large organizations are constantly searching for top executives, preferably from within the organization. They try to raise and nurture them deliberately. If the organization is decentralized, promising candidates for executive posts can be given responsibility for an entire division or major subfirm, possibly rotated among several units, and can be observed for their ways of coping with the challenges. In this way, decentralization enlarges the pool of potential candidates and permits more sensitive and informed selection, increasing the chances that the best executives will be at the top. Insofar as candidates who did not quite make the top are not likely to be demoted, the middle-management levels may be populated by the less capable and mediocre talents. This may decrease flatness.

9.3 OVERALL VIEW

We hope to have given the reader the impression that a scientific approach to questions of decentralization has potentialities that, despite important limitations, are preferable to the conventional type of thinking that underlies much of what is being done in practice. We have tried to suggest that decentralization need not be merely a matter of the redistribution of power or control. That is, the issues are far more complex than a simple centralization-decentralization dichotomy would imply. However, a scientific basis for more rational action can nevertheless be developed. The nature of our approach has resembled that used by economists' optimization (Samuelson, 1971). The approach hinges on the possibility of finding a social welfare function to be maximized that is subject to constraints or relative to which a specified aspiration level is to be attained. Since we cannot now specify such a welfare function, we can consider a range of such functions and look for the degree of specialization that maximizes most of the range.

242 / Conclusions and Perspectives

Where prior studies dealt with the overall, general problem, the degree of logical precision was often insufficient for a more rigorous logical-deductive approach, and interesting mathematical models tended to deal with only one aspect of the total problem. We have tried to combine these two approaches. We hope to have added clarity by introducing priorities in the selection and formulation of key problems.

A diversity of *specialized functions* is needed to cope with complex needs. Institutions capable of but one function are certainly doomed to fail, because at least one problem will eventually occur requiring more specialized capabilities than are available.

Feedback is not merely a convenience or luxury. Modern control systems cannot function without it; a missile with an 800-mile range can be targeted within a few hundred yards only with sophisticated feedback-control circuits similar to those of the human eye and brain.

Tall hierarchies topple more easily than flat ones; unless top management makes vastly fewer poor decisions than would local decision makers who are close to the service, their mistakes have vastly more impact and are much more devastating. Sooner or later, top management will err and bring down much of the hierarchy, while the damage of errors at lower levels is more readily detected, contained, repaired, and even avoided. Most likely, no strict hierarchy endures for long: eventually feedback loop appears from the top to clients or other concerned citizens who participate in organizational redesign and to whom top management becomes accountable in some way. Similar arguments apply to the instability of organizations in which there is little delegation and which allow no participation.

Nearly all the colonial empires have been transformed into commonwealths or their even more decentralized equivalents. During the last 100 years the number of nation-states as well as the number of business organizations and local agencies in the world has increased faster than the world's population and this is likely to continue, at least to some extent.

While the number of active corporations has tripled from 1950–1973, the percentage of total corporate assets owned by the largest "asset size-class" has increased only by 25 percent. This concentration of assets has been cost-effective in the period from 1965 to 1975. The 100 corporations that rank highest in total sales presently have 65.7 percent of the total assets and 72.5 percent of the net income of the 500 U.S. corporations ranking highest in total sales (*Statistical Abstract*, 1976). While we cannot claim to be able to capture all of the complexities with the few dozen variables and models we have developed, we can say with greater confidence after having done this analysis than before what is impossible, what is likely, and what is desirable.

An extreme degree of centralization is impossible for an extended period of time because of the instability, vulnerability to err, and maladaptiveness to rapid change that is inherent in such structures. Pluralization provides insurance against local malfunction or malfeasance. There is more safety in numbers. If there are at least two agents or facilities at each site in an organization, the functions required of that site can still be performed even if one agent is out of commission or errs. With but one agent, it is only a question of when a functional failure will occur.

A similar argument holds for *dispersion*, where elimination of all facilities in an entire geographic location would not necessarily damage the entire organization beyond repair. The human brain appears to be organized this way. It is pluralized in that neurons are omnipresent and their functions are so widely dispersed that even a hemispherectomy enables some of its survivors to function in society (e.g., one is an executive and is completing an advanced degree in library science).[2]

Mergers do occur among firms.[3] Among countries the advantages of such mergers (for arguments based on a Machiavellian model that focuses on power of countries, see Bremer, 1977) often do not seem to outweigh the disadvantages. According to a study by leading economists, the size of a country has no effect on its economic productivity. For example, if two economically unproductive countries were to merge, the resulting country would not necessarily be more productive, even though the combined market, labor force, available capital, and so on, would be larger (E. A. Robinson, 1960). To gain the advantages of larger aggregates and more centralized control without giving up independence and autonomy to deal with global problems (that affect several countries or organizations at once), such as forecasting and possibly control of weather, air and water pollution, or armaments control—or universal problems (that occur repeatedly in many cities, countries, organizations), such as solid-waste disposal, transportation planning, health services—effective international research organizations such as IIASA have been set up. These serve as prototypes for what is to come. They need involve no more than the countries or organizations that are directly concerned with the problems.

Extreme decentralization of the kind preached by decentralists (Barsodi, 1948; Goldsmith, 1972; Goodman, 1970; Henderson, 1974; Röpke, 1960) is also impossible if our assumptions are accepted, primarily because the social costs are prohibitive and not worth the benefits. The range of possibilities lies between the two extremes.

A desirable point in the range of possibilities is characterized by a degree of pluralization that increases with load, dispersion that matches the distribution of demand for service, and functional specialization that corresponds to the level of knowledge and the difficulty of the problems that this level makes it possible to solve. The degree of functional specialization, like the degree of pluralization, is measured by the number of agents in different specialties that are optimally dispersed over the range of functional specialties. Knowledge advances at the frontier of or between specialties (Price, 1965). This makes it possible to solve problems that had previously resisted attack. With every advance in knowledge we become aware of problems we did not think of before and are not able to resolve. Too much specialization is counterproductive because it decreases both effectiveness and efficiency in picking and solving the most important problems in favor of very narrow problems of little long-range significance for human affairs. Too little specialization does not provide us with enough capabilities.

The most desirable level of feedback is such that less will cause a server to commit more errors through insufficiently informed decisions that are no longer sensitive to their consequences and such that more will just increase the server's errors and/or delays through overloading him or her. This may also lead to prejudice, stereotyping, and rigid classifications and formalization. Lack of responsiveness, with no options and no decisions at all when needed, is a most likely and undesirable effect.

Regarding flatness of hierarchical structure, the most desirable number of levels is not so low as to incur excessive costs in horizontal communication or bring a lack of coordination. Nor is it so high as to incur excessive costs of higher-level managers who are not so exceptional and the costs of instabilities and alienation that result from long vertical distances. The ability to delegate depends on the delegator's ability to trust the delegate and the delegate's ability to live up to that trust by his or her performance. Ideally, the members of an organization should be self-selected and should have selected one another so that relations of mutual trust exist and, above all, remain warranted. Thus, the most desirable degree of delegation is a nearly equal distribution of competence over the levels.

Participation in both kinds of decision making, that is, the actual providing of service and organizational redesign, is what decentralist ideologues usually clamor for. But rational and objective arguments can also be advanced that a certain degree of participation is desirable. Together with more active feedback dialog, it makes the difference between a physician and a veterinarian. Too little participation contributes to the feeling of alienation and helplessness that adds up to a very heavy social cost. As Piaget and Skinner have taught us, learning is an active process. Participation in rendition of services affords the

9.3 Overall View / 245

client an opportunity to improve the quality of services while reducing their cost. The client of medical services, for example, is in the best position to increase the success of primary prevention programs by modifying his or her lifestyle; even in treatment the client's cooperation is essential, at least by complying with prescribed drug regimens and similar medical management procedures.

There are some arguments on the opposite side. Too much participation lets "too many cooks spoil the broth." If participation is not to be biased in favor of the most competent, an influx of useless or harmful inputs to decision making must be expected. Screening such communications sometimes may be more difficult and costly than screening the sources in the first place. If such messages are allowed to filter through, there is a heavy expected social cost of the consequences of poor decisions. If they are sifted, with the necessary rejections, at either the stage of input or barring certain people from participation in the first place, the issue shifts to who should do the screening.

This then means participation in redesign. Thus, the same considerations for and against participation apply, but with much higher stakes and risks. Moreover, having allowed incompetent people to participate in deciding who the gatekeepers will be, and assuming that this has brought in a few incompetent gatekeepers, and through them incompetent decisions, an organization finds it very difficult to undo such damage and reverse the actions taken that brought it about. The cost of decreasing the involvement of people after they have become participants may greatly exceed the cost of nonparticipation beyond a certain degree of participation; the point at which these costs balance leads to the most desirable degree of participation in this regard. Where speed and efficiency in the short run are decisive, arguments for greater decentralization and less participation will have greater weight; where long-run viability and continuing learning capacity count for most, the opposite should be the case.

If changes in organizational structure lead to consequences that are moderately undesirable, they will stimulate the generation of forces to cause shifts in the reverse direction. The result may be an oscillation, as Herbert Kaufmann (1973) has suggested, between shifts toward decentralization, a backlash reaction engendered by the frustrations and dashed hopes of high expectations sought after by insufficient means, followed by another push toward decentralization, and so forth. Insofar as learning from such mistakes occurs, the oscillatory swings become less extreme, more dampened, and eventually settle on a relatively stable structure. The time between swings may be a decade or two at present and decrease to a few years in the next few decades.

9.4 RECOMMENDATIONS

The most valuable suggestion we can make to someone faced with the decision of whether or not to decentralize their service organization is to take account of their clients' opportunity costs. Surveys of physicians' clients have shown their greatest complaint to be the servers' disregard of the value of the clients' time by keeping them waiting for unacceptably long hours (often after traveling unacceptably long distances) for a very few contact minutes with physicians. If costs were no consideration, a private service organization in any field would do well to provide rapid, responsive service to forestall any complaints in the first place. This could best be done by measuring the value of lost time to clients and taking concrete steps to reduce it, not by questionaires to express satisfaction or dissatisfaction.

This need not necessarily mean special catering to clients whose time is most valuable or whose need for speedy help is greatest. It could mean making all services more responsive to all people through pluralization, such as employing enough servers or controlling load so that it does not exceed 80 percent of the server's capacities. Functional specialization, geographic dispersion, feedback correction, and some delegation of jurisdiction and equipment might be additional ways to increase responsiveness.

However, since highly responsive service usually involves additional costs, persons who design, install, and/or conduct a service system will have to decide how these costs are to be apportioned. The answers may depend on the relative priorities assigned to various aspects of the systems and the services provided. In some cases, the higher costs of faster responses may be compensated for by reducing the number of feedback cycles or negotiating passes between server and client, or by other savings that may prove less inconvenient than would be a continuation of the original amounts of delay.

If the cost of error were insignificant, those in charge of government service organizations would be well advised to minimize delays in issuing licenses, documents, arriving at decisions or judgments, and so forth. The loss of income to a barber or restaurant awaiting a license to operate is real. In many instances, dissatisfied clients cannot turn to a competitor who provides faster, more responsive service, as is the case for services supplied by nongovernment organizations. Nor will complaints or riots help much. And elections are too rare and elected officials often too far removed from the servers in contact with clients to have much effect. We therefore recommend, to government officials who now are accountable to clients, decentralization decisions to make the servers more immediately accountable to the clients, such as in-

9.4 Recommendations / 247

stalling simple mechanical or electronic feedback systems reporting waiting time and client satisfaction.

Decentralization has a chance to work only if key people involved at all levels agree and try to make it work. Therefore, it is not just a decision of a manager responsible for decisions about organizational structure. Where morale is low, an outside organizational consultant should be brought in who can set up programs with clearly specified behavioral objectives aimed at generating mutual trust and a sense of group community reflected in the increased use of "we" rather than "I." A significant literature on intervention in organization has developed over the past two decades, starting with the pioneering work of Argyris (1961, 1970) up to the present (Friedlander and Brown, 1974).

Behavior modification programs to improve vertical communication could be tried. This would involve specification of precise goals, such as a meeting between a manager and the subordinates every day at a fixed time and place. These meetings could be devoted to clarification of objectives, procedures, performance evaluation, expectations, and so forth. Similar efforts should be tried to change attitudes, from "what is good for the organization is good for the clients (and staff)" to "what is good for the client is good for the organization (and staff)."

Another recommendation, based on an analysis by Wildavsky (1976), is to avoid the use of modern "information systems" in the narrow sense, since these are often misinterpreted (e.g., in connection with PERT, "Management by Objectives," "Program Budgeting") as substitutes for policy analysis in comparing programs. "Management information" systems are misnamed because they are not information systems at all but only data base systems, and it takes policy analysis to convert data into information. The data base systems sold to management under the various acronyms (MIS, MBO, PPBS, SI, CPM) are often used as tools to tighten top management's control of a centralized organization. They are not genuine information systems to help improve the quality of services and reduce the *total* social cost of providing them. According to Wildavsky, *policy analysis* is a reaction against such data systems and for the continual reformulation of hypotheses— learning by constant revision of our image or representation of the world—through action. It is to be hoped that managers will avoid becoming entrapped by these data base systems that help them to strengthen or support previously held positions rather than help them to ask new questions and form new positions.

One of the most important recommendations based on our study is to avoid building rigidity into the structure of an organization. Strength is better attained through flexibility. This means the capability of responding elastically, adaptively to external loads rather they yielding by irreversible deformations of structure. Hence, an organization must above all be guided by values, goals, ideals that are relatively stable and reflect a long-range plan or dream it strives for as if it would exist forever. At the same time, it must be able to rapidly shift its resources and temporarily change its structure so that it cannot only survive from day to day, but also learn in so doing. As a material basis for such a learning capacity, the organization must have adequate—or at least substantial—excess capacity, redundancy, and/or recommittable resources at its disposal. It will need these resources both in regard to the services it has to deliver and to the information-processing and self-restructuring operations it may have to perform.

Taken together, our findings can be used in several ways. One way would be to derive from them a checklist of variables for which specific values have to be found for any particular system of service or administration for any particular area, period of time, and type of service, so that with their aid an optimal system could be designed. Another way would be to study an ongoing system over time, so as to find out which of its important variables had changed, by how much, or at least in what direction, and what further such changes could be expected. From this approach one could at least learn whether some increase or decrease in the numbers, dispersion, functional specialization, hierarchical organization, and so on, of the system would be likely to improve the cost-effectiveness of its performance. Finally, richer data bases, more complex computer simulations, and more sophisticated mathematical models could be developed. Some suggestions for research in these directions are listed in Appendix 9.1.

At most, our work has made only a beginning in the development of a rational theory of decentralization. But perhaps we have shown that such a theory is possible, and we have offered some reasons to think that the major trends of social, economic, and technological development in the present and the foreseeable future will make the deliberate search for reasonable levels of decentralization more important than ever before.

Appendix 2.1

Derivation of the Optimum Degree of Pluralization

If we interpret n as a real variable rather than as a positive integer, so that the total cost is a continuous, twice differentiable function of n, then we can find the value of n that minimizes the total cost by setting its derivative with respect to n equal to zero and solving for n. The derivative is $kDL/4vn^2 + C$, and setting that equal to zero gives $kDL/4v = Cn^2$ and it follows that $n = \sqrt{kDL/4Cv}$, as in the approximation to Equation 2.3.

The exact solution is given by the following theorem. If the increase in fixed cost equals the decrease in operating costs due to increasing by 1 the number, n, of optimally dispersed facilities in the presence of a uniform demand distribution, then n must satisfy:

$$n(n - 1) < kDL/4Cv < n(n + 1)$$

If $\frac{1}{2}(\sqrt{1 + kDL/Cv} - 1)$ is an integer, then that is the optimal value of n.

A variation of the above cost equation is obtained by taking account of income distribution. Let $N_0(W)$ be the number of clients who earn between W and $W + dW$ dollars per month. This is likely to be a Pareto distribution, such as shown in Figure A2.1.1.

Let us now partition the abscissa or wage scale into "classes," and let $\overline{W}_i$ be the average wage in the ith class, or

$$\int_{W_i}^{W_{i+1}} W N_0(W) dW \bigg/ \int_{W_i}^{W_{i+1}} N_0(W) dW$$

249

250 / Appendix 2.1

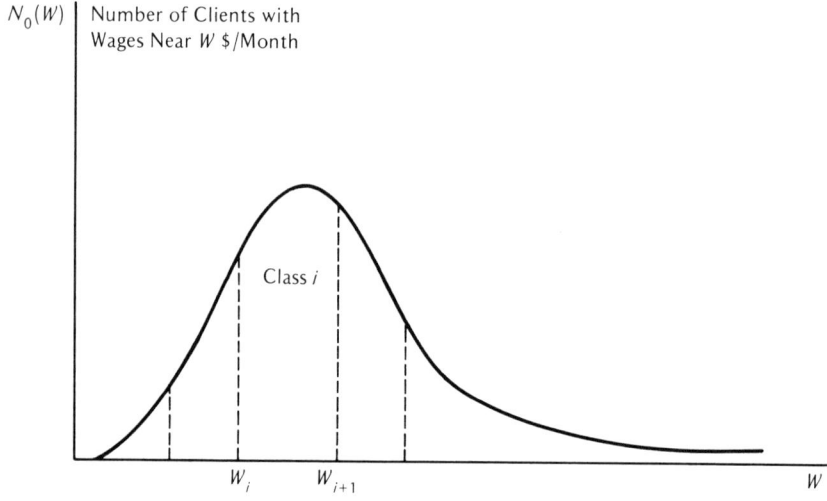

Figure A2.1.1. Illustrating a skew (Pareto) income distribution.

Instead of adding the operating cost to the organization, we add it to the cost of the clients' lost time. We take the client's lost time to be proportional to $\overline{W}_i$ and return to the use of c_{op} dollars per request for the operating cost to the organization. We also assume that clients in different classes are serviced by different facilities, reflected in different fixed costs, c_i. Thus, mentally ill patients who are poor tend to receive less costly electroshock treatments while those who are rich may receive more costly psychoanalysis (Hollingshead and Redlich, 1958). The fixed cost component of the total cost is thus nC_i and the client's part of the operating cost is $\delta \overline{W}_i DL/2nv$ dollars per month. Here, δ is the factor of proportionality relating the cost of the client's time lost in waiting to $\overline{W}_i$, and we used the factor of 2 rather than 4 in the denominator to indicate that both forwarding and return time is to be taken into account. To the total cost must now be added $c_{op}L$:

Total cost = $nC_i + \delta \overline{W}_i DL/2nv + c_{op}L$

Differentiating this with respect to n and setting the result equal to 0 gives:

$$C_i = \delta \overline{W}_i DL/2n^2 v$$

Derivation of the Optimum Degree of Pluralization / 251

Solving for n gives:

$$n = \sqrt{\frac{\delta \overline{W}_i DL}{2C_i v}} \qquad \text{(A2.1.1)}$$

For low-income classes, $\overline{W}_i$ and C_i are both small, though C_i cannot be made too small without impairing service quality. For high-income classes, both $\overline{W}_i$ and C_i are large, but when C_i exceeds a certain value, no further benefits are obtained. Thus, the ratio $\overline{W}_i/C_i$ will tend to be constant over the middle-income ranges, decrease for the lower classes, and increase for the upper classes. If only i varies, with δ, D, L, v staying fixed, then it follows that n is slightly less for the poor and slightly greater for the rich. We tend to pluralize (decentralize in this sense) for the affluent and centralize for the poor.

Appendix 2.2

Location of Service Facilities in the Plane

Suppose that the density, $D(i,j)$, of demand is given for each point (i,j) of a rectangle. Superimposed on the rectangle is an $m \times k$ grid, with (i,j) the coordinates of a vertex on that grid. The total load is the sum of all the demand densities:

$$L = \sum_{i=1}^{m} \sum_{j=1}^{k} D(i,j)$$

Two aspects of location theory must be dealt with simultaneously—finding a number, n, of service facilities and locating them, so as to minimize total cost. This is the sum of the fixed cost of maintaining all the facilities and of the clients' travel costs to reach the nearest facility. The former depends on the client load or demand at each location.

A Fortran program for this was developed by Howard Fredrick at the University of Michigan. It starts with one facility, and it iteratively considers n facilities, dividing the rectangle into n service regions, computing for each its center of gravity where the facility is located. It then computes the mean travel costs for clients as a linear function of distance and monitors the segments of the demand density surface that crossed boundaries of service regions to utilize the facility of another service region. When such crossings occur, the partition into service regions is modified. Costs are printed out, and the user stops the program when the cost starts to go up again.

Appendix 3.1

Derivation of Optimal Number of Functionally Specialized Facilities

To simplify, let $b = \rho$ and assume that there is only one facility servicing requests that range uniformly over the ρ specialties. If the facility is to provide the appropriate services, it will have to make some adjustment from one request to the next and it would be best to start it in the center of the scale. On the average, this adjustment will involve a transition of $\rho/4$ specialties, by the assumption of uniform distribution. Now the average time of adjustment will be $\rho/4v_f$, where v_f is the functional adjustment speed in adjustment steps per hour. If c_f is the cost in dollars per hour of making the requisite functional adjustment for a single step along the scale of $1 \ldots \rho$ specialties and L is the number of requests per month, then the monthly adjustment cost for the single facility will be $c_f \rho L/4v_f$ in dollars per month.

Now if we allow for more than one facility, the load can be shared. If n is the number of facilities, the adjustment cost is $c_f \rho L/4v_f n$ dollars per month. Clearly this decreases as the number of facilities increases; actually the costs could decrease even more radically if we provided for rerouting of requests to minimize adjustments.

Let C be the cost, in dollars per month, of maintaining one facility, and assume that the cost of maintaining n facilities is nC. As in previous calculations of this nature, we assume that the optimum number of facilities will be that value of n for which the cost of maintaining an additional station is offset by the reduction in adjustment cost.

Hence the increase in maintenance cost incurred by increasing the number of facilities by 1 will be $(n + 1)C - nC = C$ dollars per month, and it is to be offset by the decrease in adjustment cost, which is

$$\frac{c_f\rho L}{4v_f n} - \frac{\rho c_f L}{4v_f(n + 1)}$$

That is,

$$n^2 + n - c_f\rho L/4v_f C \text{ should be } 0$$

which has the solution:

$$n = \frac{1}{2}(\sqrt{1 + c_f\rho L/v_f C} - 1) \qquad (A3.1.1)$$

If $c_f \rho L/Cv_f$ is very large, then approximately

$$n \doteq \frac{1}{2}(c_f\rho L/Cv_f)^{1/2}$$

If $c_f\rho L/4Cv_f = 12$, for example, then $n = 3$ is a solution (exact). Similarly, for $c_f\rho L/4Cv_f = 80, 120, 168, 224, 288, 360, 440, 528, 624, \ldots, n \doteq 4, 5, 6, 7, 8, 9, 10, 11, 12, \ldots$, respectively.

Appendix 3.2

Joint Minimization of Cost with with Respect to n_d and n_f

The total cost is $n_d n_f C + (L/4)((c_d D)/v_d n_d) + \rho c_f / v_f n_f$. This may be approximated as a differentiable function of n_d and n_f when $c_d D / v_d$ and $c_f \rho / v_f$ are large, for then the error committed by using partial derivatives instead of finite differences is quite small. It is a realistic assumption when D and ρ are large, the costs not too low, and the speeds not too high.

The partial derivative of the cost with respect to n_d is $n_f C - L c_d D/(4 v_d n_d^2)$. With respect to n_f, it is $n_d C - L c_f \rho / 4 v_f n_f^2$. The four second-partial derivatives are c, c, and $L c_d D / 2 v_d n_d$, $L c_f \rho / 2 v_f n_f^3$, and they are all positive, indicating that the value obtained by setting the first derivatives to 0 is a minimum. Multiply n_f by n_d to obtain $n_f n_d = L^2 c_d c_f D \rho / 16 v_d v_f n_d^2 n_f^2 c^2$. Using $n = n_d n_f$ and cross-multiplying, we obtain

$$n^3 = L^2 c_f c_d D \rho / 16 v_f v_d c^2 \tag{A3.2.1}$$

On taking the cube root of both sides, the result follows.[1]

Appendix 3.3

Effect of More Dimensions and Economies of Scale

So far we have dealt with just one-dimensional geographic regions and a single scale for functional specialties. Geographic regions are at least two dimensional, and functional space may require several dimensions. Let m_d be the dimensionality of the geographic space (taking values 1, 2, or 3) and m_f that of the functional adjustment space. Using a technique similar to that used in Appendix 3.2, we obtain for the optimal number of facilities:

$$n = (L/4C)^{m/m+1} (Dc_d/v_d)^{m_d/(m+1)} (\rho c_f/v_f)^{m_f/(m+1)} \qquad (A3.3.1)$$

where $m = m_d + m_f$.

If $m_d = 2$ while m_f increases greatly, then n tends toward $L\rho c_f/4C$. Hence, if m_f is large enough, it no longer has a large effect. If L is the dominant trend, then the plurality of facilities needed increases. Similarly, an increase in the number of specialties favors pluralization. Increased dimensionality of functional adjustment space makes the trend toward this aspect of decentralization more pronounced in that it replaces growth of the number of facilities as the square root of load, by growth as a higher power (less than 1) of load, up to a linear function of load. This, if m is large, doubling the request load doubles the least-cost number of facilities to be deployed over the specialties and the geographic region.

This suggests replacing the assumption that n equal facilities, agents, or units cost n times as much as one by an assumption that introduces economy of scale. If a large number of identical facilities are ordered at once, the unit price is often lowered. This would not apply to human agents as well as it does to mass-producible hardware. Indeed, the promise of the savings due to economies of scale is often used as a major reason for centralization. The following assumption represents an extreme case that gives the greatest economy of scale, one that might apply to mining and collecting moon rocks:

$$C_n = C/n \text{ dollars per unit}; \quad C = C_1$$

This says that n units cost just C, the same as one unit. Under this assumption, both n_d and n_f should be made as large as possible, for that minimizes the operating cost. In the case of moon rocks, the numbers are limited by the carrying capacity of the space vehicle, the time available to collect and load them, and so on.

More generally, we can express the variation of unit cost with n by

$$C_n = Cn^{-\alpha}, \quad 0 < \alpha \leq 1$$

A value of $\alpha = 1/2$ has been used in the literature. The optimal value of n that minimizes total cost is now

$$n = (L^2 c_f c_d D\rho / 16 v_f v_d C^2)^{1/(3-2\alpha)} \quad \text{(A3.3.2)}$$

But if $\alpha > 1$, the aggregate fixed cost declines for an increasing number of units. In all those cases, the optimum number of facilities tends, in theory, to infinity, or in practice, to the number of clients. This is a situation analogous to personal radios or telephone extensions, where the optimum is limited only by the population and the number of radios or telephones each individual can reasonably be expected to own. Only if $\alpha < 1$ is n meaningful as an optimal number of facilities in our model, since there is a local minimum in this case.

It is of interest to solve the above cost minimization equations simultaneously for n_f and n_d. The ratio n_f/n_d, of functionally dispersed facilities to spatially dispersed ones, is given by $4r_0^{(2-\alpha)/(1-\alpha)}$ where $r_0 = (c_f \rho v_d / c_d D v_f)$. This ratio, r_0, measures the degree of idiosyncrasy or individuality. If it is large, there is considerable diversity relative to dispersion over space. The ratio r_0 is that of the corresponding costs, and this formula states that n_f/n_d varies as the square of that ratio if $\alpha = 0$ (when there are no economies of scale), as the cube of that ratio if $\alpha = 1/2$ (when the unit cost decreases as the inverse square root of the number of facilities).

If $\alpha = -1$, which corresponds to $C_n = Cn$, the cost per facility *increases* with the number of facilities, as might be the case for custom-designed or highly specialized or personalized facilities. In that case, $n_f/n_d = 4(r_0)^{3/2}$. Note that as α increases from -1 to $1/2$, n_f/n_d rises with r_0 as a higher power. Such conditions of rising cost per facility might be realistic for creating additional highways, medical schools, law courts, or universities.

If we fix the ratio n_f/n_d a priori, and call it i, then $n_f = in_d$, and hence $n = in_d^2$ and $n_d = n^{1/2} i^{-1/2}$, and $n_f = n^{1/2} i^{1/2}$.

The value of n for which the total cost is minimum is:

$$n = (Li^{1/2}k_d(1 + r_0/i))/4C \qquad (A3.3.3)$$

It is easily shown that viewing this value of n as a function of i, n is smallest when $i = r_0$. If i/r_0 declines below 1, n increases because the demand for diversity will set free additional variable cost elements that may now be used to cater to the unchanged demand for geographic dispersion. For instance, if people should lose their taste for diversity of goods offered by supermarkets, the number of neighborhood grocery stores carrying limited stock might again increase.

Appendix 5.1

Effect of Load on Optimum Flatness

Here we present the technical details to support the results that give the change in optimum flatness with request load. We address the question of whether the rate of change in the optimum number of hierarchical levels increases with L.

We are able to answer this question by an analytic technique that bypasses the need to calculate the optimal number of hierarchical levels. The latter calculation—which requires a far more complex model with many more assumptions and detailed analyses—will be presented in Appendices 5.3 and 5.4. The method to be used is an adaptation of the calculus of variations as applied in mathematical economics (Samuelson, 1970). To start, we summarize the basic variables of our organizational model.[1]

λ: the number of hierarchical levels.
$C(\lambda)$: the total cost of maintaining the operating of a λ-level organization.
L: the request load, in requests per month.
l: one of the λ levels; varies from 1 to λ.
$T(l, \lambda)$: the time (hours) it takes a server at level l in a λ-level organization to service a request averaged over all requests and all servers at level l.
$K(\lambda, L)$: the overhead, fixed cost, in dollars per month of maintaining the organization.

$c(l)$: the cost, in dollars per hour, of maintaining one server at level l; this corresponds to what we previously called C.
c'_{wa}: the cost, in dollars per hour, of a client's time.

The fixed component of the total cost $K(\lambda, L)$ may well increase as λ increases to $\lambda + 1$, as the organizational hierarchy gets taller. Could there be a compensating decrease in the other operating components of the total cost? We would expect the total cost of a 1-level organization, $C(1)$, to exceed $C(2)$, or else it would not pay to maintain two levels rather than make do with just one. We therefore ask for that value of λ—denote it by λ^*—for which $C(\lambda)$ is minimum; even though we do not try to derive an explicit formula for λ^*, we ask for the sign of $d\lambda^*/dL$, the rate of change of λ with respect to L when $\lambda = \lambda^*$.

To calculate sgn $d\lambda^*/dL$ we make the mathematical assumption that $T(l, \lambda)$ is a continuous, integrable, twice-differentiable function of real variables l and λ. Regarding l and λ as continuously variable when they must be integers introduces an error that is, however, acceptable in the sense that it does not affect our answers to the question about sgn $d\lambda^*/dL$.

From an hourly rate of $c(l)$ dollars per hour and a rate of $T(l, \lambda)$ hours per request, it follows that $c(l) T(l, \lambda)$ is the unit cost, in dollars per request, averaged over all the requests serviced by a server at level l and over all servers at level l. Summing these costs at each level for all the λ levels is given as $\int_1^\lambda c(l)T(l, \lambda)dl$ dollars per request. It is an integral rather than a sum because we assumed a continuum of levels between 1 and λ. Multiplying this by L requests per month gives $L\int_1^\lambda c(l)T(l, \lambda)dl$ as the monthly payroll cost, assuming that the number of servers employed is just what is needed to clear the load L, with neither congestion nor idleness anywhere.

To obtain the total cost, $C(\lambda)$, we must add to this $K(\lambda, L)$ dollars per month for the capital cost of buildings, fixed equipment, and so on. We must also add an additional cost borne by the clients in waiting for a response, assuming that they are not productively occupied while waiting and that either they or their employers lose the amount $Lc_{wa}T(\lambda)$ dollars per month, where $T(\lambda) = \int_1^\lambda T(l, \lambda)dl$. Hence, the *total* cost to the community in dollars per month, is

$$C(\lambda) = Lc'_{wa}T(\lambda) + L\int_1^\lambda c(l)T(l, \lambda)dl + K(\lambda, L) \qquad (A5.1.1)$$

We now show[2] that the value of λ for which this cost is least increases with L if and only if $\delta^2 K/\delta\lambda\delta L < (1(L)(\delta K/\delta\lambda)$.

Let λ^* be the value of λ that makes this least. This value of λ will vary with L, as $\lambda^*(L)$. To minimize C with respect to λ, we calculate:

$$C_\lambda = \frac{\delta C}{\delta \lambda} = L\frac{d}{d\lambda}g(\lambda) + K_\lambda \qquad (A5.1.2)$$

where

$$g(\lambda) = c_{wa}T(\lambda) + \int_1^\lambda c(l)T(l, \lambda)dl \qquad (A5.1.3)$$

Effect of Load on Optimum Flatness / 261

and

$$K_\lambda = \delta K/\delta \lambda \quad \text{(A5.1.4)}$$

λ^* is the value of λ that makes this 0 and for which $C_{\lambda\lambda} > 0$ as well.
To determine qualitatively how λ^* changes with L is to determine the sign of $d\lambda^*/dL$. That is, we ask if this least-cost number of levels increases or decreases with a slight increase in the request load. To obtain this rate of change let us treat the equation that defines λ^* as a function of L as an identity and differentiate it totally with respect to L. We get:

$$L\frac{d^2g}{d\lambda^2}\frac{d\lambda^*}{dL} + \frac{dg}{d\lambda} + K_{\lambda\lambda}\frac{d\lambda^*}{dL} + K_{\lambda L} = 0 \quad \text{(A5.1.5)}$$

where

$$K_{\lambda L} = \frac{\delta^2 K}{\delta\lambda\delta L}$$

Solving for $d\lambda^*/dL$ gives

$$\frac{d\lambda^*}{dL} = -\frac{g'(\lambda) + K_{\lambda L}}{Lg''(\lambda) + K_{\lambda\lambda}} \quad \text{(A5.1.6)}$$

Here the prime denotes total differentiation and the subscripts partial differentiation.

A simple calculation shows that $g'(\lambda) = -K_\lambda L$ and $C''(\lambda^*) = Lg'' + K_{\lambda\lambda}$. Substituting, we obtain

$$\frac{d\lambda^*}{dL} = -\frac{K_{\lambda L} - K_\lambda/L}{C''(\lambda^*)} \quad \text{(A5.1.7)}$$

Because $C''(\lambda^*) > 0$, it follows that the sign of the rate of change of λ^* with L is:

$$\text{sgn}\frac{d\lambda^*}{dL} = -\text{sgn}(K_{\lambda L} - K_\lambda/L) \quad \text{(A5.1.8)}$$

It follows that λ increases with L if and only if $K_{\lambda L} < K_\lambda/L$.
To obtain some insight from this result we examine some of its implications in special cases where the mathematical form of the fixed cost as a function of λ and L is such that the implications can be derived. Suppose first that fixed cost can be written as a sum of two costs, one varying only with λ and the other only with L.

$$K(\lambda,L) + K_1(\lambda) + K_2(L) \quad \text{(A5.1.9)}$$

While this assumption is made for mathematical reasons only, we could interpret $K_1(\lambda)$ as the fixed cost of "status symbols," such as carpets, and so on, that would vary only with the number of hierarchical levels but not with load, while $K_2(L)$ is the fixed cost of the plant, which may vary only with the load but not the number of levels, and the total fixed cost for certain kinds of organizations is the sum of these two costs and nothing else. It follows that

$$K_{\lambda K} = \frac{\delta}{\delta \lambda} \frac{\delta K_1}{\delta L} + \frac{\delta K_2}{\delta L} = \frac{\delta}{\delta \lambda}(0 + K_{2L}) = 0 + 0 = 0$$

and $K_\lambda = \delta/\delta\lambda \, (K_1 + K_2) = \delta K_1/\delta\lambda + 0$. Substituting into Equation A5.1.8 we have:

$$\text{sgn } d\lambda^*/dL = -\text{sgn } (0 - L^{-1}\delta K_1/\delta\lambda)$$

It seems plausible that $K_1(\lambda)$ increases with λ, so that $\delta K_1/\delta\lambda$ is positive. Hence sgn $d\lambda^*/dL$ is also positive. In words, a trend toward increased service loads (increasing L) tends to favor taller organizations (the rate of growth of the least-cost number of hierarchical levels with L is increasing).

Another assumption about the form of $K(\lambda, L)$, made for purely mathematical reasons in order to learn more about the implications of Equation A5.1.8 is

$$K(\lambda, L) = h(\lambda)L \qquad (A5.1.10)$$

This is interpreted as stating that the fixed cost is in direct proportion to the load, but where the proportionality "constant" depends on the number of levels according to some function $h(\lambda)$. It follows from this assumption that $K_{\lambda L} = \delta/\delta\lambda(\delta/\delta L)h(\lambda)L = d/d\lambda \, H(\lambda)$, and $K\lambda = Ldh/d\lambda$. Substituting into the right-hand side of Equation A5.1.8, we have

$$\text{sgn } d\lambda^*/dL = -\text{sgn } (dh/d\lambda - L^{-1}Ldh/d\lambda) = 0$$

This means that the least-cost number of hierarchical levels does not change with request load under this assumption, regardless of how $h(\lambda)$ depends on λ.

The above two assumptions were made for analytical reasons only. A realistic assumption about how K varies with λ and L is shown graphically in Figure A5.1.1. Here we plot the fixed cost against request load for $\lambda = 1, 2, 3, 4$. For a one-level organization, we would expect this to increase, with a growing rate of increase because additional servers will be needed to cope with the larger load; the number of possible dyadic contacts among servers on the same level increases as the square of their number; and if more than two servers must be coordinated by lateral search and coordination, the number of possible triplets, quadruplets, and so on, will increase with still higher powers of the number of servers (see the curve for $\lambda = 1$).

For a two-level organization, we expect $K(L, 2)$ to increase with L as did $K(L, 1)$ until a certain level of request load, at which the economics of coordination

Effect of Load on Optimum Flatness / 263

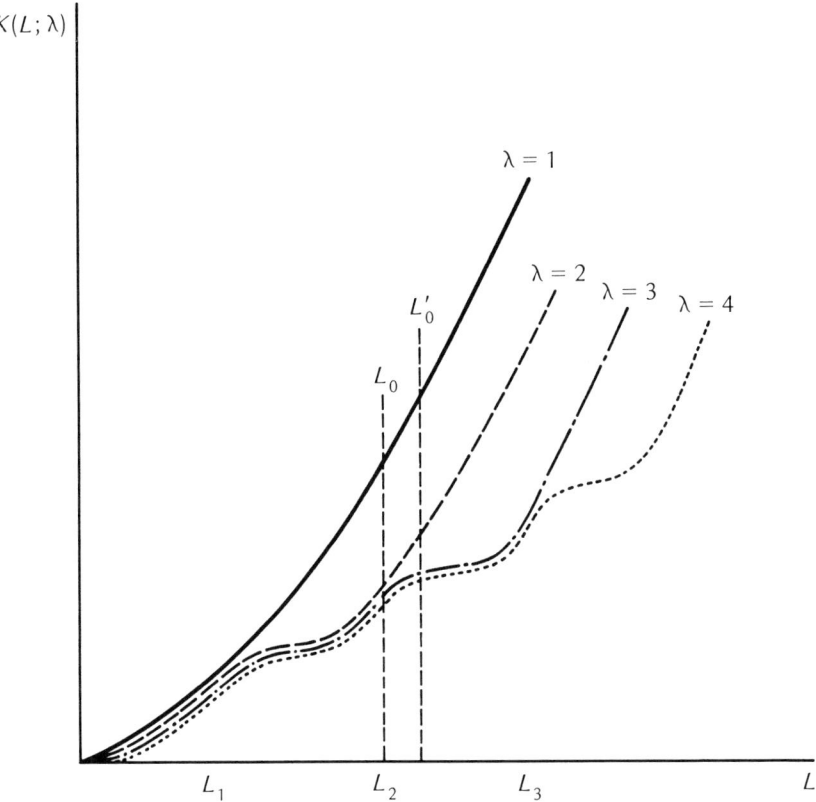

Figure A5.1.1. A plausible relation between fixed cost and request load for organizations with varying tallness.

from level 2 take effect and the rate of growth of $K(L, 2)$ with L levels off for a range of request loads, then to increase again as before, because the communication and coordinating capacities of level 2 become overloaded and saturated.

For a three-level organization, we expect $K(L, 3)$ to grow as did $K(L, 2)$ until the start of a second range of request loads, at the end of which it resumes the upward growth curve. This is shown in Figure A5.1.1.

If we draw a vertical line on this graph, say $L = L_0$, and examine the intersections of this family of curves as λ increases, we note a decrease in fixed costs, $K(L, \lambda)$. Moreover, these decreases get less; that is, if we fix L, $\delta K(L, \lambda)/\delta \lambda$ is negative but increases. If we draw another vertical line to the right of the one just drawn, say at $L = L_0'$, we note a faster rate of increase in $\delta K/\delta \lambda$. The rate of increase, $\delta K(L, \lambda)/\delta \lambda$, with respect to L increases. This means that $\delta/\delta L(\delta K/\delta \lambda)$ increases. Thus $K_{\lambda L}$ in Equation 5.1.8 is positive and quite large. Now K_λ is also positive, but K_λ/L may be less than $K_{\lambda L}$, especially if L is large. Hence $K_{\lambda L} - K_\lambda/L$ is positive and sgn $d\lambda^*/dL$ is negative according to Equation A5.1.8. This means that the tallness of an organization would tend to decrease with load under these assumptions.

Appendix 5.2

Effect of Number of Sorters and Diagnosticians

It is of some interest to explore the effect of the number of agents in stages 1 and 2, even without regard to hierarchies at each stage. The simplest model is to assume the existence of ρ functional specialties, as in Chapter 3, with n_f diagnosticians (stage 2 agents) assigned to specialty $f, f = 1, 2, \ldots, \rho$. Let n_s be the number of sorters (stage 1 agents), each of whom sorts the requests reaching him or her into one of the ρ categories. If C_s and C_f are the fixed costs ($ per month) associated with each of these agents, then the total fixed cost is $n_s C_s + \Sigma_{f=1}^{\rho} n_f C_f$ dollars per month.

Suppose now, as in Chapter 2, that requests orginate uniformly in space and time, from D-mile strip, at a combined rate of L requests per month, being forwarded to the nearest of the n_s uniformly deployed sorters at a speed of v miles per hour and at an operating cost (to servers and clients) of k dollars per hour. This adds an average operating cost of $kDL/4vn_s$ dollars per month to the total cost, taking account only of forwarding time.

Let L_f denote the number of requests per month that fall into category f, with $\Sigma L_f = L$. Assume that the sorters make no errors. If the n_f diagnosticians specialized in f are also distributed uniformly over the D-mile stretch, then an additional average operating cost is incurred in forwarding a request from a sorter to the nearest diagnostician, and this is $kDL_f/4vn_f$ for specialty f. Hence the total cost is

$$K(n_s, n_1, \ldots, n_\rho) = n_s C_s + \sum_{f=1}^{\rho} n_f C_f + kDL/4vn_s \sum_{f=1}^{\rho} L_f/n_f$$

With the help of differential calculus, we find that if n_s and n_f are approximately $\frac{1}{2}\sqrt{kDL/C_s v}$ and $\frac{1}{2}\sqrt{kDL_f/C_f v}$, respectively, then the total cost is least. The total number of agents is approximately

$$\frac{1}{2}\sqrt{kD/v\,(L/C_s + \sum_{f=1}^{\rho} L_f/C_f)}$$

If L_f/C_f does not vary with f—that is, if specialists for rare requests cost less than those for frequent ones, in proportion to frequency—then the number of agents varies directly with ρ and with $\sqrt{L}$. More realistically, if C_f were independent of f, and the volume of requests that originated from each of the ρ categories were equal, then $L_f = L/\rho$ and the number of agents would increase as $\sqrt{L}$ and as $\sqrt{\rho}$. If most of the requests came from the same few specialties regardless of ρ, then the number of agents would increase with L but not with ρ.

To the total we should add the expected errors in sorting. A larger number ρ of specialties should reduce such errors, though it might increase each C_f. A larger value of C_s may reduce the probability of errors in sorting. Moreover, it may pay to introduce backup agents. What a less costly and presumably less competent sorter cannot do is reserved for a higher-level sorter. The lowest-level sorters may respond with a simple Yes-No decision, with the ρ specialties arranged into a binary tree (e.g., if $\rho = 8$ medical specialties, each level 1 sorter makes three Yes-No decisions to pinpoint the appropriate category, i.e., emergency, functional/organic, etc.). Thus there may be good reasons for hierarchies among sorters. In a sense, diagnosis is high-level sorting with the important addition of a recommended pattern of servicing the request.

The pattern to be specified may involve two or more complementary operations, which may have to be performed simultaneously or in a specified sequence. Serving a customer a good restaurant meal requires coordination of meat and vegetables arriving simultaneously, both freshly cooked, at the same table. All these services together then lead to the payoff that will induce guests to repeatedly pay the price charged. In the absence of coordination, a random combination of such services would command a much lower price in the market. To illustrate a temporal correspondence, consider a diagnostician or correspondence specifier who states that a manuscript for a book should be printed prior to binding.

To earn the reward for such coordination it is necessary to specify which operations have to be performed in what combinations over space and time. The necessary pattern may already be prerecorded and utilize standardized, prefabricated decisions or goods such as the ubiquitous roast beef, for example. If the request load predominately involves well-known precoded combinations, the task of specifying them can be decentralized; if expensive new combinations must be worked out, more centralized specialties for issuing prescriptions may be needed.

Appendix 5.3

A Model for Calculating Optimum Flatness Analytically

To calculate the optimal number of levels, we need a simpler model, specified by variables and assumed relations among these levels. We will introduce the variables a few at a time, as needed for the model to be discussed. The following variables are common to all the models, and for completeness, we repeat some of the variables that had previously been introduced.

λ: the number of hierarchical levels (to be calculated).

λ^*: the optimal number of hierarchical levels (so as to minimize total cost).

l: any level, $l = 1, 2, \ldots, \lambda$. $l = 0$ denotes the clients.

s: any stage, $s = 1, 2, \ldots, 5$. $s = 0$ denotes the request.

$A_{l,s}$: any server at level l, in stage s.

$c_{l,s}$: the cost, in dollars per hour, of maintaining a server, say $A_{l,s}$, at level l, in stage s.

$n_{l,s}$: the number of servers at level l, stage s (calculated).

$T_{l,s}^w$: the time (hours) it takes $A_{l,s}$ in direct working activity (not communication) to service a request, averaged over all such servers and requests.

$T_{l,s}^{sll}$: the time (hours) $A_{l,s}$ spends in communicating laterally, with other servers at the same level, $A'_{l,s}$, or with him or herself (thinking) to service one request, averaged over servers and requests.

$T_{l,s}^{ud}$: the time (hours) $A_{l,s}$ spends in communicating vertically—reporting upward and listening to instructions downward and listening to reports from below—in servicing a request, averaged over clients and requests.

$T_{l,s}$: the total time $A_{l,s}$ spends, averaged per request.

$T^o_{l,s} = T_{ls} - (T^w_{ls} + T^{sf}_{ls} + T^{ud}_{ls}) = A_{l,s}$'s "idle" or "renewal" time per request.

In what follows, n and T may be viewed as functions of λ, and they may vary with l and s. When we need to call attention to that variation or functional relation, we will indicate that explicitly by writing the variables within parentheses next to the functional symbol, as in $T(l, \lambda)$; we also use subscripts, as in the above list so that $T_{l,\lambda}$ is the same as $T(l, \lambda)$, reserving the latter notion to its use as an integrand rather than as a summand.

An explicit formula for λ^*, the number of hierarchical levels that minimizes total costs, is valuable for the insights it provides into the relation between λ^* and the numerous other variables and parameters on which it depends. The value of such a formula depends, of course, on the realism of the assumptions from which it follows and the sensitivity of the conclusions to the necessarily unrealistic mathematical details in these assumptions.

The total cost, in dollars per month, of running a λ-level organization is

$$C(\lambda) = Lc(0)T(\lambda) + L \sum_{l=1}^{\lambda} c(l)T(l, \lambda) + K(\lambda, L) \qquad (A5.3.1)$$

Here, we use $c(o)$ in place of c'_{wa} for the cost of the client's time and $T(\lambda) = \Sigma^\lambda_{l=1} T(l, \lambda)$, the total time to service a request, averaged over all servers and requests. We do not need to use integrals instead of summations for the mathematical optimization technique, ordinary calculus, to be used here. That is why we tend to use subscripts in what follows, to denote c_l as a function of l, for example. Thus, $T(l, \lambda)$ or just $T_l(\lambda)$ is equal to $\Sigma_s T_{l,s}$.

We wish to find λ^*, that value of λ for which $C(\lambda)$ is minimum. If we regard $C(\lambda)$ as a twice continuously differentiable function of λ, then we can determine a minimum, if one exists, by finding the value of λ for which the first derivative $dC/d\lambda$ is 0 and the second derivatives are such that the cost is a minimum rather than a maximum, that is, $d^2C/d\lambda^2 > 0$.

We now make some strong assumptions about how $T_{l,s}$ varies with λ in order to capture plausible conditions under which it pays to add a level to the hierarchy because the cost of vertical communication more than compensates the costs of horizontal communication thus saved. First, assume that $T^{ud}_{l,s}(\lambda)$ decreases with l, which means that the time per request that $A_{l,s}$ spends in communicating vertically is less if $A_{l,s}$ is higher up. Similarly, assume that $T^{sfl}_{l,s}(\lambda)$ decrease with l; also the higher up $A_{l,s}$, the less time is spent per request in horizontal communication, in direct proportion to $T^{ud}_{l,s}(\lambda)$. The exact form of the decrease with l is not entirely arbitrary. If we assume that all communications are "through normal channels," so that each $A_{l,s}$ communicates up or down just one level, then the time spent in downward communication by all the $A_{l,s}$ must equal the time that all the A_{l-1}'s spend in upward communication. If we denote by g the time (hours per request) one server in a two-level organization spends in vertical communication, and if we do not distinguish between listening or reading and speaking or writing when measuring time spent on communication, then $T_2^{ud}(2) = T_1^{ud}(2) = g$.

In a three-level organization, we still take $T_1^{ud}(3) = g$, but we assume that $T_2^{ud}(3) = \gamma g$, where γ is a vertical communication time multiplier for level 2, a number greater than 1. Now the time spent by A_2 in just downward communication must also be g. The time spent by A_2 in downward and upward communication together must add up to γg. Hence the time spent by A_2 in just upward communication must be $\gamma g - g$ or $(\gamma - 1)g$. Now that must also equal $T_3^{ud}(3)$, because A_3 is the top man in three-level organization and can communicate vertically only downward. Hence $T_3^{ud}(3) = (\gamma - 1)g$.

If we had a four-level organization, then we assume again that the total time spent by T_3 in vertical communication is γ times the time spent by T_2 in upward communication, or $\gamma \cdot (\gamma - 1)g$. It follows that the time spent by A_3 in upward communication is thus $\gamma(\gamma - 1)g$ less the time in downward communication, or $(\gamma - 1)g$; that is $(\gamma - 1)^2 g$. The general formula is:

$$T_l^{ud}(\lambda) = \begin{cases} g, & \text{if } l = 1 \\ \gamma(\gamma -)^{l-2}g & \text{for } l = 2, 3, \ldots, \lambda - 1 \\ (\gamma - 1)^{\lambda - 2}g & \text{for } l = \lambda, \text{ provided} \geq 2 \end{cases}$$

The assumption about how $T^{sfl}(\lambda)$ varies with l is:

$$T_l^{sfl}(\lambda) = \begin{cases} \alpha^{\lambda - 1}a & \text{for } l = 1 \quad \lambda = 1 \\ \epsilon T_l^{ud}(\lambda) & \text{for } l = 2, \ldots, \lambda, \lambda = 2, \ldots \end{cases}$$

Here α is a multiplier, smaller than 1, denoting how much less time for lateral and self-communication a server at level 1 will spend after another level has been added to the organization. The present formula assumes that this per-added-level multiplier remains unchanged, regardless of how many levels the organization already has.

In an organization of more than one level, ϵ is the multiplier by which vertical, up-and/or-down communication time increases for any server at levels 2 and above, in comparison.

The assumption about the time it takes A_l in direct working activity, averaged over all servers, levels, stages, and requests, to service a request is:

$$T_l^{w}(\lambda) = \beta^{\lambda - 1}(w - w_0) + w_0 \quad \text{for } l = 1 \text{ and } 0 \text{ for } l > 1$$

Here, β is a constant, interpretable as the work-time multiplier; $\beta < 1$. This states that only bottom-level servers spend time in *direct* working activity. The others all coordinate or supervise other servers, thus contributing to service only indirectly. Among the level 1 servers, those in stage 4 probably take a greater share of direct client contact service than those in other stages, but we are for now dealing only with averages. It also asserts that people spend less time on such work in organizations with many levels.[1]

All these assumptions are shown for the special cases $\lambda = 1, 2, 3, 4$ in Table A5.3.1.

Table A5.3.1. Relations among Communication and Work Times

	λ = 1			λ = 2			λ = 3			λ = 4		
	T_l^{sn}	T_l^w	T_l^{ud}	T_l^{sn}	T_l^w	T_l^{ud}	T_l^{sn}	T_l^w	T_l^{ud}	T_l^{sn}	T_l^w	T_l^{ud}
l = 4										$\epsilon(\gamma-1)^2 g$	0	$(\gamma-1)^2 g$
l = 3							$\epsilon(\gamma-1)g$	0	$(\gamma-1)g$	$\epsilon(\gamma-1)g$	0	$\gamma(\gamma-1)g$
l = 2				ϵg	0	g	$\epsilon \gamma g$	0	γg	$\epsilon \gamma g$	0	γg
l = 1	a	w	0	αa	w_2	g	$\alpha^2 a$	w_3	g	$\alpha^3 a$	0	g
	λ = 1			λ = 2			λ = 3			λ = 4		

A Model for Calculating Optimum Flatness / 271

a: time (hours per request) one server spends in lateral communication in a one-level organization.
w: time (hours per job) one server spends in work in a one-level organization.
w_0: time (hours per job) one server spends in work in an organization with very many levels.
g: time (hours per job) one server spends in vertical communication in a two-level organization.
α: horizontal communication time multiplier for the bottom level; $\alpha < 1$.
β: work-time multiplier for the bottom level; $\beta < 1$.
γ: vertical communication time multiplier for level 2; $1 < \gamma < 2$.
ϵ: ratio of horizontal to vertical communication time for $l = 2$ to λ.
δ: wage multiplier for levels $l > 1$.
c: wages of workers at level 1 ($/hour)

Using the assumptions made in the text that relate to T_l^{ν} to λ, we have:

$$w_2 = \beta(w - w_0) + w_0;\ w_3 = \beta^2(w - w_0) + w_0;\ \text{and}\ w_4 = \beta^3(w - w_0) + w_0$$

The explicit equation for $T_l(\lambda) = T_l^{\nu}(\lambda) + T_l^{\mathit{sl}}(\lambda) + T_l^{\nu d}(\lambda)$ is given by A5.3.3.
We also need an explicit assumption about c_l, and take it to be a geometric increase with or

$$c_l = \delta^{l-1}c\ \text{dollars per hour}$$

Here δ is a wage multiplier. It is greater than 1.
Finally, assume that $T_l^{\rho} = 0$, that there is no idle time, so that

$$T_l(\lambda) = T_l^{\nu}(\lambda) + T_l^{\mathit{sl}}(\lambda) + T_l^{\nu d}(\lambda) \tag{A5.3.2}$$

Substituting the previously stated assumptions gives:

$$T_l(\lambda) = \begin{cases} \beta^{\lambda-1}(w - w_0) + w_0 + \alpha^{\lambda-1}a + \begin{array}{l} 0\ \text{if}\ \lambda = 1 \\ g\ \text{if}\ \lambda > 1 \end{array} & \text{for}\ l = 1 \\ (\epsilon + 1)\gamma(\gamma - 1)^{l-2}g & \text{for}\ l = 2, 3, \ldots, \lambda - 1 \\ (\epsilon + 1)(\gamma - 1)^{\lambda-2}g & \text{for}\ l = \lambda \end{cases} \tag{A5.3.3}$$

If we take $K(\lambda, L)$ and $c(0)$ to be 0 to simplify the calculation, we have

$$C(\lambda) = Lc \sum_{l=0}^{\lambda} \delta^{l-1} T_l(\lambda)$$

To minimize $C(\lambda)$, therefore, is to minimize $\Sigma_{l=1}^{\lambda}\ \delta^{l-1}\ T_l(\lambda)$. The value of λ for which $C(\lambda)$ is the minimum must satisfy the equation

$$\frac{dC(\lambda)}{d\lambda} = 0 \quad \text{or} \quad \sum_{l=1}^{\lambda} \delta^{l-1} \frac{\partial T_l(\lambda)}{\partial \lambda} + \delta^{\lambda-1} T_\lambda(\lambda) = 0$$

272 / Appendix 5.3

Differentiating Equation A5.3.3 term by term with respect to λ results in

$$\frac{\partial T_l}{\partial \lambda} = \begin{cases} (w - w_0)\beta^{\lambda-1} \ln\beta + a\alpha^{\lambda-1} \ln\alpha & l = 1 \\ 0 & \text{for } l = 2, \ldots, \lambda - 1 \\ (\epsilon + 1)(\gamma - 1)^{\lambda-2} gl\, n(\gamma - 1) & l = \lambda \end{cases}$$

Because $\beta < 1$, $\alpha < 1$, and $1 < \delta < 2$, all logs are negative and $\delta T_l/\delta\lambda < 0$ for $l = 1, \lambda$, and 0 otherwise. The key assumption of the previous section is satisfied. Let us now substitute into the equation:

$$0 = L\frac{\partial}{\partial\lambda}\sum_{l=1}^{\lambda} c_l T_l(\lambda) = L\sum_{l=1}^{\lambda} c_l \frac{\partial T_l(\lambda)}{\partial\lambda} + c_\lambda T_\lambda(\lambda)$$

$$0 = c_1\left[(w - w_o)\beta^{\lambda-1}\ln\beta + a\alpha^{\lambda-1}\ln\alpha \right.$$
$$\left. + c_\lambda(\epsilon + 1)(\gamma - 1)^{\lambda-2} g \ln(\gamma - 1) + (\epsilon + 1)(\gamma - 1)^{\lambda-2} g\right]$$

$$= L\left[c((w - w_o)\beta^{\lambda-1}\ln\beta + a\alpha^{\lambda-1}\ln\alpha) \right.$$
$$\left. + \delta^{\lambda-1} c(\epsilon + 1)(\gamma - 1)^{\lambda-2} g \ln(\gamma - 1) + \delta^{\lambda-1} c(\epsilon + 1)(\gamma - 1)^{\lambda-2} g\right]$$

To be able to solve this explicitly for λ, let us arbitrarily assume that $\alpha = \beta$, collect terms, and simplify:

$$0 = (w - w_o + a)\alpha^{\lambda-1}\ln\alpha + \delta^{\lambda-1} g(\epsilon + 1)(\gamma - 1)^{\lambda-2}(\ln(\gamma - 1))$$

or

$$0 = A\alpha^{\lambda-2} + B(\delta(\gamma - 1))^{\lambda-2},$$
where $A = (w - w_0 + a)\alpha \ln\alpha$ and $B = g(\epsilon + 1)\delta \ln(\gamma - 1)e$

Since $\alpha < 1$, $\ln\alpha < 0$ and A is negative. If $(\gamma - 1)e > 1$, $B > 0$ and we can take the logs of both sides of $-A\alpha^{\lambda-2} = B\delta(\gamma - 1)^{\lambda-2}$ to get $\ln(-A) + (\lambda - 2)\ln\alpha = \ln B + (\lambda - 2)\ln\delta(\gamma - 1)$.

Thus, if $(\gamma - 1) > 1/e$ or $1 + 1/e < \gamma < 2$, we can solve for λ^*. It is $\lambda^* = 2 + (\ln(-A) - \ln B)/(\ln\delta(\gamma - 1) - \ln\alpha)$ or, substituting for A and B,

$$\lambda^* = 2 + \frac{\ln\dfrac{(w - w_o + a)\alpha \ln(1/\alpha)}{g\delta(\epsilon + 1)\ln e\,(\gamma - 1)}}{\ln\dfrac{\delta(\gamma - 1)}{\alpha}} \quad (A5.3.4)$$

To interpret this, let $w = 1$, $w_0 = 1/2$, $a = 1/2$, $g = 1/2$, and $\gamma = 1.5$. These are plausible values. Then

$$\lambda^* = 2 + \frac{\ln\dfrac{\alpha \ln(1/\alpha)}{.15\delta(\epsilon + 1)}}{\ln\dfrac{\delta}{2\alpha}}$$

A Model for Calculating Optimum Flatness / 273

What is the effect of ϵ, the substitution ratio of horizontal to vertical communication time, upon λ^*? We would expect ϵ to exceed 1, since vertical communication is supposed to be resorted to only if any time spent on it will save on the average a larger amount of horizontal communication time. As ϵ increases while α and δ stay fixed, λ^* varies as the negative logarithm of ϵ or λ^*; that is, it decreases linearly with every order of magnitude increase in the ratio of horizontal to vertical communication.

From the special case analyzed there, it appears that if other factors are the same and only the ratio of horizontal to vertical communication is increased by an order of magnitude (factor of 10), then the optimal number of levels decreases by a constant. The greater the time spent in horizontal relative to vertical communication, the flatter the optimal organization, and it pays to keep tall organizations only if there is immensely more vertical than horizontal communication.

What is the effect of δ, the wage multiplier? As δ increases while α and ϵ stay fixed, both the numerator of the fraction decreases, and the denominator increases, both tending to decrease λ^*. That, too, is plausible. The more costly it gets to add upper-level servers, the less it will pay to maintain tall organizations and shorter ones are favored.

What is the effect of α, the horizontal communication time multiplier for the bottom level? This multiplier is less than 1. It is that ratio of the time spent on horizontal communication by a server in a one-level organization to that of a bottom-level server in a two-level organization. Thus, if the server in a one-level organization spends 8 minutes per request in horizontal communication and $\alpha = .75$, then the bottom-level server in a two-level organization spends only 6 minutes on horizontal communication; $\alpha = 6\ 1/8$. Our result implies that as α increases from 0 to $1/e$, $\alpha ln\ 1/\alpha$ increases and then decreases as α varies from $1/e$ to 1, while $ln\ (\delta/2\alpha)$ decreases with α. The numerator changes less with α than does the denominator. Thus, on balance, λ^* tends to increase if only α increases. In words, if the effect of tallness on the time spent in horizontal communication among bottom-level servers is strong (α is near 0 and increasing) taller organizations tend to pay off.

If we examine Equation 5.3.4 for the effect of w on λ^*, it becomes clear that the optimal height increases (logarithmically) with the time per request required in direct work in a one-level organization. It decreases with the corresponding work time required in a multilevel organization. It also increases with the time per request that a server in a one-level organization needs to spend in horizontal communication; it decreases with the time per request required for vertical communication in a two-level organization. All these are direct consequences of our assumptions, and are no less plausible, though some are a little less evident.

Our assumptions determine the average total time per server per request. We still assume that no server is idle, nor being waited for. Then the number of servers at level l is also specified, by

$$n_l = LT_l$$

The ratio, n_l/n_{l+1}, gives the average number of immediate subordinates per supervisor or superior, commonly known as "span of control." Let us call it χ_l. That number is determined entirely by our assumptions.

For an optimal tallness organization, it is:

$$\frac{n_{l-1}}{n_l} = \chi_l = \begin{cases} \dfrac{\alpha^{\lambda^*-1}(w - w_0 + a) + w_0 + g}{(\epsilon + 1)\gamma(\gamma - 1)g} & \text{for } l = 2 \\[2ex] \dfrac{1}{\gamma - 1} & \text{for } l = 3, 4, \ldots, \lambda^* - 1 \\[2ex] \dfrac{\gamma}{\gamma - 1} & \text{for } l = \lambda^* \end{cases}$$

The span of control has been observed empirically (Urwick, 1956) to be about 3 at the top. It is limited by the capacity of a supervisor and psychosocial considerations. From this we estimate γ by setting $\gamma/\gamma - 1$ equal to 3, obtaining $\gamma = 1.5$. It would imply an average span of control of $1/.5 = 2$ at middle-management levels.

So far, we have taken all requests to be of equal difficulty and made no attempt to characterize the distribution of the request load according to kind and length of services required. We assumed servers at a given level and stage to be interchangeable. Suppose that the fraction of the request load that is uniform, standardized, or identically routine increases over time. Suppose that the sorters and load schedulers allocate requests so that all the servers under a given supervisor have to do the same thing, and repeatedly. Then the amount of time a higher-level server has to spend on supervision decreases, while the time per request spent by his or her subordinates decreases only slightly. If the supervisors do not spend the time thus freed on planning or other higher-level activities, then fewer of them are needed. The span of control increases. The total number of hierarchical levels will decrease.

What, however, determines an upper bound to the number of hierarchical levels?[2] Why do we rarely see organizations with more than 20 levels? The number of levels is limited by interaction capacities and the variety of interaction types. It is possible that for a given distance there is a type of interaction that is effective at that distance. If that is so, then an ensemble of interaction types will generate a collection of partly decomposable subsystems, each with its own hierarchy. Rather than growing too tall by increasing the number of levels as well as the total size of a single organization, the tree starts to divide into a number of smaller subtrees that interact, resulting in the kind of structure that has been called segmented (many, diverse groupings), polycephalons (many heads or decision-making organs), or reticulate (coupled through a network) (Gerlach, 1970).

Appendix 5.4

The Optimum Number of Hierarchical Levels Determined by Computer Simulation

Gain in Reduced Work Time and Horizontal Communication Due to Vertical Communication. Let $A_{l,s}$ denote one of the $n_{l,s}$ service agents, or servers, at stage s level l of a five-stage, λ-level service organization. Each such agent is assigned to a service station with an associated waiting area in case queues develop. Instead of assuming analytically tractable relations between the times per request that an agent spends on lateral and vertical communication and on direct client service, we now use more realistic assumptions.

We start with the probability that it takes between t and $t + dt$ hours of lateral communication for an agent to first acquire the information needed from peers to serve a client. Let $P_h(t)$ be the probability of an agent having received the needed information by horizontal communication by time t. If we assume that the probability, p_h, of the agent obtaining the needed item during the interval $(t, t + dt)$ does not change with t and these events are independent in nonoverlapping time intervals, then $P_h(t) = 1 - (1 - p_h)^t$, taking $dt = 1$. This is approximately $1 - e^{-p_h t}$. We can interpret $1/p_h$ as the time it takes for $P_h(t)$ to increase from 0 to $.63 \doteq 1 - 1/e$ (because $p_h(t) = 1 - e^{-1}$ when $p_h t = 1$ or $t = 1/p_h$), something like the half-life of lateral communication, or the average horizontal communication time it takes an agent to obtain an acceptable amount of information to service a request.

The probability, $P_v(t)$, that it takes between t and $t + dt$ hours of *vertical* communication for an agent to first acquire information needed to serve a client is similarly derived. The corresponding average vertical communication time it takes an agent to obtain an acceptable amount of information to service a request is $1/p_v$. Both p_h and p_v are input parameters to the computer program. In the results we report, they were taken to be .9 and .1, respectively, because, as is shown in the sensitivity study of p_h/p_r, this is a sensitive zone. We felt that these values would introduce less bias in the study of the effect of other parameters. We also interpreted these values as averaged over all agents, stages, requests, and levels.

The independence of the events of successful service completion in nonoverlapping time intervals is unrealistic because probability of success should be larger in a time interval following one in which there was thinking or communication than one in which there was not. The error introduced by the less realistic assumption is, however, not large enough to change our main conclusions.

The computation of the total average time per request proceeds as follows. The vertical communication time per request was chosen to start with. In most of the runs that were made, this was taken to be eight minutes; the average total time is directly proportional to that number. Next, the probability of getting the needed information by either horizontal or vertical communication was set equal to .95, which is $P_h(t) + P_v(t) - P_{hv}(t)$, and is closely related to P_t as previously defined. Here $P_{hv}(t)$ is the probability that it takes between t and $t + dt$ hours to first acquire the needed information by communicating horizontally and vertically at the same time. Assuming independence, $P_{hv}(t) = P_h(t)P_v(t)$. Given T^{ud} we can calculate $T^{sfl} = 3/p_h - (p_v/p_h)T^{ud}$, which is derived next.

Start with:

$$P_h(T^{sfl}) + P_v(T^{ud}) - P_h(T^{sfl})P_v(T^{ud}) = .95$$

This expresses the probability of an agent getting the information needed to service a request by either T^{sfl} hours of horizontal communication or T^{ud} hours of vertical communication or both, assuming both to have independent effects. Substitute $P(t) = 1 - e^{-pt}$:

$$(1 - e^{-p_h T^{sfl}}) + (1 - e^{-p_v T^{ud}}) - (1 - e^{-p_h T^{sfl}})(1 - e^{-p_v T^{ud}}) = .95$$

or

$$2 - e^{-p_h T^{sfl}} - e^{-p_v T^{ud}} - (1 - e^{-p_h T^{sfl}} - e^{-p_v T^{ud}} + e^{-p_h T^{sfl}} e^{-p_v T^{ud}}) = .95$$

After cancellations, this becomes:

$$-e^{-p_h T^{sfl}} e^{-p_v T^{ud}} + 1 = .95$$

or

$$e^{-p_h T^{sfl}} = e^{p_v T^{ud}}(1 - .95)$$

Taking natural logs of both sides,

$$-p_h T^{sfl} = p_v T^{ud} + \ln(.05) \doteq p_v T^{ud} - 3$$

Solve for:

$$T^{sfl} = \frac{3 - p_v T^{ud}}{p_h} = 3/p_h - p_v/p_h T^{ud}$$

The ratio p_v/p_h can be interpreted as the value of vertical relative to horizontal communication. We then calculate the average time per request spent on direct service to the client according to $T^w = A - BT^{sfl} - CT^{ud}$. In most of the runs, $A = 10, B = .5, C = .2$. The three times are then added to give the total time/request:

$$T = T^{sfl} + T^{ud} + T^w$$

Given the load L, the number of servers is calculated not according to LT, which assumes that the server is fully occupied 100 percent of the time with the idle time, $T^o = 0$, but according to $1.2LT$ or some variant of that, which assumes 17-percent idle time or 83-percent utilization, so as to avoid excessive swings (variance) in the waiting lines.

Let $\delta_{l,s}$ be the probability of a client appealing an incorrect decision by $A_{l,s}$ and $\delta'_{l,s}$ the probability of a client appealing a correct decision by $A_{l,s}$. The result of an appeal is to move the request to $A_{l+1,s}$. If a decision by $A_{l,s}$ is not appealed, the request is transferred to $A_{l,s+1}$. If the last decision maker is the top man, A_λ, then the client must accept the decision and the request moves on. If $A_{l+1,s}$ grants the client's appeal, then the decision of $A_{l,s}$ is reversed, and steps to improve $E_{l,s}$ are taken. These steps involve: (1) comparing $E_{l,s'}$ with a "permissible" error rate for $A_{l,s}$. (2) If $E_{l,s}$ exceeds $\epsilon_{l,s}$, then this $A_{l,s}$ who has strayed too far above that permissible rate is replaced by another agent whose error rate is $\epsilon_{l,s}$. This replacement is made with probability $\theta_{l,s}$ or a fraction $\theta_{l,s}$ of the time. This is to simulate the use of policy directives by $A_{l+1,s}$ or his or her hiring/firing power in order to alter the subsequent error rate of the organization in a favorable direction.

The values of E, δ, δ', ϵ, and θ are specified as input to the computer model and taken to be averages over all requests, agents, levels, and stages.

From these numbers, we calculate the number of agents required to handle the request load so as to keep queue length within some tolerable limit, according to:

$$n_{l,s} = \frac{1.2 \times \text{Avg. load at } l,s \times \text{Avg. time per request (min.)}}{\text{Number of minutes per month}}$$

The expected load will, in general, exceed L because an additional load is generated internally through recycling and revisions of requests. The factor

1.2 stems from an 83-percent utilization of each server's time to cushion the effect of excessive swings in the waiting time. That enables us to calculate the total fixed cost of maintaining the service organization. The fixed cost is the salary cost of the agents who are needed to meet the needs of the clients. The salaries of civil service employees were used in this calculation with level 1 agents receiving grade 1 salaries while level 7 agents receive grade 18 salaries (top level). Linear extrapolations were used at any time when more than seven levels were to be considered. One time period was assumed to be equivalent to one month. Thus, load represents the monthly number of clients to be serviced by the facility.

Table A5.4.1. List of Variables

Input

λ = number of hierarchical levels in the organization.
$C_{l,s}$ = agent's hourly salary at level l, stage s.
$c(o)$ = clients' average hourly opportunity cost.
$\delta_{l,s}$ = probability (client appeals decision at level l, stage s, given that the decision is in fact in error).
$\delta'_{l,s}$ = probability (client appeals decision at level l, stage s, given that the decision is in fact correct).
$E_{l,s}$ = error rate at level l, stage s.
ϵ_s = normative error rate at level 1, stage s.
$1/p_h$ = half-life coefficient of exponential function used in determining the probability that acceptable information is retrieved due to the lateral communication in which the agent engaged.
$1/p_v$ = analogous to $1/p_h$, except dealing with vertical rather than horizontal communication.
$T^{ud}_{l,s}$ = V = amount of time spent in up-down communication to service one client at level l, stage s.
CE = cost of allowing a poorly treated case to be returned to the environment.
A, B, C = where these are defined as follows,
 $T^{lc}_{l,s} = A - (B \times T^{ud}_{l,s}) - C \times T^{sfl}_{l,s}$,
$T^{sfl}_{l,s}$ = amount of time spent in lateral communication to service one client at level l, stage s.
$T^{lc}_{l,s}$ = amount of time spent in direct working activity to service one client at level l, stage s.
$\theta_{l,s}$ = probability ($E_{l,s}$ will be corrected to $\epsilon_{l,s}$, given that $E_{l,s} > \epsilon_{l,s}$) after correcting decision at level l, stage s.
L = client load.

Output

1. Number of agents at each level and stage in the facility.
2. Fixed cost of operating facility (sum total of all agents' salaries over the time period being studied).
3. Client opportunity cost (time spent in facility by all clients × opportunity cost/unit time).
4. Poor treatment cost (number of poorly treated cases being discharged × cost of poor treatment/unit).
5. Total cost (fixed cost + client opportunity cost + poor treatment cost).

Optimum Number Determined by Computer / 279

To this we add the cost of the clients' time while waiting for their request to be serviced. As before, we assume that they do not occupy themselves usefully for the duration of the service and that their loss increases at an average rate of $c(0)$ or c'_{wa} dollars per hour.

The client cost is calculated as follows. As a client enters the facility the time is noted. The entire sequence of client arrivals is so determined. Similarly, client departures are noted. A comparison is made between the arrivals and the departures. This leaves the cumulative amount of time spent in the facility by all clients. This sum total is then multiplied by the average opportunity cost of the client. This opportunity cost per unit time is an input parameter. The product of this calculation is called the "client opportunity cost."

The cost of poorly treated cases is also an output of the computer program. Clients who leave the facility after one or more errors in treatment have been made without being corrected are regarded as poorly treated. This number, when multiplied by CE (the unit cost of discharging an improperly treated case) equals the cost of poor treatment to the client. This cost comprises one component of the total cost.

What follows is a summary of the input, the output, the assumptions, and a sketch of the algorithm in flow diagram form for calculating the output (see Tables A5.4.1, A5.4.2, and Figure A5.4.1).

The flow chart (available on request from the authors) of the original computer model used a Monte Carlo technique to generate the various desired

Table A5.4.2. Model Based Upon These Assumptions

1. Monthly load remains uniform.
2. Once a client has entered the facility, the only means for leaving is through being discharged from stage 5.
3. Client appeals are permitted at all levels of the facility.
4. The facility concerns itself only with the service to client function.
5. Clients will choose the shortest queue available when more than one queue exists at a particular node. Moreover, a client will remain in that queue until serviced, even under the situation where other queues become shorter during the course of the waiting period.
6. All agents at a given node perform similarly (only differences in performance are due to random chance).
7. The prospect of having a decision appealed does not alter an agent's decision.
8. After being returned by the stage 5 monitor for readministering service, the error rates remain unchanged for that client.
9. Historical antecedents play no role in a client's behavior in appealing decisions.
10. Historical antecedents play no role in an agent's error behavior unless policy directives are passed down by an agent's supervisor.
11. All activities engaged in by agents can be categorized under one of the following: direct work vertical communication, horizontal communication (including thinking), idleness.
12. Agents communicate only with the following people: themselves, agents on their own level, agents in their service stage, contacts outside of the formal organization.
13. The probability of receiving acceptable information is a function of time. Moreover, this function takes on the form of a negative exponential curve.

280 / Appendix 5.4

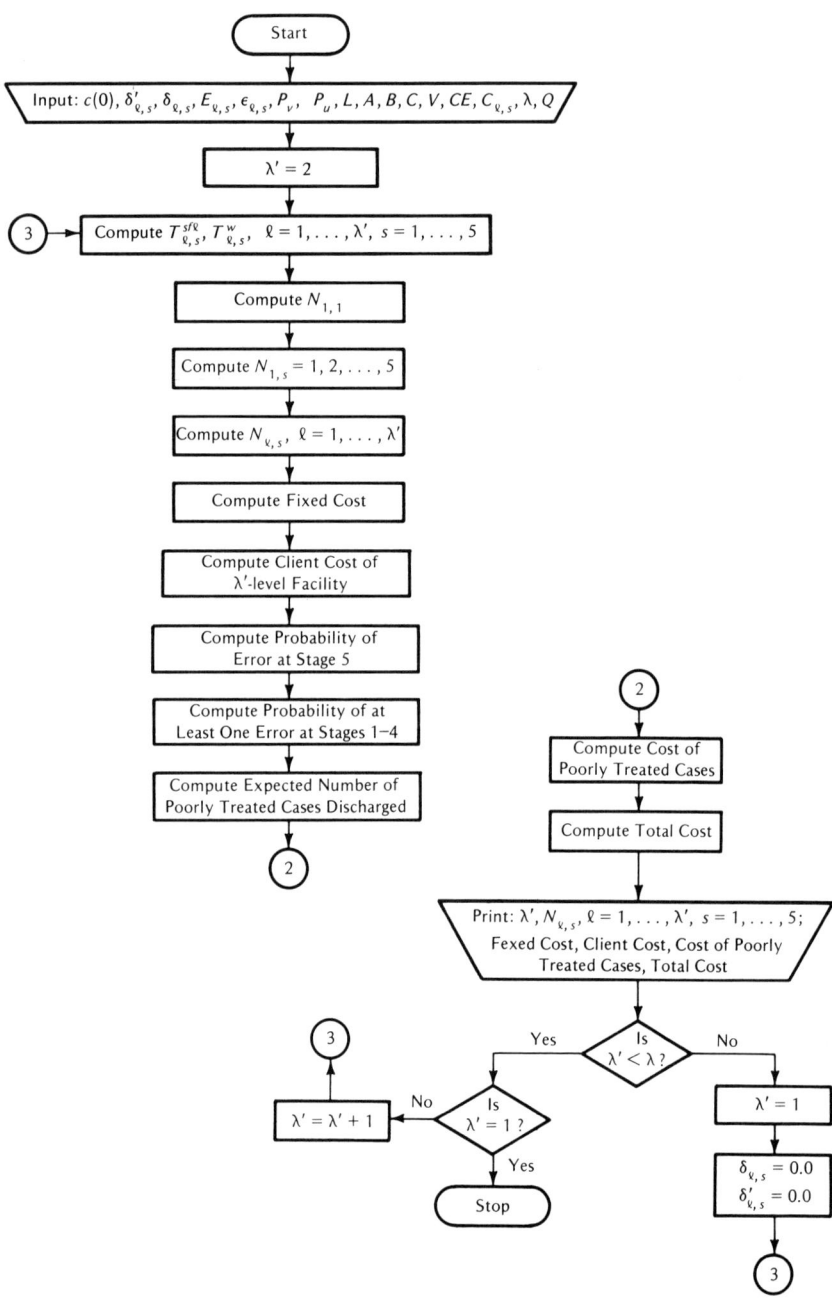

Figure A5.4.1. Flow chart utilized to design final computer model (also see Appendix 6.4).

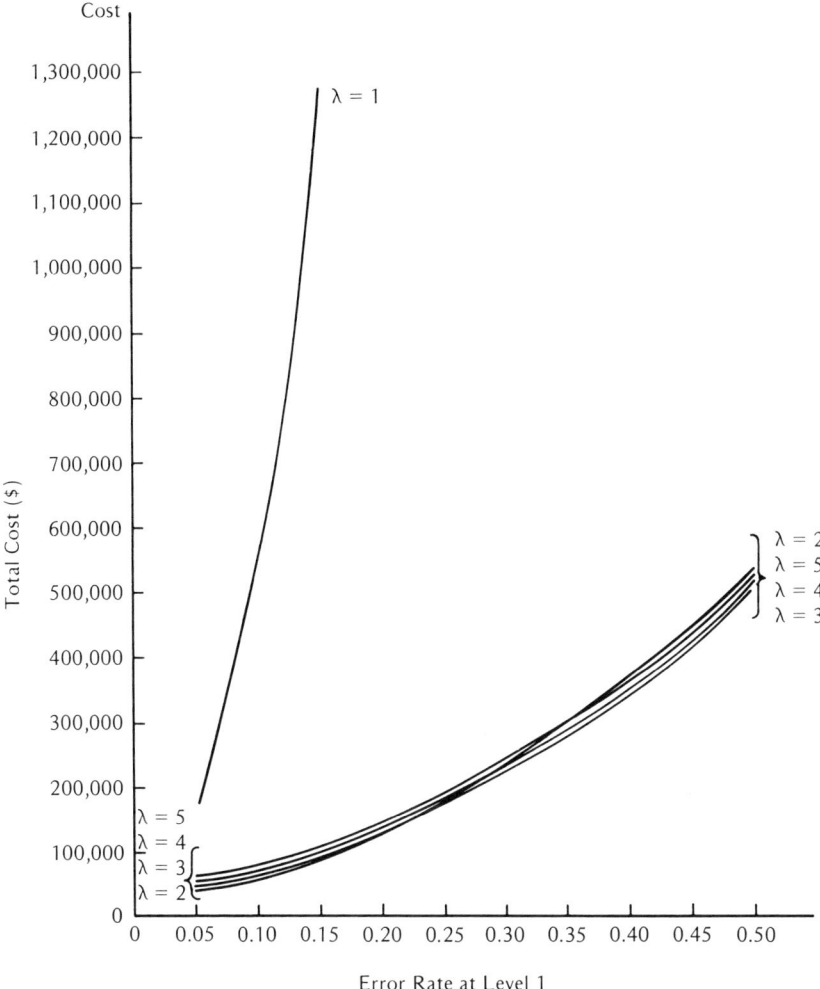

Figure A5.4.2. Total cost vs. error rate at level 1 for varying degrees of flatness.

costs. In order to study the effects that large increases in client load have on the optimal number of hierarchical levels, it became necessary to design a computer model based upon expected values (see Figure A5.4.1).

The transition from the Monte Carlo technique to the computational probabilistic model involved only two minor variations in the input parameters. The first variation was to delete the parameter $\theta_{l,s}$, the probability that the error rate at level 1, stage s will be changed to the normative error rate after correcting a decision at level 1. This complicated the probabilistic model while making little difference in the actual output. The second variation was to disregard the average waiting time each and every time a client entered a queue, since the computer was no longer required to maintain an accounting of the flows of clients through queues. This variable has been referred to as Q.

What follows are the results of running the computer program when δ, the probability of the client's appealing a decision when it is in error, is .75 and δ', and the probability of the client's appealing a decision given that it was correct is .05. The probability rates p_h and p_v of an agent obtaining information needed to service a request during any small (unit) time period by horizontal and vertical communication were taken to be, respectively, .1 and .9. The load was set at 1000 requests per month. The opportunity cost of a client's time was taken to be $5 per hour. In every case, $E_{2,s}$, the probability of error by an agent at level 2 at any stage s, was set to equal .03 and .01 for all higher levels. For level 1 it was set equal to ϵ, the permissible error probability, and that was varied from .05 to .50.

The program computed the total cost, in dollars per month, the fixed cost, the client opportunity cost, and the cost to clients of poorly treated cases for organizations with one, two, three, four, and five hierarchical levels. The results are shown in Table A5.4.2 and Figure A5.4.2.

Note that as the permissible error rate by a level 1 agent increases toward .15, the use of a one-level, nonhierarchical organization becomes increasingly costly, especially to the client. The client costs as shown in Table A5.2 result only from the time the client (or the client's request) resides in the organization; as the agents in a one-level organization make more errors, including the agents in stage 1, they also tend to dismiss requests erroneously more often, thus shortening the time spent in the organization. This is paid for, however, by a vast increase in the cost of poorly treated cases. We have denoted by CE, the cost per poorly treated case (and the organization through malpractice suits), and have added to the total cost column $CE \times$ the number of poorly treated cases. CE is taken to be equal to $10,000 in all of the computer runs.

Appendix 6.1

Delegation and Suboptimization

Suppose that the organizational aims indeed optimized an objective function, say $f(x_1, x_2, x_3, x_4)$ such as profit or net worth, where $x_1, \ldots, x_4$ are allocated resources or information inputs. A single manager cannot know or control $x_1, \ldots, x_4$ with complete certainty, but he can rewrite $f(x_1, x_2, x_3, x_4)$ as $f(x_5, x_6)$, where $x_5 = g(x_1, x_2)$ and $x_6 = h(x_3, x_4)$. Then the manager can hire two subordinates, one of whom can know or control x_1, x_2 with greater certainty, and the other x_3, x_4. The manager need then know or control only x_5 and x_6. By having each subordinate optimize g and h, subject to his or her own constraints, the f is optimized, but this technique of suboptimization works only if: (1) f can be so factored; (2) there are no significant interactions between the suboptimized system and other variables in the total system (Smithies, 1970). These conditions are rarely met. They also apply to decentralization. The decentralized manager optimizes a function that differs from $g(x_1, x_2)$ that would be suboptimized by having additional variables of local interest that did not effect g, and by giving different weights to x_1 and x_2 and the additional variables.

Appendix 6.2

Derivation and Analysis of Expression for Net Utility of a Service Organization with Distributed Memories

As a vehicle for validating our analysis, we consider a hypothetical organization of library resources as a concrete instance of the more general class of service organization to which our analysis applies. There are N_0 potential users of these resources. Each user has a personal collection of books, reprints, and so on, amounting to m chunks of storage on the average. Here a chunk is a string of several bits that fit together. An example might be a paragraph in an encyclopedia. Assume that each user, whenever needing something requiring these resources, turns first to his or her own collection and that this user generates, on the average L'_0 requests per month. Altogether, $L'_0 N_0$ requests per month, which we denote by L, are to be serviced.

Let a be the probability that a user's need would be satisfied by a memory with minimal storage capacity of one chunk. However, a will be 1 only in cases of certainty and less than 1 in all others. If we assume that all search steps are mutually independent, it follows that the probability of the user's need being satisfied by a memory of m chunks is $1 - (1 - a)^m$. That is, at least one chunk that meets the need is contained among m independent chunks. If we interpret a to be the probability that a randomly chosen need for information is met by any given encyclopedia article or that a particular inquiry is satisfied by a randomly chosen encyclopedia article, then this expression is the probability that the need is met by an encyclopedia with m articles. Graphically, this probability will appear as a well-known convex curve of the probability of finding submarines in a section of the ocean or books in a library. This curve at first rises steeply and then flattens out asymptotically toward 1 as m increases.

If, with probability $(1 - a)^m$, the need is not met by that private source, the user turns to the nearest public or private source that is shared with several other users. We view these private or public sources as being at a level higher in a hierarchy than that of the user. This new source has $b_1 m$ bits of storage, where b_1 is the ratio of storage capacity at level 1 to storage capacity at level 0. Here we take the user to be at level 0, while level 1 refers to the bottom of the organization that is to meet the user's needs when his or her own resources are inadequate. We could interpret this level 1 source to be a library of b_1 encyclopedias. On the average, $(1 - a)^m L$ requests are forwarded to level 1.

Let n_1 be the number of these nearest public or private libraries or agents at level 1. Let L_1 denote the maximum number of requests per month that one agent at that level receives to process. All n_1 of them must process the $(1 - a)^m L_0' n_0$ requests on the average that the n_0 users cannot satisfy with their private sources and which they sent up; here L_0' is the number of requests generated per month by each user, with $L = L_0' n_0$.

The probability that a level 1 center receiving such a request cannot service it will be $(1 - a)^{b_1 m}$, under our assumptions. We now combine this analysis with our previous considerations regarding geographic dispersion, by assuming that any request is equally likely to originate at any point along a D-mile line, and goes to the nearest of the n_1 service centers. If it is serviced at a first-level service center, then the expected delay will be $D/4n_1 v$ hours, where v is the speed, in miles per hour, at which the request moves to the nearest center. If c is the variable cost of rendering the service (to the user and to the service organization for which k was used in Chapter 2), then $Dc/4n_1 v$ times the expected number of requests per month is the total cost. For the first level that is:

$$\frac{Dc}{4n_1 v} (1 - a)^m L_0' n_0 (1 - (1 - a)^{b_1 m})$$

Proceeding to the next level, observe that, on the average, only $L_0' n_0 (1 - a)^m (1 - a)^{b_1 m}$ requests per month are forwarded to level 2 centers by the n_1 first-level centers. If each of these first-level centers appeals to the nearest second-level center, and there are n_2 of the latter, then the cost of the expected delay here is:

$$\frac{DcL_0' n_0 (1 - a)^m (1 - a)^{b_1 m}}{4n_2 v} \text{ dollars per month}$$

Also if L_2 is the number of requests per month such a second-level agent can service without causing congestion, then n_2 should be such that:

$$n_2 L_2 \geq L_0' n_0 (1 - a)^{m(1 + b_1)}$$

Let u be the average utility of an adequate response, and u' the disutility of an inadequate response from the organization if there are λ levels in place of the two we had discussed. Suppose further that the cost of a center (dollars per month per center) is proportional to its memory, with a coefficient of proportionality d_k that depends on level k. The fixed cost is then $\Sigma_{k=1}^{\lambda} d_k b_k$ dollars per month.

Let U_1 denote the net utility. Let $L = L_0' N_0$ and $b_0 = 1$. The utility from all $\lambda + 1$ levels is (N_k and n_k are used interchangeably in this appendix):

$$uL\left(1 - (1-a)^{m\sum_{k=0}^{\lambda} b_k}\right) \text{ dollars per month}$$

The corresponding disutility is:

$$u'L(1-a)^{m\sum_{k=0}^{\lambda} b_k} \text{ dollars per month}$$

The two together are:

$$L\left(u - (u+u') \prod_{k=0}^{\lambda} (1-a)^{mb_k}\right)$$

The fixed-cost component to be subtracted is:

$$m \sum_{k=1}^{\lambda} d_k b_k N_k \text{ dollars per month}$$

and the variable cost component is:

$$\frac{DcL}{4v} \sum_{k=0}^{\lambda-1} (1-a)^{m\sum_{i=0}^{k} b_i} \frac{(1 - (1-a)^{mb_{k+1}})}{N_{k+1}}$$

$$= \frac{DcL}{4v} \sum_{k=0}^{\lambda-1} \frac{\prod_{i=0}^{k}(1-a)^{mb_i}(1-(1-a)^{mb_{k+1}})}{N_{k+1}}$$

The general expression for the net utility is, therefore

$$U_1 = uL\left(1 - (1-a)^{m\sum_{k=0}^{\lambda} b_k}\right) - u'L(1-a)^{m\sum_{k=0}^{\lambda} b_k} - m\sum_{k=1}^{\lambda} d_k b_k n_k$$

$$- \frac{DcL}{4v} \sum_{k=0}^{\lambda-1} (1-a)^{m\sum_{i=0}^{k} b_i} \frac{(1-(1-a)^{mb_{k+1}})}{N_{k+1}}$$

where $b_0 = 1$ and where $L = L'_0 n_0$, the total request load in requests per month. We can now ask what values of $b_1, \ldots, b_n, n_1, \ldots, n_n$ will maximize U_1 for given values of $u, a, m, d_k, D, c, L'_0, n_0, v$.

If we assume that U_1 and its derivatives are continuously differentiable in $b_1, \ldots, b_H$, and $N_1, \ldots, N_H$, we may find the maximum of U_1 if it exists, by setting $\partial U_1/\partial b_k = 0$ and $\partial U_1/\partial N_k = 0$ for $k = 1, \ldots, H$. We can write the derivatives as:

$$\frac{\partial U_1}{\partial b_k} = -m(u - u')Lln(1 - a) f(H) - N_k d_k m$$

$$- \frac{DcLm\,ln(1-a)}{v} \sum_{j=k}^{H-1} \frac{f(j)}{n_j + 1} = 0$$

and

$$\frac{\partial U_1}{\partial N_k} = -m d_k b_k + \frac{DcL}{v} \frac{f(k-1)}{N_k^2}, \text{ where } f(k)$$

where $f(k) = \prod_{i=0}^{k} (1-a)^{mb_i} = (1-a)^{m \sum_{i=u}^{k} b_i}$

Hence,

$$N_k^2 = \frac{DcL\,f(k-1)}{mvd_k b_k}, \text{ where } k = 1, \ldots, N$$

Setting the $2N$ equations equal to 0 and substituting for N_k, $k = 1, \ldots, N$, gives N simultaneous transcendental equations to be solved for $b_1, \ldots, b_n$. It is difficult to get further insights into the nature of the solution without making more specialized assumptions. Symbol-manipulating programs such as MACSYMA may be useful here.

It is plausible that if each agent at level k has larger memory then few such agents should be needed, provided there are enough to handle the load.

To obtain a better overview, the key variables and implications are summarized in Table A6.2.1.

Because $am \doteq .003$, the approximations we discussed previously may hold provided that b_k remains less than 100. To gain further insights, consider now the special case of $\lambda = 2$. In this case it is possible to derive expressions for b_1/b_2 and n_1/n_2 that are surprisingly simple. If we linearize $f(k)$, and take $u' = 0$, then we have the approximation:

$$U_1 = uL[am + (1 - am)(ab_1 m) + (1 - am)(1 - ab_1 m)ab_2 m]$$

$$- N_1 d_1 b_1 m - N_2 d_2 b_2 m - \frac{DcL}{2v}\left[\frac{(1-am)}{N_1} + \frac{(1-am)(1-ab_1 m)}{N_2}\right]$$

Table A6.2.1 Key Variables and Implications

Variable	Definition	Typical Value	Trend of Change
m	Number of chunks of memory at the level of the client	3000	Constant
a	Probability that a random need is met by some chunk	10^{-6}	Decrease
b_k	Ratio of storage capacity at level k to that at bottom level $k = 1, 2, \ldots, H$		
λ	Number of levels, excluding that of the client		
L_0'	Number of needs per user per month	10	Increase
N_0	Number of users or clients	10^3	Increase
D	Length of total service region (mi)	10^3	Constant
v	Speed at which a need is forwarded (miles per hour)	10	Decrease
c	Cost of user's time (dollars per hour)	10	Increase
d_k	Cost of time of an agent and equipment at level k, in dollars per month per chunk of memory for $k = 1, 2, \ldots, H$	.02	Increase
N_k	Number of agents at level k		
u	Utility to client of an adequately met need (dollars per request)	20	Increase
L	$N_0 L_0'$, total load, requests per month	10^4	Increase

Now:

$$\frac{\partial U_1}{\partial b_1} = uL[(1-am)am - (1-am)(am)(ab_2 m)] \quad (A6.2.1)$$

$$- N_1 d_1 m + \frac{DcLam(1-am)}{2vN_2}$$

and

$$\frac{\partial U_1}{\partial b_2} = uL[(1-am)(1-ab_1 m)am] - N_2 d_2 m \quad (A6.2.2)$$

We can now solve the system of four simultaneous equations. The result, in the form of b_1/b_2 and N_1/N_2, is surprisingly simple:

$$\frac{b_1}{b_2} = \frac{d_1}{d_2}\left[1 - \frac{Dcd_1}{2u^2 avL(1-am)}\right] \quad (A6.2.3)$$

and

$$N_1/N_2 = auL(1 - am)(2u^2va(1 - am)L - Dcd_1)/2uvd_1d_2 \quad (A6.2.4)$$

Had we measured the utility per request, the result for b_1/b_2 would be the same.
To derive the result in Equations A6.2.3 and A6.2.4, we start with:

$$\frac{\partial U_1}{\partial N_1} = -d_1b_1m + \frac{DcL}{2v}\frac{(1-am)}{N_1^2}$$

$$\frac{\partial U_1}{\partial N_2} = -d_2b_2m + \frac{DcL}{2v}\frac{(1-am)(1-ab_1m)}{N_2^2}$$

Setting these derivatives equal to 0 and solving for N_1^2, N_2^2, we get:

$$N_1^2 = \frac{DcL(1-am)}{2vd_1b_1m} \quad N_2^2 = \frac{DcL(1-am)(1-ab_1m)}{2vd_2b_2m} \quad (A6.2.5)$$

Square both sides of $\partial U_1/\partial b_2 = 0$ from Equation A6.2.2 and substitute for N_2^2 to get

$$(uL(1-am)(1-ab_1m)am)^2 = \frac{DcL(1-am)(1-ab_1m)}{2vd_2b_2m} \cdot d_2^2m^2 \quad (A6.2.6)$$

Simplify:

$$2vu^2L(1-am)(1-ab_1m)a^2mb_2 = Dcd_2 \quad (A6.2.7)$$

Substitute for N_1 and N_2 into $\partial U_1/\partial b_1 = 0$ from Equation A6.2.1 to get:

$$uLam(1-am)(1-ab_2m) - d_1m$$

$$\sqrt{\frac{DcL(1-am)}{2vd_1b_1m}} + \frac{DcLam(1-am)}{2v}\sqrt{\frac{2vd_2b_2m}{DcL(1-am)(1-ab_1m)}}$$

Solve Equation A6.2.5 for b_2 to get $b_2 = Dcd_2/(2vu^2aF(1-ab_1m))$, where $F = am(1-am)L$ as a convenient abbreviation. Substitute this into the above, and simplify, to get:

$$uF(1-amDcdc)/(2vu^2aF(1-ab_1m))$$

$$= d_1m\sqrt{\frac{DcL(1-am)}{2vd_1b_1m}} - m\sqrt{\frac{DcFad_2}{2v(1-ab_1m)}}\sqrt{\frac{Dcd_2}{2u^2vaF(1-ab_1m)}}$$

Further:

$$uF - \frac{mDcd_2}{2uv(1 - ab_1m)} = d_1m\sqrt{\frac{DcL(1 - am)}{2vd_1b_1m}} - \frac{mDcd_2}{2v(1 - ab_1m)u}$$

and

$$uF = d_1m\sqrt{\frac{DcL(1 - am)}{2vd_1b_1m}}$$

Square both sides and solve for b_1:

$$b_1 = \frac{d_1^2m^2DcL(1 - am)}{2u^2F^2vd_1m} = \frac{Dcd_1}{2Lu^2a^2vm(1 - am)} \qquad (A6.2.9)$$

Note that b_1 increases with c. This is plausible, because as the cost of the client's time increases, it pays to put more memory resources at the (bottom) level closest to the client. As L increases, b_1 decreases, and if u increases, b_1 decreases substantially.

Now substitute Equation A6.2.9 for b_1 into Equation A6.2.7 for b_2:

$$b_2 = \frac{Dcd_2}{am(2u^2av(1 - am)L - Dcd_1)} \qquad (A6.2.10)$$

Note that b_2 also decreases as u^2L and increases with c.

Finally:

$$b_1/b_2 = \frac{d_1}{d_1}\frac{am(2u^2av(1 - am)L - Dcd_1)}{am2u^2Lav(1 - am)}$$

After further simplification, the first result, Equation A6.2.3, follows.

Now substitute for b_1 from Equation A6.2.9 into Equation A6.2.5 to get, after simplification:

$$N_1 = \frac{auL(1 - am)}{d_1} \qquad (A6.2.11)$$

Note that N_1 increases with Lu and is insensitive to c. Also this time, N_1 varies directly with L rather than as its square root as it did when b_1 and b_2 played no role.

From Equations A6.2.8 and A6.2.9 we substitute for b_1 and for b_2 into Equation A6.2.5. After considerable algebraic simplification we find:

$$N_2 = \frac{2u^2av(1 - am)L - Dcd_1}{2uvd_2} \qquad (A6.2.12)$$

Again, N_2 increases directly with L and u, but now it decreases with c. From Equations A6.2.11 and A6.2.12, Equation A6.2.4 follows.

The b_1/b_2 ratio is a simple measure of decentralization in this two-level organization. If it is 0, then we have centralized structure with all the memory concentrated at the upper level; if it is 1, then it is moderately decentralized, with memory evenly spread over both levels; if it is greater than 1, then most of the memory is at the bottom level, a case of far-reaching decentralization. We find from the formulas for b_1/b_2 the following results:

1. As L increases, b_1/b_2 increases toward d_1/d_2 as an asymptote. In a very large battle or natural catastrophe, when the load on medical personnel of all kinds is high, it pays to throw more resources forward, as close to the immediate operating level as possible. If the request load L is small, on the other hand, the service organization has little to do, and it pays to place more memory at the higher levels. The asymptote d_1/d_2 is the ratio of unit memory costs. If the memory of the top-level agent costs twice as much per unit of memory (and is presumably twice as effective though not necessarily efficient) as the memory of the bottom-level agent, then, when the load is high, we should have the most decentralized structure it pays to have, with twice as much memory at the top as at the bottom. The more equalitarian are the pay and cost structures at different levels, the more memory facilities should be located at the bottom level of the organization.

2. As c increases up to a limit and loads remain low, b_1/b_2 decreases until it is zero. If the cost of the client's time is high, all the memory should be allocated at the top and little at the bottom. Busy and important clients will tend to try to go "straight to the top" of the organization in order to obtain service.

3. As u, the client's utility of the service increases, b_1/b_2 increases. The distribution of memory shifts toward the lower level. The ratio $N_1 N_2$ increases with L as L^2. This means that, for large loads, the pyramid rapidly broadens, with many agents at the bottom level and few at the top. The ratio also increases as u^2. If the clients value the service highly, this again favors a decentralized structure. As c, the cost of the clients' time increases, N_1/N_2 decreases and increasing c favors a top-heavy organization.

Appendix 6.3

Model for Determining Shifts of Memory to Minimize Cost

Our aim is to find conditions under which an increase in M_1, the memory at level 1, results in lowered total costs. To derive an expression for the total cost C, we summarize, once more, the needed variables:

c_l: cost of maintaining A_l, a server at level l, dollars per hour
n_l: number of servers at level l
k_l: cost per case that A_l treats poorly, dollars per case
E_l: fraction of cases that A_l treats poorly,

Then

$$C = \sum_l (c_l n_l + k_l E_l L_l) \text{ dollars per hour}$$

where L_l is the load, that is, number of requests per hour, reaching all servers at level l.

We now summarize the assumptions of our model. The first asserts that A_l's salary is proportional to his or her memory, M_l, or years of experience, education plus special skill and talent that M_l is assumed to measure, according to:

$$c_l = cM_l$$

where c is the cost per chunk per hour, for "storage."

Model For Determining Shifts of Memory / 293

The second assumption is that A_l is never idle, nor are there lines of clients waiting for the service. That means approximately:

$$n_l = L_l T_l$$

where T_l is the average service time per request for A_l, hours per request. (We neglected the safety factor 1.2 to guard against excessive swings in waiting time.)

Third, we assume that a more experienced, better server, one characterized by larger M_l, can service requests faster, according to:

$$T_l = aM_l^{-b}$$

where a is a constant interpretable as how many hours it would take a server with 1 byte of memory to service a request; and b is proportional to the rate at which T decreases with increases in M for such a one-byte server.

Fourth, we assume that more experienced servers (higher M) make fewer errors, according to:

$$E_l = dM_l^{-e}$$

where, as above, d is a constant interpretable as the fraction of cases that a server with 1 byte of memory would treat poorly; and e is proportional to the rate at which E decreases as M increases for such a 1-byte server.

Appendix 6.4

Derivation of the Amount of Memory to Be Transferred

With the above assumptions, the expression for C is:

$$C = ac \sum_l M^{1-b} L_l + d \sum_l k_l L_l M_l^{-e}$$

For two levels:

$$C = acM_1^{1-b}L_1 + dk_1 L_1 M_1^{-e} + acM_2^{1-b}(L - L_1) + dk_2(L - L_1)M_2^{-e}$$

To render this amenable to analysis without a computer, let us take $d = 0$ and $b = 1/2$. Then:

$$C/ac = M_1^{\frac{1}{2}} L_1 = M_2^{\frac{1}{2}}(1 - L_1)$$

and

$$C'/ac = (M_1 + m)^{\frac{1}{2}} L_1 + (M_2 - m)^{\frac{1}{2}}(L - L_1)$$

If L_1 is sufficiently small, then $C'/ac < C/ac$, and it pays to transfer memory from level 2 to level 1.

If we treat C'/ac as a differentiable function of m, viewed as a real variable, then we can derive an expression for m at which C'/ac is minimum, given M_1, M_2, L, L_1, a, c.

Derivation of the Amount of Memory to Be Transferred / 295

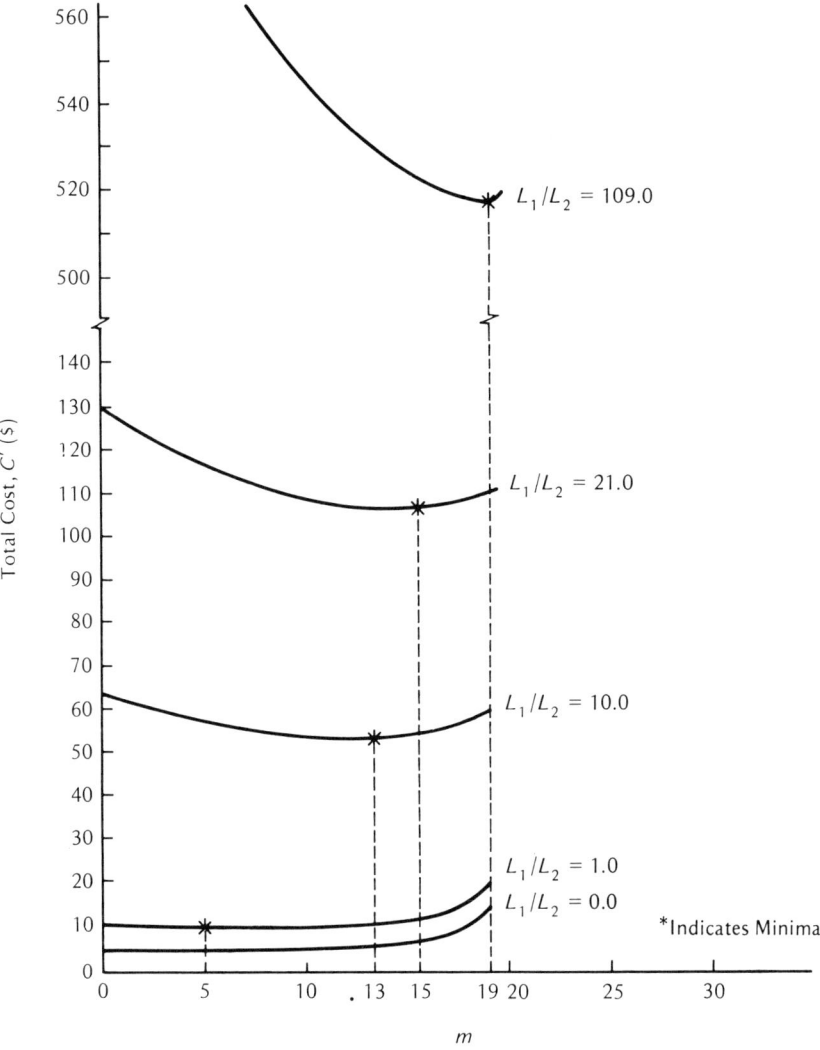

Figure A6.4.1. Total cost vs. amount of memory delegated.

To minimize $(M_1 + m)^{\frac{1}{2}}L_1 + (M_2 - m)^{\frac{1}{2}}(L - L_1)$, differentiate with respect to m, to obtain $\frac{1}{2}(M_1 + m)^{-\frac{1}{2}}L - \frac{1}{2}(M_2 - m)^{\frac{1}{2}}(L - L_1)$. Set this equal to zero, square both sides, and solve the equation:

$$\frac{L_1^2}{M_1 + m} = \frac{(L - L_1)^2}{M_2 - m}$$

for m, to obtain:

$$m = \frac{M_2 L_1^2 - M_1(L - L_1)^2}{L_1^2 + (L - L_1)^2} = \frac{M_2 L_1^2 - M_1 L_2^2}{L_1^2 + L_2^2}$$

$$= \frac{M_2(L_1/L_2)^2 - (M_1/M_2)}{(L_1/L_2)^2 + 1}$$

It pays to transfer if $L_1/L_2 \geq \sqrt{M_1/M_2}$. It is plausible that $M_2 > M_1$, so that $M_1/M_2 < 1$. If $L_1 > L_2$, which is also plausible, then there should be delegation. The greater M_2, the more we should delegate.

We assumed $d = 0$ for analytical purposes only, realizing that this is implausible. To analyze the general formula:

$$c' = ac[(M_1 + m)^{1-b}L_1 + (M_2 - m)^{1-b}L_2]$$
$$+ d[k_1 L_1(M_1 + m)^{-e} + k_2 L_2(M_2 - m)^{-e}]$$

a computer program was written and run for $A = 1, B = 1/2, c = .001, E = 1/2, d = 1/2, k_1 = 10^4, k_2 = 10^4, M_1 = 10^6, M_2 = 2 \times 10^6$, with L_1/L_2 varying from 0 through 1, 10, 21, to 109 and m varying from 1 to 19 for each value of L_1/L_2. The results are shown in Figure A6.4.1. The minimum of C' occurs at $M_2 = 0, 5, 13, 15, 19$, for $L_1/L_2 = 0, 1, 10, 21$, and 109, respectively. The corresponding values for the minimum C' are: 4.95, 10.61, 54.95, 107.39, and 519.72. The greater L_1/L_2, the more we should delegate.

Appendix 6.5

Does It Pay to Delegate More Than One Level Down?

The variables and notation used are those in the previous sections of this chapter, except for the new variable:

$e_{ll'}$: the average time in hours for A to explain a request to $A_{l'}$, $l' < l$

We recapitulate the basic assumptions:

1. If A_l does not delegate, it costs $c_l T_l = (cM_l)(am_l^{-b}) = acM_l^{1-b}$ dollars per request.
   If A_l does delegate to $A_{l'}$, it costs $c_l e_{ll'} + c_{l'} T_{l'}$ dollars per request.
2. A new assumption is that $e_{ll'} = \delta M_l^{-b} m_{l'}^{-b}$, which asserts that the explanation time decreases if either the speaker, listener, or both have increased memory. We may interpret δ as the time (hours per request) it would take a speaker with a 1-byte memory to explain the request to a listener with a 1-byte memory.
3. We make the additional assumption that $M_l = lM$ $(=(l + 1)m)$.

The cost per request if A_l delegates to $A_{l'}$ and $A_{l'}$ does not delegate further is:

$$cM_l \delta M_l^{-b} + cM_{l'} a M_{l'}^{-b} = cM_{l'}^{-b}(M_l^{1-b} + aM_{l'})$$

We now ask when this is less than acm_l^{1-b}, the cost of nondelegation. The reader can readily verify that the condition that it pays A_l to delegate to $A_{l'}$ is:

297

$$\delta/a < M^b(l'^b - l'l^{b-1})$$

where δ/a is the ratio of the time to explain a request to the time to service it if both speaker and listener had a 1-byte memory; M is the memory of the level 1 servers; and b is the rate at which response time decreases with memory for a server with a 1-byte memory.

Delegation to One Level Down. Since values of 10^6 bytes are plausible for M, even quite small values of b, for example, $b = 1/6$, would make the right-hand side approximately $(1 - l'/l)$, which varies from $1/2$ at $l = 2$ to as little as $1/\lambda$ at $l = \lambda$. As long as the time to explain is less than $1/\lambda$ of the time to do the service alone, where λ is the height of the organization, it pays to delegate. But this is very approximate.

More exactly, suppose that A_l delegates down to the level just below, so that $l' = l - 1$. A_2 should delegate if $\delta/a < M^b(1 - 2^{b-1})$, which is, for $b = 0$ and $1/2$, $\delta/a < 1/2$ and $\delta/a < .31\sqrt{M}$. However, b cannot exceed 1 and when b is $\log_2 (ln\ M/ln\sqrt{2M})$ (slightly less than 1 for large M) the right-hand side is maximum when b exceeds that, and it decreases to 0 as b increases to 1 and becomes negative thereafter. If the requests are quite uniform or simple, then δ should be less than a and A_2 should delegate.

A_3 should delegate if $\delta/a < M^b(2^b - 2.3^{b-1})$, which is $1/3$ for $b = 0$ and about $.27\sqrt{M}$ for $b = 1/2$ and ≤ 0 if $b \geq 1$. The right-hand side has a maximum when $b = ln(3ln\ 2M/2ln\ 3M)/ln3/2$, which is still close to 1 for large M. For the highest-level servers, the condition becomes most stringent. For A_7, it is $\delta/a < M^b(6^b - (6 \times 7^{b-1}))$. The right-hand side is $1/7$ for $b = 0$, and, of course, 0 for $b = 1$. For A_7 to delegate, if $b = 0$, a request should take at least seven times as long to service it him or herself than to explain it to A_6, which seems plausible for higher-level servers.

Does it ever pay to delegate more than one level down? In special cases we can calculate the value of l' so that $\delta/a = M^b(l'^b - l'l^{b-1})$, the condition that realizes the greatest cost savings. If we take $b = 1/2$, we can derive a quadratic equation in l'. Solving it for $M = 10^6$ indicates that we should never delegate further down than one level under these conditions.

Appendix 9.1

Suggestions for Future Research: A Proposed Analytic System

The computer programs that we have constructed and used to report results in this book are freely available to anyone with access to the Michigan Terminal System.[1] Since they are written in FORTRAN they can be exported for use with many other computer systems. This should encourage others to check and extend our results to other configurations of parameters; more importantly, it should stimulate others to improve upon our programs and the algorithms and models on which they are based.

A9.1 A PROPOSED ANALYTIC SYSTEM

We suggest that a complete collection of such models, both analytical and in the form of computer programs, be integrated into a coherent overall program that can help to provide a consulting service of the following kind.

A9.1.1 A Question-Asking Program. Organizations concerned with questions of decentralization would present their requests to a question-asking program. It would elicit from such clients values for the key parameters in the models that are available. It would then report to the client the results of running programs likely to interest the client.

The question-asking program would ask about the type of service a user's organization performs; the set of potential clients for that service, the load to be expected; the needed equipment, tangible and intangible; the fixed and operating costs to be expected; the need for coordination, pluralization, dispersion; how poorly or sharply the request classes are defined, their number, priorities, and dispersal, to mention but a few.

A9.1.2 An Analytic Program. A second program would seek to analyze the answers. It would be aimed to answer technical questions about the relative benefits and costs of proposed shifts in the degree of decentralization. Essentially, it would compute and display a "response surface" that expresses net utility as a function of many variables and permits the user to explore it. It would remind users of their and the program's assumptions, values, and compromises and their consequences. It should make them aware of trades that they must make and permit them to play out what could happen. It could acquaint them with profiles of other organizations and show how their own organization compares to them, and it should remind them of the importance of collecting and entering high-quality input data. Even more importantly, it should stimulate them to think of asking questions and viewing problems in ways they had not previously imagined. Quite possibly, experience with the program and subsequent discussions about it, might bring out users' latent resourcefulness in inventing original insights and solutions to their problems for which the program served only as a trigger or catalyst.

Dewayne Hendricks[2] has written a computer system of this kind with the following properties: (a) It is interactive so that the user can pose various types of questions to the model and get immediate feedback. (Unless the user is fluent in a high-level language such as SNOBOL4, this would require an intermediary to "translate" the user's questions; if the question involves changing the model by replacing an assumption, for example, to explore the model's sensitivity to that assumption, then the response will be less than immediate.) (b) It is flexible and extensible. It should enable the intermediary-programmer to not only configure various structures but also modify the underlying model with great ease. (c) It should access a data base storing previously defined systems and results for later reexamination and modification. (d) It defines a class of structures by assigning indefinite values to attributes. (e) It can retrieve specific data from a description, such as the mean service time for a particular server. (f) It manipulates lists, sets, strings, and numbers. (g) It displays results in easily read graphical form.

A9.1.3 An Experimental System. The organizational structure of the proposed experimental system, viewed as a service, should exhibit the degree of decentralization we recommended. Pluralization, dispersion, and specialization would be embodied in the number of terminals located for convenient access to users with associated intermediary programmers who can make both input and output highly responsive to them. They would be as active (interventionist, in contrast to passively responsive) as individual users would like, and they would provide feedback and personal interactions of great sensitivity and human quality. The administrative structure would be quite flat, with most of the responsibility delegated to the intermediaries who work directly with the users.

The users, as well as the intermediaries, would participate not only in major decisions in the operation of the experimental system but also in its overall design and redesign. Indeed, to ensure responsiveness to users' needs, they should eventually not only bear the cost of capitalizing and operating the system but also feel that it is their own creation and tool as much as it is that of their colleagues whose primary concern is design, operation, and research.

A9.1.4 A Reporting System. Another program responsible for long-term follow-up would elicit, from the clients, the actions taken relevant to decentralization and the consequences experienced. All this data would be compiled, analyzed, and used to improve the analytic capabilities. It would also create a forum in which clients can share one another's experiences, on-line, and a consortium for growing a data base of great value for empirical researchers.

A9.2 SUGGESTED RESEARCH: FURTHER ANALYTICAL EXTENSIONS

An important extension of our work is to explore the effect of minimizing cost by jointly varying three or more of the variables corresponding to our eight aspects of decentralization. Another is to introduce mathematically defined variables and assumptions corresponding to the numerous mechanisms that we have described only verbally.

A9.2.1 On Specialization. An outstanding example of this would be a more thorough analysis of specialization. Too much specialization on the part of too many diverse specialists leads to costs beyond the sum of the costs of maintaining the many highly paid specialists; coordination and management cost must be added. The patient who must go to a different specialist for treatment of each organ is not likely to feel well served as an entire person, particularly if the specialists do not communicate their findings or coordinate their recommendations with one another, and if they do not act in synchrony or concert to help the patient's health, which depends on the interactions among bodily systems and organs. Nature does not respect the disciplinary specialties of experts. Too little specialization, on the other hand—for example, just one general practitioner or "Jack-of-all Trades"—may not be able to render certain specialized services when the need arises no matter how many adjustment steps the physician takes. It may simply exceed the practitioner's capacity or the time required may exceed the time available.

A9.2.2 On Delegation. Our models of delegation should be extended to more than two-level organizations. They should be combined with models for participation and for computing the optimal flatness. The notion that different functions can be decentralized in different degrees should also be introduced, though that introduces considerable complexity into the models. The realistic condition that agents often "wear several hats," that is, coordinate certain activities of certain other persons some of the time, introduces even greater complexity but it needs to be investigated.

A9.2.3 On Divided Clienteles. Another line of research would deal with service systems servicing a divided clientele. Suppose the clients form a relatively uniform group or one with a normal distribution of needs and resources; then our models apply directly. If they are sharply divided in these matters, then optimal solutions for one group will not be optimal for the other. In such divided societies, our models may permit a better understanding of a possibly significant aspect of interest conflicts.

A.9.2.4 On Advanced Simulation and Modeling. The considerable body of literature on computer simulation and probabilistic analysis (e.g., Sauer, 1976; Schkolnick, 1976) should be utilized more fully to derive results at a mathematical level that is more advanced than we have done here. A good vehicle for further studies is the analysis of roving facilities, such as ice cream vendors, ambulances, or bookmobiles. Operations research to determine how many units, what size and specialization should be deployed, and where and when they should be moved requires deeper investigation of at the least the following generally applicable problem areas. How do potential clients of roving facilities know that they exist? Where and when is one conveniently accessible? What are the fluctuations and swings in demand and how are they smoothed or aggravated by a roving facility? What are the economics and how do they interact with political and social aspects? Excellent starting points for such work are the studies of how to deploy municipal emergency services by the RAND Institute in New York (e.g., Chaiken, 1971—there are over 40 other references, as well as many that relate to decentralizing the courts, health services, schools, transportation, housing, and others).

A9.3 SOME SUGGESTED EMPIRICAL INQUIRIES

The analytic system proposed in Section A9.1 would begin to build up a data base for empirical studies that could eventually serve as a consortium for both users and researchers. It could provide a continually updated and systematic record of cases such as are now recorded in books for students of business administration (Seiler, 1967). The compilation of such data may use values of variables that are not yet embodied in analytic models or computer simulations, much as our models employ variables in which the values have not yet been reliably measured.

A9.3.1 Variables. To accommodate existing empirical data about organizations, as well as to stimulate their collection, we propose the following three classes of variables. (1) Describing human clients and servers: their skills, knowledge, behavior patterns, needs, values, expectations, images, or representations of the world. (2) Organizational: the service agency's goals, strategies, salary levels, incentive and reward systems, leadership styles, peer review mechanisms, influence and acceptance by and of others, social status, required skill levels, and working conditions. (3) Technological: level of automation, speed of obsolescence, change in work volume, extent of retraining due to technological unemployment, educational requirement, effect on working conditions, departmental structure, and nature and number of supervisors.

Interactions among these variables should also be recorded. These include the existence of coordinating committees; the degree of consistency between organizational inputs and servers' predispositions, organizational norms and traditions; variety, autonomy, communication, learning time, responsibility associated with jobs; emergence of informal group; cohesiveness and several others.

A9.3.2 Levels and Performance. Though we have searched the literature without success, we believe that it should be possible to find accurate records of the number of hierarchical levels in various organizations throughout history.[3] It should be easy to examine the correlation between flatness and organizational performance in armies, navies, industrial corporation, and governments. Similarly, it may be possible to find data that correspond to the other seven aspects of decentralization that could be correlated with organizational performance. Techniques such as those used by Hage (1971, 1976) should be applied and extended to test hypotheses implied by our theoretical approach in comparison with his. Cross-cultural (Roberts, 1970) and anthropological studies that discuss the effects of centralized leadership or its lack (Steward, 1936; Service, 1962, 1958; Sahlins, 1961; Middleton and Tait, 1958) should also be connected, with profit, to further extensions of our analysis.

Figures correlated with centralization of countries might be obtained from various existing sources (Banks and Textor, 1960; Kaufman, 1963, 1973; Grodzins, 1963). Though such data is of nonuniform quality, very significant correlations are not likely to escape even very crude measures and gross approximations. At least two approaches are available. One relies on documents and informants. The other is based on survey techniques, using interviews and questionnaires (Pennings, 1973).

A9.4 SUGGESTED EXPERIMENTAL STUDIES

While the difficulty of conducting controlled experiments on large real organizations is obvious, smaller communication nets can be investigated in a laboratory. Thus, such investigations as Harshbarger's (1971) can be extended to observe the effect of all our eight main variables on the effectiveness of a group in providing a required service. For example, a group organized in a certain way can be asked to provide the experimenter, acting in the role of a client, with a specified service to be provided. Such findings as the increased effectiveness of decentralized nets for solving *complex* problems should be verified, using different characterizations of decentralization and complexity. Experimental studies of the effect of feedback on team performance (Egerman, 1966) and the effect of authoritarian versus democratic modes of leadership (Bavelas and Barrett, 1951; Leavitt, 1955; Cohen and Bennis, 1959; Etzioni, 1965; Festinger, 1950; Kahn and Katz, 1960; Guetzkow, 1960; Mulder, 1963; Mears, 1971) should be extended and combined with the decentralization variables we have proposed.

A9.5 APPLICATIONS RESEARCH

Perhaps the most important next step in further research in the direction we have begun is the particularization of our general models to specific operational service organizations with important decentralization problems.

A9.5.1 Decentralization in Health Services. With the help of computer simulations and operations research techniques (Mills, 1975; Fetter and Thompson, 1965), considerable progress has been made toward the design of more cost-effective health services. One study of a gynecology clinic, for example, showed that scheduling patients so that there is an interarrival time of 30 minutes produced very few delays and that two examination rooms provided as good a service as larger modules. The trends toward health maintenance organizations (HMOs), professional service review organizations (PSRO), neighborhood health centers, consumerism in health care, the effective use of community intervention with the help of mass media (Farquhar, 1977), and the potential of telemedicine (Bashshur, 1976) make this a very promising area of research.

It has been established that the average cost per hospital patient treated for a given condition decreases with the number of such cases (*Science*, February 28, 1975, p. 730). Would this suggest concentrating many clients with the same condition in one hospital? Different hospitals would then specialize in different conditions, and the patients or their insurance companies would seem to gain. This has been done for burn injuries. The reasons for such centralizing rearrangements are, however, balanced by reasons against it, such as the greater distances that patients might have to travel unless all the hospitals were near one another. It is, though, an interesting problem of practical import that can also advance a general theory.

There are many other problems with these attributes, and there is a strong foundation on which to build. In addition to the previously mentioned RAND Institute studies in New York and the work at Yale, there is promising work from new health services research centers (Horvath, 1971, 1973) and other studies (e.g., Gustafson et al., 1975; Fryback and Gustafson, 1975).

A9.5.2 Decentralization in Education. This has received the greatest attention in recent years and generated the greatest heat. Loads can be most readily estimated in this application area. Pluralization corresponds to the number of schools, rooms, teachers, texts, and duplicate materials. Dispersion refers to where the schools are located relative to students' residences. Specialization refers to the diversity of special courses offered and the number of teachers who are specialists in some subject. Feedback refers to the quality of interaction between students and teachers, whether it is many to one as in large lecture courses or individualized with a great deal of warm, sensitive human attention. Flatness refers to the number of levels above the classroom teacher, up to the superintendent of schools. Delegation refers to how much authority and responsibility the teacher exerts in choice of courses, texts, standards, tests, syllabi, and so on. Participation refers to the extent of the teachers' influence in major educational policy decisions and in redesign and restaffing of the entire school board. Parents, educational researchers, concerned community leaders—even students—are all participants in the system in various degrees. The effectiveness of the system could be measured by the sum of the contributions made by the school system's graduates over their lifetimes relative to other school systems in communities with the same demographic characteristics. In this way, the effect of these eight dimensions could be investigated.

Problems of decentralization in educational services may not provide as good a research vehicle as the problems of health services, because outcomes are much harder to evaluate, and because there is less opportunity for systematic inquiry; but certain special problems are both important and researchable. Questions of bussing and how to reach decisions about what languages to use in schools as well as issues of displinary policymaking and enforcement and the dissemination and utilization of educational research appear amenable to fruitful inquiry.

A9.5.3 Information Systems. This is an area in which a great deal can be done and learned. Information systems are found everywhere. The study of intelligence systems in various branches of government, particularly the conditions for intelligence failure and for the relation between decentralization and success in early crises warning, is rich in potential findings.

Libraries and information centers have different degrees of decentralization in various countries, and a comparative study could reveal differences in cost and benefit of both practical and scientific value. Large-scale centralization of mechanized document retrieval facilities was not recommended (A. D. Little, 1964) in 1964; whether that recommendation still holds is worthy of investigation. Our simplest model for pluralization applies to a science library, where it could perhaps help to persuade hard-boiled administrators to increase budgets when they realize that the cost of a client's time is not zero.

Decentralized libraries are expensive from the librarians' viewpoint, but not from the user's viewpoint, whose interests a good librarian constantly has in mind and who may feel alienated in a centralized, impersonal library. Yet users' increased mobility may enable both scientists and humanists to become attracted by a specialized "research material repository" just as the Smithsonian's Museum of Natural History with its millions of research specimens or a large accelerator or astronomical observatory attracts them to come to such a central facility.[4] Quite possibly, we could have numerous decentralized reading rooms with terminals as well as larger repositories, and an interesting research question is to determine the best mix of these two.

Networks of computer and communication systems have already been discussed and offer many research opportunities. The Education Resources Information Center network is quite decentralized and has proved very cost-effective (Marron and Burchinal, 1967). More recent studies and comparisons would be valuable. This also holds for international information systems (Gottschalk, 1970).

Finally, the human nervous system is a decentralized information system. It is, in part, a service system in the sense that government and regulation and coordination and control are services. Studying it from this point of view may provide useful analogies and perhaps even unexpected insights into the relation between mind and brain.

In general, questions of decentralization arise in a vast range of disciplines; from the sociology of the family, tribes, clans, and ethnic groups to governance of industrial corporations, universities, countries, and multinational alliances. They arise wherever we observe complex organizational structures. It is from the interplay between the search for generally applicable principles and the attempts to solve very concrete real problems that progress toward a general theory is most likely to emerge.

Notes

PREFACE

1. Settling for a level of aspiration, as discussed by Herbert A. Simon in *Models of Man* (New York: John Wiley, 1957).
2. Excellent books, such as *Decentralization in Management Systems* by W. T. Morris, or *Organizational Planning* by J. W. Lorsch and P. R. Lawrence, already have presented mathematical analyses of particular organizational structures. However, they do not stress political aspects, nor do they use a system viewpoint aimed at a general theory. Major literature from the social sciences, such as the work of James W. Fesler, is rich in concrete insights and experience, but does not bring the power of mathematical analysis to bear. For these reasons we think that our book still can add something to the general understanding of its subject.

CHAPTER 1

1. See, for example, Albert Wohlstetter, "Illusions of Distance," *Foreign Affairs* 46, 2 (1968):242-255.
2. For critical surveys, see for example, James W. Fesler, "Approaches to the Understanding of Decentralization," *Journal of Politics* 27 (August 1965):536-566; Henry J. Schmandt, "Municipal Decentralization: An Overview," *Public Administration Review* 32 (1972):571-587; Donald Haider, "The Political Economy of Decentralization," *American Behavioral Scientist* 15, 1 (September 1971):108-129.

3. In some recent discussions, it has seemed all too easy to use "quality of life" as a device for deciding in favor of the latter kind of policy when the lives threatened are considered by some to be of low quality (e.g., aged, ill, or mentally retarded).
4. If a principle or a theory in science or ethics were to be considered completely invariant, regardless of any changes in conditions, it would turn into a language. Thus "matter" in the philosophy of "dialectic materialism" today does not mean completely the same as it did in the eighteenth century, and the reinterpretations of the Biblical commandment "Thou shalt not kill" have been legion.
5. "There are voices today urging us not only to eschew conscious intervention but also to distrust and limit the uses and consequences of reason itself," states Grobstein, and he concludes that "a stereoscopic vision that includes both 'creative pessimism' and 'creative optimism' is now required" (Grobstein, 1977, p. 32).
6. We are indebted to a grant from the University of Michigan's Office of Religious Affairs to explore "Decentralization and the Values of Authority and Autonomy: A Study of Reciprocal Effects" as part of the University's Values Year, 1975-1976. Robin Crickman participated in this study and examined the effect of computer conferencing on broadening people's views of value-laden issues.
7. Sometimes this is a reciprocal relationship: clients are convinced of the high quality of service *because* of its cost and rarity.
8. Actually, a great deal of confusion exists in the literature concerning the precise meaning of the term "decentralization." Schmandt (1972) takes it to mean all types of power distribution, admitting that it might also refer to the delegation of authority to the lowest level within a system. Haider (1971), on the other hand, takes a more political view and perceives a decentralized system as one in which (1) there exist local bodies with power over the subsystem they find themselves in; or (2) services and programs provided by the system are responsive to local demand. Morris (1968) understands decentralization to mean the splitting off of segments of an organization; the split-off divisions operate more or less autonomously, in coordination with the parent structure, like satellites. Kaufman (1963) defines six major aspects of centralization, in terms of the respective degrees to which there is central direction and/or conduct of (1) specification of tasks of subordinates and procedures to be followed by them; (2) recruitment and promotion of members of the organization; (3) revenues and disbursements; (4) reporting, inspection, and record keeping; (5) review and prior clearance of questions and decisions by field personnel; and (6) fostering of loyalties of staff to the top leadership.
9. Because an organization has many types of agents, there may be a different degree of pluralization associated with each type. Thus a clinic may have three sorters or receptionists, five diagnosticians, six operatives, one inspector who also doubles as supervisor, a load scheduler, and a planner.
10. Thus, if there are three receptionists in a single clinic, their degree of dispersion is 1. If two are at one site and the third is at another site, then it is 2.
11. See F. Levy and E. H. Truman "Toward a Rational Theory of Decentralization: Another View," *The American Political Science Review* 65, 1 (March 1971):172-179; and Albert O. Hirschman, *Exit, Voice and Loyalty* (Cambridge, Mass.: Harvard University Press, 1970).
12. The notions of the scope and weight of participation, similar to those of the scope and weight of power, have been developed from earlier ideas by Harold D. Lasswell, Abraham Kaplan, and Robert A. Dahl. See H. D. Lasswell and A. Kaplan, *Power and Society* (New Haven: Yale University Press, 1950); R. A. Dahl, "The Concept of Power," *Behavioral Science* 2 (1957):201-215; K. W. Deutsch, *The Analysis of Inter-*

national Relations, 2nd ed. (Englewood Cliffs, N.J.: Prentice-Hall, 1978), pp. 28–32, 36–44; and *Politics and Government*, 2nd ed. (Boston: Houghton Mifflin, 1974), pp. 71–74.

CHAPTER 2

1. In a sense, the idea of a "center" is a geometric concept, based on some notion of distance or closeness among clients and servers. The importance of physical distance among communicating individuals has been studied extensively, for example, by Robert Sommer, "Small Group Ecology," *Psychological Bulletin* 67, 2 (1967):145–152. Though more generalized notions of distance have been studied, for example, by Deutsch and Isard, *Behavioral Science*, 6 (November 1961):308–311, the importance of simple geographical distance cannot be overestimated, despite the emergence of technologies for telecommunication and automated transport, for example, see Kochen, "On Determining Optimum Size of New Cities," in *Is There an Optimum Level of Population?*, edited by S. F. Singer (New York: McGraw Hill, 1971), p. 364; (see also Chapter 4). The physical growth of modern hospitals has meant that hospital staff members have to walk greater distances. For example, in one hospital surgical interns walked an average of six miles per day, which has some effect on patient care (private communication, W. J. Foley, "Distances Walked By Surgery Interns on Duty," University of Michigan Hospital, 1976). Data on patient travel has also proved to be useful in helping hospitals and community planning agencies reach a joint decision about the geographic area over which services will be provided (e.g., D. L. Drosness and J. W. Lubin, "Planning Can Be Based on Patient Travel," *The Modern Hospital*, 106 (April 1966):92–94.) The general concept of "communicative distance"—which is the inverse of "closeness" is discussed in Chapter 4 (see also footnote 1 in Chapter 3).
2. If these values are determined in the labor market, an executive's time will appear to be more valuable than that of an as yet unrecognized free-lance artist. Summing over their lifespans would lead to the conclusion that the life of one has greater economic value than that of the other. From the point of view of democratic politics and culture, everyone's life and hence everyone's lost time ought to be valued equally. From the viewpoint of social utility, anyone's life and time should be valued in proportion to this person's probable usefulness to the life expectancy or life quality of other people. In practice, a variety of compromises between these viewpoints may be expected.
3. The effects of levels of aspiration and education could be analyzed as separate variables. In a decentralized society, more people are likely to have attained at least some education than in a centralized society. With increased education among the masses of people comes awareness of a gap between what could be and what is, leading to higher aspiration levels and expectations. Falling hope when these are not met may contribute pressure to even further decentralization. Excessive decentralization, however, may be counterproductive in that it does not allow for the concentration of resources needed to develop new services.
4. There is an increasing body of literature in human geography devoted to the description of mathematical properties of the distribution patterns of people and their activities. Attempts have been made to determine the size, shape, and number

of administrative areas within a territorial unit, to measure the efficiency of the particular arrangements, and to compare them with alternative spatial arrangements.

In many studies deriving measures for the geometry of areas, there is an assumption that earth space can be treated as Euclidean. This means that parallel lines never meet; that the shortest distance between two points is a straight line; that distances between points can be calculated from Pythagoras's theorem. However, cities may be joined by dirt roads or superhighways, in which case the simple straight-line distance may be inadequate for handling variables such as the time, cost, or effort of moving between these places. Similarly, these factors may not be accurately reflected in a two-dimensional division of space; the same administrative area may take on different shapes when the criterion to define units shifts from time to cost minimization.

Abler, Adams, and Gould (1971) in their book *Spatial Organization* discuss the problem of boundaries for administrative units and locating facilities to achieve specific objectives. They define this general location-allocation problem thus: "How shall we allocate one set of facilities to serve a second set of people?" From a geographer's point of view, the difficulty with a problem of this type is that many things can vary: (1) the number of things to be assigned; (2) the size of capacity of the facilities; and (3) the locations to which the facilities must be allocated.

While examining some of the spatial aspects of administration, Massam (1975) outlines a series of six stages to be "considered as a sequence of results in a competition between a completely centralized administrative system with a single administrative center and no local subdivision, and complete decentralization, whereby each individual provides all the goods and services he requires." He compares the state of the area to the stage of the administrative system as they vary over time. This evolutionary approach facilitates tackling the problem of trying to identify and explain specific trends in spatial organizations with well-established statistical tests.

Massam also classified services as follows:

	Distribution System			Examples
	Number of Origins	Number of Destinations	Number of Purposes of Trip	
1.	Many	Few	Single or Many	Hospitals, Schools, Libraries, Clinics, Voting Polls, Welfare Offices; Fire Stations,
2.	Few	Many	Single	Police Stations
3.	Few	Many	(servicing many per trip)	
4.	Few			Garbage Collection, Mail Delivery, Snow Removal; Taxation units, Pollution control

5. The strip includes enough land on either side of the highway to include the population requesting service. There is data, in the form of punched cards, to describe how population density varies along Route 40 from Baltimore to San Francisco (W. Tobler, private communication).

6. Simon's thoughtful comments on the various tendencies making for actual, rather than merely possible, centralization are wholly compatible with our analysis. The latter merely adds some emphasis on several no less real tendencies that may work in the opposite direction.
7. On centralization and communication at earlier levels of technology, Lewis Mumford comments: "Action at a distance, through scribes and swift messengers, was one of the identifying marks of the new mega-machine (the centralized state) . . . 'The scribe, he directeth every work that is in this land,' an Egyptian New Kingdom composition tells us . . . They made possible the constant 'report to political headquarters' essential for a centralized organization": *The Myth of the Machine* (New York: Harcourt Brace, 1967), p. 192. Also compare Harold A. Innis, *Empire and Communication* (Oxford: Oxford University Press, 1950).
8. The following formula gives the average waiting time (in months) with n facilities.

$$w(n) = \frac{s\left(\frac{a}{s}\right)^n}{(n-1)!(ns-a)^2} \cdot \frac{1}{\frac{1}{n!}\left(\frac{a}{s}\right)^n \frac{ns}{ns-a} + \sum_{k=0}^{n-1}\frac{1}{k!}\left(\frac{a}{s}\right)^k} \quad (2.7)$$

We wish to minimize the total cost

$$K(n) = Lc'_{wa}E(n) + Lc_{op} + nC \quad (2.8)$$

where

c'_{wa} = cost of client's time, in dollars per hour
c_{op} = operating cost per request
$E(n) = w(n) + 1/s$
  = average client time spent in system from arrival to completion of service

9. If properly used it is an important and valuable method. It has been used in attempts to mathematically explain organizational decentralization in an hierarchical structure (Krouse, 1972). In the context of optimizing a production function the distinction between suboptimization, interpreted as delegating an optimization responsibility, and decentralization has been clarified (Smithies, 1970). But suboptimization can often lead to very misleading results. When certain complex real problems are made mathematically tractable by focusing on a few variables while others are ignored, called "externalities," or assumed to remain unchanged or to be negligible, and a key variable is calculated so as to optimize some objective function, subject to constraints, we often are suboptimizing when we think we are optimizing. If the variables that were ignored were taken into account, a different result might well be obtained. The economist Kenneth Boulding once remarked that he has seen the face of the devil, and it is suboptimization. (In this context, Hell might be considered a suboptimal location.)
   We would like to thank the *Journal of Regional Science* for permission to use some of our suboptimization results.
10. Several measures of the extent to which facilities are dispersed have been proposed. The simplest is the mean deviation from the centroid. Another is the mean distance between facilities. In two dimensions several "indexes of centrality" have been used, particularly in experimental and mathematical studies of communication networks in small groups (Bavelas, 1951; Flament, 1963; Beauchamp, 1965). One such index applies to a graph with n points for which the distances, d_{ij}, are given between all pairs of points and i, j. The index is $n(n-1)/\Sigma_{ij}d_{ij}$.

CHAPTER 3

1. For the definition of Euclidean space, see note 4 in Chapter 2. Note also that ordinary geographic distance, which entered into our analysis of pluralization and dispersion, is increasingly used in planning services. For example, it has been found that inner-city men and blacks of either sex are more likely to commute to suburban jobs than women or whites, and this has implications for transportation planning (McKay, 1973).
2. A more realistic assumption would be that many varieties of functional requests would have to be mapped into a more restricted service space, consisting of the relatively few varieties of services available. The implications of this process of mapping functional requests into functional facilities—similar to the mapping of requests from service districts into pluralized and/or dispersed service stations—would constitute another research problem.
3. For simplicity, we assume that the capital cost of each serving unit, regardless of its total scope and type of specialization, is the same. We continue to assume that $b = \rho$ for all facilities.

CHAPTER 4

1. See K. W. Deutsch, *The Nerves of Government*, 2nd ed. (New York: The Free Press, 1966), pp. 99–101; and F. C. Redlich and D. X. Freedman, *Theory and Practice of Psychiatry* (New York: Basic Books, 1966).
2. For a more generalized concept of distance, see Deutsch and Isard (1961).
3. This calculation assumes roughly the usual average of 6 bits per character, 80 characters per line, and 42 lines per page. For further discussion, see Manfred Kochen (ed.), *The Growth of Knowledge* (New York: John Wiley, 1967); also Manfred Kochen, "New Techniques for Processing Bibliographic Information," in F. Kilgour (ed.), *Proceedings of the Symposium on Data Processing Information in University Libraries* (Philadelphia: Drexel Institute of Technology, 1968).
4. Kas Kalba has called our attention to a video tape of a courtship that developed over television, and the teaching of a new ballet step was taught by a teacher in New York's Lincoln Center to a live class in Denver.
5. B. M. Russett et al., *World Handbook of Political and Social Indicators* (New Haven: Yale University Press, 1964), pp. 46–48.
6. *United Nations Demographic Yearbook*, 1966 (New York: 1967), p. 95.
7. Approximate rates, computed from data in the *Statistical Abstract of the United States 1967*, pp. 58, 86, 505, 508–509, 561, and 586; and ibid., 1968, pp. 6, 550, and 573; and *Uniform Crime Reports for the United States*, 1960, p. 2, and ibid., 1965, p. 3.
8. We wish to thank the *Society for General Systems Research* for permission to use some of the results in their 1975 Proceedings (Kochen and Deutsch, 1975).

CHAPTER 5

1. F. Auerbach, "Das Gesetz der Bevölkerungskonzentration," *Petermans Mitteilungen* 59 (1913):74–76; A. J. Lotka, *Elements of Physical Biology* (Baltimore, 1925), pp. 306–307 (reprinted as *Elements of Mathematical Biology*, New York: Dover, 1956); G. K. Zipf, *National Unity and Disunity* (Bloomington, Ind.: Principia Press, 1941);

Notes / 313

B. Mandelbrot, "Final Note on a Class of Skew distributions," *Information and Control 4* (1961):198–216, also his "A Class of Long-Tailed Probability Distributions and the Empirical Distribution of City Sizes," Research Note NC-95, Yorktown Heights, New York, May 23, 1962, Thomas J. Watson Research Center.
2. Herald Hage, Michael Aiken, and Caro Bagley Marrett, "Organization Structure and Communication," *American Sociological Review* 36, 5 (1971):869.

CHAPTER 6

1. If the sorters issue no alarm, then M can take the initiative instead of responding to a situation. Analysis of this is sufficiently different and complex to require separate treatment. This is also the case for dealing with unanticipated situations calling for general alarm. We therefore confine this analysis to situations calling for responses to a special alarm, a local alerting message.
2. According to classical economic theory, utility is subjective. An interpersonal notion of utility would be defined as expected utility of outcome averaged over groups.
3. An example was President de Gaulle's question to Dean Acheson about President Kennedy's policy in the Cuban missile crisis in 1962, "Did you come to inform me or to consult me?" After the reply affirming the former, de Gaulle eventually removed France from NATO.
4. See T. N. Clark, "Centralization Encourages Public Goods, But Decentralization Generates Separable Goods," Report W2-25, New Haven, Yale University, Institute for Social and Policy Studies, November 1972. For a definitive study of the notion of "public good" see Olson (1971).
5. Where such a subjective feeling of control may not—or no longer does—correspond to any substantial probability of reinforcing real life experiences, it may continue to be held, valued, or defended against cognitive dissonance, in accordance with well-known psychological processes, such as repression, denial, or distortion of evidence. Moreover, even a very small proportion of continuing reinforcements may suffice to maintain an unrealistic habit of thought. Skinner found this to be so with continuing or even increased effectiveness of attenuated probabilistic reinforcement schedules.
6. $C' = ac (M_1 + m)^{1-b} (L_1 + fm) + dk_1(L_1 + fm)(M_1 + m)^{-e} + ac(M_2 - m)^{1-b}(L - L_1 - fm) + dk_2(L - L_1 - fm)(M_2 - m)^{-e}$
7. If these conditions are met, then $f = [(L - 2L_1)acM^{-b} - (L + 2L_1)dk_1 M^{-(e+1)}]/DEN$, where $DEN = 2acmM^{-b} + dk_1 M^{-(e+1)} (M + m)$ and $M = (M_1 + M_2)/2$.
8. We would like to thank *Behavioral Science* for permission to use some of the results in a recently published paper (Kochen and Deutsch, 1977a).

CHAPTER 8

1. If capital, skills, and abilities are at a high level among, say, a group of farmers, and their work habits are modern and efficient, then they tend to favor their status quo or improve their condition: "rich" farmers get "richer," both in the United States and the Soviet Union. If their work habits are traditional or conservative, then they may go bankrupt and move to the cities. If capital or the equivalent in skills is low, as it is among migrant farmers, and if their work habits are modern, then they, too, move to the cities; if, however, they are traditional and attached to the land, then they tend to have more children and get "poorer."

314 / Notes

It is of interest to inquire how the distribution of participation affects the distribution of wealth, power, access to service, and service quality. A shift toward centralization, that is, toward a skewed or uneven distribution of participation, would probably skew each distribution to the right: the poor get poorer as the rich get richer. If capital investments are unequally distributed over space, a mobile population will shift toward the sites of greater capital concentration until the probability of access to capital for marginal residents at each site is equal. This population movement will shift the distribution of capital and the distribution on which these processes converge, and if it does, it may be one of considerable concentration.

CHAPTER 9

1. An empirical study that factor analyzed 46 organizations in the United Kingdom (Pugh et. al., 1968) was among the first to question Max Weber's conception of a one-dimensional characterization of organization structure. Their scales and methods were extended by others (e.g., Reimann, 1973). Factor analysis based on data using such scales as "functional specialization," "formalization of role definition," "lack of autonomy," "centralization," "functional dispersion," and "hierarchical control" led to three factors: decentralization, specialization, and formalization. Careful analysis of the evidence, however (Mansfield, 1973), does not warrant treatment of the main variables as vectors or of dismissing Weber's conception of bureaucracy, the degree of which is negatively correlated (weakly) with centralization.
2. Private communication from Aron Smith, University of Michigan, April 1977.
3. The size of a firm is related to the organizational structure, to a greater degree even than is technology (Child and Mansfield, 1972).

APPENDIX 3.2

1. We wish to thank *Management Science* for permission to reprint these results here (Kochen and Deutsch, 1973).

APPENDIX 5.1

1. Elsewhere in the Book, we have used subscripts to indicate a variable argument of a function, as in c_l. In this appendix, we will use functional notation, $c(l)$ consistently, reserving the use of subscripts to indicate partial derivatives, $c_l = \partial c/\partial l$, as in the convention in mathematics. For variety, δ and ∂ as well as subscripts were used interchangeably in this chapter.
2. We wish to thank *Management Science* for permission to reprint some of the results from our article (Kochen and Deutsch, 1975).

APPENDIX 5.3

1. Empirical research (Blau and Schoenherr, 1971) had suggested that large organizational size, resulting from large L, promotes an economy of scale in administration,

but further research (Kasarda, 1974) suggests that even though there are proportionately fewer managers in large organizations, the proportion of other clerical and professional staff increases.
2. Recent formulations that use high-level mathematics for optimizing the number of hierarchical levels in a file to minimize search time have been analyzed by Howard Resnikoff, head of the Division of Information Science and Technology of the U.S. National Science Foundation (private communication, January 1980). If we liken finding an item in, say, a card file with tab separators (2-levels) to reaching an appropriate service agent in an organization, then the mathematical techniques can be transferred.

APPENDIX 9.1

1. For details, contact the authors.
2. Dewayne Hendricks was on our project at the University of Michigan in 1973-1974 and is presently with the Amdahl Company.
3. Finding accurate records of the number of hierarchical levels should be especially easy for the case of military history (Janowitz, 1959).
4. Private communication from Phyllis Richmond, March 29, 1973. An example of such a repository would be the "ideal" information retrieval test collection that has been proposed by Karen Sparck-Jones to the British Library Research and Development Division (1977).

Bibliography

Abler, R.; Adams, J. S.; and Gould, P. R. *Spatial Organization.* Englewood Cliffs, N.J.: Prentice-Hall, 1971.

Ackerman, R. W. "Influence of Integration and Diversity on Investment Process." *Administrative Science Quarterly* 15 (1970): 341–350.

Advisory Committee on National Growth Policy Processes to the National Commission on Supplies and Shortages. *Forging America's Future: Strategies for National Growth and Development.* Washington, D.C.: U.S. Government Printing Office, December 1976.

Aiken, M., and Mott, P., eds. *The Structure of Community Power.* New York: Random House, 1970.

Ardell, D. B. "The Metropolitan Council CHP Experience—A Search for Balance between Control and Delegation." *American Journal of Public Health* 62 (1972): 516–521.

Argyris, C. "Explorations in Consulting-Client Relationship." *Human Organization* 26 (1961): 121–313.

———. *Intervention Theory and Method.* Reading, Mass.: Addison-Wesley, 1970.

Note: The abbreviation "LT" refers to S. T. Hsu, *Bibliography on Location Theory* (1976); "LC" refers to "Planning for Location Change in the Delivery of Medical Care," in *Exchange Bibliography 100* (1969).

Arrow, K. J. "Optimization, Decentralization and Internal Pricing in Business Firms." In *Contributions to Scientific Research in Management*. Los Angeles: UCLA, Western Data Processing Center, 1961, pp. 9–18.
──────. "Control in Large Organizations." *Management Science* 10 (1964): 397–408.
──────. *The Limits of Organization*. New York: W. W. Norton, 1974.
──────, and Hurwicz, L. "Decentralization and Computation in Resource Allocation." In *Essays in Economics and Econometrics*, edited by R. W. Pfouts. Chapel Hill: University of North Carolina Press, 1960, pp. 34–104.
Ashby, W. R. *Design for a Brain*. New York: John Wiley, 1952.
Auerbach Publications Inc., "54 Ways to Reduce DP Costs." Philadelphia: Data Processing Management, Auerbach, 1976.
Bales, R. F.; Stradtbeck, F. L.; Mills, T. M.; and Roseborough, M. "Channels of Communication in Small Groups." *American Sociological Review* 16 (1951): 461–468.
Banfield, E. C. *Big City Politics*. New York: Random House, 1965.
Banks, A. S., and Textor, R. B. *Cross-Policy Survey*. Cambridge, Mass.: M.I.T. Press, 1960.
Barnard, C. I. *The Functions of the Executive*. Cambridge, Mass.: Harvard University Press, 1938.
Barsodi, R. *Education and Living*. Melbourne, Fla.: Melbourne University Press, 1948.
Bashshur, R. "Acceptance and Impact of Telemedicine in a Rural Community." Paper presented at the 4th Annual Telecommunication Policy Research Conference, Airlie, Virginia, April 24, 1976.
Bauer, R. A., et al. *Second Order Consequences: A Mathematical Essay on the Impact of Technology*. Cambridge, Mass.: M.I.T. Press, 1969.
Baum, B. H. *Decentralization of Authority in a Bureaucracy*. Englewood Cliffs, N.J.: Prentice-Hall, 1961.
Baumol, W. T., and Wolfe, P. "A Warehouse Location Problem." *Operations Research* 6 (1958): 252–263.
Bavelas, A. "Communication Patterns in Task-Oriented Groups." In *The Policy Sciences*, edited by H. D. Lasswell and D. Lerner. Palo Alto: Stanford University Press, 1951.
──────, and Barrett D. "An Experimental Approach to Organizational Communication." *Personnel* 27 (1951): 366–371.
Beauchamp, M. A. "An Improved Index of Centrality." *Behavioral Science* 10 (1965): 161–163.
Beckmann, M. *Location Theory*. New York: Random House, 1968. (LT)
Bell, D. *The Coming of Post-Industrial Society*. New York: Basic Books, 1973.
Belloc, H. *The Servile State*. Boston: LeRoy Phillips, 1913.
Benello, C. G., and Roassopoulos, D. *The Case for Participatory Democracy*. New York: Grossman, 1971.
Berlinski, D. *On Systems Analysis*. Cambridge, Mass.: M.I.T. Press, 1976.
Berry, B. J. L. "Urban Hierarchies and Spatial Organization in Developing Countries." Paper delivered at the Rehovot Conference on Urbanization and Development in Developing Countries, Rehovot, Israel, August 16–24, 1971.

Berry, B. L. *Geography of Market Centers and Retail Distribution.* Englewood Cliffs, N.J.: Prentice-Hall, 1976. (LC)
Blau, P. M., and Schoenherr, R. A. *The Structure of Organizations.* New York: Basic Books, 1971.
Blau, P., and Scott, R. W. *Formal Organizations.* San Francisco: Chandler Publishing Co., 1962.
Boseman, F. G., and Jones, R. E. "Market Conditions, Decentralization, and Organization Effectiveness." *Human Relations* 27 (1974): 665–676.
Boulding, K. E. *Economic Analysis.* New York: Harper, 1955.
Boulding, K. E. *Conflict and Defense: A General Theory.* New York: Harper, 1962.
Brecht, B. *Caucasian Chalk Circle.* Translated by E. Bentley and M. Apelman. New York: Grove Press, 1966.
Bremer, S. *Simulated Worlds.* Princeton: Princeton University Press, 1977.
Bresnick, D. "Decentralizing the City: Who Gets Control?" *National Civic Review* 10 (1973): 486–490.
Brownell, S. M. "Desirable Characteristics of Decentralized School Systems." *The Education Digest* 36 (1971): 8–11.
Brzezinski, Z. "The American Transition." *New Republic* 157 (December 1967): 18–21.
Buber, M. *I and Thou.* New York: Scribner, 1958.
Bucci, G., and Streeter, D. N. "A User-Oriented Approach to the Design of Distributed Information Systems." RC 5887, IBM Thomas J. Watson Research Center, Yorktown Heights, N.Y. 10598, April 15, 1976.
Burgess, R. L. "Communication Networks and Behavioral Consequences." *Human Relations* 22 (1969): 137–159.
Cairncross, A. K. *Essays in Economic Management.* New York: State University of New York Press, 1971.
Carzo, R., Jr. "Some Effects of Organization Structure on Group Effectiveness." *Administrative Science Quarterly* 7 (1963): 393–424.
———, and Yanouzas, J. N. *Formal Organization: A Systems Approach.* Homewood, Ill.: Richard D. Irwin, 1967, pp. 392–394.
———. "Effects of Flat and Tall Organization Structure." *Administrative Science Quarterly* 14 (1969a): 178–191.
———. "Effects of Flat and Tall Organization Structure." *Administrative Science Quarterly* 14 (1969b): 427–442.
———. "Justification for the Carzo-Yanouzas Experiment on Flat and Tall Structures." *Administrative Science Quarterly* 15 (1970): 235.
Chaiken, J. *Number of Emergency Units Busy at Alarms Which Require Multiple Servers,* March 1971, Rand Report R-53-NYC/HUD (New York City: Rand Institute); also *Allocation of Emergency Units,* p-4745, December 1971.
Chandler, A. D. *Strategy and Structure.* Cambridge, Mass.: M.I.T. Press, 1962, pp. 241–276.
Child, J. "Strategies of Control and Organizational Behavior." *Administrative Science Quarterly* 18 (1973): 1–17.
Christaller, W. "Die Hierarchie der Städte." *IGU Symposium in Urban Geog-*

raphy. Lund, 1962, pp. 3–11. See also *Central Places in Southern Germany,* translated by C. W. Baskin. Englewood Cliffs, N.J.: Prentice-Hall, 1966.

Cillié, F. *Centralization or Decentralization.* New York: Teachers College, Columbia University, 1940, p. 96.

Clark, T. N. *Community Structure and Decision Making.* San Francisco: Chandler Publishing Co., 1968.

———. *Centralization Encourages Public Goods, But Decentralization Generates Separable Goods.* Report W2-25. New Haven: Yale University Institute for Social and Policy Studies, November 1972.

Clear, D. K. "Decentralization Issues and Comments." *Clearinghouse* 44 (1970): 259–267.

Cohen, A. M., and Bennis, W. "Continuity of Leadership in Communication Networks." *Human Relations* 12 (1959): 359–365.

Colby, K. M.; Watt, J. B.; and Gilbert, J. P. "A Computer Method of Psychotherapy: Preliminary Communication." *Journal of Nervous and Mental Disease* 142 (1966): 148–152; in *Psychological Abstracts* 40 (1966): 11223.

Collins, G. L. "Cost Analysis and Efficiency Measures for Hospitals." *Inquiry* 5 (1968): 50–62. (LC)

Cooper, L. "Location-Allocation Problems." *Operations Research* 11 (1963): 331–344. (LT)

———. "Solution of Generalized Locational Equilibrium Models." *Journal of Regional Science* 7 (1967): 1–18. (LT)

Cooper, M. "Organizational Patterns of Academic Science Libraries." *College and Research Libraries* 29 (1968): 357–363.

Corey, K. E., and Stafford, H. A. "Planning for Location Change in the Delivery of Medical Care." In "Exchange Bibliography 100," Council of Planning Librarians, Monticello, Ill., August 1969.

Cyert, R. M., and March, J. G. *A Behavioral Theory of the Firm.* Englewood Cliffs, N.J.: Prentice-Hall, 1963, pp. 36–38.

Dahl, R. A. "The Concept of Power." *Behavioral Science* 2,3 (1957): 201–215.

———. "Power." In *International Encyclopedia of the Social Sciences,* vol. 12, edited by D. L. Sills. New York: Crowell, Collier and Macmillan, 1968, pp. 405–415.

Dalton, G.; Barnes, L.; and Zaleznik, A. *The Distribution of Authority in Formal Organizations.* Boston: Harvard University Division of Research, 1968.

Davis, H. "Time-Sharing Moves Toward Centralization." *Scientific Research* 4 (1969): 25–29.

Dearden, J. "Computers: No Impact on Divisional Control." *Harvard Business Review* (January–February 1967): 99–104.

Dearing, P. M., and Francis, R. L. "A Network Flow Solution to a Multifacility Location Problem Using Rectilinear Distances." *Transportation Science* 8 (1974): 126–141. (LT)

deBakey, M., and Gotto, A. *The Living Heart.* New York: David McKay, 1977.

Dennis, J. B. "A Position Paper on Computing and Communications." *Communications ACM* 11 (1968): 370–377.

Deutsch, K. W. "The Value of Freedom: Some Long-Range Implications for the

Social Sciences." In *Science, Philosophy and Religion in Their Relation to the Democratic Way of Life,* edited by Lyman Bryson. New York: Kraus Repr., 1947.

―――. "Some Quantitative Constraints on Value Allocation in Society and Politics." *Behavioral Science* 7 (1966): 245-252.

―――. *The Nerves of Government.* 2nd ed. New York: Free Press, 1966, pp. 99-101.

―――. *Nationalism and Social Communication.* 2nd ed. Cambridge, Mass.: M.I.T. Press, 1966.

―――. *The Analysis of International Relations.* Englewood Cliffs, N.J.: Prentice-Hall, 1968, pp. 24-28, 33-39.

―――. *Nationalism and Its Alternatives.* New York: Alfred A. Knopf, 1969.

―――. "Some Quantitative Constraints on Value Allocation in Society and Politics." In *Politics, Personality and Social Science in the 20th Century: Essays in Honor of Harold D. Lasswell,* edited by A. Rogow. Chicago: University of Chicago Press, 1969.

―――. *Politics and Government.* 3rd ed. Boston: Houghton-Mifflin, 1974, pp. 71-74.

―――, and Burrell, S. A., et al. *The Political Community and the North Atlantic Area.* Princeton: Princeton University Press, 1957. Reprinted 1970 by Greenwood, Westport, Conn.

―――, and Isard, W. "A Note on a Generalized Concept of Distance." *Behavioral Science* 6 (November 1961): 308-311.

―――, and Kochen, M. "Review of *On Systems Analysis* by D. Berlinski." *Behavioral Science* 22 (1977): 309-310.

―――, and Meadow, W. "On the Appearance of Wisdom in Large Bureaucratic Organizations." *Behavioral Science* 1 (1961): 72-78.

deVise, P. "Methods and Concepts of an Interdisciplinary Regional Hospital Study." *Health Services Research* 3 (1968): 166-173. (LC)

Dimond, P. R. "Responsible Governance: A Plan for Decentralization of New York City's School System." University of Michigan, School of Education, unpublished paper for Urban Planning Seminar, December 2, 1968.

Downs, A. *Inside Bureaucracy.* Boston: Little, Brown, 1967.

Drosness, D. L., and Lubin, J. W. "Planning Can Be Based on Patient Travel." *The Modern Hospital* (April 1966): 106.

Dutton, J. M., and Starbuck, W. H. *Computer Simulation of Human Behavior.* New York: John Wiley, 1971.

Easton, D. *Systems Analysis of Political Life.* New York: John Wiley, 1965.

Egerman, K. "Effects of Team Arrangement on Team Performance—A Learning Theoretic Analysis." *Journal of Personality and Social Psychology* 3 (1966): 541-550.

Ehrle, R. A. "Management Decentralization: Antidote to Bureaucratic Ills." *Personnel Journal* 49 (1970): 396-397.

Ellul, J. *The Technological Society.* New York: Alfred A. Knopf, 1954.

―――. *The Political Illusion.* New York: Alfred A. Knopf, 1965.

Elzinga, D. J., and Hearn, D. W. "Geometrical Solutions for Some Minimax Location Problems." *Transportation Science* 5 (1972): 379-394. (LT)

Etzioni, A. *A Comparative Analysis of Complex Organizations.* Glencoe, Ill.: Free Press, 1961.

———. "Dual Leadership in Complex Organizations." *American Sociological Review* (1965): 688–698.

Fagin, H. E. "Hospital Location Involves Planning for Community Health Needs." *Southern Hospitals* 37 (June 1969): 19–22. (LC)

Fantini, M., and Gittell, M. *Decentralization: Achieving Reform.* New York: Praeger, 1973.

Farquhar, J. W. "The Stanford Three-Community Study: A Multifactor Cardiovascular Risk Education Campaign." In *Proceedings of the University of Michigan Services Research Conference,* edited by W. Horvath. Ann Arbor: University of Michigan Health Services Research Center, 1977.

Feingold, E. "A Political Scientist's View of the Neighborhood Health Center as a New Social Institution." *Medical Care* 8 (March-April 1970): 108–116.

Feller, W. *An Introduction to Probability Theory and Its Applications,* vol. 2. New York: John Wiley, 1966.

Ferkiss, V. C. *Technological Man: The Myth and the Reality.* New York: George Braziller, 1969.

Fesler, J. W. *Area and Administration.* Alabama: University of Alabama Press, 1964.

———. "Approaches to the Understanding of Decentralization." *Journal of Politics* 27 (1965): 536–566.

———. "Centralization and Decentralization." In *International Encyclopedia of the Social Sciences,* vol 2, edited by D. Sills. New York: Macmillan and Free Press, 1968, pp. 370–379.

Festinger, L. "Informal Social Communication." *Psychological Review* 57 (1950): 271–282.

Fetter, R. B., and Thompson, J. D. "The Simulation of Hospital Systems." *Operations Research* 13 (1965): 689–711.

Feynman, R. P.; Leighton, R. B.; and Sands, M. *The Feynman Lectures on Physics.* Reading, Mass.: Addison-Wesley, 1963, pp. 3–10, 46–48.

Fiske, P. H., and Root, W. L. "Identifiability of Slowly Varying Systems." *Information and Control* 32 (November 1976): 201–230.

Flament, C. *Applications of Graph Theory to Group Structure.* Englewood Cliffs, N.J.: Prentice-Hall, 1963.

Foa, U. G. "Interpersonal and Economic Resources." *Science* 171 (January 29, 1971): 345.

Foley, W. J. "Distances Walked by Surgery Interns on Duty." Private communication, University of Michigan Hospital, 1976.

Francis, R. L., and White, J. D. *Facility Layout and Location.* Englewood Cliffs, N.J.: Prentice-Hall, 1974. (LT)

Friedlander, F., and Brown, L. D. "Organization Development." *Annual Review of Psychology* 25 (1974): 313–341.

Friedrich, C. J. *Man and His Government.* New York: McGraw-Hill, 1963.

Fryback, D., and Gustafson, D. H. "Development of the Index of Medical Under-Service." *Health Services Research* 10 (1975), 168–180.

Furniss, N. "The Practical Significance of Decentralization." *Journal of Politics* 37 (1974): 958–982.
Galbraith, J. R. "Environmental and Technological Determinants in Organization Design." In *Studies in Organization Design*, edited by P. R. Lawrence and J. W. Lorsch. Homewood, Ill.: Richard D. Irwin, 1970.
Garrison, W. L., et al. *Studies of Highway Development and Geographic Change.* Seattle: University of Washington Press, 1959. (LC)
Gerlach, L. P. "Corporate Groups and Movement Networks in Urban America." *Anthropological Quarterly* 43 (July 1970): 123–145.
Ghiselli, E. E., and Siegel, J. P. "Leadership and Managerial Success In Tall and Flat Organization Structures." *Personnel Psychology* 25 (1972): 617–624.
Giscard D'Estaing, O. *La Décentralisation des pouvoirs dans l'enterprise.* Paris: Les Edition d'Organisation, Collection INSEAD Management, 1969.
Goldsmith, E. A. *A Blueprint for Survival.* Boston: Houghton-Mifflin, 1972.
Goodman, P. *People or Personnel: Decentralizing and the Mixed System.* New York: Random House, 1965.
_____. *New Reformation.* New York: Random House, 1970.
Gottschalk, C. "System Analysis Considerations In a Decentralized International Information System." *Proceedings ASIS Annual Meeting.* Washington, D.C., 1970, pp. 211–213.
Greenberger, M. "Computing in Transition." *Science* 181 (September 28, 1973a): 4106:1207.
_____; Aronofsky, J.; McKenney, J. L.; and Massy, W. F. "Computer and Information Networks." *Science* 182 (October 5, 1973): 4107:27–35.
Grobstein, C. "The Recombinant-DNA Debate." *Scientific American* 237 (July 1977): 22–33.
Grodzins, M. "Centralization and Decentralization in the American Federal System." In *A Nation of States*, edited by R. A. Goldwin. Chicago: Rand McNally, 1963.
Guetzkow, H. "Differentiation of Roles in Task-Oriented Groups." In *Group Dynamics*, edited by D. Cartwright and A. Zander. Evanston, Ill.: Row, Peterson, 1960.
Gurr, T. R. *Why Men Rebel.* Princeton: Princeton University Press, 1970.
Gustafson, D. H., et al. "Design of a Health Policy Research and Development System for Wisconsin." *Inquiry* 12 (September 1975): 251–262.
Guthrie, J. W. "American School Costs Compared." *Current History* 63 (July 1972): 39.
Hage, J. "An Axiomatic Theory of Organizations." *Administrative Science Quarterly* 10 (1965): 289–320.
_____; Aiken, A; and Marrett, C. B. "Organization Structure and Communications." *American Sociological Review* 36 (1971): 860–871.
Haider, D. "The Political Economy of Decentralization." *American Behavioral Scientist* 15 (September/October 1971): 108–129.
Hannon, J., and Fried, L. "Should You Decentralize." *Computer Decisions* 9 (February 1977): 40–42.

Harlegard, S. *Zentralisieren oder Dezentralisieren*. Bern: P. Haupt, 1971.
Harris, C. "Decentralization." *Public Administration* 3 (April 1925): 17–33.
Harshbarger, D. "An Investigation of a Structural Model of a Small Group Problem Solving." *Human Relations* 24 (1971): 43–63.
Hart, D. K. "Theories of Government Related to Decentralization and Citizen Participation." *Public Administration Review* 32 (1972): 603–621.
Hauriou, M. *Étude sur la Décentralization*. Paris: V. Giard and E. Briere, 1892.
Havighurst, R. J. "The Reorganization of Education in Metropolitan Areas." *Educational Digest* 36 (1971): 5–8.
Heierli, U. "Towards a Low Energy Development for the Third World." *CIDA* 1 (1974/1976): 5.
Henderson, H. "The Entropy State." *Planning Review* 2 (April/May 1974): 1–4.
Herbert, A. W. "Management Under Conditions of Decentralization and Citizen Participation." *Public Administration Review* 32 (1972): 622–637.
Hessacker, F. L. "Hitching up the Small School Districts: Shared Services." *American Education* 6 (April 1970): 18–21.
Hillier, F. S. "Economic Models for Industrial Waiting Line Problems." *Management Science* 10 (1963): 119–130.
Hirschman, A. O. *Exit, Voice and Loyalty*. Cambridge, Mass.: Harvard University Press, 1970.
Hollingshead, A. B., and Redlich, F. C. *Social Class and Mental Illness*. New York: John Wiley, 1958.
Hoover, E. M. *The Location of Economic Activity*. New York: McGraw-Hill, 1948.
Horvath, W. J. "The Current Situation in Psychiatry and Its Effects on the Delivery of Mental Health Services in the Next Decade." *Psychiatry in Medicine* 2 (1971): 138–145.
———. "Some Methodological Problems in the Evaluation of Community Health Care." *Medical Program Technology* 2 (1973): 13–17.
Hotelling, H. "Stability in Competition." *Economics Journal* 39 (1929): 52–53.
Howard, L. C. "Decentralization and Citizen Participation in Health Services." *Public Administration Review* 32 (1972): 701–717.
Hsu, S. T. *Bibliography on Location Theory*. Paper prepared for NSF-CBMS Conference on the Mathematics of Optimal Facility Location, Notices of the American Mathematical Society, June 28–July 2, 1976. (LT)
Hull, A; Saarinen, K.; and Mason, G. "Analysis and Simulation of the Wednesday Afternoon Arthritis Clinic at University Hospital." Ann Arbor: Technical Report No. 10, University of Michigan Functional and Resource Analysis, February 1975.
Hummon, N. P. "Criticism of 'Effects of Flat and Tall Organization Structure'." *Administrative Science Quarterly* 15 (1970): 230–234.
Hurwicz, L. *Decentralized Resource Allocation*. New Haven: Yale University Press, 1955. Cowles Commission Discussion Paper, No. 2112.

Ink, D., and Dean, A. L. "A Concept of Decentralization." *Public Administration Review* 30 (1970): 60–63.
Innis, H. A. *Empire and Communication.* Oxford: Oxford University Press, 1950.
Isaacs, R. B. "The Neighborhood Theory. An Analysis of Its Adequacy." *Journal of American Institution Planners* 14 (1948): 15–23.
Isard, W., et al. *Methods of Regional Analysis: An Introduction to Regional Science.* Cambridge, Mass.: M.I.T. Press, 1960.
Janowitz, M. "Changing Patterns of Organizational Authority: The Military Establishment." *Administrative Science Quarterly* 3 (1959): 473–493.
Jehlik, P. J., and McNamara, R. L. "The Relation of Distance to the Differential Use of Certain Health Personnel and Facilities and to the Extent of Bed Illness." *Rural Sociology* 17 (1952): 261–265. (CL)
Jones, H. R. "A Study of Organization Performance for Experimental Structure of Two, Three and Four Levels." *Academy of Management Journal* 12 (1969): 357–365.
Kahn, R. L. "Organizational Development: Some Problems and Proposals." *Journal of Applied Behavioral Science* 10 (1974): 485–502.
_____, and Boulding, K. E. *Power and Conflict in Organizations.* New York: Basic Books, 1964.
_____, and Katz, D. "Leadership Practices in Relation to Productivity and Morale." In *Group Dynamics,* edited by D. Cartwright and A. Zander. Evanston, Ill.: Row, Peterson, 1960.
Kaplan, S. A. "Don't Let Patients Push You Around." *Medical Dimensions* (March 1975): 27–28.
Kasarda, J. D. "The Structural Implications of Social System Size: A Three-Level Analysis." *American Sociological Review* 39 (1974): 19–28.
Katchalsky, A. "Thermodynamics of Flow and Biological Organization." *Zygon* (1971): 99–125.
Katz, D., and Kahn, R. L. *The Social Psychology of Organizations.* New York: John Wiley, 1966.
Katzenstein, P. *Disjointed Partners: Austria and Germany Since 1815.* Berkeley: University of California Press, 1976.
Kaufman H. *Politics and Policies in State and Local Government.* Englewood Cliffs, N.J.: Prentice-Hall, 1963, p. 12.
_____. "Administrative Decentralization and Political Power." *Public Administration Review* 29 (1969): 3–14.
_____. *Administrative Feedback.* Washington, D.C.: Brookings Institution, 1973.
Kerr, C. "Industrial Conflict and Its Mediation." *American Journal of Sociology* 60 (1954): 230–245.
Klein, S. "Mini Revolution in the Computer World." *New York Times* (February 13, 1977), Section 3, p. 1.
Knorr, K. *The War Potential of Nations.* Princeton: Princeton University Press, 1957.
_____. *The Political Economy of International Power.* New York: Basic Books, 1973.

Knuth, D. *The Art of Computer Programming.* Reading, Mass.: Addison-Wesley, 1968.
Kochen, M. "An Information-Theoretic Model of Organizations." *Transactions of the Professional Group on Information Theory* 1 (1954): 67, American Institute of Electrical Engineers.
―――. *Some Problems in Information Science.* Metuchen, N.J.: Scarecrow Press, 1965.
―――. "Newer Techniques for Processing Bibliographic Information." In *Proceedings of the Symposium on Data Processing in University Libraries,* edited by F. Kilgour. Philadelphia: Drexel Institute of Technology, 1968.
―――. "On Determining Optimum Size of New Cities." In *Is There and Optimum Level of Population,* edited by S. F. Singer. New York: McGraw-Hill, 1971.
―――. "Directory Design for Networks of Information and Referral Centers." *Library Quarterly* 42, 1 (1972): 59–83.
―――. "Cognitive Learning Processes: An Explication." In *Artificial Intelligence and Heuristic Programming,* edited by N. V. Findler and B. Meltzer. Edinburgh: Edinburgh University Press, 1971b, pp. 261–317. Revised German translation, 1973.
―――, ed. *The Growth of Knowledge.* New York: John Wiley, 1967.
―――, and Deutsch, K. W. "Toward a Rational Theory of Decentralization: Some Implications of a Mathematical Approach." *American Political Science Review* 63, 3 (1969): 734–749.
―――. "Decentralization and Uneven Service Loads." *Journal of Regional Science* 10, 2 (1970): 153–173.
―――. "Pluralization: A Mathematical Model." *Operations Research* 20, 2 (1972): 276–292.
―――. "Decentralization by Function and Location." *Management Science* 10 (April 1973): 841–856.
―――. "A Note on Hierarchy and Coordination: An Aspect of Decentralization." *Management Science* 21 (1974): 106–114.
―――. "Interpretive Distance and Informational Decentralization." In *Systems Thinking and the Quality of Life.* Proceedings of the Annual Meeting of the Society for General Systems Research, 1975.
―――. "Delegation and Control in Organizations with Varying Degrees of Decentralization." *Behavioral Science* 22 (July 1977): 258–269.
―――, and Donohue, J. *Information for the Community.* Chicago: American Library Association, 1976.
―――. "Decentralization: A New Analytic Approach." Presented at the Meeting of the International Political Science Association, Moscow, August 1979; submitted to *Large Scale Systems,* February 1980.
Komorita, S. S. "Weighted Probability Model of Coalition Formation." *Psychological Review* 81 (1974): 242–257.
Koopmans, T. C., ed. *Activity Analysis of Production and Allocation.* New York: John Wiley, 1951. Cowles Monograph No. 13.
―――, and Beckman, M. J. "Assignment Problems and the Location of Economic Activities." *Econometrica* 25 (1957): 53–76.

Krouse, C. G. "Complex Objectives, Decentralization, and the Decision Process of the Organization." *Administrative Science Quarterly* 17 (1972): 544–554.
Kuhn, H. W. "A Note on Fermat's Problem." *Mathematical Programming* 4 (1973): 98–107. (LT)
Lammers, C. J. "Power and Participation in Decision Making in Formal Organizations." *American Journal of Sociology* 73 (1967): 201–216.
Larson, T., and Anderson, A. "Procedural Guide for the Evaluation and Statewide Accreditation of Courts and Administrative Hearing Facilities." Ann Arbor, Mich.: Draft, Institute for Continuing Legal Education, University of Michigan, 1977.
Lasswell, H., and Kaplan, A. *Power and Society: A Framework for Political Inquiry.* New Haven: Yale University Press, 1950.
Lawrence, P. R., and Lorsch, J. W. *Organization and Environment.* Homewood, Ill.: Richard D. Irwin, 1967.
——. *Developing Organizations: Diagnosis and Action.* Reading, Mass.: Addison-Wesley, 1969.
Leavitt, H. J. "Small Groups in Large Organizations." *The Journal of Business* 28–29 (1955): 8–17.
Lee, E. C. *Management Decentralization: New York City Police Department.* New Haven: Yale University Institute for Social and Policy Studies, Report WC2-14, November 1971.
Levinthal, E. C.; Carhart, R. E.; Johnson, S. M.; and Lederberg, J. "When Computers Talk to Computers." *Industrial Research* 17 (November 15, 1975): 35–42.
Levy, F., and Truman, E. H. "Toward a Rational Theory of Decentralization: Another View." *The American Political Science Review* 65 (1971): 172–179.
Likert, R. *New Patterns of Management.* New York: McGraw-Hill, 1961.
——. *The Human Organization.* New York: McGraw-Hill, 1967.
Litterer, J. A. *The Analysis of Organizations.* New York: John Wiley, 1965.
Lorsch, J. W., and Lawrence, P. R. *Organizational Planning.* Homewood, Ill.: Richard D. Irwin, 1972.
Lösch, A. *The Economics of Location.* New Haven: Yale University Press, 1954.
Lowrie, S. G. "Centralization versus Decentralization." *American Political Science Review* 16 (August 1922): 384.
Lundquist, L. *Means and Goals of Political Decentralization.* Lund: Lund Political Studies 12, 1972.
Maass, A. E. *Area and Power: A Theory of Local Government.* Glencoe, Ill.: Free Press, 1959, pp. 9–26.
MacMahon, A. W. *Delegation and Autonomy.* Bombay: Asia Publishing House, 1961.
Macy, J. W., Jr. "To Decentralize and to Delegate." *Public Administration Review* 30 (1970): 438–443.
Maddick, H. *Democracy, Decentralization and Development.* London: Asia Publishing House, 1963.
Mandel, M. D. "Cost Analysis of Regionalized Versus Decentralized Abortion Programs." *Medical Care* 13 (1975): 137–148.

Mann, J. K., and Yett, D. E. "The Analysis of Hospital Costs: A Review Article." *The Journal of Business* 41 (1968): 191–202. (LC)
Manne, A. S. "Plant Location Under Economics-of-Scale—Decentralization and Computation." *Management Science* 11 (1964): 213–235.
Mansfield, R. "Bureaucracy and Centralization—Examination of Organizational Structure." *Administrative Science Quarterly* 18 (1973): 477–488.
―――, and Child, J. "Technology, Size, and Organization Structure." *Sociology* 6 (1972): 369–393.
March, J. G., and Simon, H. *Organizations*. New York: John Wiley, 1958.
Marien, M. "The Two Visions of Post-Industrial Society." Unpublished manuscript, May 1977.
Marron, H., and Burchinal, L. "ERIC—A Novel Concept in Information Management." *Proceedings of American Documentation Institute* 4 (1967): 268–272.
Marschak, J. "Efficient and Viable Organizational Forms." In *Modern Organizations*, edited by A. Etzioni. Englewood Cliffs, N.J.: Prentice-Hall, 1963.
―――, and Radner, R. *Economic Theory of Teams*. New Haven: Yale University Press, 1972.
Marschak, T. *Steps Toward a Theory of the Optimum National Location Pattern*. Technical Report #1. Palo Alto: Stanford University, Economics Department, December 1951.
―――, "Centralization and Decentralization in Economic Organization." *Econometrica* 27, 3 (1959): 399–430.
Maslow, A. *Motivation and Personality*. New York: Harper and Row, 1954.
Massam, B. *Location and Space in Social Administration*. New York: John Wiley, 1975.
Massie, J. L. "Management Theory." In *Handbook of Organizations*, edited by J. G. March. Chicago: Rand McNally, 1965.
McFarland, A. S. "Power, Critical Decisions and Leadership: An Analysis of Empirical Pluralist Theory." Ph.D. Thesis, University of California at Berkeley, 1966.
McGuire, C. B., and Radner, R., eds. *Decision and Organization*. New York: American Elsevier Co., 1972.
McKay, R. V. "Commuting Patterns of Inner-City Residents." *Monthly Labor Review* (1973), Reprint 2926. Washington, D.C.: U.S. Department of Labor, Bureau of Labor Statistics, pp. 43–48.
Mears, P. "Structuring Communication in a Working Group." *Journal of Communication* 24 (1971): 1.
Merriam, C. E. *Political Power: Its Composition and Incidence*. New York: McGraw-Hill, 1934.
Mesarovic, M. D., and Macko, D. "Foundations for a Scientific Theory of Hierarchical Systems." In *Hierarchical Structures*, edited by L. L. Whyte; A. G. Wilson; and D. Wilson. New York: American Elsevier Publishing Co., 1969.
Middleton, J., and Tait, D., eds. *Tribes Without Rules*. London: Routledge and Kegan Paul, 1958.
Miller, G. A.; Galanter, E.; and Pribram, K. *Plans and the Structure of Behavior*. New York: Holt, Rinehart and Winston, 1960.

Miller, G. K., and Chomsky, N. "Finitary Models of Language Users." In *Handbook of Mathematical Psychology*, vol. 2, edited by R. D. Luce. New York: John Wiley, 1963, pp. 419–491.
Miller, J. G. "The Nature of Living Systems." *Behavioral Science* 16 (1971): 277–301.
Mills, R. *The CML Tutorial: A Teaching Model for the Organizational Modelling Language*. New Haven: Report, Yale University School of Organization and Management, January 1975.
Morgenthau, H. J. *Politics Among Nations*, 5th ed. New York: Alfred A. Knopf, 1973.
Morrill, R. L., and Earickson, R. "Locational Efficiency of Chicago Hospitals: An Experimental Model." *Health Services Research* 4 (1969): 131.
———, and Rees, P. "Influence of the Physician on Patient to Hospital Distance." Working Paper I. 16. Chicago: Chicago Regional Hospital, 1968.
Morris, W. T. *Decentralization in Management Systems*. Columbus: Ohio State University, 1968.
Morse, P. *Queues, Inventories and Maintenance*. New York: John Wiley, 1958.
Moses, L. N. "A General Equilibrium Model of Production, Interregional Trade and Location of Industry." *Review of Economics and Statistics* 42 (1960): 373–397.
———. "Spatial Economics: General Equilibrium Approach." In *International Encyclopedia of the Social Sciences*, edited by D. L. Sills. vol. 15, New York: Macmillan, 1968, pp. 95–107.
Mulder, M. *Group Structure, Motivation and Group Performance*. The Hague: Mouton, 1963.
Mumford, L. *The Myth of the Machine*. New York: Harcourt Brace, 1967, p. 192.
Murphy, J. "School Planning by the People." *Education Digest* 37 (1972): 14–17.
Myrdal, G. *Rich Lands and Poor*. New York: Harper, 1957.
———. *Challenge of World Poverty*. New York: Pantheon, 1970.
Negandhi, A. R., and Riemann, B. C. "A Contingency Theory of Organization Re-Examined in the Context of a Developing Country." *Academy of Management Journal* 15 (1972): 2.
———. "Task Environment, Decentralization and Organizational Effectiveness." *Human Relations* 26 (1973): 203–214.
New York Times, September 16, 1976, p. 52.
Nordlinger, E. A. *Decentralizing the City: A Study of Boston's Little City Halls*. Cambridge, Mass.: M.I.T. Press, 1972.
Nystuen, J. D. "Identification of Some Fundamental Spatial Concepts." *Papers of the Michigan Academy of Science, Arts and Letters*, 1963, pp. 373–384; also in *Spatial Analysis*, edited by B. Berry and A. Pred. Englewood Cliffs, N.J.: Prentice-Hall, 1968. (LC)
Olson, M. L., Jr. *Logic of Collective Action: Public Goods and The Theory of Groups*. Cambridge, Mass.: Harvard University Press, 1971.
O'Neill, G. K. "The Colonization of Space." *Physics Today* 27 (September 1974): 32–40.
———. "The High Frontier." *The CoEvolution Quarterly* 3 (Fall 1975): 4–29.

Ostrom, V. "Can Federalism Make a Difference." *Publius* 3 (1973): 197–234.
Packer, A. H. "Applying Cost-Effectiveness Concepts to the Community Health System." *Operations Research* 16 (March/April 1968): 227–253.
Panico, J. A. *Queueing Theory.* Englewood Cliffs, N.J.: Prentice-Hall, 1969.
Parkinson, C. N. *Parkinson's Law.* New York: Houghton-Mifflin, 1957.
Penchansky, R., and Axelson, E. "Old Values, New Federalism, and Program Evaluation." *Medical Care* 12, no. 11 (1974): 893.
Pennings, J. "Measures of Organizational Structure." *American Journal of Sociology* 79 (1973): 636–704.
Penty, A. J. *Old Worlds for New: A Study of the Post-Industrial State.* London: G. Allen and Unwin, 1917.
———. *Post-Industrialism.* London: G. Allen and Unwin, 1922.
Perrow, C. "Is Business Really Changing." *Organizational Dynamics* (Summer 1970): 31–44.
———. *Complex Organizations: A Critical Essay.* Glenview, Ill.: Scott, Foresman, 1972.
Peter, L. J., and Hull, R. *The Peter Principle.* New York: Morrow, 1969.
Pfiffner, J. M., and Sherwood, F. P. *Administrative Organization.* Englewood Cliffs, N.J.: Prentice-Hall, 1970.
Piaget, J. *Genetic Epistemology.* New York: Columbia University Press, 1970.
Platt, J. "Social Traps." *American Psychologist* 28 (1973): 641–651.
———. "Mechanisms of Social Transformation." In *Annual Report of the Mental Health Research Institute.* Ann Arbor: University of Michigan, 1977.
Polanyi, M. "Life's Irreducible Structure." *Science* 160 (June 21, 1968): 1308–1312.
Porter, L. W., and Lawler, E. E. III. "The Effects of 'Tall' versus 'Flat' Organizational Structures on Managerial Satisfaction." *Personnel Psychology* 17 (1964): 135–148.
Press, C. "The City Within a Great City: A Decentralist Approach to Centralization." *Centennial Review* 7 (1963): 113–130.
Presthus, R. *Men at the Top: A Study in Community Power.* New York: Oxford University Press, 1964.
Price, C. R. "Conferencing via Computer: Cost Effective Communication for the Era of Forced Choice." In *The Delphi Method: Techniques and Applications,* edited by A. A. Linstone and M. Turoff. Reading, Mass.: Addison-Wesley, 1975.
Price, D. de Solla. "Networks of Scientific Papers." *Science* 149 (July 30, 1965): 510–515; reprinted in *The Growth of Knowledge,* edited by M. Kochen. New York: Wiley, 1967, pp. 145–155.
Price, J. L. *Handbook of Organizational Measurement.* Lexington, Mass.: D. C. Heath, 1972.
Pugh, D. S., et. al. "Dimensions of Organization Structure." *Administrative Science Quarterly* 13 (1968): 65–105.
Radner, R. "Team Decision Problems." *Annals of Mathematical Statistics* 33 (1962): 857.
Rapoport, A. *Fights, Games and Debates.* Ann Arbor: University of Michigan Press, 1960, pp. 166–170.

---, and Chammah, A. M. *Prisoner's Dilemma: A Study of Conflict and Cooperation.* Ann Arbor: University of Michigan Press, 1965, pp. 9–30.

Redlich, F. C., and Freedman, D. X. *Theory and Practice of Psychiatry.* New York: Basic Books, 1966.

Reimann, B. C. "On the Dimensions of Bureaucratic Structure: An Empirical Reappraisal." *Administrative Science Quarterly* 18 (1973): 462–476.

Revelle, C. S., and Swain, R. W. "Central Facilities Location." *Geographical Analysis* 2 (1970): 30–42. (LT)

Richards, P. G. *Delegation in Local Government: Country to District Councils.* London: G. Allen and Unwin, 1956.

Riker, W. *Theory of Political Coalitions.* New Haven: Yale University Press, 1962.

---. *Federalism, Origin, Operation, Significance.* Boston: Little, Brown, 1964.

Roberts, K. H. "Looking at An Elephant—Evaluation of Cross Cultural Research Related to Organizations." *Psychological Bulletin* 74 (1970): 327.

Robinson, E. A. *Economic Consequences of the Sizes of Nations.* New York: St. Martin's Press, 1960.

Rook, A. *Transfer Pricing: A Measure of Management Performance in Multidivisional Companies.* London: British Institute of Management, 1971.

Röpke, W. *A Humane Economy.* Chicago: Henry Regnery, 1960.

Roszak, T. *The Making of a Counterculture.* Garden City, N.Y.: Anchor Books, 1969.

Rubenstein, A. H. "Organizational Factors Affecting Research and Development Decision-Making in Large Decentralized Companies." *Management Science* 10 (1964): 618–633.

---, and Haberstroh, C. T., eds. *Some Theories of Organization.* Homewood, Ill.: Richard D. Irwin, 1966.

Ruefli, T. W. "A Generalized Goal Decomposition Model." *Management Science* 17 (1971): 505–517.

Russett, B. M., et al. *World Handbook of Political and Social Indicators.* New Haven: Yale University Press, 1964, pp. 160–161.

Sade, R. M. "Medical Care as a Right: A Refutation." *New England Journal of Medicine* 285 (1971): 1288–1292.

Sahlins, M. "The Segmentary Lineage: An Organization of Predatory Expansion." *American Anthropologist* 63 (April 1961): 322–345.

Samuel, Y., and Mannheim, B. F. "A Multidimensional Approach Toward a Typology of Bureaucracy." *Administrative Science Quarterly* 15 (1970): 216.

Samuelson, P. A. *Foundations of Economic Analysis.* New York: Atheneum, 1970, pp. 15–19, 39–43. (Originally published by Harvard University Press, 1947.)

---. "Maximum Principles in Analytical Economics." *Science* 173 (September 10, 1971): 991–997.

Santone, L., and Berlin, G. "Location of Fire Stations." In *Systems Analysis for Social Problems.* Washington, D.C.: Washington Operations Research Council, 1970, pp. 81–91. (LT)

Sauer, C. H. *Characterization and Simulation of Generalized Queuing Net-*

works. Report RC 6057. Yorktown Heights, N.Y.: IBM Research Center, 1976.

Savas, E. S. "Simulation and Cost-Effectiveness Analysis of New York's Emergency Ambulance Service." *Management Science* 15 (1969): 608–627.

Schelling, T. C. *Micromotives and Macrobehavior*. New York: W. W. Norton, 1978.

Schkolnick, M. *A Clustering Algorithm for Hierarchical Structures*, Report RJ 1806. Yorktown Heights, N.Y.: IBM Research Center, July 16, 1976.

Schleh, E. C. "The Essence of Decentralization." *Advanced Management* 24 (1959): 8–10.

Schmandt, H. J. "Municipal Decentralization: An Overview." *Public Administration Review* 32 (1972): 571–588.

Schumacher, E. F. *Small Is Beautiful: Economics As If People Mattered*. New York: Harper and Row, 1973.

Schutz, W. C. *Interpersonal Underworld*. (Original title: *FIRO: A Three-Dimensional Theory of Interpersonal Behavior*.) Palo Alto: Science and Behavior Books, 1967.

Seiler, J. A. *Systems Analysis in Organizational Behavior*. Homewood, Ill.: Irwin and Dorsey, 1967.

Selznick, P. *Leadership in Administration: A Sociological Interpretation*. New York: Harper and Row, 1957.

———. "Foundations of the Theory of Organizations." In *Complex Organizations*, edited by A. Etzioni. New York: Holt, Rinehart and Winston, 1964.

Service, E. R. *Profiles in Ethnology*. New York: Harper and Row, 1958.

———. *Primitive Social Organization*. New York: Random House, 1962.

Shannon, C. E., and Weaver, W. *The Mathematical Theory of Communication*. Champaign/Urbana: University of Illinois Press, 1949.

Shannon, G.; Bashshur, R. L.; and Metzner, C. A. "The Concept of Distance as a Factor in Accessibility and Utilization of Health Care." *Medical Care Review* 26 (1969): 143–161. (LC)

Shapley, D. "Computers in Medicine: Hospitals Cope with Costs, Quality Review." *Science* 187, 4178 (February 28, 1975): 730.

Shapley, L. S., and Shubik, M. "A Method for Evaluating the Distribution of Power in a Committee System." *American Political Science Review* 48 (1954): 787–792.

Shubik, M. "Games, Decisions, and Industrial Organization." *Management Science* 7 (1960): 4.

———, and Thompson, G. L. "Games of Economic Survival." *Naval Research Logistics Quarterly* 6 (1959): 111–123.

Sidel, V. W. "The Barefoot Doctors of the People's Republic of China." *The New England Journal of Medicine* 286 (1972): 1292–1300.

Simon, H. A. "Comments on the Simulation of Human Thinking." In *Management and the Computer of the Future*, edited by M. Greenberger. New York: MIT Press and Wiley, 1962, pp. 95–114.

———. "The Architecture of Complexity." *Proceedings of the American Philosophical Society* 106, no. 6 (1962): 467–482.

———. *The Sciences of the Artificial*. Cambridge, Mass.: M.I.T. Press, 1969, pp. 99–107.

——— . *The Shape of Automation for Men and Management.* New York: Harper and Row, 1975.
———; Guetzkow, H.; Kosmetsky, G.; and Tyndall, G. *Centralization vs. Decentralization in Organizing the Controller's Department.* New York: Controllership Foundation, 1954.
———; Smithburg, D. W.; and Thompson, V. A. *Public Administration.* New York: Alfred A. Knopf, 1950.
Skinner, B. F. *Beyond Freedom and Dignity.* New York: Alfred A. Knopf, 1971.
Skolka, J. V. "Long-Term Effects of Unbalanced Productivity Growth: On the Way to a Self-Service Society." ASPELT European Meeting, Geneva, December 15–20, 1974.
Smith, G. A. *Managing Geographically Decentralized Companies.* Cambridge, Mass.: Riverside Press, 1958.
Smith, J. M. "The Theory of Games and the Evolution of Animal Conflict." *Journal of Theoretical Biology* 47 (1974): 209–221.
Smithies, A. "Boundaries of the Production Function and Utility Function." In *Explorations in Economics.* New York: McGraw-Hill, 1936.
——— . *PPBS, Suboptimization and Decentralization.* Rand Report, RM-6178-TR. Santa Monica: Rand Corporation, April 1970.
Sommer, R. "Small Group Ecology." *Psychological Bulletin* 67, 2 (1967): 145–152.
Sparck-Jones, K. and Bates, R. G. *Report on a Design Study for the 'Ideal' Information Retrieval Test Collection.* BLR & D Report No. 5428. Cambridge: Cambridge University, October 1977.
Starbuck, W. H. "Organizational Growth and Development." In *Handbook of Organizations,* edited by J. C. March. Chicago: Rand McNally, 1965.
——— . "Mathematics and Organization Theory." In *Handbook of Organizations,* edited by J. C. March. Chicago: Rand McNally, 1965, pp. 335–386.
Statistical Abstract of the United States. Washington, D.C.: U.S. Government Printing Office, 1967, pp. 58, 86, 505, 508–509, 561, 587.
Statistical Abstract of the United States. Washington, D.C.: U.S. Government Printing Office, 1968, pp. 6, 550, 573.
Stevens, S. S. "Mathematics, Measurement and Psychophysics." In *Handbook of Experimental Psychology,* edited by S. S. Stevens. New York: John Wiley, 1951, pp. 23–30.
Steward, J. *The Economic and Social Basis of Primitive Bands.* Berkeley: University of California Press, 1936.
Stidham, S. *Statistical Models for Queueing Systems with Non-Linear Waiting Costs,* Technical Report No. 1. Palo Alto: Stanford University, December 2, 1968.
Strauss, A. "Medical Ghettos." *Trans-Action* 62 (May 1967): 7–15. (LC)
Suojanen, W. W. "Substantive Decentralization in the Large Corporation." *Advanced Management* 21 (1956): 16–22.
Syski, R. *Introduction to Congestion Theory in Telephone Systems.* Edinburgh: Oliver and Boyd, 1960.
Tannenbaum, A. S. "Control in Organizations." *Administrative Science Quarterly* 7 (1962): 236–257.
——— et al. *Hierarchy in Organizations.* San Francisco: Jossey-Bass, 1974.

Tauber, M. M. "Centralization and Decentralization in Academic Libraries: A Symposium." *College and Research Libraries* 22 (1961): 334–338.
Teitz, M. B. "Locational Strategies for Competitive Systems." *Journal of Regional Science* 8 (1968): 135–148.
Trinkl, F. H. "Hierarchical Resource Allocation Decisions." *Policy Studies* 4 (1973): 211–221.
Truman, D. B. *Administrative Decentralization.* Chicago: University of Chicago Press, 1940.
Tullock, G. *The Politics of Bureaucracy.* Washington, D.C.: Public Affairs Press, 1965.
Udy, S. *The Organization of Work.* New Haven: Human Relations Area Files Press, 1959.
Uniform Crime Reports for the United States. Washington, D.C.: Federal Bureau of Investigation, 1960, p. 2.
Uniform Crime Reports for the United States. Washington, D.C.: Federal Bureau of Investigation, 1965, p. 3.
United Nations Demographic Yearbook 1966. New York: United Nations, 1967.
Urwick, L. F. "The Manager's Span of Control." *Harvard Business Review* 34 (1956): 41.
Von Neumann, J., and Morgenstern, O. *Theory of Games and Economic Behavior.* Princeton: Princeton University Press, 1947.
Vosburgh, W. W., and Hyman, D. "Advocacy and Bureaucracy, The Life and Times of a Decentralized Citizen's Advocacy Program." *Administrative Science Quarterly* 18 (1973): 433–448.
Wager, L. W. "Organizational 'Linking Pins': Hierarchical Status and Communicative Roles in Interlevel Conferences." *Human Relations* 25 (1972): 307–326.
Webber, M. M., and Webber, C. C. "Culture Territoriality, and the Elastic Mile." In *Taming Megalopolis,* edited by H. W. Eldredge. Garden City, N.Y.: Anchor, 1967, pp. 35–53.
Weber, M. *A Theory of Social and Economic Organizations.* Glencoe, Ill.: Free Press, 1946.
Weizenbaum, J. *Computer Power and Human Reason.* San Francisco: W. H. Freeman, 1976.
Wheeler, H. *Dissaggregation vs. Decentralization.* Santa Barbara: Center for the Study of Democratic Institutions, June 1974, pp. 14–16.
Whisler, T. L. "Measuring Centralization of Control in Business Organizations." In *New Perspectives in Organization Research,* edited by W. W. Cooper et al. New York: John Wiley, 1964.
White, O. F., Jr. "Organization and Administration for New Technological and Social Imperatives." In *Public Administration in a Time of Turbulence,* edited by D. Waldo. Scranton, Penn.: Chandler, 1971, pp. 151–168.
Whitin, T. M. *The Theory of Inventory Management,* 2nd ed. Princeton: Princeton University Press, 1957.
Whyte, L. L.; Wilson, A. G.; and Wilson, D., eds. *Hierarchical Structures.* New York: American Elsevier Publishing Co., 1969.

Wildavsky, A. Working paper 53, University of California at Berkeley. Paper presented at the Annual Meeting of the Society for Information Science, San Francisco, October 1976.
Wilensky, H. L. *Organizational Intelligence*. New York: Basic Books, 1967, pp. 58–62.
Wilson, W. *Congressional Government*. New York: Meridian Books, 1956.
Winthrop, H. *Ventures in Social Interpretation*. New York: Appleton-Century-Crofts, 1968.
Wohlstetter, A. "Illusions of Distance." *Foreign Affairs* 46 (1968): 242–255.
Wolin, S. S. *Politics and Vision*. Boston: Little, Brown, 1960.
Yates, D. T., Jr. *Decentralization: An Analytical Framework*. Report WC2-10. New Haven: Yale University Institute for Social and Policy Studies, May 1972.

――――. *Decentralization in Cities*. Report W2-11. New Haven: Yale University Institute for Social and Policy Studies, May 1972.

――――. "Making Decentralization Work: The View from City Hall." Working paper of the Center for the Study of the City and its Environment. New Haven: Yale University Institute for Social and Policy Studies, April 1973.

――――. *Political Innovation and Institution Building: The Experience of Decentralization Experiments*. Report WC3-41. New Haven: Yale University Institute for Social and Policy Studies, 1973.

Yin, R. K. "Some Remarks on Evaluating Administrative Decentralization." RAND paper P-4844. New York: RAND Institute, June 1972.

――――; Hearn, R. W.; and Meinetz, P. "Administrative Decentralization of Municipal Services: Assessing the New York City Experience." *Policy Sciences* 5 (1974): 57–70.

Zadeh, L. A. "Fuzzy Sets." *Information and Control* 8 (1965): 338–353.
Zand, D. E. "Collateral Organization: A New Change Strategy." *Journal of Applied Behavioral Science* 10 (1974): 63–89.
Zeleny, M. "Toward Self-Service Society." *Proceedings National Conference on the Service Sector of the Economy*, forthcoming.

Index of Mathematical Symbols

a	Average rate of arrival of requests, req./mo., 50	$c(l)$	Cost of a service at level l, 260
a	Probability a random request is met by one chunk of memory, 30, 285	$c_{l,s}$	Cost of an agent at level l and stage s, 267
		$c(o)$	Opportunity cost of client's time, 141
A	Parameter relating T^{ud}, T^{sfl}, 141–155, 278	c_{op}	Operating cost, \$/req., 38
		c'_{op}	Cost of a server, \$/hr., 30
$A_{l,s}$	Agent or server at level l, stage s, 140, 267	c_{sf}	Cost of suffering due to unmet request, \$/req., 38
α	Horizontal communication time multiplier, 269–271	c'_{wa}	Cost of client's time, \$/hr., 30, 260
		C	Fixed cost/station, \$/mo., 31, 44, 249
b	Amount of memory, chunks, 30, 285	C	Parameter relating T^{ud} to T^{sfl}, 141–155, 278
b	Maximum adjustment range of server, 73, 253	C_n	Fixed cost per server if n are ordered, 39
B	Memory needed by N persons, 105	$C(\lambda)$	Cost of λ-level organization, 260
B	Parameter relating T^{ud} to T^{sfl}, 141–155, 278	CE	Cost of poorly treated case, 141–155, 278
B'	Memory of common data base, 105	χ	Span of control, 274
β	Worktime multiplier, 269–271		
		D	Distance of service region, 30, 44, 45
c_d	Cost of forwarding, \$/hr., 76		
c_f	Cost of adjustment step, \$/hr., 73, 76, 253	δ	Probability of erroneous appeal, 141–155; defined, 277, 278

δ'	Probability of correct appeal, 141–155; defined, 277, 278	n_p	Number of servers at peak load, 65
δ	Used interchangeably with ∂, 260, as partial deriv. operator, 314	N	Number of individuals in service organization, 103
∂	Partial differentiation, 287, 314	$N_{l,s}$	Number of servers at level l, stage s, 267
δ	Wage multiplier, 270–271	N_0	Number of clients in a region, 30
		ν	Number of request classes, 92
E	Environment, 170		
E	Expectation operator, 50	p_h	1/half-life of horizontal communication, 139, 141–155, 275
$E_{l,s}$	Error rate by agent at level l and stage s, 140	p_v	1/half-life of vertical communication, 139, 141–155, 275
E_1	Error rate at level 1, 141–155, 277		
E_2	Error rate at level 2, 141–155, 277	ψ	Ratio of shorter to longer side in a rectangular region, 49, 50
E_3	Error rate at levels 3 or above, 141–155		
ϵ	Error rate at level 1, 141–155	q	Quality of service, 107
ϵ	Multiplier by which vertical communication time increases with lateral communications, 269–271	r	Service as a response, 170
		R	Value of client's time, \$/hr., 30, 109
f	Load factor, 57	ρ	Number of specialties, 73, 253
f	Rate at which memory load changes, 182	s	Average service rate, req./server/mo., 50
$f(x)$	Demand density, 59		
F	Number of feedback cycles, 74	s	Stage of service processing, 140, 267
g	Vertical communication, time in a two-level organization, 269	s	State or condition of world, 170
		S	Service (rate) time, 11, 37
g'	Derivative, $dg/d\lambda$, 261		
$g(\lambda)$	Cost, 260	T	Response time, 11
γ	Vertical communication time multiplier, 269–271	T^d	Time in downward communication, hrs./req., 30
		T^l	Time on lateral communication, hrs./req., 30
h	Height of spikes, 66		
		$T(l,\lambda)$	Time to service q request at level l in a λ-level organization, 259
λ	Number of levels in hierarchy, 31, 141–155, 259, 267	T^s	Time on thinking communication, hrs./req., 30
λ^*	Optimum number of levels, 260, 267		
		T^{sfl}	Time for lateral communication or thinking, 138, 267
m	Number of types of servers, 92		
m_d	Dimensionality of geographic space, 256	T^u	Time in upward communication, hrs./req., 30
m_f	Dimensionality of functional space, 256	T^{ud}	Time for up and down or vertical communication, 138, 141–155, 267
M	Amount of memory transferred, 182, 285		
		θ	Probability that an incompetent server is replaced, 277, 278
M	"If-then" machine, 170		
M_i	Memory at level i, 182		
		u	Average utility, \$/req., 30
n	Number of servers, 37, 44	u	Fraction of a region that is populated, 60
n_i	Number of servers in dimension i, 49	U	Net utility, 109, 286

v	Average speed to forward request, mph, 31, 44, 249	V	Nonhomogeneity measure, 62
v	Time spent in vertical communication, 278	w	Average time by server in work, hrs./req., 30
v_d	Forwarding speed, mph, 76	$w(n)$	Waiting time for n servers, 311
v_f	Adjustment speed, steps/hr., 4, 76, 253	w_0	Minimum work time/request, 269
		W	Wage class, 250–251

Author Index

A

Abler, R., 310
Aborn, M., xxi
Achison, D., 313
Ackerman, R. W., 177
Adams, T. S., 30
Aiken, M., 86, 139, 177, 313
Ardell, D. B., 184, 215
Argyris, C., 247
Arrow, K. J., 27, 174, 175, 192
Ashby, W. R., 97, 106, 170
Auerbach, F., 312

B

Bales, R. F., 96
Banfield, E. C., 177
Banks, A. S., 303
Barnard, C., 213
Barrett, D., 304
Barsodi, R., 243
Bashshur, R. L., 304
Bauer, R. A., 220
Bavelas, A., 21, 88, 304, 311

Beauchamp, M. A., 311
Bell, D., xviii, 4, 5, 224
Belloc, H., 4
Bennis, W., 304
Berlinski, D., 120
Berry, B. L., 123
Blau, P. M., 25, 314
Boseman, F. G., 176
Boulding, K. E., 8
Brecht, B., 26
Bremer, S., 243
Bresnick, D., 167
Brown, L. D., 247
Brownell, S. M., 124
Brzezinski, Z., 201
Buber, M., 88
Bucci, G., 235
Burchinal, L., 306
Burrell, S. A., 121

C

Cairncross, A. K., 29, 31
Carzo, R., 127

Chaiken, J., 302
Chammah, A. M., 189
Chandler, A. D., 119, 122
Child, J., 314
Chomsky, N., 186
Cellia, F., 91
Clark, T. N., 177, 313
Clear, D. K., 214
Cohen, A. M., 304
Colby, K., 94
Cooper, L., 82
Corey, K. E., 42
Crickman, R., xxi, 308
Cyert, R. M., 164

D

Dahl, R. A., 187, 308, 309
Davis, H., 80, 82
Dean, A. L., 19, 134
Dearden, J., 235
DeBakey, M., 95
Dennis, J. B., 235
Deutsch, K. W., 42, 62, 72, 98, 101, 119, 120, 121, 122, 166, 187, 192, 196, 208, 237, 309, 312, 313, 314
Downs, A., 97, 124, 212
Drosness, D. L., 309

E

Earickson, R., 91
Easton, D., 192
Egerman, K., 304
Ehrle, R. A., 134, 139
Eitner, P., xxi
Ellul, J., 208
Etzioni, A., 96, 168, 304

F

Feingold, E., 219
Feller, W., 56
Ferkiss, V. C., 220
Fermat, P., 41
Fesler, J. W., 9, 20, 205, 307
Festinger, L., 304
Fetter, R. B., 304
Fiske, P. H., 119

Flament, C., 311
Foa, U. G., 196
Foley, W. J., 309
Fredrick, H., xxi, 252
Freedman, D. X., 312
Fried, L., 40, 234
Friedlander, F., 247
Friedrich, C. J., 187, 205
Fryback, D., 304
Furniss, N., 20, 107, 165, 175

G

Galanter, E., 97, 186
Galbraith, K., 216
deGaulle, C., 313
Gerlach, L. P., 120, 274
Ghiselli, E. E., 127
Gogal, N., 11
Goldsmith, E. A., 243
Goodman, P., 243
Gottschalk, C., 306
Gould, P. R., 310
Greenberger, M., 175, 235
Grobstein, C., 308
Grodzins, M., 303
Guetzkow, H., 304
Gurr, T. R., 196
Gustafson, D. H., 304
Guthrie, J. W., 199, 220

H

Hage, J., 86, 91, 93, 139, 162, 303, 313
Haider, D., 41, 201, 307, 308
Hallock, Cecilia, xix
Hannon, J., 40, 234
Harris, C., 25
Harshbarger, D., 88, 93, 303
Hart, D. K., 208, 240
Hauriou, M., 25
Havighurst, R. J., 170
Hearn, D. W., 183
Heierli, U., 80
Henderson, H., 243
Hendricks, D., 300, 315
Herbert, A. W., 221
Hessacker, F. L., 98
Hirschman, A. O., 13, 86, 308,
Hitler, A., 189

Hollingshead, A. B., 90, 101, 150
Horvath, W. J., 304
Howard, L. C., 219
Hsu, S. T., 41
Hull, A., 135
Hummon, N. P., 127
Hurwicz, L., 27
Hyman, D., 220

I

Ink, D., 19, 134
Innis, H. A., 311
Isard, W., 72, 309, 312

J

Janowitz, M., 315
Jones, R. E., 176

K

Kahn, R. L., 96, 304
Kalba, K., 312
Kaplan, A., 196, 201, 208, 308
Kaplan, S. A., 88
Kasarda, J. D., 315
Katz, D., 96, 304
Katzenstein, P., 122
Kaufman, H., 28, 29, 202, 221, 245, 303, 308
Kennedy, J. F., 313
Kerr, C., 200
Klein, S., 235
Knorr, K., 195
Knuth, D., 56
Kochen, M., 42, 62, 65, 120, 187, 237, 309, 313, 314
Komorita, S. S., 89
Krouse, C. G., 311
Kuttner, B., xxi

L

Lammers, C. J., 200
Lasswell, H., 196, 201, 208, 308
Lawler, E. E., 127
Lawrence, P. R., 176, 307
Leavitt, H. J., 304

Levinthal, E. C., 231
Levy, F., 24, 308
Likert, R., 96, 200
Lincoln, A., 217
Lorsch, J. W., 176, 307
Lotka, A. J., 312
Lowrie, S. G., 25
Lubin, J. W., 309
Lundquist, L., 192

M

Machiavelli, N., 185, 243
Machlup, F., xviii
Macko, D., 119
Macy, J. W., 184
Mandelbrot, B., 313
Mannheim, B. F., 26
Mansfield, R., 314
Mao Tse-tung, 206
March, J. G., 164, 168
Marien, M., 4, 5
Marrett, C. B., 86, 139, 313
Marron, H., 306
Marschak, J., 27
Marschak, T., 42
Maslow, A., 196
Mason, G., 56
Massam, B., 310
Meadow, W., 166, 321
Mears, P., 304
Meinetz, P., 183
Merriam, C. E., 25
Mesarovic, M. D., 119
Middleton, J., 303
Miller, G. A., 97, 186
Miller, J. G., 119, 120
Mills, T. M., 304
Morgenstern, O., 198
Morgenthau, H. J., 187, 195
Morrill, R. L., 71, 72
Morris, W. T., 27, 307, 308
Mulder, M., 304
Mumford, L., 311
Murphy, J., 219
Myrdal, G., 124

N

Neghandi, A. R., 27, 28, 176
Neumark, E., xxi

Nivola, P., xxi
Nordlinger, E. A., 25, 183, 187

O

Oettinger, A., xviii
Olson, M. L., 313
Orwell, G., 98
Ostrom, V., 201

P

Panico, J. A., 51
Parkinson, C. N., 8
Pennings, J., 303
Penty, A. J., 4
Perkel, B., xxi
Perrow, C., 79, 134
Peter, L. J., 135
Piaget, J., 119, 244
Plato, 206
Platt, J. R., 33, 98
Polanyi, M., 121
Porat, M. U., xviii
Porter, L. W., 127
Pribram, K., 97, 186
Price, D. deSolla, 244
Pugh, D. S., 314

R

Radner, R., 27
Raizman, C., xxi
Rapoport, A., 88, 189
Redlich, F. C., 90, 101, 250, 312
Rees, P., 72
Reimann, B. C., 27, 28, 176, 314
Resnikoff, H., 315
Richards, P. G., 215
Richmond, P., 315
Riker, W., 89, 201
Roberts, K. H., 203
Robinson, E. A., 243
Root, W. L., 119
Ropke, W. A., 243
Roszak, T., 220
Rubenstein, A. H., 19, 175
Ruefli, T. W., 177
Russett, B. M., 122, 312

S

Saarinen, K., 56
Sahlins, M., 303
Samuel, Y., 26
Samuelson, P. A., 18, 241, 259
Sauer, C. H., 302
Savas, E. S., 82
Schelling, T. C., 124
Schkolnick, M. A., 302
Schmandt, H. J., 307, 308
Schoenherr, R. A., 25, 314
Schumacher, E. F., 5, 41
Schutz, W. C., 86
Scott, R. W., 168
Seiler, J. A., 302
Selznick, P., 221
Senghaas, D., 98
Service, E. R., 303
Shapley, D., 190
Shubik, M., 190
Siegel, J. P., 127
Simon, H. A., 45, 95, 122, 168, 175, 307, 311
Singer, S. F., 309
Skinner, B. F., 6, 244, 313
Skolka, J. V., 9
Smith, A., 314
Smith, G. A., 181
Smith, J. M., 187
Smithburg, D. W., 45
Smithies, A., 283, 311
Sommer, R., 309
Sparck-Jones, K., 315
Spitzer, A., xxi
Stafford, H. A., 42
Starbuck, W. H., 321
Stevens, S. S., 72
Steward, J., 303
Streeter, D. N., 235
Suojanen, W. W., 19
Syski, R., 56, 58, 65

T

Tait, D., 303
Tannenbaum, A. S., 165, 200
Tauber, M. M., 82
Textor, R. B., 303
Thompson, J. D., 45, 304

Tobler, W., 310
Trinkl, F. H., 177
Truman, E. H., 24, 25, 308

U

Urwick, L. F., 168, 274

V

von Neumann, J., 198
Vosburgh, W. W., 220

W

Wager, L. W., 96, 125
Wallace, F., xxi
Washington, E., xxi
Weber, M., 314

Weizenbaum, J., 94
Wheeler, H., 5
White, J. D., 220
Whyte, L. L., 120
Wildavsky, A., 216, 247
Wohlstetter, A., 307
Wolin, S. S., 221

Y

Yanouzas, J. N., 127
Yates, D. T., 26, 140
Yin, R. K., 167, 183

Z

Zand, D. E., 125
Zeleny, M., xviii, 9
Zipf, G. K., 312

Subject Index

A

Absenteeism, 27, 177
Abuse of power, 26
Accessibility, 23, 180, 220, 234
Accountability, 215, 234, 242
Adaptiveness, 91, 116, 202, 216, 239
Adjustment space, 69, 253. *See also* Salesmanship
Adversary relations, 194, 195. *See also* Conflict
Advising, advisors, advisory committees, 173
Advocacy, 220
Affirmative action, 7
Affluence, 251. *See also* Poverty
Agents, agencies, 7, 35
Aggregation, 21, 121, 243. *See also* Clustering
Agreements, 194
Agrarianism, 4
Alabama, 220
Alarm: general, 130, 171; local, 130, 171, 313
Alaska, 220

Alienation, 17, 25, 165, 220, 244, 305
Allocation, 17
Amalgamation, 121
Amazon, 63
Ambiguity of laws, 236
Ambulances, xix, 24, 66, 231
Anticipated contingencies, 172
Anthropology, 303
Antiscientism, 6
Antitrust legislation, 240
Apathy, 222
Appeals, 140, 143, 277; probability, effect of, 158
Appellate courts, 236
Applications, 304
Architects, 219
Arrival rate, 51
Aspiration level, 241, 309
Asymmetry of power relation, 188
Australia, 63
Authority, 124, 134, 138, 165, 168, 190, 192, 202, 228, 235, 304, 308
Automation, 116, 216
Autonomy, 6, 7, 20, 168, 192, 199, 205, 208, 243, 303, 308, 314

348 / Index

B

Backlash, 245
Bandwidth, 96
Bargaining, 202
Barriers to decentralization, 214
Bell Telephone, 99, 235
Belongingness, 196
Beneficiaries, 14
Bonds, 121
Brain, 318; analog to, 224, 243, 306
Breakdown, 67, 116, 194
Bribery, 68
Budgeting, 26
Bureaucracy, 6, 8, 25, 26, 27
Business, small vs. big, 6
Business organization, 122, 242
Busing, 305
Byzantium, 16, 230

C

Capacity: distribution, 167; excess, 56, 234, 248; reserve, 64
Cascades, 22
Cases: clients as, 212; closed, 133; defined, 9, 10
Catalysis, of progress, 91
Caution, 130
Center, 41, 309
Center of gravity, 42
Centrality, index of, 311
Central place hierarchies, 123
Central processing units, 234
Channels, transport, 100
Chicago, 177
China, 206
Christ, 230
Chunks of memory, 181, 284, 292
Cities, medium sized, 124
Citizen participation, 184
Clients, xvii, 13, 95, 211
Clinics, 143, 231
Closeness, 309. *See also* Distance
Clustering, 120
Coalitions, 89, 190
Coding, 74
Cognitive dissonance, 313
Cohesiveness, 221
Colonies, colonialism, 143, 242
Command, 167

Commission error, 140
Commitment, 169, 192
Commonwealths, 242
Communications, 23, 85, 325; and control, xvii, 21, 171; at a distance, 94, 99; networks, 21, 303; volume, 139
Community, 4, 5, 239; school boards, 26; task forces, 26
Compassion, 130
Compatibility, 97
Compensation, 214
Competence, distribution of, 244
Competition, 27, 176, 216
Complaints, 26, 133, 140
Complementarity, of communications, 100
Complexity, 91, 93, 96, 222, 239, 304
Compromises, 209
Computer: centers, 230, 231; communication terminals, 231; conferencing, 99, 104, 235; distribution, 235; facilities, 82; networks, xix; simulation, 275
Computerization, 5
COMSAT, 107
Concentration, 3; of power, 198
Conflict: behavior, 26, 122; of interest, 217; prevailing in, 186; relative to power, 203; resolution, 124, 133
Conformity, 26, 221
Congestion, 22, 24, 64, 67, 121, 131
Conscience, 191
Conscious intentions, 97, 239
Consensus, 18, 21, 99, 192, 247
Consent, informed, 209
Conservatives, 199
Consonance, 8, 121
Consultation, 173
Consumerism, 219, 304
Contacts, 213
Contingency theory, 176
Contracts, 86
Control, 20, 28, 134, 138, 143, 175, 179, 223; controller, 186; corporate, 234; defined, 168; hierarchical, 314; as power, 241; self- vs. external, 86; social, 139; structural, 26; unobtrusive, 79; as a value, 214
Convergence, 90, 192
Conversational interaction, 85, 215
Coordination, 23, 67, 68, 124, 125, 139, 173, 238, 244, 301; negative, 127; positive, 125

Corporate decentralization, 20; of corporations, 242
Corruption, 26
Cost(s), 103, 142–155; of data processing, 318; vs. disutility and price, 32; fixed, 38, 44; operating, 38, 40, 44
Cost–benefit analysis, 2, 216, 223, 248
Courts, 229, 257
Creativity, 107
Crimes, 218; growth of, 116
Crisis management, 218
Cultural uniformity, 207
Customizing, 174, 234, 257

D

Data bases, 104, 234, 247
Data processing, 19, 229
Debates, 88, 215
Decentralist dogma, as secular religion, 4, 5, 20, 224, 244
Decentralization, 20; barriers to, 214. *See also specific types of decentralization*; Index of decentralization
Decision makers, 3, 4, 165, 208
Decision: points, 23; rules, 130
Decoding, 100
Decomposability, 95, 122
Defense, 155. *See also* Military
Deconcentration, 192
Deference, 196, 212
Definition, sharpness of, 300
Degradation, 219
Dehumanization, 96
Delay, 22, 24, 37, 67, 143, 217
Delegation, 22, 23, 28, 135
Delegational decentralization, 173, 178, 240, 244, 283, 301; as a mapping, 238
Delivery time, 43
Demand, 38, 163, 252
Democracy, participatory, 309
Democratization, 4, 208, 304
Dentistry, 202
Departmentalization, 169
Depreciation, 38, 64
Desires, 9
Devolution, 183
Diagnosis, 130
Diagnosticians, 12, 265
Dialog, 88, 89, 95
Diffusion of power, 198

Digital Equipment Corporation, 235
Dignity, 6
Directness, 21
Discounts, 40
Disillusionment, 194
Disparities, 221
Dispersion, 17, 22, 36, 63, 70, 80, 228, 236, 243, 257; functional, 314; as a mapping, 237
Disputes, 124
Dissemination of information, 305
Dissociation of information, 169
Dissonance: of bonds, 121; of services, 9
Distance: channel, 100; Euclidean; informational, 96, 100, 203, 309; intentional, 97; "Manhattan," 49; social, 203
Distributedness, 18, 234, 235
Distribution: binomial, 123; of capacities, 167; log-normal, 123; "multiuniform," 60, 62; Pareto, 123; uneven, 59, 314; uniform, 43, 253
District courts, 236
Disutility, vs. cost and price, 32
Divergence of interaction, 90. *See also* Convergence
Diversification, 28, 139, 177
Diversity, 242, 257
DNA, 121
Document retrieval, 305
Domination, dominance, 86, 195
Double bind, 193, 194
Downtime, 66
Downward communication, 268

E

Ecologism, 6, 211
Economic decentralization, 20
Economics of scale, 50, 75, 76, 226, 234, 256, 314
Education, 292, 305, 309. *See also* Schools
Effectiveness: behavioral vs. economic, 177; organizational, 27; of vertical communication, 161
Efficiency, 20, 240, 245
Egypt, 45
Electronic funds transfer, 240
Elitism, elites, 6, 139, 199
Emergent properties, 224
Emergency, 140
Employees, turnover of, 27, 177

England, 205. See also United Kingdom
Enlightenment, 196
Entropy. See Negentropy
Equalitarianism, Equality, 18, 207, 291
Education Resources Information Center (ERIC), 306
Erlang loss formula, 56
Error(s), 16, 24, 92, 116; control of, 66, 139; correction of, 139; detection of, 139; rates, 140, 142-155; transmission, 97, 101
Ethical considerations, 3
Ethnic uniformity, 207
Evaluation, 133, 165, 169
Exclusiveness, 179; of power, 198
Executives, 165
Expectations, 213, 221, 309
Expendability, 216
Experience, 138, 214, 240, 292
Expertise, 218
Explanation, to subordinates, 183
Export-import, 123
Externalities, 211, 311

F

Factor analysis, 314
Failures, mean time between, 67
Farmers, 313
Federalism, 7, 201
Feedback, 22, 28, 51, 86, 92, 95, 116, 228, 238, 243, 244; administrative, 325; negative, 90, 91, 168; positive, 90, 91
Files, 234
Finance, 29, 41
Firefighting, 153, 232
Firms, mergers of, 243
First-order effects, 14
Fixed-sum game, 201
Flatness, 23, 29, 127, 135, 228, 244, 259; as a mapping, 237
Flexibility, 247
Fluctuations, 37, 58, 114, 176
Football team, 231
Formalization, 97, 244, 314
Fragmentation, 17, 122, 169, 173
France, 230
Freedom, 5, 6
Free goods, law of, 212

Frustration, 220
Functional: mapping, 237; centralization, 70; decentralization, 20; request space, 73; service space, 73; specialization, 22, 23, 67, 139, 244. See also Administrative decentralization
Functionalization, 26
Futurism, 6

G

Game theory, 189
Garbage, 167, 243
Generalists, 74, 237
General Motors, 175
Geometry, Euclidean, 41
Germany, 189, 230
Global problems, 243
Goods, 196
Governments, xix, 21, 26, 246; municipal, 231; small vs. big, 6
Greece, ancient, 206
Greed, 195
Grievances, 26
Gross National Product, per capita, 79, 116
Groups, small, 93, 96
Growth, 115
Guidelines, 28
Guilt, 193

H

Harvard University, 83
Health service, xix, 89, 129, 171, 243, 304; arthritis clinic, 2, 56; local centers, 140
Hedonism, 6
Hemispherectomy, 243
Hierarchies, 17, 21, 22, 28, 68, 234; effect on cost of, 152, 157
Hiring/firing decisions, 217
History, 178
Horizontal communication, 86, 165, 244, 275
Hospitals, 72, 143, 232, 304
Households, 232

I

IBM, 18, 175
Ideology, 4, 223
Idleness, 56, 67, 131
IIASA, 243
Illegitimacy, 194
Illnesses: prevention of, 87; risk of, 87
Images, 134
Impersonality, 26
Incentives, 174
Income, per capita, 115; distribution, 220, 249
Independence, 7, 243; statistical, 50
Index: of decentralization, 28, 176, 225; of centrality, 311
India, 200
Individuality, 257
Industrial decentralization, 20, 213
Industrialization, 63
Inequalities, inequities, 218, 220
Influence, 25, 165, 194, 200, 210
Information: and referral, 238; dissociation of, 169; distance, 204; gathering of, 183; processing of, 27, 248; recombination of, 169; service industry, 235; systems, 216, 305; as a value, 196
Internally generated workload, 162
Innovativeness, 91, 97, 102, 163, 203, 206
Input loads, 155, 162. *See also* Request loads
Inspectors, inspection, 12, 133, 308
Intake channels, 163, 174
Integration, 121
Intelligence, 178, 305
Intentions, 95, 97, 186, 239
Interaction, divergence of, 90
Interagency communication, 183
Interests, 124, 240; centers of, 168; fragmentation of, 169
Internal decentralization, 20. *See also* Administrative decentralization
Interpersonal relations, 27
Interpretation, costs of, 103
Intervention, 247
Intimacy of scale, 41
Invariance, as indicator of power, 203
Invariants, 308
Invention, 163. *See also* Innovativeness
Inventories, 64
Investments, visible vs. invisible, 102

Invisible hand, 179
Israel, 27, 200

J

Japan, 45
Jefferson–Hamilton debates, 4
Job satisfaction, 165, 177
Jurisdiction, 122, 181, 183, 203
Justice, 218

K

Kindness, 130
Know-how, 176, 178
Knowledge: scientific, 218, 239, 244; synthesis of, 89

L

Labor, division of, 67, 96, 125
Languages, 103, 308
Lateral communication, 125, 267
Laws, ambiguity of, 236
Leaders, 208
Learning, 164, 204, 214, 247
Legislative decentralization, 20
Legislatures, legislation, 175, 190
Legal services, xix, 102
Legitimacy, 207
Levels, 267
Leveling, 18
Liberty, 208
Libraries, xix, 305; roving, 66, 82, 212
Life: quality of, 107; value of, 3, 153
Lifestyles, 87, 245
Line vs. staff, 134
Linguistic uniformity, 207
Linkages, 125, 238
Little, Arthur D., 305
Little city halls, 26
Load: effect on hierarchies, 159; factor, 56; schedules, 12, 68, 131; of work or requests, 9, 37, 259
Local government, 214; agencies, 242
Location: change, 42; theory, 41, 252, 310
Log-normal distribution, 123
Los Angeles, 177

M

Love, 196
Loyalty, 29, 168, 308
Luxuries, 257

Mail order houses, xix
Mail service, 103
Maintenance, 131
Maladaptiveness, 243
Management, managers, 131, 135, 224, 301; by objectives, 247; consulting firm, 231; information systems, 247
Man–machine interaction, 88
Manpower, 27
Marginal costs, 13
Markets, 124, 176, 186
Materialism, 196
Medical services, 219. *See also* Health; Physicians
Memory, 23, 103, 168, 173, 174, 178, 181, 284, 292
Mental health centers, 19
Mental Health Research Institute, xxi
Mergers, 28, 243
Meritocracy, 221
Military, 153, 205, 213, 315
Modes of organizational operation; authority/production, 125; knowledge/problem, 125
Mohammed, 230
Momentum, analog of, 102
Money, 196
Monitoring, 130, 171
Monte Carlo methods, 279
Moral considerations, 3, 6
Morale, employee, 27
Multidimensionality, 106
Municipal: government, 231; services, 25, 59, 82, 140, 175, 177
Mutual support groups, 18
Museums, 306
Mythologies, shared, 104

N

Nation-states, 242
National Science Foundation, xxi
Needs, 9

Negentropy, 225
Negotiations, 202
Neighborhood, 124; action, 140; clinics, 304; corporations, 26; decentralization of, 25; stores, 258
Network, 21, 120; friendship, 231; telephone, 104
New York City, 26, 140, 183
Nonhomogeneity, 62
Nonuniformity, 81
Normativity, 26, 223

O

Objective functions, 177, 283
Ombudsman, 140
Operations, 132
Operatives, 12
Opinion: giving, 125; leaders, 21; seeking, 125
Opportunity cost, 32, 95, 245; calculated, 150; of time, 116
Optimal unit cost vs. client: load, 160; redundancy, 22
Optimism, creative, 308
Order, 5, 225
Organizations: malaise in, 194; two-level, 156, 162
Originality, 107
Oscillation, 245
Overhead, 234
Overload, 16
Ownership, 179

P

Pakistan, 200
Palestinians, 200
Panic reaction, 172
Paradoxes, 7
Parallel, 22
Parasitic bonds, 195
Pareto's law, 123, 249
Parks, 183
Participants, xvii, 13, 25, 240
Participation: by teachers, 91; in decision making, 22, 23, 116, 170, 173, 228, 244, 308, 313; in redesign, 22, 28, 116, 210, 228

Participational decentralization, 174, 207–238
Patronage, 26
Peak: location, 63; periods, 63, 68
Performance, 248; evaluation of, 133
Personality, 86
Personnel allocations, 183
Perspective, broad, 138
Persuasion, 168, 194
PERT, 247
Pessimism, creative, 308
Physicians, relation to patients, 87, 212, 213, 231, 244, 245
Planning, planners, 132; comprehensive vs. specialized, 215; long-range, 28, 134, 162; physical, 26; urban/regional, 123
Pluralization, 17, 22, 35–68, 70, 204, 228, 249, 256; as a mapping, 237; informational, 105
Pocket calculators, 231
Poisson process, 55, 139
Police, xix, 66, 143, 153, 183, 212
Policymaking, 8, 124, 173; analysis of, 216, 247; output, 177
Political decentralization, 20, 167
Politics, 114, 221
Pollution, 243
Polycephalism, 120
Polymorphism, 121, 235
Pompousness, 194
Population growth, 116
Positive reinforcement, 215
Postindustrialism, 4
Poverty, 251, 314
Power, 3, 138, 139, 186–223, 228, 240, 243; concentration of, 198; domain of, 197, 204; exclusiveness, 198; gross vs. net, 189; as an invariant, 203; over nature, 189; range of, 197, 202; relative, 189; scope of, 197, 204; striving for, 217, 219; viability of, 198; weight of, 196, 202
Powerlessness, 165
Precision, 106
Predictability, 180
Preemption, 179
Prejudice, 244
Pressure, accommodation of, 202
Prestige, 196
Prevailing, in a conflict, 186
Prevention, 245

Price vs. cost and disutility, 32
Primacy, 123
Priorities, 68, 183
Prisoner's dilemma, 210
Privacy, 179
Privilege, 179
Problem(s): anticipated, 130; ill-structured, 125; solving, 224; unanticipated, 130
Procurement, 19
Product mix, 28
Production, 28; function of, 238
Productivity, 40, 243
Professionalism, 6, 180
Professional service review organizations (PSRO), 304
Programming, programs, 139, 186, 234, 252; budgeting, 247
Promotion possibilities, 165, 308
Protest, 26. *See also* Complaints
Psychic integrity, 194
Psychoanalysis, 250
Public: goods, 177, 313; pressure, 211; private, 24
Pyramid, 23

Q

Quality: control, 12; of life, dimensions, 196, 308; of service, 85, 106, 179, 180
Question-asking, 299
Queueing, 24, 51, 56, 68

R

Racism, 143
Rand Institute, 304
Rank-size distribution, 206. *See also* Pareto's law; Zipf
Rapport, 106
Recall, recombination of information, 169
Record keeping, 29
Recruitment, 308
Recruiting of executives, 165
Rectitude, 196
Reductionism, 6
Redundancy, 56, 248
Referral, 10, 133, 172
Reformers, 199

Region, 42
Regional planning decentralization, 20
Reinforcement: negative, 193; positive, 193
Reliability, 17, 66, 67, 106
Religion, priests, churches, 4, 5, 212
Replacement, 131
Reporting of relation, 210, 308
Representatives, 25
Requests, 9; unmet, 58; loads, 67, 75, 116, 239
Research and development, 19
Research Institute, 231
Resources, 122, 183; allocation, 177; as power, 195; recommitable, 248; tangible, 164; uncommitted, 164
Respondent, to controller, 186
Response: defined, 132; surface, 300; time, 24, 51
Responsibility, 124, 173, 193, 210–211, 228
Responsiveness, 10, 11, 23, 25, 73, 96, 169, 180, 202, 220, 246
Review, 308
Revolutions, 220
Reward, gross, 126
Rhodesia, 200
Rigidity, 247
Riots, 219
Risks, 64, 67, 138, 175
Robots, 94
Roles, 213
Romanticism, 6
Rome, 16
Routine sorting, 130
Roving ambulances, 3
Rulers, 208
Ruthlessness, 194

S

Salary, 292
Salesmanship, 130, 177; policies of, 28
Sanitation, 167, 183. *See also* Garbage
Satisficing, xviii
Scales, 72, 226
Scheduling, load, 131
School(s), 91, 169, 199, 211, 214, 220, 257; community boards, 140; districts, 124; planning, 219

Science, 5
Scope, 69, 72, 101, 202, 308; value, 196
Screening, 245
Second-order effects, 14
Secular religion, 4, 5
Security, 196, 234
Segmentation, 120
Self-: actualization, 196, 224; concepts, 214; confidence, 216; determination, 4; interest, 217; restructuring, 248; service, 9, 89, 215; sufficiency, 6
Selling, 130
Separable goods and services, 177
Servers, 211; single, 56
Services: as a value, 196; costs, 24; defined, 8; dissonance of, 9; organization, 7, 211; rate, 50; regions, 74, 75; society, 4, 5, 9, 224; stations, 42; systems, 12, 185, 223; time, 10, 11
Sharing, 98, 210
Shock treatments, 250
Sick care vs. health care, 219
Skew distributions, 10
Skill, 196, 216
Slack, organizational, 164
Small groups, 93, 96
Smoothing, 64, 67
Socialization, 139
Social: contacts, 213; traps, 33; uniformity, 207; welfare function, 31, 32, 241, 309
Sorters, 12, 92, 130, 171, 265
South Africa, 220
Sovereignty, 214
Span of control, 127, 162, 166, 167, 179, 274
Spatial decentralization, 20. *See also* Administrative decentralization
Specialists, 74
Specialization, 67, 228, 242, 244, 266, 301, 314
Speed, 245
Sponsors, 207, 210
Spontaneity, 106
Stability, 176
Stacks, 56
Staffing, 181, 211
Staff vs. line, 134, 234
Stages, 267
Standards, 216, 217, 234; professional, 133; relaxation of, 166; setting of, 28, 240

Star nets, 21
Status, 196; pyramid, 139
Steepness of hierarchy, 165
Stereotyping, 244
Storage and retrieval, 182, 292
Strategists, 12
Stratification, 91
Structural redesign, 24
Structure, structuralism, 199
Submission, submissiveness, 195
Suboptimization, 62, 81, 175, 283, 311
Subsidiarity principle, 183
Suburbanization, 63, 199, 312
Supervision, supervisors, 132, 162
Supreme Court, 236
Surgery, 171, 309
Survey Research, 303
Survival, 196
Switching points, 100
Switzerland, 45, 103, 231
Symbiotic bonds, 195
Synchronization, 127
Synthesis, of knowledge, 89
Systems capacity, 24
Systems theory, xviii

T

Tactical supervisors, 12
Talent, 292
Tallness, 127, 242
Task specification, 308
Tastes, 240
Taxation, 199, 232
Taxis, 231
Technology, 98, 217, 239
Telecommunication, 309
Telemedicine, 304
Telephone congestion theory, 56
Tensions, 217; dynamic, 204
Termination, 133
Third World, 324
Thucydides, 206
Time: consuming vs. saving, 215; horizon, 4; sharing, 231; turnaround, 11, 92, 108; value of, 309
Top management, 308
Training of executives, 165, 241
Transaction Network Service, 240

Transfer: of memory, 182; of staff, 181; prices, 176
Transportation, 93, 99, 243, 257, 312; speed, 116
Treasury, central, 29. *See also* Finance
Treatment, poor; costs of, 142–155
Troubleshooting, 135
Trust, 101, 190, 244, 247
Turnaround time, 11, 92, 108
Turnover, employee, 27, 177
Two-level organizations, 156, 162
Tyranny, 194

U

Uncertainty, 163, 176
Underutilization, 65
Unevenness, 59
Uniformity, 43, 59, 97, 162, 207
United Kingdom, 26, 314
United States: Army, 231; Congress, 231; court system, 231; farmers, 313; universities, 232
Universal problems, 243
University departments, 231, 257
University of Michigan, xxi
Upward communication, 268
Urbanization, 122
USSR, farmers in, 313
Utility, 108

V

Vaccinations, 24
Values, 4, 7, 196, 211, 240; authority and autonomy, 308; political, 207
Value of time, 95, 109
Variance: breadth of, 106; in waiting time, 56
Variety, 79, 92, 97, 106, 213, 240
Vending machines, 231
Vertical: communication, 125, 133, 153, 156, 269; integration, 177
Veterinarians, 215, 244
Viability, 216; of power, 198
Voting: electronic, 218; extent of, 220; participatory, 209
Vulnerability, 165

W

Wage multipler, 273
Waiting: formula for, 311; lines, 16, 49, 51, 56, 65; room, 58; time, 58, 246
Wantonness, 194
Wealth, 196
Weapons, 243
Weather, 243
Wheel Nets, 21
Wideband communication, 104
Will, 187

Wisdom, 166, 176
Worker control, 20
Workload, 24
World views, shared, 104
Worth, net, 174, 283

Z

Zero-sum games, 201
"Zoning of power," 25

About the Authors

Manfred Kochen is a member of the faculty of the University of Michigan, where he is Professor of Information Science, Research Scientist at the Mental Health Research Institute, and a member of the Urban/Regional Planning Department. He is chairman of the Electorate Nominating Committee of the American Association for the Advancement of Science, Section T, and managing editor of *Human Systems Management*. Professor Kochen is the author or editor of six books, including *Information for Action and Principles of Information Retrieval*, and has contributed over one hundred articles to professional journals. He received his Ph.D. in applied mathematics from Columbia University.

Karl W. Deutsch is the Stanfield Professor of International Peace in the Department of Government at Harvard University, and the Director of the International Institute for Comparative Social Research at the Science Center Berlin. He holds a Jur.Dr. from Charles University in Prague, a Ph.D. from Harvard University, an Ll. D. from the University of Illinois, and several honorary degrees. Professor Deutsch's publications include *The Nerves of Government*, *The Analysis of International Relations, Politics and Government*, and *Tides Among Nations*. His most recent research involves global modeling, international peace, and the politics of emerging nations.

About the Science Center Berlin

The Wissenschaftszentrum Berlin (Science Center Berlin), a non-profit corporation, serves as a parent institution for institutes conducting social science research in areas of significant social concern.

The following institutes are currently operating within the Science Center Berlin:

1. The International Institute of Management,
2. The International Institute for Environment and Society,
3. The International Institute for Comparative Social Research.

They share the following structural elements: a multinational professional and supporting staff, multidisciplinary project teams, a focus on international comparative studies, a policy orientation in the selection of research topics and the diffusion of results.